Procrastinators Daily Devotion

REVELATIONS, REFLECTIONS & PRAYERS
OF A LIFELONG PROCRASTINATOR
ON THE ROAD TO VICTORY!

Barbara G. Gelnett

WestBow Press books may be ordered through booksellers or by contacting:

WestBow Press
A Division of Thomas Nelson & Zondervan
1663 Liberty Drive
Bloomington, IN 47403
www.westbowpress.com
844-714-3454

ISBN: 978-1-6642-8614-6 (sc)
ISBN: 978-1-6642-8615-3 (hc)
ISBN: 978-1-6642-8613-9 (e)

Library of Congress Control Number: 2022922979

Print information available on the last page.

WestBow Press rev. date: 01/24/2025

INTRODUCTION

As far as I can remember procrastination has been a part of my life. As a child, whenever there was a chore to do, that chore was delayed. My mother would get the dirty dishes ready for me to wash in a hot, sudsy sink with protective rubber gloves placed on the counter. By the time I got to the sink, there was no bright white foam covering the yucky dishes. The water was so cold, who needed rubber gloves? Hiding in the bathroom with a comic book or sneaking into a room to watch TV were my favorite forms of escape.

In school, homework was never at the top of my agenda. My standard practice was to wait until the last possible minute, or not do it at all. I may have wanted to play the piano because I loved music, but after listening to my ever-present grandmother repeatedly nagging, "Barbara, Barbara, are you going to practice the piano?" "You know your father pays good money for those lessons." "When was the last time you practiced?" I sabotaged my musical possibilities. If procrastinating my piano practice annoyed her, that seemed perfect payback for her annoying me.

In college and in graduate school, I was queen of the all-night cram sessions, and was well known for my late papers and excuses. Academic pressures often came with brutal migraines. I felt guilty for the deceptive excuses (or outright lies) and putting other people through various disappointments for my lateness. But, I did not feel any motivation to change. Until... as a teacher my tendency to let grading wait until the last minute became a real burden. At the end of each term, grades and report cards were stressfully accomplished with such overwhelming anxiety, I would swear to myself "never again." However, it was always the same next term.

My procrastination had cost me: stress, frustration, elevated blood pressure, and constant disappointment in myself for not being able to change. Leaving important matters until the last minute was robbing me of peace and would create a cloud of anxiety-induced motivation, instead of developing self-regulation. While I certainly have accomplished much to be proud of in my life, many creative goals still weigh heavily on my mind, because they have not been realized. Belief in my own possibilities is annually ignited by those, "Your dreams really can come true" Oscar speeches. But, because so many projects have stalled, chronic disappointment has been deposited in my soul, wounding my heart.

I clearly remember approaching the New Year of 2011, telling my pastor's daughter, Bella Wilson, while we were serving in the Kids ministry together, "I'm going to write a Procrastinators Daily Devotion. If I write a little bit every day, in 365 days, there will be a complete book!" I started with much enthusiasm knowing that, "Surely I am not the only Christian out there whose life and productivity has been severely hampered by this terrible habit of putting things off."

Realizing that this project had the potential to spiritually impact countless people freeing them from stagnation into unlimited productivity, my initial motivation was strong. Unfortunately, I am a procrastinator, so I did what we do. We keep putting things off until tomorrow and another tomorrow, until the motivation fades away and dies. Looking at a list of unfulfilled goals approaching New Year's Eve 2012 was very depressing. The project was then tucked away for another few years and re-booted in 2014. Not a good year to re-boot, due to teaching full-time, taking post graduate classes, moving across the country, and having a family member with serious health issues.

While my efforts to sustain work on this devotional project failed again, it did move me to get toe to toe with God and question his will for my life. "Will I ever be a published author?' "Which books, scripts, projects should I complete?" "Will I ever be able to stop putting off projects that can fulfill my hopes and dreams?" Thank God I did not procrastinate about moving to New England to be close to my elderly mother; for some things there simply is no tomorrow. She died within a year of my arrival.

As I approached New Year's Day in 2017, I faced great confusion. With so many different writing projects circling around in my head, I prayed hard that God would reveal to me where to focus my attention, and which project was it that *he wanted me to pursue through completion*. On the first Sunday of the New Year 2017, there was both expectation and a touch of dread. This is where I must pause to simply thank God for the local church.

My husband and I attend *Wave Norfolk*, and on the first Sunday of the month all of the Wave churches are tuned into our main campus to listen to Pastor Steve Kelly. His topic that first Sunday morning of the year, "Procrastination!" God, thank you for removing all doubt in the direction I must take with my writing! The combination of Steve Kelly's sermon, with the realization that it had been six years since I first started my procrastination devotional book, that was all I needed to chart my course for the next year and beyond.

Procrastination is something that must be overcome in the life of those who follow Christ. Time is too short to delay. When I thought of all that the Body of Christ has left undone due to this "acceptable" flaw of character, there was a sadness that quickened my heart and spirit to finally do something about it. This book is the result of overcoming something in myself, something that many others also need to overcome.

Imagine freedom from procrastination within the entire Church, what a formidable force we would be in this world! I have faith that the scriptures, reflections, and prayers in this book will ignite victory within believers that will help change our world and greatly expand God's Kingdom on earth. I heartily thank God for the wisdom, strength and support provided to me from the local churches that I have been a part of over the years in various parts of this country including: my current church *Wave Norfolk, Wave Church* in Virginia Beach, *Next Level* in New Hampshire, *Newport Church* in California, and for all the local churches from Maine to Texas that I attended while seeking God's direction for my life.

May you also be set free to do this day, and for the rest of your life, that which God is calling you to do. In Jesus' name... Amen.

JANUARY 1

A New Year

Not that I have already obtained all this, or have already arrived at my goal, but I press on to take hold of that for which Christ Jesus took hold of me... But one thing I do: Forgetting what is behind and straining toward what is ahead, I press on toward the goal to win the prize for which God has called me heavenward in Christ Jesus.
–Philippians 3:12—14, *New International Version* (NIV)

How many times have you concocted a New Year's resolution only to see it become nonexistent within days? In 2011, I told myself that this was the year. *Yes, I will do this! I will write my blog every day, and in 365 days, an entire devotional book will be complete. At last, my procrastinating tendencies will be defeated once and for all.* Yeah, that didn't happen. It was earnestly tried in 2014 too. What? It turned into 2017, and it still wasn't finished it? Yes, on and on, unfortunately that is simply what happens. What we put off until tomorrow doesn't get done tomorrow; it often doesn't even happen in years down the road.

This year, I must slay this monstrous hindrance known as procrastination. Whatever the reason: fear of failure, laziness, selfishness, psychological quirks, rationalizing, etc. It must be stopped in the now– never in the tomorrow. I need help overcoming a life pattern that has robbed me of seeing my dreams come true. I am tired of plans fading away, of projects gathering dust, and of ideas half-baked. The only way to stop it is with today. So today... I did it! Hooray for me. Let us pat ourselves on the back for our baby steps of achievement. It will be brick by brick. We must forget our past, and move forward, having faith that we will be fit to finish the work that we are called to do in this life.

Dear Lord, You know that I am fearful of starting down this road once again. I am burdened by feelings of failure that I have absolutely no desire to feel again. Please give me the courage to put my dreams, and my "hoped for" results out there once again, today. Guard all of us from the power of putting things off into tomorrow. Let us accomplish all that You have called us to do today, today. In Jesus' name... Amen.

JANUARY 2

The Power of Dedication

God, my Master, you let me in on the beginnings, you let me see your greatness, you let me see your might... Please, let me in also on the endings, let me cross the river and see the good land over the Jordan.
–Deuteronomy 3:23—25, *The Message* (MSG)

As I contemplated the start of a New Year, the memory of squandered resolutions and a need to find something to dedicate myself to for this year, I thought, *What about this year?* Leary of making another resolution that would prematurely give birth to failure, I paused. It is my husband's habit to read aloud a devotional every morning. This year it's *Jesus Calling*, written by Sarah Young. As he was about to proceed I said, "No. Don't read January 1. Just read the stuff at the beginning of the book, the introduction or something." I had no idea what was there.

The beginning of the book contained the author's dedication of the book to her mother. She lovingly expressed her appreciation, which was enhanced by papers she had found after her mother's death. Her mother had made handwritten copies of her Sarah's devotional writings. When my husband read the words, "Her oft-expressed desire to write children's books never came to fruition." I broke down and cried as if I was seeing my own life about to be cut short, and deeply felt a depressing emptiness for not attaining my life's goals. My procrastination could be sentencing me to a sadly incomplete and unfulfilled life. I could not let that happen. I needed to dedicate myself to overcoming procrastination and help others who are also hindered by this flaw as well, starting now and seeing it through to the finish.

Dear Lord, Thank you for leading me to the right words at the right time. Thank you for your faithfulness in my devotional time, to speak clearly to me. Thank you for giving me a goal that will be fulfilled by your Holy Spirit, by your guidance, and by my decision to do something on a daily basis that will break the power of procrastination over my life. Thank you that you are a great God, that you can do mighty things. I pray that you let me see, that at the end of my life, I will have accomplished all that you have called me to do, and I will create a means to spread your kingdom on earth as it is in heaven. In Jesus' name... Amen!

JANUARY 3

This Time Next Year

But my covenant I will establish with Isaac, whom Sarah will bear to you by this time next year.
–Genesis 17:21 (NIV)

I always feel presumptuous thinking a certain thing that I hope for, or believe is God's will for my life, equals a "Promise of God." To want something very deeply may cloud one's judgement as to whether it is truly God's will for one's life (his promise) or self-will (our desired outcome.) When something I thought was God's will has taken so long... year after year, and hasn't yet manifested, it is easy to doubt.

Thank God that the Bible is full of examples of people who held on to their heart's desire as if it was surely God's promise, as well as those that heard very clearly and knew beyond a shadow of a doubt. These people of the covenant believed, because if God said it, they believed it. Abraham and Sara are the primary examples of believing despite not seeing results year after year. Hannah cried her heart out to God to have a child, then heard Eli speak God's promise directly to her. The angel Gabriel announced the conception of Jesus to Mary, a promise she believed and was later confirmed by her cousin Elizabeth. God's promises seem to always give birth to something. First we must believe, then complete our part by giving that promise life by our own actions.

Dear Lord, Help us to discern your will in all things. Give us eyes to see as you see, and ears to hear your voice. Let us spend more time in your written Word, that we may perceive your spoken words and promises. Let us create the life and the destiny you have made clear to us. The more we know where we are going, the easier it will be to attend to what we must attend to, and make your promises come to pass. In Jesus' name... Amen.

JANUARY 4

Look Back to Look Forward

I know what I'm doing. I have it all planned out–plans to take care of you, not abandon you, plans to give you the future you hope for.
–Jeremiah 29:11 (MSG)

Pay close attention to me now: I'm creating new heavens and new earth. All the earlier troubles, chaos, and pain are things of the past, to be forgotten. Look ahead with joy. Anticipate what I'm creating...
–Isaiah 65:17 (MSG)

In ancient Roman religion and mythology, Janus is the god of beginnings and transitions, which also means he presides over gates, doorways, endings, and time. He is usually a two-faced god since he looks to the future and the past. We get the name for the month of January based on this Roman god. If we don't know where we have been, how can we really map our course for the future? My past teaches me that procrastination has been a weight, and an obstacle, hindering me from living the kind of life God desires for me to have. As I start this year, I pray that my victory over procrastination will become a trail that is blazed for others to follow. It is my deep desire to lead others away from the drive to escape and avoid, toward a place of productivity and satisfaction.

Dear Lord, Direct our vision into the future that you want for us. Help us to plainly see what our procrastinating ways have cost us. Help us strive for freedom from all the hindrances we have created for ourselves. May we learn lessons from our past, but never dwell there. Keep us looking forward, with joyful anticipation for the new things that you have created. In Jesus' name... Amen.

JANUARY 5

On the Road to Somewhere

My sad life's dilapidated, a falling-down barn; build me up again by your Word. Barricade the road that goes Nowhere; grace me with your clear revelation. I choose the true road to Somewhere, I post your road signs at every curve and corner. I grasp and cling to whatever you tell me; God, don't let me down! I'll run the course you lay out for me if you'll just show me how.
–Psalm 119:28—32 (MSG)

Times of sadness for me are often the result of the same dilemma... What do I do? Time is so precious, and today I have nothing scheduled, so what do I do? There are the "have to do's," the "want to do's" and the "probably should do's." Too many possibilities make my head swim, I'm often unsure of my next step, and at the end of the day I feel regret about what didn't get done.

Today I chose to take one more step in the direction of fulfilling my goal of finishing this project, so I write. This is not just for me, but for the procrastinators everywhere that want a life more surrendered to God, more focused on finishing than starting a project. As a reader, you are connecting with something that will help you overcome a character defect that holds your potential hostage. As a writer, I am celebrating my victory over procrastination today by actually following through on my commitment to write. We can both celebrate the fact that we made a choice moving us forward in the right direction. I now choose to do that one thing that needs to be done, and I will not put it off. God posted a road sign for me, and I followed it. You did too.

Dear Lord, I thank you that you have not made us puppets, but people of strengths and weaknesses and a will of our own. Choices are everywhere. Sometimes we get overwhelmed by all the options that are before us at every turn. God, give us your heart's desire for our lives. Give us vision to see the future that you have mapped out before us. Let us stay close to you, that our will would be in sync with yours. In Jesus' name... Amen.

JANUARY 6

Better Than Belief

Trust in the Lord with all your heart and lean not on your own understanding; in all your ways submit to him, and he will make your paths straight.
–Proverbs 3:5—6 (NIV)

But he gives us more grace. That is why Scripture says: 'God opposes the proud but shows favor to the humble.' Submit yourselves, then, to God. Resist the devil, and he will flee from you. Come near to God and he will come near to you.
–James 4:6—8 (NIV)

Jesus replied, 'Very truly I tell you, no one can see the kingdom of God unless they are born again.'
–John 3:3 (NIV)

There is a spiritual mystery in the act of surrendering to God and being born again. In a world where the idea of submission is often repugnant, it is hard for people to accept the thought that the best way to enter a relationship with God is through total surrender. Many people believe in God, yet cannot see that surrender is better than belief. To surrender your heart, your will, and your entire life to Jesus, enables the spirit within to come alive. There is true victory when we take ourselves off the throne, then place the King of Kings in a position of authority over our life. While belief in Jesus is a great place to start, it is by surrender that you assure yourself of a glorious finish. Whatever your desires and plans are, his are better because God knows best. Any trials, sufferings, and disappointments life may throw at us, submitting to him marries us to his highest purpose for our lives. Believing in Jesus is good, a life totally yielded to the lover of our soul is so much better.

Dear Lord, You are an all knowing, mysterious God. Your ways are higher than ours, often beyond comprehension. I am glad that we are not required to understand you, but to lovingly surrender to you. I confess that obedience is so much easier when I yield myself totally to you. May all those that believe in you grow in their relationship by submitting themselves totally to you. May all who follow you enjoy the benefits of an intimate relationship with you by being born again. May there be a multitude of testimonies of your transforming power by those who choose to move beyond belief, to surrender. In Jesus' name... Amen.

JANUARY 7

Running to Win

Do you not know that in a race all the runners run, but only one gets the prize? Run in such a way as to get the prize. Everyone who competes in the games goes into strict training. They do it to get a crown that will not last, but we do it to get a crown that will last forever. Therefore, I do not run like someone running aimlessly; I do not fight like a boxer beating the air. No, I strike a blow to my body and make it my slave so that after I have preached to others, I myself will not be disqualified for the prize.
–I Corinthians 9:24—27 (NIV)

Television time is very often sports watching time in my home. I admire athletes for many reasons. Often athletic performances seem superhuman to me. Whether it is the aesthetic beauty of an Olympic gymnast, the precision of a perfect 40-foot putt, the teamwork necessary to score a goal, the strength, design, and discipline of a great football play, or the unscripted excitement. I could go on and on about the value of sports. It is truly amazing the hard work and discipline necessary to be an athlete who excels in their field. I say that I could never be that disciplined, or even come close to their level of commitment.

It is foolish for me to compare myself to them, but it is wisdom to be inspired by their example. Their goals are quite different from mine, but I too want to win a prize! I want to accomplish everything God has called me to do, and without an athlete's extreme dedication, the prize that I so desire will always be out of reach. Let me not be the hapless greyhound chasing after a mechanical rabbit that can never be his to possess. How sad a life would that be? Spiritually speaking, within the realm of godly service, innovative creativity, and monumental task completion, I want to grasp that Oscar, hold that Vince Lombardi trophy, feel that gold medal placed around my neck.

Dear Lord, Please be that wind beneath my wings that I need to soar higher. Help me to establish firm goals, help me to realize that time is too precious to fill with attractive worthless things. Whisper constant reminders of the better choice, and the benefits of self-discipline, mold my attitude toward self-discipline so that I will highly regard it, rather than shun it. In Jesus' name… Amen.

JANUARY 8

The Main Thing

Show me, LORD, my life's end and the number of my days;
let me know how fleeting my life is.
–Psalm 39:4 (NIV)

Probably the older you get, the more you think about "How much time do I have left to my life." The younger you are, the general feeling is, "I have my whole life ahead of me." Both perspectives really are slightly skewed. Whether you are sixteen or sixty years old, all you have is today. Obviously if one is going to write a novel like *Roots,* or *Moby Dick* (loved them both by the way) one needs years to complete a monumental task. Take the Crazy Horse Memorial statue still a work in progress for over seventy years in South Dakota. It was started in 1948 by a sculptor named Korczak Ziolkowski and as of the day I am writing this, not completed. It's a good thing that a young woman named Ruth fell in love with him and bore him ten children, four of which were dedicated to completing his work, along with twenty-three of his grandchildren. When it is complete it will be one of the largest statues in the world.

Those of us who procrastinate must get over the idea that we need to see immediate results, and instant gratification for our efforts. The following words of Ziolkowski's widow are very enlightening & encouraging. "The important thing is that we never stop. That's the main thing. And if you looked at it as strictly a view of being finished, you could get awfully distracted waiting for that day to come. This way, you're pleased with every little step of progress that you make."

Dear Lord, Today her words are my prayer. Help us to never stop pursuing the path you have laid out for us. Let us not get distracted by the length of this path. Keep us focused on every little step of progress. Thank you for allowing us to enjoy the pleasure of progress. In Jesus' name… Amen.

JANUARY 9

Oh, It's Too Late

They've pitched camp all around her, and plan where they'll 'graze.' And then, 'Prepare to attack! The fight is on! To arms! We'll strike at noon! Oh, it's too late? Day is dying? Evening shadows are upon us? Well, up anyway! We'll attack by night and tear apart her defenses stone by stone.'
–Jeremiah 6:4—5 (MSG)

I don't know how I could decide that it was time to start writing my blog at 11 A.M. this morning and while I was at my computer to write, somehow... some way... everything that crossed my path trumped that decision. Boom, here I am, 11 P.M. and it wasn't finished! I read this quote in Jeremiah, and it echoes my day. "We'll strike at noon!... Oh, it's too late? Day is dying? Evening shadows are upon us?" Like, it happened that fast. When the decision is made to fight at noon, then it is already evening, then comes the darkness of night! ... How does that happen? I don't know, but it seems to happen to me a lot. It happened today.

Dear Lord, Please help me to see the swift river of time. I jump in at one spot, and before I know it, I am carried downstream, far away from my destination, landing nowhere near my intended spot. Are my procrastinating ways so deeply driven into my character, they pull the strings of my will? Give me eyes to see what is happening every moment, free me from this blindness that makes the "next thing to do," turn into the thing I do twelve hours later. Help me to understand this defective process within me, so it can be defeated! God, please help everyone who struggles with this hindrance, that we may all be able to tear it apart, stone by stone! In Jesus' name… Amen.

JANUARY 10

First Things First

But seek first His kingdom and His righteousness, and all these things will be added to you. So do not worry about tomorrow; for tomorrow will care for itself. Each day has enough trouble of its own.
–Matthew 6:33—34, *New American Standard Bible* (NASB)

A few years ago, I went through an extremely hard emotional time. Although I had told myself for years that there should be a place, and a time, for me to daily read my Bible and journal my thoughts, feelings, and prayers. It was not until my spiritual back was against the wall, my marriage on the line, and my future hanging by a thread, that I actually developed time devoted to hearing from God as part of my daily routine. With that discipline, God gave me revelations. What a positive impact that time with Bible and notebook in hand has made! I do not berate myself if a day or two is skipped because it is ingrained deeply now and skipped times do not equate to falling off the track anymore. The track has been laid, used, and is now part of my life. It is something I just do. I wish that I could say that it is the first part of my day, every day, but not so. After all, I am a procrastinator.

Why did it take so long to finally do something of such value, even though it had been my intention for decades? I am a procrastinator. It is what we do, to our own detriment, time after time. I don't know about you, but a life of poor time management, cutting it too close, incomplete grades, missed flights, work piling up to an unmanageable height, tension, anxiety, and a mad rush, is not the way to live. The hurrying and worrying about "blowing it" once again is bad, but not doing anything about it, is even worse. With God's help this day can be the start of changing for the better.

Dear Lord, Help me to do "first things first" every day. Help me to always turn my thoughts and my attention to you and devote myself to your kingdom business daily. Spending quality time with You first means starting each day right. Please use my right starts to keep me from worrisome times throughout my day. In Jesus' name… Amen.

JANUARY 11

It's All About Timing

But God is not finished. He's waiting around to be gracious to you. He's gathering strength to show mercy to you. God takes the time to do everything right– everything. Those who wait around for him are the lucky ones.
–Isaiah 30:18 (MSG)

If there is something that I have difficulty with, it is "timing." In so many different areas, poor timing has plagued me. My first pregnancy certainly wasn't planned by me or my husband, but it was in God's time. I am still trying to figure out how we have been on the costly, bad side of timing for some of our house purchases. I have thrown many *Whys?* and *How comes?* up to God over the years. Timing that works to my advantage has really seemed to allude me throughout my life. Yet, in my heart and deep in my spirit I know that God's timing is perfect, after all he is the author of time.

No matter how behind I am, in whatever task I am tackling, time in prayer, time in reading God's Word, surrounding myself with music that praises God and uplifts my spirit, is never a waste of time. Attending God's presence makes me more in tune with who God is, and who I should be. I trust God's timing is perfect. I desire to be a person that by his mercy, his perfect timing may just rub off a little bit, into my imperfect self.

Dear Jesus, You knew just what to say, just what to do at every given moment. You and the Heavenly Father are so unified, doing just the right thing at the right time. Be gracious unto me and grant me that insight to be in harmony with your plan, your will, and your timing. In Jesus' name… Amen

JANUARY 12

It's a Beautiful Morning

When one rules over people in righteousness,
when he rules in the fear of God, he is like the light of morning at sunrise
on a cloudless morning, like the brightness after rain
that brings grass from the earth.'
'If my house were not right with God,
surely he would not have made with me an everlasting covenant,
arranged and secured in every part;
surely he would not bring to fruition my salvation
and grant me my every desire.
–2 Samuel 23:3—5 (NIV)

I am not a king, or any kind of a political leader, I do not rule over anyone. However, I need to rule over myself. Currently, confession dictates that I must declare my failure as a sovereign over myself. Whether it is procrastination, lack of control over negative thoughts, taking on burdens that are not my own, or my quick draw temper, the evidence of my lack in this arena of self-rule is quite obvious. God has surely done His part to make my house right, now it is necessary that I do my part to make my house right with God.

This morning, awakened by the light much earlier than usual, there was a sight before my eyes that was very rare. It was the absolute beauty of the sunrise, the dawning of the light of day. Like God's presence it colored the morning in a brand-new way. There was a desire to rise up, and not delay. There was motivation to address the responsibilities of the day, and to not "put it off." An aura of righteousness covered the start of the day, creating beauty for a new beginning.

Dear Lord, I do rely on you in a covenant relationship. You have paid the price for all of my sins and shortcomings on the cross, now I am yours! You have arranged and secured every part. You have brought my salvation to fruition. Please grant my desire to overcome my procrastinating ways. Whisper the ways of wisdom in my mind and spirit that I would rule myself wisely and accomplish this day what you would have me do. In Jesus' name… Amen.

JANUARY 13

This is the Day

This is the day that the Lord has made;
let us rejoice and be glad in it.
Save us, we pray, O Lord!
O Lord, we pray, give us success!
–Psalm 118:24—25, *English Standard Version* (ESV)

Sometimes when planning out my day, I overthink it and other times it is "go with the flow," with no plan at all. It is only natural to look at "MY day," to decide what I should do with it. As a Christian, I must admit that the day really isn't mine at all. My relationship to God is based on the Good News that he gave his only son to die on the cross for my sins, and I get to go to Heaven as God's freely given gift to me. In return, I have surrendered my life to God to do with it as he wills. So, really it is "His day," and not mine at all. This is the day that the Lord has made. Another free gift that he has given to me! I need to rejoice in that, be glad in him, and pray.

There is absolutely nothing inappropriate about praying for success. My life is His; the day is His. Any success I achieve will bring me personal happiness, and praise to God. Holding on to that perspective is worth working hard to achieve it, every day. It is a waste to dread the day or try to avoid the unpleasant obligations and mundane tasks ahead. It is a pleasant thing to embrace this gift of twenty-four hours that is ours, and to rejoice in it for as long as we are able.

Dear Lord, You have created all things, even this day is yours. Help me to not be possessive of my time, to realize that my time belongs to you. Every day is truly borrowed time, help me to follow your will, to use my time wisely, and that my work is blessed by success. I thank you God for the time that you have given me, help me to treasure it as I should. In Jesus' name… Amen.

JANUARY 14

Time for Order

Put your outdoor work in order and get your fields ready; after that, build your house.
–Proverbs 24:27 (NIV)

But everything should be done in a fitting and orderly way.
–I Corinthians 14:40 (NIV)

It seems as if people that procrastinate avoid establishing routines as much as avoiding undesirable tasks. I don't know why I have such an aversion to conforming to a routine. It may be that the very idea of doing something at the same time every day seems like a restriction of my freedom. If I am locked into a daily pattern, I am not free. But when I think about Creation, it is marked by times, seasons, day and night, predictable rotations and revolutions, and orbits. God is not a god of chaos, but of order. Probably half of the problems that I create for myself could be avoided with establishing a regular routine. It doesn't matter whether I am in school, employed, unemployed, or almost doing the same thing every day, I still resist making it orderly and predictable. God help me!

Dear Lord, So often the freedom I embrace leads to: nothing being accomplished, deadlines passed, assignments undone, and a lack of sleep. Help me to establish regular routines in my life that will create less confusion, less chaos, and less frustration. Lead me in a way that doesn't strain against my natural rhythms but compliments them. Help me to create daily schedules and weekly routines that will bring me into a productive life, free from the anxiety of overload from the "not done". In Jesus' name… Amen.

JANUARY 15

The Destiny of Dreamers

But let justice run down like water, And righteousness like a mighty stream
–Amos 5:24, *New King James Version* (NKJV)

He defends the cause of the fatherless and the widow, and loves the foreigner residing among you, giving them food and clothing.
–Deuteronomy 10:18 (NIV)

The righteous care about justice for the poor, but the wicked have no such concern.
–Proverbs 29:7 (NIV)

While our calendar of national holidays fluctuates, giving us Monday holidays for long weekends, on January 15, 2018, it is Martin Luther King Jr. Day. He was great leader, motivational speaker, a compelling man with flaws, and he had a dream that drove his destiny. He learned from another great leader, Gandhi, to devise a plan using nonviolent means to bring justice and equality to his people, and to change the heart and culture of the American people.

Had his dream just stayed a dream, and he didn't do anything about it, we might not even know his name today. The truth is, while there have been great strides in equality, all that he envisioned for this country in terms of justice and righteousness, is not evident yet. Some of us are letting our destiny die because our dreams have put us into a coma. We need to wake up, become active in our God-given destiny, and become a vibrant part of a living legacy, not just passive observers of a someone else's memorial.

Dear Lord, Help us to be truly awake to the dream and the destiny that you have put on our life. You have created us to make a difference in this world. We are to bring your kingdom on earth, and fill it with love, peace, justice, forgiveness, equality, and righteousness. Whether our impact is magnificent or minute, it still matters. Let us do what we must do to get our part done, expanding your kingdom, and making this world a better place. In Jesus' name... Amen.

JANUARY 16

Small Beginnings

Do not despise this small beginning, for the eyes of the Lord rejoice to see the work begin...
–Zechariah 4:10, *The Living Bible* (TLB)

If you saw a picture of my den you would probably think, "Oh, I bet her entire house is a wreck!" Not so. There was a time in my life when going to bed with a sink full of dirty dishes was standard, and when my attitude toward making my bed was like, "What for?" Presently this is not the case. During a stretch of unemployment, when time was more abundant to me, habits were developed. As soon as my feet were on the floor in the morning, I would make the bed which helped get my blood flowing even before my morning coffee. I got in the habit of cleaning the kitchen before going to bed, so that I could wake up to a nice, clean, orderly kitchen first thing. If the dishwasher is full of clean dishes, I empty it first before preparing any breakfast.

The point being... I wish I could get zapped instantaneously with some kind of "Never Procrastinate Again" ray that would totally eradicate that aspect of my life. It doesn't happen that way. It happens one step at a time. Pick one thing to work on. God will smile on that small beginning. A tiny spark can ignite a revolution. Begin by changing one thing. Seeing that change firmly planted is very encouraging. You will grow confidence for the battles ahead. "Viva la Revolution!"

Dear Lord, Help me to realize the power of beginning. Encourage me with a sense of accomplishment at every small step taken to defeat the enemy of Procrastination. Let an attitude of purpose triumph over avoidance and delay. In Jesus' name... Amen.

JANUARY 17

I'd Rather be His Delight

No ill befalls the righteous,
but the wicked are filled with trouble.
Lying lips are an abomination to the LORD,
but those who act faithfully are his delight
–Proverbs 12:21—22 (ESV)

I consider myself to be an honest person, but when you procrastinate sometimes there is a certain amount of fudge factor, if not outright lies, to cover our excuses, lateness, and unfulfilled deadlines. I had a philosophy class that I truly enjoyed in college. There was a major paper due right before the break at the end of the term. I don't know what particular excuse I gave Dr. Wagoner for not being able to finish on time (I hadn't even started), but I bought more time to finish by swearing to high heaven the paper would be completed over break, then handed in to him as soon as I arrived back on campus.

Of course I didn't spend my break finishing a philosophy paper! I was a college student on break. When the break was over, I pretended to not be back on campus yet. I hid myself in my room when I returned and didn't go to the cafeteria for meals. God forbid that my presence would be observed on my small campus. I even missed my registration for the new term, an unpleasant event where every student was herded into long lines in the gym. Protecting the illusion of my absence was paramount. When I finally handed in the paper, conceived in guilt, sweat, and deceit, I can't remember what excuse I gave for being late, again. I just remember what an ordeal it felt like. It had been such an unnecessary charade adorned with elaborate fabrications, simply because I procrastinated.

Dear Lord, Help me to realize that being a procrastinator can be more than a character weakness, it is often just sin. It can be broken promises, lies, laziness, anxiety, and it produces a bogus imitation of our best. God, I need your strength in me to not cheat in this area, help my vows and obligations be filled on time. Let me not do later, what I should do right now. In Jesus' name... Amen.

JANUARY 18

Whose Plans Prevail?

Many are the plans in a man's heart, but it is the Lord's purpose that prevails.
–Proverbs 19:2 (NIV)

According to Hara Estroff Marano, in the articl, "Procrastination: Ten Things to Know."—

> Procrastinators are made not born. Procrastination is learned in the family milieu, but not directly. It is one response to an authoritarian parenting style. Having a harsh, controlling father keeps children from developing the ability to regulate themselves, from internalizing their own intentions and then learning to act on them. Procrastination can even be a form of rebellion, one of the few forms available under such circumstances. What's more, under those household conditions, procrastinators turn more to friends than to parents for support, and their friends may reinforce procrastination because they tend to be tolerant of their excuses.

Reading this was a "Wow" moment for me! Not only was my father an authoritarian figure whose temper was fearsome, and whose belt wielding wrath had to be avoided, his mother, our "Nana," was constantly around to try to nag you into submission to all of his rules and edicts. If doing what I was supposed to do, was going to make them happy, why would I want to do that? They made my childhood miserable too often to want to do that! Household chores… I was the little diva of dragging my feet. Practice my piano lessons…not now. Sweep the driveway… later. Me, late for dinner?... you can count on it. Do my homework? Yeah right! While my sister Janet took the "good girl" road under dad's dominion to avoid our father's fury, I became the rebel. Unfortunately, we rebels, more often than not, shoot ourselves in the foot.

Dear Lord, I am so grateful to have you as my Heavenly Father. Let no remnant of rebellion from my past infect my current relationship with you. Your will is perfect for me, your plans are all good, help me to see I gain nothing from avoiding the work necessary to complete your plans for my life. Let my heart and mind be infused with your purpose. Please soothe that rebellious child that still resides within me. Your will be done. In Jesus' name... Amen.

JANUARY 19

I am Weak

But he said to me, "My grace is sufficient for you, for my power is made perfect in weakness." Therefore I will boast all the more gladly about my weaknesses, so that Christ's power may rest in me.
–2 Corinthians 12:9 (NIV)

Let me just share some lyrics from one of my favorite bands, *MxPx* from their CD, *Panic:* "Late again, Forgive me friends, For I am late again, Til' the day I die, Lord knows I'll try, 'Cause I'm still late again." Why do I identify so strongly with this particular punk band? It's because their lyrics so often reflect what is going on in my head, and sometimes it is not that pleasant. There is a certain intense frenzy in their music that feels like what is going on inside of me. I was late again last night to meet some people, stuck in a traffic jam, and aggravated because I planned too much to do in too little time. I felt like my head was going to explode, so what did I do? I pumped up the volume on my MxPx & screamed, a warrior type scream, as loud as I could. All that negative energy has to go somewhere! Much better than yelling at my dear husband for some insignificant straw that broke my procrastinating, overloaded back.

Again, to quote MxPx: "How will the story end? Where does the time go? How will the story end? All we really wanna know How will this life end?" I don't want anyone reading this to find it's all doom and gloom. While I know that I can't conquer all the frustration that comes with my procrastination, mixed with quick temper and bouts of self-condemnation, but thankfully the situation is certainly not helpless. Like additional MxPx lyrics reassure me, "You are your own best secret weapon. It's all up to you to come out swinging." It's got to be me, fighting for me, with God in my corner.

Dear Lord, I do confess that I am weak, I need your power to be made perfect in my weakness. I need to know how to access your grace. In moments of tension and frustration your grace seems so distant to me. Guide me; show me what I can do that your grace could flood my soul and cleanse me from these negative emotions. In Jesus' name... Amen.

JANUARY 20

Controlling Distractions

Like a city whose walls are broken through is a person who lacks self-control.
–Proverbs 25:28 (NIV)

No matter the issue from which procrastination springs: time management, lack of emotional management, deep rebellion, generic character flaw; we must be vigilant in keeping seemingly innocent distractions at bay. Everything under the sun can cross our path to lead us astray. Literally anything that we choose to do, to avoid the thing that we should be doing, is wrong for us to do at that moment. It may be a good thing to do, like wash the dishes, vacuum the carpet, or organize our workspace, but bad for us to be doing during that time when we know we should be doing something else.

Nothing I could write now could illustrate this point any better than a video created by Johnny Kelly in 2007. The images and words resonate within me, to recognize when I need to muster self-control. It has made me more aware of distractions that have taken me off course. Please take a look, then avoid going down one more endless rabbit hole of videos. I dare you!

View it - On Vimeo: ***Procrastination***- Johnny Kelly, 2007.

Dear Lord, Help me to exercise my self-control on a regular basis so that it would become like a strong muscle, enabling me to do what needs to be done. Let self-control be more active and prominent in my life every day, in every area. Let me stop telling myself that self-control is something I simply do not have. Help me to not give in so easily to distractions and self-gratification. Let me see distractions for what they are in my life. They are fuel for my procrastinating ways, and activities to be avoided. In Jesus' name… Amen.

JANUARY 21

A No-Kill Zone

The thief comes only to steal and kill and destroy; I came that they may have life, and have it abundantly.
–John 10:10, *Revised Standard Version* (RSV)

It seems to me as if Time and the Thief (the Enemy of human souls) are good buddies. Sometimes the Thief doesn't have to actively steal things from our lives; Time will passively do that for him, with our implied consent. It's rather insidious if you ask me. It is certainly true that procrastination creates a life that is less abundant in many ways. Whether it is losing your job through chronic tardiness, putting off getting that degree that would enhance your life and income, not paying bills on time and ruining your credit rating, or avoiding the chore of exercising and dying at an early age from a heart attack. Procrastination kills a better life.

Right now, I have written one movie script with only the first two scenes complete, a memoirs book that has only one chapter, and countless finished projects that have not advanced into the publication stage for many reasons. All of these projects have been collecting dust for years. According to Timothy Pychyl, a professor who studies procrastination at Carleton University, in Ottawa, "A lot of teachers think that kids have time-management problems, when they procrastinate. And they don't have a time-management problem. ... What they have is an emotion-management problem. They have to learn that you don't feel good all the time, and you've got to get on with it."

While I know that I definitely have time management problems that impact every task before me, emotion-management issues create a more fertile ground for procrastination in my life. Hating rejection, wishing to avoid the bad news that my efforts are not considered worthy, and fear of failure, are all emotional issues that have crippled me. Those kinds of emotional issues can sabotage a potentially abundant life for any procrastinator.

Dear Lord, Let me not care about how I am perceived by anyone but you. Free me from the fears and the emotional weaknesses that hold me down in a comfortable, unproductive place. Give me the discernment to recognize the thieves that hover over my day-to-day life, enemies poised to rob me of my destiny. Let me see the value in making time my ally instead of my adversary. Lead me in ways and decisions that bring me to an abundant, productive life. In Jesus' name... Amen.

JANUARY 22

I Never Liked Doing Nothing

I am the vine; you are the branches. Whoever abides in me and I in him, he it is that bears much fruit; for apart from me you can do nothing.
–John 15:5 (ESV)

I can do all things through Christ who strengthens me
–Philippians 4:13 (NKJV)

Sometimes meeting the goals and expectations that I put on myself seems overwhelming. It feels like some psychological warfare is going on within my brain. I really do need to check myself more often to see if I am setting myself up to fail. I remember signing up for a class that was about getting spiritually and physically fit. Our book was great, *Body and Soul,* by Dianne Wilson. The first night after talking with one of the fitness coaches that referred to my favorite food (peanut butter) as "poisonous" and looking at the highly structured, restricted diet facing me, I literally cried all the way home thinking, "Oh good. Something else I can fail at!!" The initial night was very depressing.

After becoming more open to change, following some of the prescribed food regimes, doing more exercises, I did feel better and had some much-needed weight loss. I have to admit that on my own, I am powerless over regulating how much I eat. God's intervention and help is absolutely necessary for me to change my ways. But, if I do nothing, the problem of being overweight gets worse and worse. Any goal is easier a little bit at a time. If I can lose one lb. I can lose thirty lbs., even though that amount seems overwhelming to me. The worst scenario is to do nothing.

Dear Lord, Help me to approach needed changes a little bit at a time. Help me to not "put off" what is good for me. Draw me close to you, so that you can infuse me with your truth, your life, your purpose, so that I can live a productive life. Impress upon my mind that doing nothing is not an option! Help me to not hinder myself with unrealistic expectations, and yet believe that I can truly do all things through you. In Jesus' name... Amen

JANUARY 23

Naps Are Great

When he came back to his disciples, he found them sound asleep. He said to Peter, "Can't you stick it out with me a single hour? Stay alert; be in prayer so you don't wander into temptation without even knowing you're in danger. There is a part of you that is eager, ready for anything in God. But there's another partn that's as lazy as an old dog sleeping by the fire."
–Matthew 26:40—41 (MSG)

Well, here I am; I want to be like the old dog sleeping by the fire. Do you ever envy a dog? They seem so content, like there isn't anything on their minds robbing them of peaceful dreamy rest. Not like me. Sometimes when I lay down to sleep there is a ticker tape of "to do's" and a condemning parade of "didn't do's" surging through my brain. There is definitely part of me that is "lazy as an old dog sleeping by the fire." Whenever I am facing a monumental task, or large project, I no sooner assign myself to start, and I want to take a nap, then usually do just that! I love to be asleep. It's warm and cozy, and a pure escape from reality. Am I the only procrastinator that prefers a good long nap, to digging into that looming task? Probably not.

There are times when I need to take a nap after some bad night's sleep, some tiring physical exertion. Taking a nap for the sheer pleasure of being unconscious and doing nothing, could possibly be a comforting detour taken by procrastinators. It is a side trip that I have often taken; it leads nowhere. No more escape napping would eliminate some of my "put off until tomorrow" moments. Being aware of the reason for a nap may just help me to chip away at those behaviors that need to be shed on the way to victory. Praise the Lord for little insights.

Dear Lord, Help me to stay alert. I know that there is part of me that is eager and ready for anything in you. Help me to feed that part of myself, that part that desires to please you above anything. I pray that eagerness will be a strong force within me, one that will push past the desire to close my eyes to the task at hand, one that chooses you over my own personal comfort. In Jesus' name… Amen.

JANUARY 24

Are We Wrestling or Snuggling our Demons?

Beloved, I urge you as sojourners and exiles to abstain from the passions of the flesh, which wage war against your soul.
–I Peter 2:11 (ESV)

For I do not understand my own actions. For I do not do what I want, but I do the very thing I hate. Now if I do what I do not want, I agree with the law, that it is good. So now it is no longer I who do it, but sin that dwells within me. For I know that nothing good dwells in me, that is, in my flesh. For I have the desire to do what is right, but not the ability to carry it out.
–Romans 7:15—18 (ESV)

Procrastinators are well aware of the struggles pointed out in these scriptures. Every day there may be things that we set out to do and want to accomplish, but we wiggle unsuccessfully through our schedule to fit in something that never happens. Just being aware of the battle should make the victory within our reach. Too often we head into that battle unprepared, un-prayed, and unorganized. Often I don't understand my own actions and lose my own private battles. Such is the lot of all humans. It is necessary to rise above our own limitations and prepare ahead of time to avoid common failures. Let's stop feeding our fleshly ways; it is time to strengthen our spirits. If our spirits are not fed, not encouraged, or developed to be victorious, we will not be able to overcome this weakness. Our flesh is content to sit on the couch for endless hours watching TV, go down social media rabbit holes, ignore those pesky bills, get drunk, etc. and hit the snooze button for the umpteenth time. We need to be allied with our spirit man who yearns to glorify God, and desires to defeat the "demons" in our life. Time to stop being cozy with our flesh, who is our enemy. This enemy is forever content to satisfy itself at the cost of our calling, and possibly our souls.

Dear Lord, Help us to be willing warriors in this battle against the flesh. Give us a true understanding of the cost of "snuggling with our demons." Guide us in ways that strengthen the spirit within ourselves. Draw us into your presence and fill us with your Word, which has power. Let us be encouraged by every battle won, no matter how small. Let us blaze a trail into our future with consistency and dedication to this fight. Let the feeling of accomplishment replace the ease of avoidance. In Jesus' name… Amen.

JANUARY 25

I Can, Because God Can

God can do anything, you know—far more than you could ever imagine or guess or request in your wildest dreams! He does it not by pushing us around but by working within us, his Spirit deeply and gently within us.
–Ephesians 3:20 (MSG)

Procrastination can take many forms, establish bad patterns and cause negative consequences. Because we experience the unpleasant results of these ingrained ways, we often feel that we can never change. When we are habitually late, or delaying the inevitable until it becomes painful, we may see our lives as always being handicapped by procrastinating behaviors. This is not true. It is not true because God does miraculous deeds. When I feel that change is impossible in this area, I must remember that with God, nothing is impossible. Getting depressed or hard on ourselves simply doesn't work. Being hopeful, looking forward to a better way of life, and having faith in God can create an outlook based on the wonderful possibilities of positive change. Read this scripture aloud, one more time. Let these words come alive and do their power.

Dear Lord, I am often overwhelmed by your goodness. Help me to keep your ability to do anything beyond what I can even imagine in the forefront of my thinking. Free me from the weight of past failures, and the fear of a future without victory. Thank you that by your Spirit, you do work deeply and gently within us. Help us to always remember "God can do anything." In Jesus' name... Amen.

JANUARY 26

Not by What I See

We live by faith, not by sight
–2 Corinthians 5:7 (NIV)

For in the gospel the righteousness of God is revealed—a righteousness that is by faith from first to last, just as it is written: "The righteous will live by faith."
–Romans 1:17 (NIV)

Sometimes it is easy to forget just how powerful faith really is. Faith is something active that is a creative source. Something that did not exist comes into being by faith. Even people with no faith in God have a belief that their own plans will come to pass if they just complete certain steps to get there. How much more should those of us who believe in an Almighty God, who created all life, have faith. We need to realize that God is not a giant Santa Claus in the sky, granting our selfish wishes. If we seek God and his will for our future, our will combined with his will, becomes a seed of faith in our heart, our mind, and our soul.

One good and bad thing about procrastination, it resides within us because we allow it, we have given it permission to be part of our lives. Unlike a fatal disease which occurs totally outside our will, procrastination has our will behind it to exist. By faith and our will now strengthened and enlightened by God's will, procrastination now seems like a likely candidate for eviction. I have never been a part of any eviction process, other than to see all of someone else's possessions hauled out to the curb. Within ourselves by faith and our will, we must determine that it is time for this parasitic tenant to go!

Dear Lord, You tell us that it is by increasing your Word in our hearts and minds, that our faith increases. Jesus, you told us that a mustard seed sized faith is all we need. Help me to understand and to live out the power of faith in my day-to-day life. Help me to see, by faith, my life unshackled from this defect within me. Help me to see the unseen, that I may pursue the course that you have laid out for me. In Jesus' name… Amen.

JANUARY 27

What's Trust Got to Do with It?

Trust in the Lord with all your heart
and lean not on your own understanding;
in all your ways submit to him,
and he will make your paths straight.
–Proverbs 3:5—6 (NIV)

I have been accused of being "too trusting," but I must admit I don't really understand the dynamics of trust at all. I have often taken strangers into my home, believing that it was what the Lord wanted me to do. It was just living out the Gospel in my life. I believed that he would give me discernment when any action would be harmful, or unwise. Unfortunately, that took a lot of trial and error on my part. How exactly does one trust God with their whole heart? Trust is not a noun, not a thing, not a behavior to be enacted, or a rule to be obeyed. If it was, then it would be easy to trust. It is more like a verb, a shadowy action that resides in "Attitude Land" somewhere. Possibly because my life has had a barrage of disappointments and dashed expectations, trust is harder to come by. I pray that God will grant me greater understanding of how to operate my life from a place of trust.

The second part of this verse is something that I have desired ever since I gave my life to Jesus. I want to submit all my ways to him. I need my path to be straightened out. As a procrastinator the inclination to wander, and to drift down dead-end alleys is always there. Sometimes there is no discernment of what is most important to do, or accomplish, at any given moment. The idea that we can totally submit to God and he will make our paths clear and straight, and direct us where we are supposed to be going, sounds like a miraculous blessing to me. No confusion, no delays, no useless off ramps, that sounds like what every procrastinator needs.

Dear Lord, Please put us on that straight path. Bring all of those that love you into a place of greater trust. Teach us that following your Word and submitting ourselves totally to you, means that there is no worry about the outcome. Grant us peace as we trust and obey, that all things will work out for good. Help us stay on that straight path our whole lives, until we arrive at our eternal home to stay with you forever. In Jesus' name… Amen.

JANUARY 28

I Just Want to Feel Good

You will call and I will answer you;
you will long for the creature your hands have made.
Surely then you will count my steps
but not keep track of my sin.
My offenses will be sealed up in a bag;
you will cover over my sin.
–Job 14:15—17 (NIV)

When I first became a Christian, the strongest emotion I had, being wrapped up in my brand-new faith, was exhilaration over the fact that I was forgiven. Thinking of the magnitude of all my sinful wrongdoing (believe me it was plenty) and to know that all my mistakes, past, present, and future, were covered by Jesus' sacrifice on the cross... Wow! I was high on forgiveness. There was such freedom in being unburdened of guilt. Just knowing that God's love for me covered a multitude of sins was sheer joy. Never had I felt better about life, or myself, than I did then. Salvation ushered in a euphoric state that endured for a long time.

Procrastinators tend to carry a weight of self-condemnation. They have difficulty in forgiving themselves, often because we frequently repeat the same sorts of mistakes. This over and over again procrastination can develop into a whirlpool of regret, self-recrimination, and guilt. This creates an emotional space that makes it hard to move forward, or to design positive actions for one's life. The key is forgiveness. Sometimes we just need to forgive ourselves.

Many psychologists see procrastination as a kind of avoidance behavior, a coping mechanism gone awry in which people according to Professor Timothy Pychl, "give in to feel good." Our ticket out of the whirlpool is to forgive ourselves. Forgiveness feels great! Often, it is the first step toward making an alternate type of feel-good moment on the path to doing on-time, finished work.

Dear Lord, Help me to forgive myself. Help me to realize that "feeling good" should not be my motivation for what I do, or do not do. Protect me from a heavy weight of guilt and self-condemnation that keeps me down and traps me from moving forward. Let me be ever grateful for the immense forgiveness that you have showered upon me. Lift my spirit up by the power of forgiveness. Set me free from the emotional traps that I set for myself. In Jesus' name... Amen.

JANUARY 29

Students Beware

Come to me, all you who are weary and burdened, and I will give you rest. Take my yoke upon you and learn from me, for I am gentle and humble in heart, and you will find rest for your souls.
–Matthew 11:28—29 (NIV)

I never minded starting an academic research paper. Picking a topic of interest, going to the library, finding resources, discovering facts I never knew, and even taking notes were enjoyable student activities for me. Then when the real work began: organizing notes, developing a logical order, MLA citations (ugh!), bibliographies, and doing the actual writing part, it seemed torturous. Back in the day, one had to use a very inefficient ancestor of the word processor, the typewriter, correcting every mistake was labor intensive. Since I hated the actual writing part, I was always behind schedule until panic and stress would finally extract a finished product from me at the last minute, or past the deadline. It was downright unhealthy, with the stress, the sleepless nights, and stimulants ingested to get the job done. This lifestyle puts us far from where Jesus wants us to be, which is at rest and not stressed.

> According to an article by Ana Swanson entitled, "The Real Reasons You Procrastinate"–For many people, procrastination is a strong and mysterious force that keeps them from completing the most urgent and important tasks in their lives with the same strength as when you try to bring like poles of a magnet together. It's also a potentially dangerous force, causing victims to fail out of school, perform poorly at work, put off medical treatment or delay saving for retirement. A Case Western Reserve University study in 1997 found that college-age procrastinators ended up with higher stress, more illness and lower grades by the end of the semester.

Dear Lord, Help me let go of the condemnation I feel for putting off my schoolwork until the last minute. Help me, and all students, learn to be better at planning and learning and dividing their time into manageable parts of rest and work. Help us not to dread the work needed to complete any assignment before us. Help us to create new patterns and routines that would help eliminate the force of procrastination in our lives. In Jesus' name… Amen.

JANUARY 30

Our Inner Child

When I was a child, I talked like a child, I thought like a child, I reasoned like a child. When I became a man, I put the ways of childhood behind me.
–I Corinthians 13:11 (NIV)

Epaphras greets you. He is one of you, a servant of Christ, always laboring fervently for you in prayers, that you may stand mature and complete in the entire will of God.
–Colossians 4:12, *Modern English Version* (MEV)

As an imaginative and strong-willed first grader, I probably was not the most manageable child in Miss Rollingston's class. Daydreaming was my favorite activity, and the most dreaded activity was to recreate the sentence printed on the board by sifting through a cardboard box filled with a multitude of individual letters, then arranging them in correct order on our desks. I hated that activity. One day my avoidance of this onerous task was not rewarded by the dismissal bell. Ritchie and I were held captive by Ms. Rollingston until the job was complete. I thought, "What is wrong with me? I'm smarter than Ritchie, what are we both doing here?" That mass of scrambled letters was overwhelming… true, but there was no disability here, just disinterest and putting off what needed to be done simply because I didn't want to do it!

Recently I was enjoying leading a class full of four and five-year old's. While there was a lot of fun going on, there was also a lot of children being disobedient, easily distracted, not being focused on the task at hand, and wanting to do their own thing. It occurred to me that our inner child just wants its own way, and procrastination is simply one of those childish ways. Have you ever experienced a "pick up" time with a child that doesn't want to pick up? It is delays, begging to get out of the task, hiding, whining, moving ridiculously slow, or so fast it creates an untidy, unorganized mess. Hmm... sounds like procrastination to me.

Dear Lord, Please help me to grow up. Help me to rid myself of childish ways that block me from being the kind of adult I want to be. Open my eyes to see actions in my life that are childish, so that I will not repeat those types of actions again. Maturity means not putting my immediate interests first, help me to desire maturity, so that I will be able to complete your will for my life. In Jesus' name… Amen.

JANUARY 31

Something to Show

I'm trying to be helpful and make it as easy as possible for you, not make things harder. All I want is for you to be able to develop a way of life in which you can spend plenty of time together with the Master without a lot of distractions.
–1 Corinthians 7:35 (MSG)

Our people have to learn to be diligent in their work so that all necessities are met (especially among the needy) and they don't end up with nothing to show for their lives.
–Titus 3:14 (MSG)

While there is much about my life that I am proud of so far, there is also a lurking fear that I will not complete what God has called me to do before my life is over. No matter how old or young we are, we still have the same amount of time– today. There are books, film scripts, movies to be made all inside my head, if they just stay there, what good are they? If I had finished, and not just started these projects they could have been alive and expanding God's Kingdom now. What's inside your head? What are your dream projects and plans? We all have today, and today without distractions, with no procrastination, means a life with something to show for it tomorrow.

Dear Lord, Show us the power that is in our hands today to make a difference, to create a life with something to show for it. Help us to stay focused on the dreams and plans that come from you. Give us discernment as to how to spend our time. Plant your Word in our hearts, giving us the courage and inspiration to make a difference in our world. Grant us the awareness to know when we are using distractions to avoid the most important tasks before us. In Jesus' name... Amen.

FEBRUARY 1

Paying for Nothing

A good woman is hard to find, and worth far more than diamonds.
Her husband trusts her without reserve, and never has reason to regret it.
Never spiteful, she treats him generously all her life long. She shops around for the best yarns and cottons... She's up before dawn, preparing breakfast for her family and organizing her day. She looks over a field and buys it, then, with money she's put aside, plants a garden. First thing in the morning, she dresses for work, rolls up her sleeves, eager to get started....
She's quick to assist anyone in need, reaches out to help the poor.
– Proverbs 31:10—20 (MSG)

The "good woman" in Proverbs 31 is a role model, a standard hard to attain, but her ways are an example of a blessed life. After all, she has a good husband, is a hard worker even though she has servants, and has plenty of money along with the wisdom of how to handle it. I'd like to be like her. Being wise in handling time and money is not only virtuous; it is a big part of having a life that is blessed.

Male or female, maybe we all need to check ourselves against her. Did I just pay $300 extra for a conference because I was late in registering for it, knowing for weeks that the deadline was January 31st? Did that show wisdom? Absolutely not! Where I live, a $1.85 unpaid toll turns into $27.50 if not paid within that month. Next month, voila! It turns into over $50.00 for being two months late. This is merely a small example of how bills, not paid on time, can accumulate fees and late charges, plus a swelling tide of interest. Many procrastinators have bills, parking tickets, credit cards, car registrations, etc. that sit there, unpaid. This financial procrastination becomes a sad waste because it is paying over and over again for nothing!

Dear Lord, Help me to be more like the Proverbs 31 woman. Remind me of the cost of being late in paying off my financial obligations. Help me to be wise in my spending. Give me the wisdom to realize that proper management of time and money go hand in hand. Let me see the depth of my procrastinating ways, and how widespread they are in their negative effects on my life. Help me change my ways. In Jesus' name... Amen.

FEBRUARY 2

Groundhog Day

Every part of Scripture is God-breathed and useful one way or another—showing us the truth, exposing our rebellion, correcting our mistakes, training us to live God's way. Through the Word we are put together and shaped up for the tasks God has for us.
–II Timothy 3:15—1 (MSG)

I have no problem admitting that *Groundhog Day* is one of my favorite movies. Ironically, one that I can watch repeatedly, again and again, never getting tired of it. Some movie viewers get quite bored, like– "How can you watch a movie about a guy stuck in the same day, doing the same things over and over again?" Well, to start with, Bill Murray makes me laugh. I love the theme; it is so life relevant.

Most people are prone to make the same mistakes over and over again, stuck in a loop of their own failings. Phil Connors, the arrogant, self-centered weatherman, endlessly repeats a day, until he gets it right. He develops musical talent, saves lives, brings happiness to a dying man, and gets the woman he loves to fall in love with him. After going through depression, hopelessness, and suicide, he forever gets a second chance to make things right. What's not to love about that? As Christians we are constantly given countless chances to get our life right, no matter what. Every day is a new day. We have opportunities to make the most of our gifts and talents, to generously make life better for those around us, and to experience love. This movie reminds me that correcting our mistakes and being the best that I can possibly be, is to live God's way, and that way is one of joy!

Dear Lord, Help us to see ourselves for who we really are. Take our blinders off and show us what we need to change. Let us treasure your Word, let us infuse ourselves in the wisdom and guidance you provide for us in your Word. Never let depression, futility, and discouragement gain the upper hand over our lives. May we always give you thanks for each brand-new day and all the opportunities that you give us today. In Jesus' name... Amen.

FEBRUARY 3

It May Seem Impossible

**Faith is the substance of things hoped for,
the evidence of things unseen.**
–Hebrews 11:1 King James Version (KJV)

At one time I managed a Christian club called the Fire Escape in Virginia Beach, Virginia. When I was given full authority over the venue by the founder of the organization, I believed that it was time to renovate and totally change the look of our place. The problem was, there was no money and only two weeks to complete the overwhelming project. It seemed impossible to complete this transformation, but I did have faith. Sometimes, I feel as if my faith is something that needs to be propped up and constantly prayed for to keep from falling apart. In this particular case, thank God it was not like that at all. It was visually seeing the end result that was hoped for and releasing the entire project into God's hands.

Where did the money came from? From a source I could not even imagine. A wonderful woman from Richmond, named Jannine, had a brother who was playing in a poker tournament. Apparently, he wanted to win so badly that he prayed for victory and promised God that if he won, he would give the entire amount of prize money away, $1,000. He didn't even know who to give it to, so he asked his sister, and she said, "The Fire Escape." Our entire budget was covered! We must believe for victory in our lives. We must have faith even when it seems that the situation is impossible. Changing my procrastinating ways seems impossible to me because it has been part of me for my entire life. With God, with faith, with a vision of different future, change is definitely possible.

Dear Lord, Please give us a vision of our future self, changed and free of procrastination. Give us words of encouragement. Grant us hope. Keep the helmet of salvation firmly secure. Protect us from negative thinking and an attitude of defeat. Give us direction as to which areas of our life, we should apply our faith. Grant us victory in our day-to-day battles. In Jesus' name... Amen.

FEBRUARY 4

Watch Out for Foxes and Squirrels

The little foxes are ruining the vineyards. Catch them, for the grapes are all in blossom.
–Song of Solomon 2:15 (TLB)

My life is as close as my own hands, but I don't forget what you have revealed. The wicked do their best to throw me off track, but I don't swerve an inch from your course.
–Psalm 119:108—110 (MSG)

"Procrastinators actively look for distractions, particularly ones that don't take a lot of commitment on their part. Checking e-mail is almost perfect for this purpose. They distract themselves as a way of regulating their emotions such as fear of failure." The preceding quote is from an article, by Hara Estroff Marano entitled, "Procrastination: Ten Things You Should Know." YouTube, social media, or any one of the myriad of domestic chores always needing to be done, could easily be added to e-mail as perfect distractions. The fact is, diversions are constantly within our vision. The question is, will they occupy our peripheral vision, or be our main focus?

In the wonderful animated movie *Up*, the audience gets to laugh at the dogs, so intent on their duty, then instantly sidetracked by a "Squirrel!" or a thrown tennis ball. Far too often those of us who procrastinate are like those dogs, funny in the movie, but a burden in real life. We that are in the attention deficit category, find the struggle to be distraction-free a monumental task. If we can stay on course, if we can root out those foxy digressions that keep our harvest from coming to fruition, if we can keep our eyes on the prize instead of the squirrels, one day the fruit and the prize will be ours. That's a lot of "ifs."

Dear Lord, Please give us discernment to see what is, and is not, a futile distraction. Give us the wisdom to understand what truly needs to be done now. Help us to see what is worth our time and effort today, and what should wisely be left until another day. Help us to exterminate those invading pests that take us off course and threaten the harvest of blessings you desire for us to enjoy. In Jesus' name… Amen.

FEBRUARY 5

Who Wants to Get Crushed Today?

The righteous cry out, and the Lord hears them; he delivers them from all their troubles. The Lord is close to the brokenhearted and saves those who are crushed in spirit.
–Psalm 34:17—18 (NIV)

There are times in life when everything wonderfully falls into place, other times life seems overwhelming. There have been moments when I truly felt like my spirit was being crushed to bits. Whether it was through my own wrongdoing, or difficult circumstances totally out of my control, it was equally painful. The wreckage may be emotional or spiritual, but the effects became physical. We are designed to cry, and to cry out when we feel certain emotions. I find it interesting that humans are the only animals that cry emotional tears. Over the years I have found that when I am crying from the depths of my being, it usually turns into crying out to God for help. The only upside to this situation– being close to God because of it.

What does all this have to do with procrastination? Often it doesn't, but sometimes it does. When there is too much that has gone undone, when a time crunch creates too much stress, when we cannot stand the fact that we have let ourselves down again, we heap weight upon weight burdening our spirit. These events can crush the life out of us and often bring us to tears. Life throws enough pain our way. Who wants to add to the possibility of feeling devasted due to the inability to keep procrastinating ways in check? Not me! I've been there too many times; I now desire better ways to be close to God.

Dear Lord, You have created us in your image, created us to be close to you, and I thank you for that. I thank you that you hear my cries. You know my circumstances, deliver me from personal flaws and weaknesses that bring a crushing load of trouble upon me. Save me from my self-inflicted wounds and heartaches. Please grant me your grace, and mercy, and peace, more and more every day. Thank you for your loving heart toward me. In Jesus' name... Amen.

FEBRUARY 6

Ruling Over the Flood

The Lord rules over the floodwaters.
The Lord reigns as king forever.
The Lord gives His people strength
The Lord blesses them with peace.
–Psalm 29:10—11, New Living Translation (NLT)

Recently when my street was flooding, as the water crept above the curb, submerged my sidewalk, then kept rising over my lawn and driveway, I must admit it was scary. I can barely imagine how people feel when floodwaters rise into their homes, and they must climb onto their roof for safety. As a teacher, my procrastination created a sense of drowning almost every time grades were due. I loved the teaching part, but then came the most disliked and avoided task for me– grading papers. There were times when grades were due within 48 hours, and I'd be adrift in a tidal wave of ungraded papers, trapped and surrounded. One simply cannot put off to the last minute what will take countless hours to do. The floodwaters came rushing in: confusion, panic, desperation. If only I had not avoided the inevitable. If only I had relied on God's rule over my life and sought his peace, maybe I would not be drowning.

I hated my emotional state at the end of every term, but that terrible feeling was never quite enough to make me change my ways the next term. Our finite problems are huge to us, but usually nothing to the rest of the universe. If our ways are more aligned with his ways, we are equipped to rise up and not drown. Often believers need to be reminded that God rules, he is in charge, he strengthens and blesses with peace. While we are micro-focused on our little slice of existence, our Creator rules over all ready to bless us with peace. Meanwhile, we too often struggle to keep our head above water.

Dear Lord, Help me to understand myself. Help me to stop putting myself through terrible emotional times by repeatedly avoiding what should be done in a timely manner. Help me to submit to your reign over my life, give me your strength, your peace, and your blessing. Allow me to enjoy your presence and lordship over my life. Help me to grasp hold of your ways, and free myself from a pattern of avoiding what must be done. In Jesus' name… Amen.

FEBRUARY 7

From the Inside Out

So here's what I want you to do, God helping you: Take your everyday, ordinary life—your sleeping, eating, going-to-work, and walking-around life—and place it before God as an offering. Embracing what God does for you is the best thing you can do for him. Don't become so well-adjusted to your culture that you fit into it without even thinking. Instead, fix your attention on God. You'll be changed from the inside out. Readily recognize what he wants from you, and quickly respond to it. Unlike the culture around you, always dragging you down to its level of immaturity, God brings the best out of you, develops well-formed maturity in you.
–Romans 12:1—2 (MSG)

Procrastination is manifested in a variety of ways, some of us act out all of its shortcomings, and some of us act only in specific circumstances delaying certain things. No matter how this tendency produces our actions, or inactions, it should not be any part of a follower of Jesus. Our effectiveness in building God's kingdom here on earth is severely handicapped, and possible salvations are sabotaged due to this major character flaw. People have talked themselves out of their God-given dreams and destinies. All too often laziness, avoidance, fear of failure, inability to face reality, seeking of instant gratification over long-range goals, or an existence centered on self-will, creates the parameters for our lives. It is time to say, "No more!" and embrace a "Romans 12" lifestyle and change from the inside out.

Dear Lord, Place this word deep in my heart and bring me to a place where my day-to-day life is an offering to you. Change me from the inside out, let my surrender to your will be ongoing, not a once in a lifetime decision. Help me to recognize when I am being lazy, and when I am avoiding something that should be done immediately. Free me from the fear of failure and attachment to instant gratification. Guide me to focus my attention on matters that have eternal, not temporary significance. Transform me through growing patience and self-control. Give me a vision of myself that will bring out the best in me. In Jesus' name… Amen.

FEBRUARY 8

Plan Ahead

Let me give you a new command: Love one another. In the same way I loved you, you love one another. This is how everyone will recognize that you are my disciples when they see the love you have for each other.
–John 13:34—35 (MSG)

Apparently, procrastinators aren't the only people that procrastinate, it is a fairly common phenomenon. Today I heard a statistic on the radio that surprised me. The announcer said that more than 50% of people that buy a Valentine's Day card or gift, wait until the last minute to do so. Now, I can understand if you are in a shaky relationship, and do not know how much love you want to show that person you've been dating lately. However, that statistic must include a lot of committed couples too.

I must confess that I have been disappointed a few times by lack of planning on Valentine's Day. One particular night my husband and I went from restaurant to restaurant. Each one we went to was full, and no one without a reservation was let in. Here I was, dressed in my best "going out to dinner" clothes, and we ended up in a cheap BBQ place with peanut shells all over the floor, ordering in line at the counter, food on Styrofoam plates with plastic utensils, and sports re-runs (not even live!) blaring through multiple television screens. Not at all the fine dining experience I envisioned in my head. Today gives you enough time; if you are going to make someone's Valentine's Day special, you better plan ahead, and do it now.

Dear Jesus, You have shown us complete sacrificial love. Help us to truly love one another. Pour out a special blessing on married couples, give them an extra portion of kindness, forgiveness, and selflessness. Sometimes we take our loved ones for granted, and do not put in the time, effort, and planning, to show them how much they mean to us. Help us to not wait until the last minute to show our love, help us to be deliberate and give our best to those who are important to us. In Jesus' name… Amen.

FEBRUARY 9

Millennials at Risk

The end of a matter is better than its beginning, and patience is better than pride.
–Ecclesiastes 7:8 (NIV)

Be patient, then, brothers and sisters, until the Lord's coming. See how the farmer waits for the land to yield its crop, patiently waiting for the autumn and spring rains.
–James 5:7 (NIV)

Being strengthened with all power according to his glorious might so that you may have great endurance and patience...
–Colossians 1:11 (NIV)

The December 2017 edition of the AARP Bulletin was highlighting how to boost brain power, and concentrate better, etc. Numerous studies listed, and experts interviewed, revealed a concern for millennials when it comes to dealing with distractions, and the ability to sustain focus to execute projects that require extended amounts of time. One employer complaining, "The young kids that I've worked with have the attention span of an ant." In general, the generation now raised on technology in their hands, have brains that operate differently. Constantly checking their phones, they are prone to numerous distractions, and are unable to handle slight times of boredom. Studies show that even paying quick attention to short notifications can "prompt mind-wandering and task-irrelevant thoughts." While millennials may not be prone to procrastinate as avoidance, they are at risk for: the need of immediate gratification, getting distracted from primary tasks, lack of patience, being unwilling to sustain projects requiring long term commitments... sounds like typical procrastination issues to me.

Dear Lord, You have created us to be thoughtful, intelligent beings. In this technological age we live, generations process information differently than ever before. Those whose minds have been molded by constant use of technology still need patience, still need to be able to maintain extended focus. I lift up this current generation to you. Help them to spend extended time peacefully meditating on your Word, seeking your presence free from all distractions. Help them to not depend on social media for a sense of inclusion and self-worth. Reveal to them that the only thing that they need to be plugged into 24-7, is you. Guide them to acquire the ability to be more controlled by your Holy Spirit than by the devices held in their hands. In Jesus' name... Amen.

FEBRUARY 10

Clichés Can Be True

In the beginning was the Word, and the Word was with God, and the Word was God. He was with God in the beginning. Through him all things were made; without him nothing was made that has been made. In him was life, and that life was the light of mankind.
–John 1:1—4 (NIV)

"It is never too late for a brand-new start." Is that just a cliché or true? Maybe it is both. Good advice given over and over again, gains familiarity then loses impact. Truth should have impact, but often it is avoided or ignored. We must remember as we battle our shortcomings, like procrastination, that the more we infuse ourselves to Jesus as our Lord and Master, the more we seek to do what is right, we increase the probability of doing the right thing. The more we desire to fill our heart, soul, and mind with his words, the more God's truth will rule and reign in our lives. The more time we spend with our Creator, the more of our corrupt mortal coil we shed.

How would it feel to just slough off self-defeating habits, self-deceptive thinking, to never again be tempted beyond our power to resist? It sounds glorious to me. It sounds like total freedom. It sounds like a "new life." Those of you who hang your head down in defeat because some deadline was missed, some great idea was never fleshed out, or some direction in life was derailed, you need a new start. Do you believe the cliché, "It's never too late for a brand-new start?" Believe that it is true for you. This could be your first step in the right direction. It may be a cliché, but today really could be the first day of your new life.

Dear Lord, You have created the heavens and the earth. You are mighty. Create something in me, in all of us who desire to be free of procrastination. Create an inner drive that will go headlong toward the tasks at hand and rid us of that inclination to avoid. God, may the reality that you can make all things new initiate action on our part. Make those things that you have designed us to do become urgent within us. Let avoidance no longer be what drives us. Let us be driven by a new spirit, one that will tackle the unpleasant steps first, and one that seeks the joy of a completed path. In Jesus' name… Amen.

FEBRUARY 11

What to Pray

The Lord's prayer has slightly different wording in every version. The version I pray is probably closest to the Book of Common Prayer, and there is something that my paraphrased version of the poetic King James suits me. Pray whatever version that is closest to your heart. The words below are my version.

Our Father who art in Heaven,
hallowed be thy name, thy kingdom come,
thy will be done, on earth as it is in heaven.
Give us this day our daily bread.
And forgive us our trespasses,
as we forgive those that trespass against us.
And lead us not into temptation, but deliver us from evil.
For thine is the kingdom, the power,
and the glory, forever, and ever. Amen.
–Matthew 6:9—13 (KJV)

Not matter our circumstances or our struggles, we find it necessary to reach beyond ourselves for guidance and help. Sometimes when all seems desperate, the only thing we can manage to do is cry out, "Help me Lord!" When it comes to praying, just honestly asking God for what we need in our lives, and for the needs of others, should be done with one hand reaching out in submission while the other hand is acknowledging and praising God. One thing we can be sure of, is that we can never go wrong if we pray the way Jesus taught us to pray. If he said this is how we should pray (what we know as The Lord's Prayer) surely our prayer is acceptable. When we feel that we should be praying, but don't know what to pray, this is the prayer sure to capture God's heart and will.

Dear Lord Jesus, Thank you for teaching us how to pray. Bring these words to my remembrance often. Let me say them aloud again and again and be consoled that you are Lord over all people, things, and circumstances. May your will be done on earth as it is in heaven. Amen.

FEBRUARY 12

Just a Little Late

If you are faithful in little things, you will be faithful in large ones. But if you are dishonest in little things, you won't be honest with greater responsibilities.
–Luke 16:10 (NLT)

Pursue righteous living, faithfulness, love, and peace. Enjoy the companionship of those who call on the Lord with pure hearts.
–2 Timothy 2:22 (NLT)

As I approached the turn lane into my church on Sunday evening, I was late. The entrance seemed like the procrastinators "on ramp." The service started at 6:00 P.M. and here I was at 6:05 just pulling into the parking lot. There were many of us who were a little late. When arriving late for church, you are rarely alone. I don't seem to have a problem with getting to church on time for the morning service, especially if I have responsibilities. Do I feel, *Well, evening service is not an obligation, maybe God should be happy I showed up at all?* It is just one more example of how procrastination affects the little things, as well as the big things, like being five minutes late. Since I want God to entrust me with bigger responsibilities, I need to get out of the "late lane" for evening service and get with the "early is on time" program.

Dear Lord, Keep me aware of the significance of little things. Do not let me get too casual about being on time to your house. Only you know if there was an opportunity that I missed by being late again. Help me to realize that even though being a little late for church is common, it shouldn't be. Help me to show you the honor and respect you deserve and be faithful in little things. In Jesus' name… Amen.

FEBRUARY 13

Peace Be with You

May he God of hope fill you with all joy and peace in believing, so that by the power of the Holy Spirit you may abound in hope.
–Romans 15:13 (RSV)

On the evening of that day... the doors being shut where the disciples were, for fear of the Jews, Jesus came and stood among them and said to them, "Peace be with you." When he had said this, he showed them his hands and his side. Then the disciples were glad when they saw the Lord. Jesus said to them again, "Peace be with you."
–John 20:19—21 (RSV)

I can freely admit that I have much joy and hope as part of my life, but peace is quite an elusive mystery to me. I want it; Jesus promised it to me, it is mine. How come I don't experience it? The disciples had just seen their Lord and Master die a painful traumatic death. They had lost hope, and their dreams of Jesus' reign on earth were extinguished. They were frightened, believing that any knock on the door may bring their own arrest and execution. What did Jesus say to them while they were emotionally devastated? "Peace be with you," and he said it twice. If Jesus said it to them, it must be possible for me too.

Often when I walk through my procrastinating day-to-day life, I do not start a task until I am so revved-up on adrenaline, the slightest set back erupts in anger and frustration. There is no room for peace within, with all those negative emotions flowing around. Nothing I face is as difficult as what the disciples faced immediately after Jesus' crucifixion. Most people that procrastinate keep peace at a distance; it is what we do. It's like we are saying, "Peace, back off! I'm busy now!" That is something that needs to stop.

Dear Lord, Your peace is so precious, but feels so rare. Help me to hunger and thirst for your peace, knowing that it is already mine to possess. Peace is absent in the midst of rushing around or living in a state of frustration. Deliver me from an outpouring of negative emotions, so that there is room in my heart, soul, and mind for your peace to flow in. Let me seek times of stillness and quiet, times to taste the peace that you freely offer me, so that my desire for peace will continue to grow. In Jesus' name... Amen.

FEBRUARY 14

I Wish I Could Find It

Imagine a woman who has ten coins and loses one. Won't she light a lamp and scour the house, looking in every nook and cranny until she finds it? And when she finds it you can be sure she'll call her friends and neighbors; "Celebrate with me! I found my lost coin!" Count on it— that's the kind of party God's angels throw every time one lost soul turns to God.
–Luke 15:8—10 (MSG)

This passage is an important illustration of two things. First, how frustrating it is to lose something and how much time and focus you must put into recovering it. Secondly, how paramount it is to God to seek and save the lost. If it is important to God, seeing people brought into His Kingdom, we need to be doing it. Then we will be enjoying the highest calling for a celebration, lost souls coming home to Jesus.

I can't count how many hours that I have spent looking for lost keys, glasses, phone chargers, earrings, gift cards, etc. Often items are lost simply because we do not pay attention while we are in a hurry. Sometimes when the items are found, there is more regret over the time wasted looking, than there is celebration over finding. How great it would be if… instead of seeking lost items, God was using us to seek and save lost souls. Sometimes deciding to find something later, means the trail is cold, and chances of recovering it are diminished. Time to be fishers of men, instead of fishing for that lost bill that came in the mail last week.

Dear Lord, Impress upon me the value of time, that I wouldn't waste it. Help me to concentrate on being fully engaged in every moment. Let there be a deliberateness about where I put things. Too often there is an attitude of, "I'll put this away later," or "I'll put this down here for now," and then totally forget. Help me to slow down. Help me to create an environment where there is a place for everything, and everything is put in its place. Keep me from becoming anxious and wasting time finding something that never should have been lost in the first place. Help me to seek you and your ways, more and more every day. In Jesus' name... Amen.

FEBRUARY 15

Overdue Dreams

Hope deferred makes the heart sick,
but a desire fulfilled is a tree of life.
–Proverbs 3:12 New English Translation (NET)

Blessed is the man who walks not in the counsel of the wicked... but his delight is in the law of the Lord, and on his law he meditates day and night. He is like a tree planted by streams of water that yields fruit is season, and its leaf does not wither, in all that he does, he prospers.
–Psalm 1:1—3 (NET)

Sometimes I feel like the poster child for *Hope Deferred.* There is nothing like some dashed-to-bits dreams, or financial and relational expectations left in no man's land over a long stretch, to make your heart in need of resuscitation. Even the word "deferred" is kin to the ways of a procrastinator. There are words like: delayed, tardy, postponed, overdue, late. Some of our hopes are outside of ourselves, and not subject to our will and control. Some harsh life events like a miscarriage, health crisis, divorce or death of a loved one can cause a heart to become numb. Often numbness creates a hard heart starved for a joyful event that could bring healing.

Whether we are responsible for our desires being postponed because of our own flaws or not, the result and the cure are pretty much the same. According to the psalmist, we need to stop hanging out with people contrary to God's purpose for our lives, and we need to embrace God's words as a basis for our lives. We should learn how to meditate in such a way to foster peace within. We need to put ourselves in the right place where we can flourish, not merely survive. This day I hope and pray that the Holy Spirit would be like a divining rod within, leading us to places flowing with restorative water, where we can flourish and be fruitful.

Dear Lord, No matter how often my hopes have been denied or deferred, let me never stop believing that I will possess everything that you want for me. Help me to focus on your desires for me, rather than my desires for myself. Protect my heart Lord. Entice me to a place of still waters, where you can restore my soul. Let me learn from my mistakes and help me to let go of things that were never mine to acquire. Please keep hope alive within me and allow me to see the fulfillment of some of my many dreams. In Jesus' name... Amen.

FEBRUARY 16

What's That Mirror For?

For now we see in a mirror dimly, but then face to face.
Now I know in part; then I shall understand fully, even as I have been fully understood. So faith, hope, love abide, these three; but the greatest of these is love.
–I Corinthians 13:12—13 (RSV)

We don't yet see things clearly. We're squinting in a fog, peering through a mist. But it won't be long before the weather clears and the sun shines bright! We'll see it all then, see it all as clearly as God sees us, knowing him directly just as he knows us! But for right now, until that completeness, we have three things to do to lead us toward that consummation: Trust steadily in God, hope unswervingly, love extravagantly. And the best of the three is love.
–I Corinthians 13:12—13 (MSG)

Why do we use a mirror? Is it to view ourselves, or to see how others view us? One's rearview mirror should be used to identify cars that are approaching our car, so we drive accordingly and safely. However, I can't count how many times my car's rearview mirror has become my "rushing off to work" make up mirror. God knows I am not the only one out there that does this! When red lights become your opportunity to put on your lipstick and mascara, on a regular basis, it's time to face the fact that you are a procrastinator. Time to eliminate some bad habits, which could possibly be dangerous. I should be someone who is fully ready to go, wherever I am going, before getting inside a car to get there.

Dear Lord, I thank you for your love. You see us as we really are, and still you love us. The more we develop our relationship with you, the more we will reflect you, the more deeply that we know you, the more we will trust you. Help me to cover my heart, soul, spirit, and mind with the gifts of hope, trust, faith, and love. Let me be open to loving extravagantly, no matter the cost, the way you have loved me. In Jesus' name... Amen.

FEBRUARY 17

Mood Swings

A sound mind makes for a robust body, but run away emotions corrode the bones
–Proverbs 14:30 (MSG)

Are God's promises not enough for you, spoken so gently and tenderly? Why do you let your emotions take over, lashing out and spitting fire
–Job 15:11—13 (MSG)

My research has shown that there are many different types of emotions or moods, that can hinder us in overcoming procrastination. One such emotion is depression, not in a clinical sense, but in the sense of a lingering feeling of "being down." According to psychotherapist, Mike Bundrant, who currently is a pioneer of Neuro-Linguistic Programing (NLP), the number one emotional obstacle procrastinators deal with is something he calls, "ultimate futility." To quote Mr. Bundrant, "Chronic Procrastination often has its roots in emotional life... Putting off until tomorrow what you can do today is a conscious or unconscious decision... You have an emotional obstacle in the way of your success." He lists five different emotions that often contribute to our avoidance behavior. To put it simply, when you are depressed you put things off. You may feel, "What's the point?"

This type of mood is the result of feeling like nothing you do will ultimately change your life for the better. Old disappointments have a way of lingering around, whispering in our ear to remind us of plans that never succeeded. So, why bother trying again. Certainly, no Biblical figure had more disappointments in life than Job did! He had every reason to be depressed, to give up, but he didn't. He decided, no matter how badly he felt, and no matter how many complaints to his Creator he expressed, he would continue to trust in God.

Dear Lord, Free me from lingering moods of depression that spoil my hopes for the future. Help me to disregard disappointments from the past. Please silence the whispers of failure and futility that discourage me and weigh me down. Let hope, faith, and trust in you, triumph over downcast moods. Help me to rule over my emotions, so that they will not rule me. In Jesus' name... Amen.

FEBRUARY 18

Just One Thing

Know this well, then. Take heart right now: God is in Heaven above;
God is on Earth below. He is the only God there is.
Obediently live by his rules and commands which I am giving you today
so that you'll live well and your children after you...
–Deuteronomy 4:39—40 (MSG)

Today as I assigned the time to sit down and write, I also thought of everything else that I was supposed to do today. I need to walk and feed my friend's dog while she's away, don't want to forget that! Since I have decided that writing my daily blog is the priority, everything else must fit around that one thing. There is no victory over procrastination without setting a goal, and then being relentless about fulfilling that goal. While I assigned 9:30 A.M. this Saturday morning to do my *#1- Must Do Thing,* did I actually sit down to do it at 9:30A.M.? Of course not, I'm a procrastinator. I didn't think five hours of my life would be filled with finding old pay stubs, filling out a reward points membership online, or putting batteries in toys that haven't been played with in eons. Today, I am reminded of Curly from the movie, *City Slickers,* holding up his one finger, reminding Billy Crystal's character, the secret to life is just one thing, that one most important thing, we just need to figure out for ourselves.

At least I am doing it now, it is getting done before midnight. Learning to rejoice in progress, no matter how small is very important in this battle. There are a number of things that I could have chosen as *Numero Uno.* All may be important things to do, but they were not #1. Maybe that's why we digress into an avalanche of "unnecessary" things, like I did for five hours; we just want to say, "I am the master over my time." But really, nothing beats knowing your #1- Must Do Thing has been done today.

Dear Lord, Constantly guide me toward my number one priority, day by day. Help me to set goals that are in line with your plan for my life. Help me to desire that sense of completion and satisfaction that comes from meeting my most important goal today! In Jesus' name... Amen.

FEBRUARY 19

Many Times

Now an angel of the Lord said to Philip, "Rise and go toward the south to the road that goes down from Jerusalem to Gaza"... And he rose and went. And there was an Ethiopian, a eunuch, a court official of Candace, queen of the Ethiopians, ... and he was reading the prophet Isaiah. And the Spirit said to Philip, "Go over and join this chariot." So Philip ran to him and heard him reading Isaiah the prophet and asked, "Do you understand what you are reading?" And he said, "How can I, unless someone guides me?"
–Acts 8:26—3 (ESV)

Many times, I have said something to God like, "Just tell me where you want me to be, and what you want me to do today." The act of surrendering one's time and actions seems that it should be a daily occurrence. Sometimes, I am really looking for a response that is very specific. I am hoping that the Lord will bring some action to the forefront of my thinking, with the emphasis of a command. If I can hear *God says* inside my head, then that difficult thing I have been avoiding will be much easier to start or follow through to completion.

In the scripture quoted above, the story is told of how an angel spoke to Philip and said, "Rise and go toward the south to the road that goes down from Jerusalem to Gaza." Now that is amazingly specific! The result of Philip's obedience was another man's understanding of Isaiah's Messianic prophecy, the surrender of his life to Jesus, and his baptism into the Kingdom of God. Philip had to look like a total fool for a while, to run alongside this important Ethiopian official's chariot, then jump into it! But, at God's command he went, made an aggressive contact, and taught this man about Jesus. That one encounter is probably the reason for Ethiopia being the one country in Africa to have an early and continuous presence of Christian faith.

Dear Lord, I know that following you is a matter of trust, however, I still yearn for clear and specific words and directions from you. A command, heard loud and clear, is easier to follow and seems more motivating for me. I know I am not Philip, but I too desire to hear a specific word from you today, one what will activate me to do your will, and bring salvation to many. May your will be made sure to me this day. In Jesus' name... Amen.

FEBRUARY 20

Even SpongeBob Does It

For God is at work within you, helping you want to obey him, and then helping you do what he wants.
–Philippians 2:13 (TLB)

Commit your work to the Lord, then it will succeed.
–Proverbs 16:3 (TLB)

So it is with Christ's body. We are all parts of it, and it takes every one of us to make it complete, for we each have different work to do. So we belong to each other, and each needs all the others.
–Romans 12:4—5 (TLB)

Procrastinators and the myriad of ways that they choose to distract themselves are popular subjects. There is even an episode of *SpongeBob SquarePants* about it. When faced with writing a school essay, he just can't seem to stay focused on the task at hand, even though he started enthusiastically. While some people experience periodic episodes of procrastination, for others of us, it is a chronic lifestyle. The list of distractions we come up with is endless: call a friend, walk the dog, make coffee, clean the floor, sort mail, enter a rabbit hole of YouTube videos, etc.

We need to seek God to gather the peace we need to proceed on a project, not dive into an endless pool of comforting, but unnecessary distractions. Any task that produces anxiety is ripe for avoiding. A solution that works for me is to choose the most comforting and energizing instrumental music, surround myself with sound and then dig into the work. Instrumental praise, classic symphonies, movie soundtracks (*Wonder Woman, Star Wars, Hidalgo)* have all been keys to unlock a comforting, pleasant place to work.

Dear Lord, Sometimes a project we face stimulates so much anxiety, we look for and create avenues of comfort and escape. Help us to find a way out of our stressful anxious state, to clear our minds, to soothe our spirits, and bring us closer to your calming loving presence. Help us to consciously commit our work to you. Help us when we enthusiastically start, to progress diligently, and see our work through to the finish. Holy Spirit, tug our hearts away from every distraction, and develop within us the ability to recognize when we are unconsciously avoiding our responsibilities. In Jesus' name... Amen.

FEBRUARY 21

A Break from the Past

For behold, I create new heavens and a new earth; and the former things shall not be remembered or come to mind. But be glad and rejoice forever in that which I create.
–Isaiah 65:17—18 (RSV)

Therefore, if anyone is in Christ, he is a new creation;
the old has passed away, behold, the new has come.
–2 Corinthians 5:17 (RSV)

Every valley shall be filled, and every mountain and hill shall be brought low, and the crooked shall be made straight, and the rough ways shall be made smooth.
–Luke 3:5 (RSV)

When I was a teenager, and I was involved in a bad relationship with a manipulative, abusive boyfriend, I remember crying myself to sleep some nights thinking, *God, please give me amnesia! I cannot see my way out of this situation. I need my memory wiped out, so I can just start all over. If I could just forget everything, then I could have a brand-new start.* If any evangelical Christian had come my way in those days and explained what it meant to be born again, I would have probably leaped at the chance to do that. I desperately wanted a clean slate. As long as we keep doing the same things over and over again, as procrastinators are apt to do, we create a lifestyle with one foot in the past every day. Our patterns become ruts that turn into difficult-to-climb-out-of valleys. Our undone tasks become mountainous, towering over us, keeping us from getting to the other side. That other side is where the old ways have passed away, and our new self is now free from well-worn patterns of thinking that have held us hostage. Time to claim our "new" self. Let's look forward to a smoother path with no ruts to trip us, and no mountains of our own making to deter us.

Dear Lord, Help me to rejoice in what you have created. Help me to forget and to extinguish old ways of thinking and doing. Let me be confident that you have prepared a smoother way for me. Keep me looking forward, not backward. Let my future not be determined by past mistakes, but by the person that I am determined to be in the future, the new creation that you have made. In Jesus' name... Amen.

FEBRUARY 22

The Exhilarating Finish

Never quit! No extra spiritual fat, no parasitic sins. Keep your eyes on Jesus, who both began and finished this race we're in. Study how he did it. Because he never lost sight of where he was headed— that exhilarating finish in and with God— he could put up with anything along the way.
–Hebrews 12:1—4 (MSG)

There are many reasons why people do not finish every race or journey they choose to start. Everything seems rather clearly defined and inspiring in the beginning. Then life, distractions, and domineering inner inclinations take over. Some people have the perfect storm of procrastinating patterns. This list includes: emotional immaturity, attention deficit, poor time management, rebellion against authority and others' expectations, fear of the pressures of failure or success, humiliation avoidance, a long history of disappointments. There is also the shadowy comfortable feeling that *if* you had actually finished your project, it would have been a huge success- better to cling to that, than to fail and prove yourself wrong. That last pattern is the ego-boosting twin of "fear of failure."

Dear Lord, Help me to study myself to see and understand the reasons for my procrastinating behavior. Help me to never lose sight of the prize of eternity with you. I want nothing to hinder my determination to follow you. Help me to equip myself to successfully finish every race that you have set before me. Let my goals be the ones that you have for me. Help me to rid myself of excess baggage, spiritual fat, and sins that weigh me down. In Jesus' name… Amen.

FEBRUARY 23

Little Steps

How he loves his people— His holy ones are in his hands.
They followed in your steps, O Lord. They have received their directions from you.
–Deuteronomy 33:3 (TLB)

You have made wide steps for my feet, to keep them from slipping.
–2 Samuel 22:37 (TLB)

The steps of good men are directed by the Lord. He delights in each step they take.
–Psalm 37:23 (TLB)

When you have moved several times, there are different things about each residence that stick out in your mind after you leave. One duplex that we loved in New Hampshire, had a very specific draw back. The steps leading up to the second floor were steep and extremely narrow. My feet aren't that big, but still they didn't fit on the steps and had to be placed at a strange angle in order to go up and down them. I am grateful that this is not the kind of steps that God has made for us to take. His steps are wide for our protection, he directs and delights in the steps that we take because we are his. Faced with any habit or character flaw that hinders us, he is gracious and makes a way. We need not take giant leaps in order for positive change to take place, little steps will do.

Dear Lord, Thank you for the privilege of being yours. Thank you for being so gracious and protective toward us. Help us to realize that following you can simply be a matter of "little by little." Guide us by your Holy Spirit. Encourage us by the revelation of your delight. Let all our steps be to approach you and your will for our lives, leaving our flaws and faults behind us. Help us to stay on the path you have ordered. In Jesus' name… Amen.

FEBRUARY 24

Get on With It

The bright light of Christ makes your way plain. So no more stumbling around. Get on with it! The good, the right, the true–these are actions appropriate for daylight hours. Figure out what will please Christ, and then do it.
–Ephesians 5:8—10 (MSG)

As a child I can remember that if something was designated as a chore, automatically it was something I did not want to do. My mom would fill the sink with hot, white, soapy water and have everything all ready for me when it was my turn to do the dishes. I would find a way to disappear, maybe hide out in the bathroom with a comic book or watch TV until the water was cold and dingy. Possibly I would get nagged into submission by my grandmother before I would budge from my hiding place. I had a friend who would let every dirty dish in her house pile up in the sink before washing those crusty things. She would also often wait until the city put a notice on her property before mowing her lawn, which had the appearance of an abandoned field. Let's face it, not taking care of one's chores doesn't work very well in living a mature life.

Procrastination for some people is: always being late, keeping house like a total wreck, bills staying unopened then unpaid for months. However our procrastination manifests, it is not good, and our actions can hardly be pleasing to God. When I was a child, it was more acceptable to be immature. As a "grownup," that kind of immaturity creates a wall of flimsy excuses that hinders a successful adult life.

Dear Lord, At times I must admit that I am immature, and put off my responsibilities as well as daily chores, and destiny decisions. I do not want to be that way anymore. Help me to bring order into domestic chaos and have a right attitude toward the multitude of jobs, errands, and functions that are part of a responsible adult life. Help me to keep my "to do" list manageable, so that I do not become besieged by all of my responsibilities. Please help me to avoid that crippling feeling of being overwhelmed by putting too much on my plate, so tomorrow will not deliver another unbearable load. In Jesus' name... Amen.

FEBRUARY 25

The Mind is a Battlefield

Open the gates that the righteous may enter,
the nation that keeps the faith.
You will dwell in perfect peace
those whose minds are steadfast,
because they trust in you.
Trust in the Lord forever,
for the Lord, the Lord himself, is the Rock eternal.
–Isaiah 26:2—4 (NIV)

Joyce Meyers is a popular author and speaker whose life and work are devoted to seeing Christians set free from anxieties that cause them to be less than they should be. Her book, *Battlefield of the Mind,* has been a huge help to me and countless others. Although it should be an oxymoron to be a miserable Christian, there are far too many whose lives and minds have been held captive in such a way that unhappiness and negative thinking prevail. As Joyce points it, "The mind should not be filled with reasoning, worry, anxiety fear, and the like. It should be calm, quiet, and serene." A God ordained state of mind should be one of peaceful quiet and that should be considered "normal" for Christians. If it is not, we need to examine our ways of thinking, then correct it, so that we allow God's Holy Spirit to be our predominant influence. I confess that a peaceful state of mind is not normal for me, but realizing that it should be, now has me moving in that direction.

Dear Lord, I confess that far too often my mind conjures up worrisome possibilities to dwell upon. Help me to rely on the Holy Spirit to pray on my behalf, to create a quiet, peaceful state within. I confess that too often my procrastinating ways puts me in an anxious state. Too often negative thinking robs me of the faith I need to move forward into the calling that you have put on my life. Give me the insight, wisdom and tools that I need to be victorious in the battle for my peace of mind. In Jesus' name… Amen.

FEBRUARY 26

Didn't Want to Hear That

To everything there is a season, A time for every purpose under Heaven:
A time to be born, And a time to die;
A time to plant, And a time to pluck what is planted;
A time to kill, And a time to heal;
A time to break down, And a time to build up;
A time to weep, And a time to laugh;
A time to mourn, And a time to dance;
– Ecclesiastes 3:1—4 (NKJ)

The day comes for everyone when they hear the bad news; a dear friend has died. I hate that news. But today the news stings and saddens all the more because I thought of that person frequently for the past few months, and never followed through on my impulse to contact him. It is true that he lived more than two hours away, but what is two hours in the light of Eternity? It is true that I had several trips near his hometown but there was more pressing business than making visits. Arranging a get together just seemed too inconvenient. Now I am burdened by the, "should have, would have, could have" feeling that we procrastinators often have.

Dear Lord, Help me to never miss the opportunity to be with a dear loved one, one last time. Holy Spirit guide me to reach out to those people in my life who are sick or dying, ones who need an encouraging word or a good deed. I believe that you prompted me, and I did not listen. Keep my spirit, heart, and mind tuned in to you at all times. Show me, even this very day, someone that I need to contact. Guide me to a place of no regrets, a place where I will listen to you, and make the effort to arrange a meeting that may be a last visit. Before it is time to weep and mourn, let there be times to build up, and laugh with those we love. In Jesus' name... Amen.

FEBRUARY 27

Friend or Foe

No one will be able to stand up against you all the days of your life… I will never leave you or forsake you… Have I not commanded you? Be strong and courageous. Do not be discouraged, for the Lord your God will be with you wherever you go
–Joshua 1:5—9 (NIV)

There are some things that have been developed, like common place technology, that are supposed to enhance our lives. We should be able to be more productive and carry more in our devices, so that our brains can be uncluttered. As a writer I should be thanking God every day for the ease of writing with my computer, as opposed to using an old school typewriter. Anything that makes correcting errors a breeze and fixes my inept spelling, Hooray!!

Recently however technology was a formidable enemy, frustrating my efforts, wasting my time, costing me hundreds of dollars and countless hours to correct. Between the daunting turmoil of a broken printer, outdated operating systems, incompatible devices, eight hours of non-productive Apple Care assistance, I felt like my life was being held hostage to my inadequate technology. For days, I sparred with my computer issues, and hit the canvas many times before barely winning the match. Too often my devices cause frustration instead of productivity. Something procrastinators definitely don't need is another unforeseen delay.

Dear Lord, I confess that I often resent my dependence on technology. Help me to let go of anger and frustration when my devices cannot do what I need them to do. Help me to fight discouragement. These objects are not my enemies, even though sometimes it feels as if they are against me. Please quiet the turmoil that stirs within me when the things that I depend upon, no longer function, costing me time and money I was not prepared to spend. In Jesus' name… Amen.

FEBRUARY 28

"Not All Who Wander are Lost"

Take the old prophets as your mentors. They put up with anything, went through everything, and never once quit, all the time honoring God. What a gift life is to those who stay the course! You've heard, of course, of Job's staying power, and you know how God brought it all together for him in the end. That's because God cares, cares right down to the last detail.
–James 5:10—11 (MSG)

Today's title quote, from a poem of J.R.R. Tolkien, is very familiar in our culture. It is on posters, T-shirts, even on some people's bodies- as an inspirational tattoo. However, it seems commonly misused as the reasonable excuse to simply go wherever one wants, and to do whatever one feels. In the context of Tolkien's poem, that is really not what it means at all. His original meaning is more in line with the above scripture from James. Here it is in context.

All that is gold does not glitter,
Not all those who wander are lost;
The old that is strong does not whither,
Deep roots are not reached by the frost.

From the ashes a fire shall be woken,
A light from the shadows shall spring;
Renewed shall be blade that was broken,
The crownless again shall be king.

Dear Lord, Keep us from wandering from place to place, relationship to relationship, job to job, idea to idea, or anything that takes us far from the course that you have set for our lives. Let us not judge things from their outward appearance or popularity. As we mature through this life, may our roots grow deep to weather life's storms. When we fall and fail, and our life is broken, burned out, and in ashes, may we be renewed by your light. When our life is done, I pray that we will have kept our course as we enter your kingdom and share in your majestic Glory. In Jesus' name... Amen.

FEBRUARY 29

Making up Time

And God said, "let there be lights in the vault of the sky to separate the day from the night, and let them serve as signs to mark sacred times, and days and years.
–Genesis 1:14 (NIV)

If you had one extra day, what would you do with it?

The whole process of adding an extra day every four years to our calendar seems rather strange to me. I understand why, otherwise eventually January would be in the middle of summer. I have a friend that deliberately wanted to get married on February 29th, knowing that her actual anniversary date would only come to pass every four years. It made absolutely no sense to me, but she thought that if it only happens every four years, it would somehow be extra special. They entered into marriage with a slew of problems, none of which could be healed by their vows, or lack of annual celebrations, and they are no longer married. Traditionally, leap year is the year for women to propose to men, rather than men being the ones to make that move. February 29th sounds like the ideal day for two procrastinators to be joined together, their anniversary would be just one more thing to put off for years!

Dear Lord, Just thinking about marriage and vows, leap years, and how you have ordered creation confounds me. I pray that we will make wise use of this extra day that we have in our calendar this year. I lift up the institution of marriage to you right now. Help us all to see the joining of man and woman together as a sacred, God-ordained relationship. There is such a cultural assault on your design for marriage right now. May we be people that look closely at our relationships before leaping quickly into marriage. May we take our vows seriously, constantly relying on your words and your Holy Spirit to keep our commitments on solid ground, "til death do us part." In Jesus' name… Amen.

MARCH 1

Call for Help

The work is so spread out, "I explained to them, 'and we are separated so widely from each other, that when you hear the trumpet blow, you must rush to where I am; and God will fight for us.' We worked early and late, from sunrise to sunset; and half the men were always on guard."
–Nehemiah 4:19—21 (TLB)

Two can accomplish more than twice as much as one, for the results can be much better. If one falls, the other pulls him up; but if a man falls when he is alone, he's in trouble.
–Ecclesiastes 4:9—11 (TLB).

When tackling a big project, a few times I have thought, *I wonder if this is what those Israelites felt like when they were rebuilding the walls of Jerusalem?* Like them, there may be a multitude of obstacles in our way. What present day situations do we find ourselves in that can seem too much to do on our own? We may have to move- which is a huge amount of work, or a thesis to finish, or full-time work with full-time school, or a house full of kids and a spouse that that is deployed or travels for their job. There are times when the task in front of us seems impossible. It may even seem as if enemies are surrounding us, and we need to be on guard. What is the best way to overcome the odds when they are stacked against us? Those Israelites who rebuilt that wall knew what to do, call for help. Sometimes life was not meant to be done all alone.

Dear Lord, Let us always be dependent on and secure in, your ever-present support available to us. Help us to recognize who are true friends are. Help us be the type of friend that others can depend on. Let there be others that will be there for us in our time of need. Keep us from isolating ourselves. Develop a humble spirit within us, one that would allow us to ask for help when we need it. Inspire us to long for the finished project. Help us be willing to work hard, for as long as it takes, to get the job done. In Jesus' name... Amen.

MARCH 2

What A Mess

But as for me, O Lord, deal with me as your child, as one who bears your name! Because you are so kind, O Lord, deliver me.
– Psalm 109:21 (TLB)

Now here are some blurry appropriate images to illustrate my confession. My den is a mess. These pictures were not staged. It's amazing that I can get anything done in here at all. I am forever losing things. My new glasses with progressive lenses… Where are they? Only God knows. The contract concerning the book I wrote? Hmmm, I thought I knew where it was. Obviously when you work and live in a mess like this it indicates something about your life. 1) You are a procrastinator, otherwise it would have been picked up and put in order by now. 2) You must have made a comfortable arrangement with turmoil otherwise you wouldn't be able to live with this disarray.

Dear Lord, Please deliver me from my procrastinating ways. Help me to take steps every day to organize the disorganized parts of my life. Give me the motivation to put other parts of my life on the back burner and this chaotic mess on the front. Help me to discern what should be thrown away, so I will not waste time dealing with anything that I will never need again in my life. In Jesus' name… Amen.

MARCH 3

The Cost of Complaining

For God is at work within you, helping you want to obey him, and then helping you to do what he wants. In everything you do, stay away from complaining and arguing so that no one can speak a word of blame against you. You are to live clean, innocent lives as children of God in a dark world full of people that are crooked and stubborn. Shine out among them like beacon lights, holding out to them the Word of Life.
–Philippians 2:13—16 (TLB)

Scriptures like this cause me to reflect on my tendency to complain. Having grown up in a household where my father was often critical of others, and my mother prone to self-criticism, it developed a rather "easy to be critical" attitude toward life. It seems as if my nature needs to be constantly renewed, in order to not see the negative side of things first. I believe it also leads to useless complaining, either inside my head, or spoken out loud. Work that God is calling me to do, a conflict of wills within my family, unpleasant circumstances beyond my control, can too often trigger anger, arguing, or complaining. When it comes to procrastinating, my brain can mentally construct every obstacle to keep from starting, or finishing, some work that needs to be done. When I see what happened to the children of Israel, wandering around in the desert, complaining, resisting God's will, literally procrastinating about entering the Promised Land, it makes me realize that complaining can be the quickest route away from whatever blessing or promise that God has for his people.

Dear Lord, Forgive me. I confess that I am too quick to see the negative side of situations, too quick to complain, too short sighted to see the big picture of what you have in store for me. You have created a Promised Land of fulfilled destiny in this life, and unspeakable glory in heaven for all of your people. Keep us from thinking and acting contrary to your will. Let us see our lives as you see them, let us be free from complaining and arguing. Grant us the ability to see the big picture, give us the grace to look beyond things that trigger our tendency to complain. In Jesus' name... Amen.

MARCH 4

Building Up

Now you are no longer strangers to God and foreigners to heaven, but you are members of God's very own family, citizens of God's country, and you belong in God's household with every other Christian. What a foundation you stand on now: the apostles and the prophets; and the cornerstone of the building is Jesus Christ himself! We who believe are carefully joined together with Christ as parts of a beautiful, constantly growing temple for God. And you also are joined with him and with each other by the Spirit and are part of this dwelling place of God.
–Ephesians 2:19—22 (TLB)

How do we become the best we can be? There is a combination of choices we can make to create the best possible outcome for our lives. When we veer off course, even by a little, we will miss our life's target by a wide margin. So how do we do this life in the best possible way? Seek God and become more like Jesus. Join a group of other believers of like heart and mind, whose aim is also to live the best possible life that they can. We need to get close to God by ingesting his written word, the Bible- in its variety of editions. We must pray, praise and worship God, live open honest lives, be servants, work diligently, and treat others with love, mercy, justice, and compassion. Loving others is godly, and it is the way we are known by others to be followers of Christ. Living the best lives that we can is a constant, silent testimony that inspires others to walk with us on this narrow path to eternity.

Dear Lord, Guide us to the body of believers where we are meant to be a part. Build us as individuals, use us in others' lives. Help us to realize that we are now your temple, you dwell within us. Help us to guard against offenses that would knock us out of place. Keep all anger, bitterness, and resentment out of our hearts. Keep us mold-able in your hands. Help us to do this day, what we need to do, to build ourselves and our church family. Help us to look forward, never taking for granted the privilege of being a part in building your kingdom. In Jesus' name... Amen.

MARCH 5

Slow Down Ms. G

Martha received him [Jesus] into her house. And she had a sister called Mary, who sat at the Lord's feet and listened to his teaching. But Martha was distracted with much serving; and she went to him and said, "Lord, do you not care that my sister has left me to serve alone? Tell her to help me." But the Lord answered her, "Martha, Martha, you are anxious and troubled about many things; one thing is needful. Mary has chosen the good portion, which shall not be taken away from her."
–Luke 10:38—42 (RSV*)*

It's an ironic thing that so many of us who are procrastinators are also very busy people. We often spend time doing things that we just want to do, then go into a very busy mode, to take care of what should have been accomplished already. I have worked with many teacher assistants over the years. They often had to keep up with my frantic pace when I was hurrying with so much to do, and so little time to do it. One of my favorite assistants, named Milton, would observe my anxiety and spinning mind trying to get everything in order, and say to me in his deep, gravelly voice, "Slow down Ms.G, Slow down." He was probably saying exactly what God wanted me to hear at those moments. I think that when we put the most important thing first, which is spending intimate time in a devotional posture with Jesus, we are less likely to have an anxious lifestyle. We should certainly not procrastinate about spending time with our Lord and Savior. Any time spent with him, translates into being more like him, and we would be less likely to avoid doing things that we should be doing.

Dear Lord, Sometimes I mistake spending time with you as a luxury, instead of a necessity. Help me to slow down and see what is truly important and realize that time with you isn't just teaching me information or reading, it's time to build our relationship. The more time that I spend with you, the greater the well of love and peace within me. Please keep me from setting myself up to be anxious because I avoided doing something that needed to be done. Help me to clearly see what is needful, to slow down, so that I can enjoy my own good portion of time spent with you, doing your will, and loving others. In Jesus' name... Amen.

MARCH 6

The Folly of Fools

The wisdom of a prudent man is to discern his way, but the folly of fools is deceiving.
–Proverbs 14:8 (RSV)

Therefore do not be foolish but understand what the will of the Lord is.
–Ephesians 5:17 (RSV)

Tim Urban, who does the blog Wait But Why, is one of the most insightful and entertaining teachers about procrastination. Anyone who waits until the last 72 hours to write a 90-page senior thesis surely is, in his own words, "a master procrastinator." He has two main comic illustrations of the biggest influences in a procrastinator's brain and behavior, the "instant gratification monkey," and the "panic monster." Anyone who wants a deeper, and humorous understanding of their procrastinating ways, must check out his TED talk. Go to TED.com, to view Tim Urban: Inside the Mind of a Master Procrastinator, TED talk. Feb. 2016. As we go along the easy road of instant gratification, with that big deadline looming over our heads, sometimes the only motivation to get it done is the infused adrenaline that explodes within us because of sheer panic. Personally, I've been there too many times. Don't want to go there again. In faith, with a combination of understanding our own foolish ways, and God's transforming power, change is actually possible. Believing that change is possible lays a foundation to construct a better life.

Dear Lord, I do not want to be foolish. When I let my desire for instant gratification rule my desires, my time, and my life, I am not being wise. Help me to discern why I do the self-defeating things that I do. Help me to rid myself of these thoughts and behaviors. Renew my mind. Restore my mind with your words and your wisdom. In Jesus' name... Amen.

MARCH 7

No Deadlines

You shall go out with joy, and be led forth in peace; the mountains and the hills before you shall break forth into singing, and the trees of the field will clap their hands.
–Isaiah 55:12 (RSV)

Then I will give you your rains in their season, and the land shall yield it's increase, and the trees of the field shall yield their fruit.
–Leviticus 26:4 (RSV)

In his wise discernment of procrastinators, Tim Urban points out an area of procrastination that is not nearly as noticeable as the common situation of panic induced work frenzy. We are all familiar with the last-minute productivity burst to finish before a deadline. That is the stereotyped image of a procrastinator. You may be one of those, or you may be the other type, or both. What is the other type? I am talking about the procrastinators with no deadlines.

We are a very stuck bunch of people on the border of depression. Without an imposed deadline to motivate us, there is no adrenaline rush of activity that ends in a finished project. Our dreams are unfulfilled, our frustration is usually just under the surface at all times, and there is a vague sadness woven into the fabric of our being. We may have never started, or finished, the large life goals gathering dust on a cluttered shelf somewhere. We have got to impose our own deadlines. We must have an image of ourselves fulfilling a joyful accomplishment. Without a deadline assigned to our aspirations, we will walk sadly to the grave. God has given us all that we need, but we must plan, plant, toil, and harvest or there will be no fruit to enjoy.

Dear Lord, I desire your joy and your peace, but I confess that my soul is troubled by all that I have left undone. Help me to impose deadlines on myself. Bless me with your life-giving rain, so the fruit of self-control will grow within me. I yearn for the joy of finished projects. I know that you are for me, and not against me. Help me to shine forth your truth and light and be rid of smothering regrets. In Jesus' name... Amen.

MARCH 8

In the Margins

And God said, Let there be lights in the firmament of the heaven to divide the day from the night; and let them be for signs, and for seasons, and for days, and years.
–Genesis 1:14 (KJV)

It seems as if God himself has given us an example here. He has structured an existence for us regulated by light and dark, activity and sleep. Our 24-hour segments, our 365 days a year, divide our allotted time on earth into predictable segments. There is always movement and change throughout the universe, but it is not random; it is orderly. Often our job or career adds order and gives us scheduled parameters to our day-to-day life, but some jobs do not. Recently I heard world renowned worship leader and song writer, Darlene Zscheck, speak at my church. She warned about the problems in living a "too busy" life, and the importance of leaving "room in the margins" to do important unplanned things. Whatever plan we come up with to order our lives, we must always leave room for the unexpected. We do not want to miss the God ordained encounters and moments that seem to appear out of nowhere.

Dear Lord, Help me to bring order to my somewhat chaotic life. Help me to learn how to use a schedule to make my life more productive. Please rid me of any rebellion that keeps me from submitting to a reasonable schedule. Give me discernment to know what to let go of today, to think clearly so that I may avoid the stress of rushing around and doing unnecessary things. If I do what needs to be done in its proper time, then I know you will grant me freedom from guilt during my "free time." Guide me along a well-planned path, give me the wisdom to know when you desire me to take a detour. In Jesus' name... Amen.

MARCH 9

Those Annoying Pine Needles

If you care for your orchard, you'll enjoy its fruit.
–Proverbs 27:18 (MSG)

Work your garden– you'll end up with plenty of food, play and party– you'll end up with an empty plate.
–Proverbs 28:19 (MSG)

The Bible has many references to tending living things, gardens, vines, and harvests. Today while raking the stubborn pine needles from my lawn, the idea of the importance of getting rid of the dead things, in order to produce healthy living things, became a revelation to me. Too many pine needles will kill the grass trying to grow underneath. When pine needles have been left to stick into the ground too long, and not cleared away in the in the fall, they are even harder to remove. All of a sudden dead pine needles became an object lesson for trying to rid oneself of all that hinders productivity in life.

Like our life's obstacles that are self-imposed, the longer they stick around, the more they take over, the deeper they dig in, the more they become entangled with the healthy growth, the more difficult to remove. I found with the needles, if I raked the same direction, or the same way, over and over again, there was little success in their removal. But... if I came at them from different directions, from left to right, then right to left, short strokes, then long ones, they would more easily dislodge. We cannot just try the same approach over and over again to rid ourselves of our procrastinating ways! Different methods, different angles, different plans, plus exerted effort, over and over, again and again, need to be applied. Rid ourselves of the dead stuff first, then our plans and dreams can start to live.

Dear Lord, You often taught your disciples in parables. I thank you that even in our day to day lives, and through observing nature, there are lessons to be learned. Help me to devise multiple plans and approaches to rid myself of my self-defeating ways. Help me set aside time, to research, to find tools, and discover more methods that will work for me to defeat procrastination in my life. Help me to help others find their victory as well. Guide me to work in the garden of the life that you have given me, so that my efforts will produce an abundant harvest. In Jesus' name... Amen.

MARCH 10

An Easy Out

Have mercy on me, O God, according to your loving kindness; according to the abundance of your compassion, blot out my transgressions.
–Psalm 51:1 (MEV)

Sometimes we just want to look for the loophole, the easy out, the proverbial "get out of jail free" card. That may be… telling a professor a tall tale to extend the deadline for your paper, a fabrication that you hope will cover your lateness, or a lie you tell yourself like, "I'll start my diet tomorrow." I try to make sure that I thank God for his mercy, grace, compassion, and forgiveness every day. We can never fool an all-knowing God. Sometimes it is surprising to me that we act like we can.

It is my current goal to complete a blog entry every day, with an allowance for one day off out of seven, if needed. Today I cheated because I have a default loophole. Since I started to write my blog six years ago in California, my blog is set to Pacific Standard Time. When I discovered that I could actually finish my writing at 2 A.M. and it would post as 11 P.M. on the previous day, part of me was thrilled that I had an out, a free pass for procrastinating. But, the part of me that desires to defeat this enemy in my life was disheartened. I really don't need one more avenue that leads to making procrastination easier; it is just too tempting. Today I cheated, knowing my entry won't be finished until March 11, but it will post as March 10. I could just be cheating myself, or maybe my extra three hours is just a loving God's grace period. He knows my weaknesses, thankfully he still loves me.

Dear Lord, I do thank you for your love, mercy, grace, and forgiveness. I cannot imagine my life without it. Help me to not give in to temptations that override the commitment to my personal goals. It may seem like no big deal, but I desire to be faithful in the little things and build new patterns in my life that do not give room to make procrastination easy. Keep your kingdom and my goals ever before me. In Jesus' name… Amen.

MARCH 11

A Confident Hope

I pray that God, the source of hope, will fill you completely with joy and peace because you trust in him. Then you will overflow with confident hope through the power of the Holy Spirit.
–Romans 15:13 (NLT)

Lord, I give my life to you. I trust in you, my God!... No one who trusts in you will ever be disgraced... Show me the right path, O Lord; point out the road for me to follow. Lead me by your truth and teach me, for you are the God who saves me. All day long I put my hope in you.
–Psalm 25:1–5 (NLT)

There are plenty of times in my life that I have hoped for something that did not come to pass, often I gave up hope. Why? Because that thing I prayed for, believed for, did not come to pass "yet." There is a difference between hope and a *confident hope*. A confident hope is one planted deep, nourished by faith and trust in God. The other type of hope is just a wish. We must plant a confident hope deep within our mind, heart, and spirit, then leave it up to the Lord for that hope to grow and produce as he wills. I confidently hope and trust in God, not for the end result that I wish for, but in God's unfailing love, mercy, and will to produce what is best for me.

Dear Lord, Let me yield more and more to your Holy Spirit. Let your Spirit guide me in what to do, and what I should confidently hope for in my life. Help me to release doubt and fear from my mind. Help me to have a trust in you that grows day by day, never dwindling. Heal me from past disappointments. Fill me with your Holy Spirit so that I will overflow with confident hope, joy, and peace. Use me to pass on your heavenly gifts to others, so that they would come to know you and experience a revelation of what you have called them to be. In Jesus' name... Amen.

MARCH 12

Real Time

God doesn't come and go. God lasts. He's Creator of all you can see or imagine. He doesn't get tired out, doesn't pause to catch his breath. And he knows everything, inside and out. He energizes those who get tired, gives fresh strength to dropouts.
–Isaiah 40:28—29 (MSG)

I come and go. I get very tired. Sometimes I want to be more like God so badly. God, why don't you just zap me with your attributes? I want to be more creative, wiser, more tireless. We humans are mighty weak, amazing that we have transformed the entire planet with our population and productions. We are capable of astounding Olympic feats but can get immobilized by a microscopic virus. Can we really do anything we set our minds to? As a procrastinator, I know that I increase my own frustrations by creating situations of undue stress. It doesn't matter how early I get up in the morning I am always rushing out the door in a flurry of self-directed anger because I didn't get everything done before walking out the door. All I really want is solutions. Sometimes I think the only way to combat my lack of time management is to always give myself more time. Too often when I have that elusive more time, I try to unrealistically squeeze too much into it, stressing myself into a tight restraint anyway. More time, yes, but let it be realistic time, with equally realistic expectations for what can be done within those tic-tocking boundaries.

Dear Lord, Help me to be more aware of time, how much the time of whatever needs to be done, will actually take. Real time not fantasy "I can get that done in an hour" time, when it will actually take me three hours. Help me develop habits that save time and frustration. Lead me and guide me in all my ways, to do first things first. Thank you for all the grace that you generously pour over all of my faults every day. I thank and praise you for what you have done in countless ways, what you are doing now, and what you will continue to do for me in the future. In Jesus' name... Amen.

MARCH 13

Completed

When the builders completed the foundation of the Temple, the priests put on their official robes and blew their trumpets; and the descendants of Asaph crashed their cymbals to praise the Lord in the manner ordained by King David.
–Ezra 3:10 (TLB)

Having gone through the entire land, they completed their task in nine months and twenty days.
–2 Samuel 24:8 (TLB)

and the building was completed in every detail in November of the eleventh year of his reign. So it took seven years to build.
–I Kings 6:38 (TLB)

Our God is a God that smiles on completion. The fulfillment of a plan, with all of its division of labor, necessary supplies, specific designs, and exact directions, is an event to be celebrated. In Ezra 3:10, there was still no finished project, but a sure foundation is crucial to the success of any building venture. It was perfectly right that God's people celebrated that fact. As these verses show, many stages are noteworthy, whether they take weeks, months, or years to complete. Sometimes a good start, an essential start still in its infancy, is praiseworthy and cause for rejoicing. Maybe the memory of the wonderful sense at just being able to begin, can carry us through those obstacles and difficult times as we head toward the big prize, our own completed work that puts a smile on God's face and a song of thanksgiving and joy in our hearts.

Dear Lord, Give me ears to hear, and eyes to see your plan. Stir desires deep within my heart that are your desires for my life. Help me to be a diligent builder, rejoicing at every step accomplished along the way. Let me cling to you daily; you are the Master, the creator of all things. I can be encouraged to know that you desire to work and build through me. Praise you for your glorious works. In Jesus' name... Amen.

MARCH 14

Now or Later?

The thief comes only in order to steal, and kill and destroy. I have come that they may have and enjoy life, and have it in abundance [to the full, 'til it overflows].
–John 10:10 *Amplified Bible* (AMP)

There have been many times when this verse came into my mind and I thought, "You know what Jesus, I am really not having the abundant enjoyable life that you have promised. What is the deal? I follow you, go to church, witness, read your Word, pray, and feel like I am doing everything that needs to be done on my part. When are you going to come through for me?" This self-pitying introductory thinking is usually followed by a list of things that are causing me stress and sadness.

The truth is we live in a fallen world, and we have an enemy that schemes to steal our joy, and our souls. The awareness that procrastination usually means steadily giving away our long-term rewards for instant gratification, can be the first step in taking responsibility for our own happiness. God knows self-pity never opens the door to anything good in life, but sacrificing what we desire in the moment, for the reward of a life-long goal, surely does.

"The Cause of Most of Man's Unhappiness
is Sacrificing What He Wants Most
For What He wants Now."
-Gordan B. Hinkely

Dear Lord, Help me to see all that you have done for me on the cross. You provide all that I need to get through the dark valleys in this life. Help me to be more and more aware of the times when what I want now, is interfering with what is best for me and those things that I desire the most. Give me discernment to see the value, or threat to my wellbeing, in every action. Thank you for loving me through it all, happiness or heartache. In Jesus' name... Amen.

MARCH 15

Love My Neighbor as Myself

'You shall love the Lord your God with all your heart, with all your soul, with all your strength, and with all your mind,' and 'your neighbor as yourself.'
–Luke 10:27 (NKJ)

Jesus is telling anyone who wants to live a godly life, exactly what they need to do. How can we possibly fulfill this commandment? Unless we meditate on it, renew our minds, rearrange our priorities, we cannot. These words, that appear more than once in the Bible, are literally ALL we need to do. We must plant these words deep in our heart, soul, and mind, and drench ourselves in the reality of LOVE.

In researching the ways of procrastinators there are certain words that are often linked together; they are escapism, depression, procrastination, avoidance, and self-loathing. These characteristics are woven into a web of negativity that traps us into being so much less than we can be. My faults are always screaming for attention, and it is difficult to hear that still, small, loving voice of God, yet... I must. Time to make loving God, loving myself, and loving my neighbor, the main thing, so all else will be drawn into place. By loving in these ways, the negative cycle which drives procrastination can be broken.

Dear Lord, Teach me to love myself, to free myself from that condemning voice that chastises every mistake and magnifies every flaw. You have not come to condemn me, but to pour out grace and mercy. Lead me in ways to be gracious to myself. Let your words of loving kindness fill me, nurture me, and block the lies that try to smother the person that you see when you look at me. I am an adored child of my Heavenly Father. Thank you Lord, for your generous love toward me. In Jesus' name... Amen.

MARCH 16

Killing Time

Trust in him at all times, you people; pour out your hearts to him, for God is our refuge.
–Psalm 62:8 (NIV)

For if you remain silent at this time, relief and deliverance for the Jews will arise from another place, but you and your father's family will perish. And who knows but that you have come to your royal position for such a time as this.
–Esther 4:14 (NIV)

I always thought, "Just killing time," as the response to the question, "What'cha doing?" was a lame answer. Like really, who would want to do that? It seems to me as if there are mainly two types of people that feel comfortable with murdering the possibilities given to them as they flow through life. One is the perpetually bored, the other is the complacently apathetic.

When I saw a poster in the design shop, Prince Ink, in Norfolk, that stated "Killing Time is Killing Me." The hourglass image with a hangman's noose décor got the point across nicely. I simply had to have it. It is a great illustration of the self-defeating effects of destroying the time we are given. Personally, I don't kill time, don't ever want to kill time, and will be increasingly more careful every passing day to not squander it. There is no time to kill, or to be bored or complacent.

Dear Lord, Let us have the kind of wisdom and discernment of Queen Esther. Help us to realize that whatever position we are in, humble or exalted, to make the most of "such a time as this." Help us to trust in you, follow you, pour out our heart to you, and know you daily as our refuge and strength. In Jesus' name... Amen.

MARCH 17

Let's Celebrate

Therefore do not let anyone judge you by what you eat or drink, or with regard to a religious festival, a New Moon celebration or a Sabbath day.
–Colossians 2:16 (NIV)

Their sorrow was turned into joy and their mourning into a day of celebration... observe the days as days of feasting and joy and giving presents of food to one another and gifts to the poor.
–Esther 9:22 (NIV)

"Let's have a feast and celebrate. For this son of mine was dead and is alive again; he was lost and now is found." So they began to celebrate. "Meanwhile, the older son was in the field. When he came near the house, he heard music and dancing..."
–Luke 15:22—25 (NIV)

The Bible is overflowing with references to celebrations, festivals, music, and dancing. It is mystifying to me that in many periods of Christianity's timeline, serious somberness was the defining characteristic instead of JOY! Today is St. Patrick's Day. For me it has been a traditional day to celebrate my Irish heritage, my Christianity, and life. When I was teaching in a locked facility for dangerous youth, it was one of my priorities to celebrate every possible holiday I could with my emotionally damaged, confined students. Games, green beads, homemade bread pudding, sweet creamy coffee, and an Irish movie punctuated their caged lives with love and joy, if only for one day. Celebrations are precious time spent with family, friends, loved ones, or even strangers, and they can be a strong antidote for the deep ills we harbor in our souls.

Dear Lord, Let us take advantage of every joyous reason to celebrate. Our time on earth is relatively short, and needs moments of friends, feasting, and family gathering. Help us to never be so busy with the work and routines of life, that we are not willing break from our usual day to day lives and take time to celebrate. Let us find reasons to enjoy all the unexpected little pleasures in life that we are too quick to ignore. In Jesus' name... Amen.

MARCH 18

No Matter What

Be cheerful no matter what; pray all the time; thank God no matter what happens. This is the way God wants you who belong to Christ Jesus to live... May God himself, the God who makes everything holy and whole, make you holy and whole, put you together–spirit, soul, and body– and keep you fit for the coming of our Master, Jesus Christ. The One who called you is completely dependable. If he said it, he'll do it!
–I Thessalonians 5:16—24 (MSG)

There are so many things in this passage that address problems created by procrastination. It is hard to be "cheerful" when full of anxiety because the current workload has been doubled by avoiding doing it in reasonable portions. When believers pray and are thankful to God all the time, perspective changes and more positive emotions rise. Thank God it is not up to me to make myself whole or holy, if it was ... it probably would have been at the end of my "to do" list. Being in a state of procrastination makes us feel disjointed, as if our spirit, soul, and body are moving in separate directions all at once. God has basically told us, "Pull yourself together!" He formed us to be internally unified, thereby making it possible for us to be that way.

Dear Lord, Lead me back to your Word again, and again, so that I will pray the reality of your words into my life. Mold my spirit, soul, and body into a fit unit for your service, prayerful and thankful at all times. While awaiting your return, lead me into being someone who is dependable. Help me to be a clear reflection of you and your ways, more and more every day. In Jesus' name... Amen.

MARCH 19

Wonderful Things

However, as it is written: "What no eye has seen, what no ear has heard, and what no human mind has conceived"– the things [wonderful things] God has prepared for those who love him—
–I Corinthians 2:9 (NIV)

You asked, 'Who is this that obscures my plans without knowledge?' Surely I spoke of things I did not understand, things too wonderful for me to know.
–Job 42:3 (NIV)

Lord, you are my God; I will exalt you and praise your name, for in perfect faithfulness you have done wonderful things, things planned long ago.
–Isaiah 25:1 (NIV)

Recently, a friend in church said to me, "The process just doesn't look like the promise!" Amen to that! When you've had plans and dreams on hold forever, or you've seen them crash and burn, it is hard to believe that God truly has a wonderful plan for your life. You may have thought you knew what they were; you may have a parade of missteps and false starts leading to nowhere. I just may be twirling a baton at the head of that parade! Plans may have come to nothing so far, but that doesn't mean they have expired. Experience is one thing, truth is quite another. God loves us, and God is good, and God is the creator of wonderful things, on earth as it is in heaven. We are the ones that don't see the big picture. To move forward in life, we must believe that God has wonderful things, marvelous and glorious things, in store for all of us that love him.

Dear Lord, Let any vision that I have, not in keeping with your plan, fade from my mind and no longer stir any desire for fulfillment. Give me your plan, let me see my life the way you see it. Mark my path clearly in the direction of those most wonderful things, things which you have prepared for me from long ago. Let me never lose trust in your love for me and let me always believe that wonderful things will be within my reach. In Jesus' name... Amen.

MARCH 20

Will be Done

And I'm going to keep that celebration going because I know how it's going to turn out. Through your faithful prayers and the generous response of the Spirit of Jesus Christ, everything he wants to do in and through me will be done. I can hardly wait to continue on my course. I don't expect to be embarrassed in the least.
–Philippians 1:19—20 (MSG)

These thoughts are so encouraging! Whatever we decide to do, whatever goal we lay out in front of us, as children of God, if we are obedient to start and continue on the course set by that beginning, it will be done. As long as we seek God's will, he works through us and for us.

Dear Lord, Help me to realize, at the depth of my being, that you are for me, You are generous and faithful, and inspire me to stay my course. Infuse my path with a desire to spread the gospel, and to be a true witness by what I do and say. Help me to embrace and continue my journey wherever it leads. May the sins and weights that so easily beset me be dropped by the wayside. Today, may your will be done in me. In Jesus' name… Amen.

MARCH 21

Removing Guilt

Then I acknowledged my sin to you and did not cover up my iniquity. I said, "I will confess my transgressions to the LORD." And you forgave the guilt of my sin.
–Psalm 32:5 (NIV)

Whoever conceals their sins does not prosper, but the one who confesses and renounces them finds mercy.
–Proverbs 28:13 (NIV)

If we confess our sins, he is faithful and just and will forgive us our sins and purify us from all unrighteousness.
–1 John 1:19 (NIV)

We are His. We Follow Him, the one who died on a cross for our sins. Every wrong thing we ever did, every willful detour off the righteous path laid out before us, Jesus covered it all. We rarely see Jesus portrayed as hanging naked on that cross, but he probably was. Humiliation and pain that was unbearable, he bore for us. We need to be able bare our souls and confess our sins. Living our lives from a posture of guilt is very unproductive. Procrastination is no large violation against humanity, as some horrible act of atrocity, yet whether our guilt is large or small, it hinders us from being the person we should be. This is not just about being a procrastinator, it is about coming clean with whatever we need to confess. According to a post by Dr. Timothy Pychl on the guilt of procrastination, "The emotion most strongly associated with procrastination is guilt." How do we as Christians remove the weight of guilt? The act of our confession and our repentance releases the mercy and forgiveness of God. God removes our guilt.

Dear Lord, I am so grateful that Jesus died for me. His great love in suffering for me upon the cross is beyond my comprehension; let it never be beyond my appreciation. I thank you and praise you for who you are and the tremendous depth of your love for me. Help me to stay clean before you. Let me stay washed in your Word, enveloped by your Holy Spirit, and quick to confess my sins. When I recognize that guilt is dragging me down, give me the discernment as to whether it is a useless disruption of my emotional state, or a sign that it is time for me to come clean about some sin in my life. I ask these things in the precious name of Jesus ... Amen.

MARCH 22

What Log?

Why do you see the speck that is in your brother's eye, but do not notice the log that is in your own eye? Or how can you say to your brother 'Let me take the speck out of your eye,' when there is a log in your own eye?
–Matthew 7:3—5 (RSV)

While this verse is mainly used to point out dangers in being judgmental, and faulty thinking involved in being blind to one's own flaws; it is also a sign of another problem. It reminds me of an unsettling and common social problem of "The Blame Game." Phrases that start with, "If only..." then fill in the blank with a multitude of excuses as to why we haven't done this or that, because someone else did something wrong. So really... my failure is their fault. Really? "I wouldn't have missed my flight if you hadn't kept me up so late." "I couldn't finish my paper because that professor assigned us too much work." "If only my family was more supportive I could have started my own business by now." How often do we hear those kinds of, "If... then" someone-else-is-to-blame excuses? How often do we have that kind of log in our own eye?

Dear Lord, Help me to be accurate in my self-examination. Let me look boldly at my own mistakes. Guide me on a path where I will always take responsibility for my own flaws and shortcomings. Help me to recognize when I am blaming others, and not seeing the log in my own eye, then grant me the strength to remove it. In Jesus' name... Amen.

MARCH 23

Sometimes Late Means Never

At that time the kingdom of heaven will be like ten virgins who took their lamps and went out to meet the bridegroom. Five of the virgins were foolish, and five were wise. When the foolish ones took their lamps, they did not take extra olive oil with them. ... When the bridegroom was delayed a long time, they all became drowsy and fell asleep. But at midnight there was a shout, 'Look, the bridegroom is here! Come out to meet him.'.... The foolish ones said to the wise, 'Give us some of your oil, because our lamps are going out.' 'No.' they replied. 'There won't be enough for you and for us. Go... buy some for yourselves.' But while they had gone to buy it, the bridegroom arrived, and those who were ready went inside with him to the wedding banquet. Then the door was shut. Later, the other virgins came too, saying, 'Lord, lord! Let us in!' But he replied, 'I tell you the truth, I do not know you!'
–Matthew 25:1-13 (NIV)

We are all quite familiar with the expression, "better late, than never." The earliest written reference of this quote that I found comes from the writings of a Roman historian commonly known as Livy. It is also a quote referenced online from the *Dork Diaries,* written by Rachel Renee Russel. I can see that in some cases this would definitely be true, like catching a murderer, being able to pass an important test, reconciling with a loved one. However, when it comes to being late, I think Shakespeare had a better handle on this idea, "Better three hours too soon, than a minute too late." This was aptly illustrated in Romeo and Juliet! For modern inspiration, how about a quote from Drake, "... but never late is better." If you have ever missed out on an important life experience because later turned into never, like visiting your elderly grandmother, or installing batteries on your carbon monoxide detector, the importance of not being late can be measured in terms of life or death.

Dear Lord, Help me to understand that some things cannot just be put off and delayed into another day, possibly a day that never comes. Help me to understand the difference between being late and being too late. Correct my casual thinking about the nature of being late. Let me see something that I can do today, that must be done today, so that I will have no regrets in the future. In Jesus' name... Amen.

MARCH 24

Baby Boomer or Gen X, Matters Not

The God of Abraham, Isaac, and Jacob, the God of our fathers, has glorified his servant Jesus.
–Acts 3:13 (NIV)

To him be the glory in the church and in Christ Jesus throughout all generations, for ever and ever!
–Ephesians 3:21 (NIV)

Know therefore that the Lord your God is God; he is the faithful God, keeping his covenant of love to a thousand generations of those who love him and keep his commandments.
–Deuteronomy 7:9 (NIV)

My mother was part of a generation that lived through the Great Depression and World War II. She saw the transition from Model A cars, to landing on the moon. When I look around my home and see the array of her possessions that are now mine, I picture her often and think about what a wonderful woman she was. I wonder if I am able to pass on a knowledge of her to my children's children. Like family, God is a generational and a relational being. Remembering God, His words and His deeds, is essential in order to them pass on. We are called to produce something of enduring value. We do not want to be people who just live for instant gratification and build no godly monuments to guide others when we are gone. Working with children in a Sunday School room, building a career that can benefit thousands of lives, or writing a much beloved song are all examples of actions that could impact future generations. We must not let our procrastination rob generations to come. Godly good deeds are meant for us to plant now, and to be reaped by generations not yet born.

Dear Lord, Help me to be focused beyond the present. You work from one generation to another. Your truth and words are eternal. There are so many things that I could do, guide me to do the work closest to your heart. Increase within me the desire to do acts of lasting value. Let me be engaged with every generation in a way that will multiply souls saved. In Jesus' name... Amen.

MARCH 25

Getting off the Wrong Road

For people who hate discipline and only get more stubborn, There'll come a day when life tumbles in and they break, but by then it'll be too late to help them.
–Proverbs 29:1 (MSG)

God's message: "Do people fall down and not get up? Or take the wrong road and just keep going? So why does this people go backward, and just keep going on –backward! They stubbornly hold on to their illusions, refuse to change direction... They just kept at it, blindly and stupidly banging their heads against a brick wall.
–Jeremiah 8:4-5 (MSG)

When I am on a road trip I usually stay very aware of where I am during the journey. Generally, if I make a wrong turn or miss the correct exit, I quickly adjust my direction and get back on track. It is painful for me to admit, but in life I hold on to illusions, and I'm not quickly inclined to alter my direction. Being overweight has been a lifelong issue for me. I have probably lost close to 250 lbs. over the course my life, but I always gain it back, and then gain more than I lost. I believe that it is referred to as the boomerang, or elevator, method of weight maintenance. I procrastinate changes in my diet, resist regular times of exercise and ignore the obvious effects until it is too late. Pants don't fit, knees hurt more, and my inclination to dislike myself is stirred. While I can thankfully pat myself on the back for positive steps made in overcoming procrastinating ways in some areas, being on the wrong road as far as my weight is concerned, is my reality now. On the wrong road? Going the wrong direction? We all need to periodically check our areas of stubbornness, to keep from drifting backward.

Dear Lord, I confess that I resist living a "disciplined" life. I feel as if I need deliverance from the instant gratification pleasures of food. Help me to choose a new way, a healthier way, and not to be blind to all the drawbacks of being overweight. Help me change my direction in this area, and to no longer procrastinate about losing my unwanted pounds. This is so hard for me. Please help me to curb my appetite, change some daily routines, and be strict with myself. It feels overwhelming without your intervention Lord! Please heed my cry for help in this area. In Jesus' name... Amen

MARCH 26

Everybody Makes Mistakes

Indeed, we all make mistakes
–James 3:2 (NLT)

If your boss is angry at you, don't quit! A quiet spirit can overcome even great mistakes.
–Ecclesiastes 10:4 (NLT)

Enthusiasm without knowledge is no good; haste makes mistakes
–Proverbs 19:2

As a teacher it is very easy for me to focus on mistakes. One of the challenges to teaching youth designated as "Danger to Self, Danger to Others," is the fact that they certainly don't want to be inside a classroom in a locked behavioral health facility. One thing I had in common with a lot of these students is that I absolutely hate making mistakes! I came up with a way to help my students pay attention and soothe our common problem. At the beginning of the day I would say, "If you can catch me making at least six mistakes today. Pizza party after school tomorrow." They paid such close attention to everything I did and said, it was great for the learning environment. It reinforced to them and me, that we all make mistakes. It is no big deal, and we all developed a quieter spirit toward our errors.

Unfortunately, when I am working at home and I make a mistake, I am usually not quiet at all. I don't swear or cuss, but I do yell, growl, berate myself, shout a variety of putdowns, "How could I do that?! How stupid am I?!" etc. Today, this self-anger part of the procrastination-perfectionism dual force which accomplishes nothing, reared it's ugly head. No one needs a load of self-condemnation and anger heaped on their emotional back. We most certainly need, "a quiet spirit [that] can overcome even great mistakes" and peacefully accept that we are human, and we all make mistakes.

Dear Lord, I desperately need your help today and every day. Keep the erupting fire of self-anger away when I make a mistake. Holy Spirit bring peace to my mind and heart to soothe my emotional soul. If you are not angry at me for being human, there is no way I should get so angry with myself. Help me to train myself, to pause, to accept my limitations without condemnation. Grant me a supernatural peace that triumphs over my natural inclinations. In Jesus' name... Amen.

MARCH 27

Comfort versus Comfortable

What a wonderful God we have–he is the Father of our Lord Jesus Christ, the source of every mercy, and the one who so wonderfully comforts and strengthens us in our hardships and trials. And why does he do this? So that when others are troubled, needing our sympathy and encouragement, we can pass on to them this same help and comfort God has given us.
–2 Corinthians 1:3-4 (TLB)

Sometimes a bit of comfort is exactly what we need. I don't mean choosing a "comfortable" life over a challenging one that stretches us into uncomfortable places. Being comfortable isn't the goal. The goal is to be the kind of Christian that cares, loves, and comforts others, in order to draw them into the Kingdom of God. The apostles knew it is not an easy road; it can be a difficult one and for some a torturous one. We shouldn't deny ourselves God's comfort by not reaching out for it when we are going through difficult times. If the road we are on is too comfortable, we just may be on the wrong road. It should not be the path that gives us comfort, it should be a path embracing God's gift of comfort as we travel on the challenging, narrow road.

Dear Lord, I thank you that no matter what we are going through you are a wonderful God. Pour out your mercy, grace, compassion, and comfort upon us. When we are troubled let us reach out to you for encouragement. Let us not seek sympathy from others but let us seek to show compassion and sympathy to those that are hurting. Lead us in ways that we can give help and comfort. Holy Spirit, you are the Comforter; stay close to us and let us feel your presence. In Jesus' name... Amen.

MARCH 28

What Could Have Been

The band and chorus united as one to praise and thank the Lord... Their theme was "He is good! His loving-kindness lasts forever!" And at that moment the glory of the Lord, coming as a bright cloud, filled the Temple so that the priests could not continue their work.
–2 Chronicles 5:13—14 (TLB)

Sing a new song to the Lord! Sing it everywhere around the world! Sing out his praises! Bless his name. Each day tell someone he saves.
–Psalm 96:1—3 (TLB)

Love of music has been a huge part of my life. I have managed a music venue and a band, written song lyrics, but never learned to play an instrument. Between my weird piano teacher, and listening to my grandmother nagging me to practice, I procrastinated rather than practice my piano lessons. Just thinking... what if I had practiced my piano, and learned how to play? How would my life be different? What if my love of music had been combined with some discipline, routine, and patience? I could probably play the piano today. The ability to skillfully play the piano would definitely alter my life for the better. For every person who writes that Grammy winning song, or that Oscar winning screenplay, they had days when they could have chosen to take a nap, go out with friends, or party all night. Instead, they worked on that song or screenplay. A dream realized is far greater than channel surfing for hours. Maybe overcoming procrastination has more to do with believing in one's unlimited possibilities and sacrificing self-indulgence, than the lack of time management.

Dear Lord, Help me and help all of us who are inclined to put things off, who choose what is easy for the moment. Help us to see the error of our ways and the consequences of our choices. Give us a vision of what we are called to be, and what we can contribute to this world. Instill us with a greater sense of what is at stake when we delay. Help us to speak, to plan, to plant seeds of right actions that will yield good results. Help us to believe that our dreams can come true, and that the plans you have put in our hearts are worth whatever it takes to make them happen. In Jesus' name... Amen.

MARCH 29

Sometimes

I have strength for all things in Christ Who empowers me [I am ready for anything through Him Who infuses inner strength into me; I am self-sufficient in Christ's sufficiency].
–Philippians 4:13 (AMPC)

Being stuck in a way of life that is prone to postpone so many things is often frustrating and disappointing. Every procrastinator has their particular duties or activities that they usually put off to some vague place in the future. Usually, it is in the tomorrow that never arrives. Sometimes it is hard for us to believe that change is possible, but it is. If we belong to Christ, his strength resides within us, and there is power to be tapped for whatever we need to do. Sometimes, we just aren't willing. Sometimes, we wait for the mysterious force known as motivation to lunge us forward. But, sometimes motivation doesn't appear. We should not wait for motivation; it is a trap. We just need to obey and do, whether we feel like it or not. Once we are willing, then draw on the strength of an Almighty God who dwells with in us.

Dear Lord, Forgive me for all the times I waited to be motivated, and important things were left undone. Help me to see that through the power of willingness to obey, willingness to accomplish what you want me to do, willingness to fulfill my debts and obligations, you open a door within me to your strength. Thank you that you have not left me on my own, but you have placed power within me. Teach me to daily draw upon the God-infused abilities within me. In Jesus' name... Amen.

MARCH 30

Unwise Reluctance

Work hard and cheerfully at all you do, just as though you were working for the Lord and not merely for your masters, remembering that it is the Lord Jesus Christ who is going to pay you, giving you your full portion of all he owns. He is the one you are really working for.
–Colossians 3:23—24 (TLB)

You must be even more careful to do the good things that result from being saved, obeying God with deep reverence, shrinking back from all that might displease him. For God is at work within you, helping you want to obey him, and then helping you do what he wants.
–Philippians 2:12—13 (TLB)

While the scriptures are the main source for wisdom, there is a lot of wisdom to be found in other sources as well. In Proverbs 4:7, the Bible encourages us to seek wisdom as the most important thing. While reading a book of quotes called "Springs of Roman Wisdom," I came across an interesting saying from a man known as Terence. "An easy task becomes difficult when you do it with reluctance." So many of the things that we procrastinators keep avoiding, by the time we actually get to it, it has marinated in reluctance, making it all the more unpleasant to do. If we can accept the "avoided" chore willingly, we have made a step toward victory over procrastination. Reluctance strongly increases the distaste of the job at hand. If we can perceive the value in our willingness and see that we labor for our Lord in all that we do, the burden of reluctance can be lifted, hopefully sooner rather than later.

Dear Lord, Help me to not separate all unpleasant tasks into the "I'll do this later" category. Let me realize that all my labor is counted by you. I thank you that you are willing to give me a full portion from all that is yours. Help me to realize when my reluctance is leading me down the path of procrastination. Create in me a willingness to quickly obey, and the ability to change my attitude of reluctance, to readiness. Create in me a servant's heart that does not shun unpleasant tasks. In Jesus' name... Amen.

MARCH 31

If You Are Lazy

We do not want you to become lazy, but to imitate those who through faith and patience inherit what has been promised.
–Hebrews 6:12 (NIV)

Go to the ant, you sluggard; consider its ways and be wise!
–Proverbs 6:6 (NIV)

Lazy hands make for poverty, but diligent hands bring wealth.
–Proverbs 10:4 (NIV)

When I was being interviewed by a panel of administrators at an alternative school for students that were designated a step away from permanent expulsion, I strongly desired that position and answered every question very thoughtfully. Often there was a pause before answering a question, except for one question. They asked me, "Are some students just lazy?" My quick, short, assured reply took them a bit by surprise, with no usual follow up questions. "Absolutely!" was my immediate, confident answer.

According to most experts, procrastination usually has its origins in a psychological bent due to a variety of fears, rebellion, lack of emotional regulation, self-sabotage, or a profound instant gratification drive. However, some procrastinating people are simply lazy. Until Christians who are lazy overcome the desire to do nothing, coasting through life on the easiest path possible, they will never inherit all that God has planned for them. If you are lazy, you may end up in the "wicked servant" category, never hearing the words, "Well done, good and faithful servant." If you are lazy, this prayer below is for you.

Dear Lord, Help me to see myself as I really am and help me be willing to change in ways that will make me more productive. Help me to not be lazy, but to be wise, diligent and active. Create in me a desire to be self-reliant, to generate resources that will cover my own debts, and be generous to my family, to the family of God, and to others. Holy Spirit, reveal to me when I am submitting to laziness, draw me into action so that I can overcome this character flaw in my life. In Jesus' name... Amen.

APRIL 1

Time for Resurrection

Jesus told her, "I am the resurrection and the life. Anyone who believes in me will live, even if he is dead."
–John 11:24—26 (NLT)

How does determination, commitment, and enthusiasm morph into an emotional shadow with little staying power? Maybe what we think is determination is actually just false bravado, and commitment is really, "I hope I can stick to this." What happens when our enthusiasm that was going strong, doesn't yield the expected results? It's kind of like an old balloon, a bright reminder from a wonderful event, that is now a shrunken, wrinkled dust collector in the corner of the room. It has served its purpose, but now what's the point? The point is– resurrection is possible. Thank God, our God is a being who desires to bring dead things to life. He is a God of the living and not the dead. How blessed are we, when we absorb the knowledge that the same power that rose Jesus from the dead lives in us when we belong him? We are incredibly blessed! I know it is true. My problem is often accessing what God freely gives. His power to resurrect is ours, and as believers we must have faith in order to receive it.

Dear Lord, Your Word says that faith comes by hearing the Word of God, that with faith as small as a mustard seed, I can move mountains. Without faith, it is impossible to please you. Help me to do what I can to make that seed of faith grow within me. Keep me in your Word every day, let it be infused in my heart, soul, and mind. Help me to see the deflated dreams that you have birthed in me, ones that I have cast aside, rise up filled with your resurrection power. In Jesus' name... Amen.

APRIL 2

Hide and Seek

Your word have I hid in my heart, that I may not sin against you.
–Psalm 119:11 (MEV)

Let us also lay aside every weight and sin that so easily entangles us, and let us run with endurance the race that is set before us.
–Hebrews 12:1 (MEV)

Recently someone dear to me said, "I just don't see things the same way you do. I don't think that procrastination is a sin." To which I replied, "One definition of sin is simply to miss the mark." Whether it is called a sin, or a character flaw, or a weight hindering our progress in life, it is not good. Often it leads to breaking our word, making up lies as excuses, self-defeating attitudes, unpaid obligations, failing in school, or even losing a job.

While procrastination hasn't led to all these negative consequences in my life, it has certainly led to some. The thought of my life being at an end, having never completed the work God wanted me to do, that is the worst thing for me. Doing the most important thing right now, does not come easy to those of us that struggle in this area. If I don't have victory over this now, that day of victory may never come. How can you or I overcome? Hide God's word in our hearts, and seek his will for our lives, unleash the power of prayer over our situations, now… today. Put first things first, then free ourselves from entanglements that will bring us down before we are able to finish the race.

Dear Lord, As we plant the seed of your Word in our hearts, water it by your Holy Spirit. As it starts to grow in our hearts, let it push aside the weights and hindrances we create for ourselves. Free us from distractions and deception, create in us fertile ground for your words to flourish and nourish our souls, thus giving us strength to complete our race. Help us to now establish attainable goals. May the power of procrastination be broken over our lives. In Jesus' name… Amen.

APRIL 3

Choosing Calm

But seek first his kingdom and his righteousness, and all these things will be given to you as well.
–Matthew 6:33 (NIV)

You know both God and how he works. Steep your life in God-reality, God initiative, God-provisions. Don't worry about missing out. You'll find all your everyday human concerns will be met.
–Matthew 6:32—33 (MSG)

It was one of those perfect temperature, blissfully sunny days. The air was fragrant with growing things. Spending quiet time in a comfortable chair on the deck after reading God's Word, just absorbing a peaceful calm and an attitude of gratitude, felt like– *Ahh, I am home in God's Kingdom, and it is so good.* Soon after that, one by one, the thoughts of what I needed to do kept popping into my mind. Then, it was like a complete swarm of thoughts that made me feel like some cartoon character that had just been hit on the head! Even the chirping birds flying overhead added credence to my cartoon self. No "to do" is more important than seeking God's presence. In healing and changing our procrastinating ways, we must remind ourselves, God's Kingdom comes first. Reject the swirling "to do's," quiet the chirping distractions, time to be like Mary seated at Jesus' feet, as opposed to Martha. Martha chose to be anxious and troubled about many things, but as Jesus said, "one thing is needed, Mary has chosen the good part, which shall not be taken from her."

Dear Lord, Let me never feel guilty about seeking times of your peaceful presence. Give me the right perspective about all that needs to be done and accomplished every day. Help me to realize that spending time with you builds discernment within me. Let me be someone who puts first things first, relying on you. Let the quiet joy of your presence be sought after every day of my life. In Jesus' name... Amen.

APRIL 4

No Dark Paths

By your words I can see where I'm going;
they throw a beam of light on my dark path.
I've committed myself and I'll never turn back
from living by your righteous order.

Everything's falling apart on me, God;
put me together again with your Word.
Festoon me with your finest sayings, God;
teach me your holy rules.

My life is as close as my own hands,
but I don't forget what you have revealed.
The wicked do their best to throw me off track,
but I don't swerve an inch from your course.
–Psalm 119:105—110 (MSG)

Dear Lord, Please break through the dark confusion that often clouds our path. Shine your light brightly on the path we need to take. May we not be subject to whims of feelings, but help us to deepen our commitments, guided by the righteous boundaries that you have set down. When things feel like they are falling apart, draw us back to your Word for clarity. Let us feel that we are adorned by your rules, not restricted by them. Help us to realize that you have given us free will to determine what the work of our hands will be. Protect our thinking, so that thoughts that attack our purpose and ability to focus, will be defeated. Let your way, be our way always, until we draw our last breath. In Jesus' name... Amen.

APRIL 5

Real Rest

Come to me, all you who are weary and burdened, and I will give you rest. Take my yoke upon you and learn from me, for I am gentle and humble in heart, and you will find rest for your souls.
–Matthew 11:28—29 (NIV)

Do not be anxious about anything, but in everything, by prayer and petition, with thanksgiving, present your requests to God.
–Philippians 4:6 (NIV)

When I think about how often I have felt weary, burdened, and anxious because I have procrastinated about something, it is very discouraging. Why did I never change my ways if it was causing me so much emotional harm? Probably because of all the enjoyable things that I was doing while in avoidance mode made it seem very worthwhile at the time. But, in the long run it all circles back to being weary, burdened and anxious, certainly not the life we are called to live. Today it doesn't have to be that way!

Dear Lord, Help me to carry the load you want me to carry, today. Help me to work when I should be working, so I can enjoy the deep kind of rest you offer, a rest for my soul. Let me stay in prayer, and be thankful, so that I do not drift down a negative path. Help me to live a life where I do not avoid my responsibilities, and to live a life that is diligent when necessary, so that I do not get caught in a web of negative results. In Jesus' name… Amen.

APRIL 6

No Easy Path

But in everything commending ourselves as servants of God, in much endurance, in afflictions, in hardships, in distresses.
–2 Corinthians 6:4 (NASB)

So that we ourselves glory in you in the churches of God for your patience and faith in all your persecutions and tribulations that ye endure...
–2 Thessalonians 1:4 (KJV)

These things I have spoken unto you, that in me ye might have peace. In the world ye shall have tribulation: but be of good cheer; I have overcome the world.
–John 16:33 (KJV)

God never promises us an easy path. No one should ever "sell" Jesus as a way to end all of our suffering. Due to battles within of painful emotions, negative thinking, and trying to vanquish a variety of sins from our lives, there will be unexpected woeful circumstances. No one's life can be a total pleasure cruise. Whenever we move forward to overcome our own defects of character, it is almost a guarantee that there will be storms or obstacles, which may even produce massive resistance on our part! What is the answer to this disheartening dilemma? Very simple, "Don't Quit!" Hang on to God's Word, seek his presence and "Do Not Quit." I encourage you to listen to, or read, some quotes and speeches of Winston Churchill (YouTube- Never Give In- Winston Churchill 1941 HD.) Facing the power and might of Hitler's Third Reich his words about facing enemies, proper views of success and failure, and right attitudes in the face of overwhelming odds, are truly inspiring. Our path to overcome procrastination is truly puny compared to what the British faced during WW II. It never hurts to take a great leader's advice.

Dear Lord, Help me to realize that whatever storm I am going through in life, you are there with me. Do not let me feel that I am some kind of less-favored child of yours because of what I am going through. Give me the courage to stick to my convictions of what is right for my life, no matter what comes against me. Grant me your peace during difficult times. In Jesus' name... Amen.

APRIL 7

Deep Roots

Next morning, as the disciples passed the fig tree he had cursed, they saw that it was withered from the roots! Then Peter remembered what Jesus had said to the tree on the previous day and exclaimed, "Look, Teacher! The fig tree you cursed has withered!"
–Mark 11:20-21 (TLB)

And pray that Christ will be more and more at home in your hearts, living within you as you trust in him. May your roots go down deep into the soil of God's marvelous love...
–Ephesians 3:17 (TLB)

Cruising through Facebook (a common procrastinator's escape) I came across lists of things that we need to stop doing in order to live a better life. These types of lists are almost endless, and often very similar. Interesting that often many of these things deal with procrastination and some root causes for it. Maybe we need to spend time focusing on the root of our problem, instead of the problem itself.

STOP:
* Negative self-talk.
*People Pleasing.
*Fear of failure.
*Doubting yourself.
*Negative thinking.
*Procrastination.
*Fear of success.
*Being critical

Dear Lord, I need your wisdom. Reveal to me the root cause of my procrastinating ways. Infuse me with your power to curse the root of my self-defeating behaviors. Let me rid myself of unfruitful ways. Let me determine to have my roots growing deep down in the soil of your marvelous, eternal, healing love. May I be free from negative thinking and negative self-talk, free from fear of failure. As I abide in you, may I never doubt myself as I stay on the path that you have set before me. In Jesus' name... Amen.

APRIL 8

Maybe It Needs to be Brand New

I am the Lord, who opened a way through the waters, making a path right through the sea. I called forth the mighty army of Egypt with all its chariots and horses... But forget all that– it is nothing compared to what I'm going to do! For I'm going to do a brand-new thing. See, I have already begun! Don't you see it?
–Isaiah 43: 16—19 (TLB)

Often we need something entirely new within us to stir us into action. As procrastinators, often our back burners are full of old leftovers peppered with previous starts. If there is too much clutter in the appliance known as our brain, how will we ever finish anything? Sometimes there will be a renewal of passion for a particular project due to an immediate response to our life's circumstances. For many people, the best way to have a check in their win column is to start something brand new, never attempted before. Start new, and this time, unlike the other times, see it through to the finish.

Dear Lord, Sometimes, we cannot see a victory over procrastination in our future because there are too many abandoned attempts in the past. Our way seems blocked. Oh God, give us vision. Let us see something brand new in our future. Help us to be victorious; bolster our determination with your Word. Let us not look back, but forward to completion. In Jesus' name... Amen.

APRIL 9

Not Procrastination

And I tell you, you are Peter, and on this rock I will build my church, and the gates of hell will not prevail against it.
–Matthew 16:18 (ESV)

Driving down the ramp for St. Paul's Boulevard entering the city of Norfolk, Virginia, there is an old, traditional church in view to all who enter the city. It is the Basilica of St. Mary's. For a long time, I saw its missing roof shingles and parts of it in disrepair. It made me wonder if it was a "dying church," a sad fate for too many churches. Upon visiting the church during Holy Week, I was grateful to discover just the opposite. It is a vibrant historic church, full of life inside, surrounded by magnificent awe-inspiring architecture. There was a sense of God-breathed beauty within. The founding of St. Mary's started in 1791, and the original building was built 1842. I feel fortunate to have discovered a treasure that I never knew existed. You can find photos of this inspiringly beautiful church online.

What does any of this have to do with procrastination? Well at first, I wrongly assumed this place was an example of not counting the cost before renovating, or people procrastinating about meeting the physical needs of the building. How often does a desire to build something great and long-lasting stay unfulfilled due to procrastinating? Fairly often, but this is not the case here. What I found was the importance of building a legacy, and the necessary efforts needed by future generations to maintain that legacy. Legacies are not just built by the founders; they must be maintained by the labor of each new generation. Putting time, effort, and finances, is worth whatever it takes to keep a significant inter-generational church alive in its present time.

Dear Lord, As children of God that have received a great inheritance from all the faithful believers that have come before us, let us freely do our part to maintain the good works and legacy of past generations. Help us realize our part in your great chain of history. Bless your church in all its current forms, all bodies of believers whose love for you is genuine and alive. In Jesus' name... Amen.

APRIL 10

What You Give

Give, and it will be given unto you. A good measure, pressed down, shaken together and running over, will be poured into your lap. For with the measure you use, it will be measured to you.
–Luke 6:38 (NIV)

So often this scripture has to do with financial giving. Today I see it as an encouragement to give ourselves the time and effort needed to do our best at fulfilling our God given talents, abilities, and purpose. If we are lazy in giving our devotion to the work we need to accomplish, our life's return will be meager. There is no reason to live a meager life when God promises to give us a full reward. Our efforts determine what is going to be given back to us by God. That is good news, if we can overcome our procrastinating and give our time doing what God has called us to do. A future where we give a full measure and receive a full measure of assorted unexpected blessings in return sounds like a life worth living to me.

Dear Lord, Help us realize that you are a God who delights in giving. Give us an understanding of your principles of measuring. Let us not just give in a delayed, common, or casual measure, but give our best and fullest measure. Help us to realize that when we give what pleases you, we too will find the pleasure in giving. In Jesus' name... Amen.

APRIL 11

Who is Imitating Whom?

Follow God's example in everything you do just as a much loved child imitates his father.
–Ephesians 5:1 (TLB)

And you should follow my example, just as I follow Christ's. I am so glad, dear brothers, that you have been remembering and doing everything I taught you.
–I Corinthians 11:1—2 (TLB)

In Lynn Johnston's amusing illustrations of family life know as, "For Better or Worse," she very aptly illustrated an interesting aspect of procrastination. Her son is angry, overwhelmed, and looking ready to give up over his tremendous load of homework. The mom gives him excellent advice, ending with, "If you did just a little bit every day, this would never happen." As she turns down his plea for immediate help, she enters her laundry room stacked with multiple, overloaded piles of clothes towering by the ironing board. Oops! A wide-eyed recognition of the situation hits her. She cannot help him because she has not listened to her own advice or applied it to her own life! Obviously, it is never a good thing to pass on our procrastinating ways to our children.

Dear Lord, Let me see the long-term effects of what I do, that I should not be doing. Help me to be an example to those closest to me, especially to my own children. Guard my procrastinating ways from being passed on to others, or burdening others with the results of my procrastination. Let me always imitate you. Let me exhibit behavior that is worthy of being imitated. In Jesus' name... Amen.

APRIL 12

Praise Him

Oh, thank the Lord, for he is good! His loving-kindness is forever. Let the congregation of Israel praise him with these same words: "His loving-kindness is forever." ... You did your best to kill me, O my enemy, but the Lord helped me. He is my strength and my song in the heat of battle, and now he has given me the victory. Songs of joy at the news of our rescue are sung in the homes of the godly. The strong arm of the Lord has done glorious things! I shall not die but live to tell of all his deeds.
Psalm 118:1—2, 13—17 (TLB)

At one of the lowest points in my life, tired of dealing with an apparently unsolvable situation in my marriage, difficulty in handling rebellious teenagers, ready to walk out the door, I learned a very important lesson. I was desperately seeking God for answers, and he cleared my confusion. He let me know, "Leaving your family will not work my will in your life." Jesus lifted my depression and gave me a revelation of the importance of praise. Since then, praising God every day has been a priority and a consistent protection from confusion, depression and feeling hopeless. There is something that happens, an infusion from God, a focus on a positive unseen reality that can change our world and defeat our spiritual enemies. That something, only happens during times of praise and worshipping God. Praise God always and forever. Whatever your methods of praise and worship: reading the psalms aloud, playing an instrument, surrounding yourself with all the wonderful recently produced Spirit-filled music, just do it.

Dear Lord, I thank you that you are able to banish hopelessness and crippling frustration from my soul. No matter what is going on in my life, let me always praise you. Open my eyes to see the benefits of worship and praise. May I always put my whole heart and soul into times of worship, praising you from the very depth of my being. You are worthy of all praise and honor, and in your presence, there is protection from the arrows of the Enemy, and the power of transformation. I will forever thank you that your steadfast loving kindness endures forever! In Jesus' name... Amen.

APRIL 13

Help Please

With your help I can advance against a troop; with my God I can scale a wall.
–Psalm 18:29 (NIV)

God is our strength, an ever-present help in times of trouble. Therefore we will not fear, though the earth give way and the mountains fall into the heart of the sea.
–Psalm 46:1—2 (NIV)

When is the best time to call for help? Is it when you are in the midst of dangerous circumstances, or when you realize that you are heading into a difficult situation? As procrastinators, we tend to do a variety of things *too late.* Part of defeating procrastination in our lives is simply developing wisdom, and godly wisdom can protect us from coming face to face with walls that are too arduous to climb. Wisdom says– Once we realize that we have a slim chance of meeting a deadline, call for help. Asking others for help may be more effective if you are able to see the need approaching in advance, and not currently in the midst of turmoil begging for assistance at the last minute. It is so good to know that our God is truly an "ever-present help in trouble," no matter what kind of trouble we are in, and no matter when we need help. Whether we are seeking the help of God, a friend, or colleague, let's not let pride get in the way of asking for what we need, as soon as we realize we are in need.

Dear Lord, Let me always seek wisdom in every situation. Help me to be realistic in my obligations, commitments, and deadlines. Help me to not be too proud to ask for help when I need it. I thank you that you are always there for me, and I can call upon you any time. Give me vision to see the cause and effects of my behavior and guide my actions. In Jesus' name... Amen.

APRIL 14

Embracing the Cup

Consider him who endured from sinners such hostility against himself, so that you may not grow weary or fainthearted. In your struggle against sin you have not yet resisted to the point of shedding your blood.
–Hebrews 12:3—4 (RSV)

Then he said to them, "My soul is very sorrowful, even to death; remain here, and watch with me." And going a little farther he fell on his face and prayed, "My Father, if it be possible, let this cup pass from me; nevertheless, not as I will, but as thou wilt."
–Matthew 26:38—39 (RSV)

This time of year is full of remembrances about Spring, Easter, and the Crucifixion. There can be no resurrection without a death before it. The amount of torturous suffering that Jesus went through on the cross for us is something that should never ever be taken lightly. Through his selfless obedience on that horrible cross, he bought freedom and forgiveness for all our past, present, and future sins, as well as entrance into God's Heavenly Kingdom when we die. No act on earth ever did more for anyone. Thank you, Jesus.

Dear Heavenly Father, As we contemplate the cross, remind us of the virtues of obedience, and selflessness. No matter how difficult your will was to do, your son submitted to you completely. Help us to be more like Jesus; help us to be more obedient, selfless, and always willing to do your will. Remind us daily of what Christ went through for us. Help us to realize that our pains in complying with your will are often nothing in comparison to his. Help us keep the magnitude of what your son accomplished on the cross as a precious treasure in our hearts, keeping us in your will. May your will be done in us, on earth as it is in heaven. In Jesus' name... Amen.

APRIL 15

Victory Guaranteed

In the same way the Spirit also comes to help us, weak as we are. For we do not know how we ought to pray; the Spirit himself pleads with God for us in groans that words cannot express. And God, who sees our hearts, knows what the thought of the Spirit is; because the Spirit pleads with God on behalf of his people and accordance with his will. We know that in all things God works for good with those that love him, those whom he has called according to his purpose. Those whom God had already chosen he also set apart to become like his Son... In view of all this, what can we say? If God be for us, who can be against us?
–Romans 8:26—29, 31 *Good News Translation* (GNT)

This scripture reveals the depth of God being on our side, when we are on his. We should never think that it is impossible to defeat ingrained procrastinating behaviors when he tells us just the opposite. If we are weak, he helps us in our weakness. If we don't know how to pray, we can rely on the Holy Spirit to intercede for us, then our prayers always hit the mark. He sees our hearts, more than our failings, and puts His Will for our lives in motion. If we love God, he works for our good and his purpose dwells within us. What more could we possibly need to have victory? If we are becoming more obedient, more like Jesus, self-defeating behaviors will eventually evaporate. God is on our side! Victory is guaranteed!

Dear Lord, Help me to fully realize that you are on my side. Nothing can be successful against you, and because I am yours- nothing can be successful against me. Give me the confidence to step ever closer to victory. Let your word renew and transform my thinking. Thank you God, for your constant love and support. Thank you for setting me apart for your purpose. Help me put aside all vain ambitions and embrace your purpose for my life, because your purpose doesn't fail, it will prevail! In Jesus' name... Amen.

APRIL 16

Dropping our Defense

A reliable messenger brings healing. If you ignore criticism, you will end up in poverty and disgrace; if you accept correction you will be honored. It is pleasant to see dreams come true, but fools refuse to turn from evil to attain them.
–Proverbs 13:17—19 (NLT)

As a teacher, it has often been my job to be a counselor and a corrector. Many times, a student's personal issues hindered their academic performance. Some hated hearing any criticism because it came across as an attack on their feelings of self-worth. Some couldn't care less because they knew they had done a lousy job, and others were eager to hear any comment that would help them improve their performance, giving insight into their *blind spot* areas. If we seriously want to make a better life for ourselves, and more closely follow Christ, we need to be willing students of, "What's that log in my eye doing there?" life lessons. We must be open to constructive criticism, correction, and stop being defensive about our shortcomings.

Dear Lord, Please bring healing into our lives. Let us each have a teachable spirit. I pray that dreams would finally come true in my life. Build within me the kind of character that will not stubbornly refuse just criticism. Help me to turn away from any sin or distraction that hinders me making my dreams into a reality. Let me be tuned into your words, and your wisdom, knowing your way will lead me to a place of honor. Help me to receive appropriate correction and see it as a path to personal improvement. In Jesus' name... Amen.

APRIL 17

Beware the Wounded Heart

Keep vigilant watch over your heart; that's where life starts... Keep your eyes straight ahead; ignore all sideshow distractions. Watch your step, and the road will stretch out smooth before you. Look neither right nor left; leave evil in the dust.
–Proverbs 4:23—27 (MSG)

If we need to spend too much time nurturing and healing our own wounded heart, we are not being effective in advancing God's Kingdom. Like injured warriors recovering in a hospital, we have been taken out of the battle. Snares that can trap us and keep us from prevailing in our life's purpose are everywhere. It takes a strong heart and clear vision to bring to us to a place of victory. In my second attempt to write a blog that would result in a year's worth of entries, I quit and felt the sting of failure. Why? Because it was important to me that people would be reading it, that I was helping others overcome procrastination as much as myself. I was discouraged when day after day no one left any comments, it seemed as if, *If I'm not helping anyone else with this effort, then, why bother?* I lost heart, got distracted, and abandoned my goal; that's not going to happen this year. Despite an often-wounded heart, and lack of feedback, this time the end is in sight; the goal is now clear. Victory is ahead; quitting is not an option. God revealed to me that without my own victory, I cannot help others. My life's efforts cannot be measured by the approval of others, I only have one Lord and Master. Knowing that I am being obedient to the task he has called me to do is healing my heart.

Dear Lord, Help me to guard my heart, to press on even when there are wounds to overcome. Generate within me that warrior spirit, and infuse me with a drive to overcome all obstacles and distractions. Keep my goals and purpose constantly before me; give me courage to keep moving forward. Keep me steadfast, looking to you for the joy and strength to sustain me. Help me to not consider any reason to quit, deeply embed within me the concept, "Quitting is not an option!" In Jesus' name... Amen.

APRIL 18

For My Future Self

By an act of faith, Isaac reached into the future as he blessed Jacob and Esau.
–Hebrews 11:20 (MSG)

What a God we have! And how fortunate we are to have him, this Father of our Master Jesus! Because Jesus was raised from the dead, we've been given a brand-new life and have everything to live for, including a future in heaven–and the future starts now! God is keeping careful watch over us and the future. The Day is coming when you'll have it all– life healed and whole.
–1Peter 1—5 (MSG)

According to an article entitled, "The Real Reasons You Procrastinate–and How to Stop" by Ana Swanson published on April 27, 2016, psychologists are developing models to unlock the mysterious forces behind procrastination. One such model is centered on a person's relationship between their present and future selves. Procrastinators often, "have little concern, understanding or empathy for that future self." Generally a focus on how one feels today overrides any emotional connection people may have to their future self.

Hal Hersfield, a psychologist from UCLA that specializes in this present-future self relationship dynamic says, "in some ways I treat my future self as if he is a fundamentally different person... not going to benefit or suffer from the consequences of my actions today." Research currently shows that individuals who are more in sync with their future selves have fewer procrastinating behaviors. Too bad the original Hebrews who came out of slavery from Egypt didn't make that kind of connection. Because they never had the faith to receive God's Word for their Promised Land, sadly they died in the desert never receiving all that the Lord meant for them to possess.

Dear Lord, Let me be aware of my future self, and ever aware that my actions today do impact my life in the future. Let me not keep putting off important, life-giving actions. Help me to consciously create behaviors for which my future self will be thankful. Let every day I live be planting a seed of blessing for the person I become down the road. Let me not live a disconnected life, but a life forged one link at a time, day by day, that creates a strong connection from past, to present, and into the future. In Jesus' name... Amen.

APRIL 19

Got to Find a Way Out

God, you're my last chance of the day. I spend the night on my knees before you. Put me on your salvation agenda; take notes on the trouble I'm in. I've had my fill of trouble... I'm caught in a maze and can't find my way out, blinded by tears of pain and frustration.
–Psalm 88:1—2, 9 (MSG)

The seed cast in the weeds represents the ones who hear the kingdom news but are overwhelmed with worries about all the things they have to do and all the things they want to get. The stress strangles what they heard, and nothing comes of it.
–Mark 4:18—19 (MSG)

The journey of life for those of us that procrastinate seems to be an encumbered one. We have difficulty laying aside those sins and weights that so easily beset us. That is combined with the too often rush of being late, then layered with pressures of not producing something that should have been produced by now. We can create within ourselves an untidy, volatile package of frustration that can be easily ignited with the slightest setback. Like today, when I dropped a container of tacks all over my floor and I turned into an emotional volcano. Not a good foundation for living a life of peaceful fulfillment that is meant for us. I put myself in the category of someone who has received the good seed of the kingdom and planted it in fertile soil where it is destined to thrive. However, when frustrations build within me, it's as if for that stressful angry instant, the Word is being choked out, and the power of the kingdom is temporarily absent within me. Sometimes it is tears and frustration, not the freedom from anxiety that I desperately need.

Dear Lord, I need to be saved from the layers of stress and frustration I seem to heap upon myself. Your peace is all too often an elusive mystery to me. Too often my behaviors produce unnecessary pressures and stress that strangle your peace. Give me discernment in every moment so that I will not create thorny, painful weeds in my heart and mind that choke out the power of your words. God help me to rid myself of overwhelming emotions that block out the light of your peace. In Jesus' name... Amen.

APRIL 20

Progress Equals Joy

The work is being carried on with diligence and is making rapid progress under their direction.
–Ezra 5:8 (NIV)

Convinced of this, I know that I will remain, and I will continue with all of you for your progress and joy in the faith.
–Philippians 1:25 (NIV)

Be diligent in these matters; give yourself wholly to them, so that everyone can see your progress.
–I Timothy 4:15 (NIV)

Whether we are building a wall in God's temple, finally making it to the gym to work out on a regular basis, or finishing a thesis, it is all about progress. Progress and procrastination are in opposition to each other. When we apply the words mentioned here: work, diligence, continue, and attitudes like "give yourself wholly," progress is the natural result. We don't have to be perfect; we just need to be making progress. You may want to lose 40 lbs. but thank God if you have lost 7 lbs. and you are making progress! You want to finish writing your novel? Thank God and rejoice you have completed 3 chapters! You want to earn a college degree? Thank God you have finally enrolled, and you are about to start your first classes! What else does progress result in? Joy in the faith. Guilt and conviction may prod us to start, but it is all about joy to keep us going. Any progress truly equals joy. Lord knows we all need joy!

Dear Lord, Help me to not dwell on how far I have to go, help me to rejoice in how far I have come. Keep me from the trap of self-condemnation over unmet goals, free me from a burden of guilt. Let me realize to the depths of my being, that being negative over my mistakes profits me nothing. Let every step I make in the right direction be planting seeds of diligence toward my life's goals. Open my eyes and my heart to embrace the joy of progress, no matter how small. Give me the strength to continue in the right direction and give myself wholly over to progress. In Jesus' name... Amen.

APRIL 21

Grace Wins

At that point Peter got up the nerve to ask, "Master, how many times do I forgive a brother or sister who hurts me? Seven?" Jesus replied, "Seven! Hardly. Try seventy times seven."
–Matthew 18:21—22 (MSG)

In prayer there is a connection between what God does and what you do. You can't get forgiveness from God, for instance, without forgiving others. If you refuse to do your part, you cut yourself off from God's part.
–Matthew 6:14—15 (MSG)

But sin didn't, and doesn't, have a chance in competition with the aggressive forgiveness we call grace. When it's sin versus grace, grace wins hands down.
–Romans 5:20 (MSG)

As Christians we understand that forgiveness is at the very core of our faith. The cup at the Last Supper was for the forgiveness of sins. Jesus was painfully dying on the cross saying, "Father forgive them, for they know not what they do." What illustration could possibly be more powerful? It is immensely interesting to me that current research shows, that one of the most effective things that procrastinators can do is forgive themselves for procrastinating. In a study made by Timothy Pychyl and others, "students who reported forgiving themselves for procrastinating for a first exam ended up procrastinating less for a second exam." Forgiving oneself reduces negative feelings and guilt which are triggers for procrastinating. It is not a matter of feeling whether or not you deserve forgiveness. It belongs to you!

Dear Lord, Help me to realize that I deserve forgiveness as much as anyone else. Let me not be stingy with the precious grace you offer me on a daily basis. Forgiving myself means the ability to move forward. Help me to realize when I have put myself into a trap of guilt and self-condemnation. Help me to realize that you desire for me to be dependent on your grace. Let your grace enfold me like a warm blanket, wiping away negative feelings that would hold me back. In Jesus' name... Amen.

APRIL 22

Certainty of Eternity

This is the testimony in essence: God gave us eternal life; the life is in his son. So, whoever has the Son, has life; whoever rejects the Son, rejects life... you who believe in God's Son will know beyond a shadow of a doubt that you have eternal life, the reality and not the illusion. And how bold and free we then become in his presence, freely asking according to his will, sure that he is listening.
–I John 5:11—14 (MSG)

When I discuss the concept of eternity with non-believers, two things I usually bring up: the sign for infinity, and Einstein's theory of the law of conservation of mass and energy. If we accept the concept of infinity, whether in drawing that little figure eight icon, or the *endless* expanse of space, it seems perfectly logical that some things go on and on... forever. Assuming that Einstein was correct, and matter and energy cannot be created or destroyed, just change form, somehow this theory also applies to those who are deceased. When the body is worn out, and stops functioning... where does the *person* go? The energy, the personality, the soul, or spirit that animated that body... surely it hasn't ceased to exist? While infinity, and eternity are heady topics to discuss, how do they add value to our lives right now? If eternity is real, and we all have an eternal destination, what could possibly be more important than that? Let us make the utmost of our limited time on earth, so that the greatest number of souls make it to a heavenly eternal home.

Dear Lord, Help me to realize that our time here on earth is short and should not be squandered. Help me to see what needs to be done in my own life that is of eternal significance. Teach me to be an effective witness that my labor will result in souls being saved and heaven being populated. Let me not be lured into obsessing over temporal matters. Create a discernment within me for matters of eternal consequences, and a desire for eternal rewards instead of ephemeral pleasures. In Jesus' name... Amen.

APRIL 23

The Size of the Task

Then he continued, "Be strong and courageous and get to work. Don't be frightened by the size of the task, for the Lord my God is with you; he will not forsake you. He will see to it that everything is finished correctly..."
–1 Chronicles 28:20 (TLB)

So let it grow, and don't try to squirm out of your problems. For when your patience is finally in bloom, then you'll be ready for anything, strong in character, full and complete.
–James 1:4 (TLB)

The size of a task definitely intimidates me. My first response may be, *How can I get out of doing this?*" Realistically, there will always be something that seems to require more than we feel able to do. Whether that is a doctoral thesis, or passing a GED exam, or finishing a quilt before a special occasion, we all have tasks that seem like a giant impossibility. My husband is quite the opposite in this area; it would benefit me greatly to be more like him. Looking at our deck, with its need to be power washed, sanded and stained, made me want to crawl into bed and take a nap. Not him, he worked at it a little bit at a time. The job seemed even more intimidating to me because I thought it should be finished as quickly as possible and done all at once. That view was unrealistic. Like many procrastinators, patience in a long-term project is vital, and it is not my strength. I need to be constantly reminded, it is not the size of the task, but the steady progress that is important. It is not all up to me. When I rely on God, he will not forsake me, but will see to it that I am furnished with everything I need to finish.

Dear Lord, Help me to no longer be frightened by the size of the work in front of me. Remind me that you are present every step of the way, and that each step is valuable, not just the one at the finish. I confess my lack of patience, and the petulant attitude that often accompanies my lack of it. Help me to see my problems, tasks, and trials, as opportunities for growth in character. I pray that I will constantly do the work necessary to free myself from the weight and hindrance of procrastination. May I continue to look to your words, your presence, and the comfort of your Holy Spirit to sustain me. In Jesus' name... Amen.

APRIL 24

Know Your Enemy

Every God-begotten person conquers the world's ways. The conquering power that brings the world to its knees is our faith. The person who wins out over the world's ways is simply the one who believes Jesus is the Son of God.
–I John 5:5 (MSG)

So Joshua and the Israelite army continued the slaughter and completely crushed the enemy... Then Joshua said, "Remove the rocks covering the cave, and bring the five kings to me"... When they brought them out, Joshua told the commanders of his army, "Come and put your feet on the kings' necks... Don't ever be afraid or discouraged," Joshua told his men. "Be strong and courageous, for the Lord is going to do this to all your enemies." Then Joshua killed each of the five kings.
–Joshua 10:20—26 (NLT)

These scriptures indicate some powerful truths for our lives. As believers and followers of Jesus Christ we have power. Our faith is the storehouse of that power. Secondly, God desires for us to have complete victory over our enemies; they are also his enemies, and they should be totally eliminated. I am glad that I don't have to wage a war where I am assigned to slaughter a multitude of people. But I must be battle-ready to war against strongholds in the spiritual realm. There are powers and principalities bent on my destruction, as well as the ruin of my testimony and legacy. Procrastination is an enemy. My plan is to gain transformative knowledge of the causes and effects of procrastination, fill my mind with God's Word, find support from others to rally at my side, and pray effective fervent prayers that will tear down fortresses where this enemy has occupied territory within me. My enemy **will** be overpowered and evicted.

Dear Lord, Help me to prepare in every way I can, so that I may defeat this enemy in my life. Help me to root it out of every corner where it is hiding and influencing my life. Let my pursuit be ruthless to eliminate procrastination from my life. Give me a revelation of the power that resides within me! Let faith be a strong component of my life, and not a silent partner. Let me know the exhilaration of the conqueror's victory! Sustain my spirit so that I can have a priceless testimony that will help lead others into their own victories. In Jesus' name... Amen.

APRIL 25

Glorious Growth

I am the true vine, and my Father is the vinedresser. Every branch of mine that bears no fruit he takes away, and every branch that does bear fruit he prunes, that it may bear more fruit...
I am the vine, you are the branches. He who abides in me, and I in him, he it is that bears much fruit, for apart from me you can do nothing.... These things I have spoken to you, that my joy may be in you, and your joy may be full.
–John 15:1—2, 5, 11 (RSV)

While recovering from knee surgery, my very helpful neighbor asked me, "Is there anything I can do for you?" I thought, let's go big, something I couldn't do even if my knee was 100%. I said, "The crepe myrtles in our back yard are overgrown and really need to be trimmed back." He said he would do that for me. True to his word, he showed up with an extended chain saw, and hacked the living daylights out of them. They were so pruned, with way more cut off than I expected, I feared that they would never grow back! I couldn't complain; he did it for free and did multiple hours of work afterwards just to dispose of the jungled mass of tree debris.

Looking at the barren trees I thought, "Well, God only knows how many seasons will pass before I see any blossoms in my backyard again." Weeks later I am truly amazed at the glorious growth these resilient trees have displayed. God's design is to cut away what is unnecessary to increase fruitfulness. Trees and plants naturally respond to pruning, people... not so much. What am I willing to cut away so I can be more fruitful? Am I willing to offer myself to abide in the vine, submitting to painful, or life altering pruning, so that I too can exhibit glorious growth at my Heavenly Father's hands. While recovering in the pain of my useless condition, God revealed some things that needed to be pruned. The bountiful branches of new life that will soon flower have raised my faith and expectations. I sense a joy in the possibility of my own glorious growth. Pruning isn't optional for Christians; it is necessary.

Dear Lord, Thank you for being an all-knowing Creator. You have designed all things and know what they need to flourish and be fruitful. Thank you for Jesus, you are the living Word and sacrifice for all our sins. May we be followers willing to be pruned, ones who desire to abide in the vine, ones who submit to your hands to be fruitful. May we know the glory of being one with you and experience the joy of being a part of your fruitful vine. In your name Jesus, Amen!.

APRIL 26

Making My Path Straight

As it is written in the book of the words of Isaiah the prophet: "A voice of one calling in the wilderness, 'Prepare the way for the Lord, make straight paths for him.'"
–Luke 3:4 (NIV)

Consider it pure joy, my brothers and sisters, whenever you face trials of many kinds, because you know that the testing of your faith produces perseverance. Let perseverance finish its work so that you may be mature and complete, not lacking anything. If any of you lack wisdom, you should ask God, who gives generously to all without finding fault, and it will be given to you.
–James 1:2–5 (NIV)

Sometimes life becomes a rough path, strewn with a variety of disappointments and unmet desires that tend to whittle away our faith. Naturally, we desire all the blessings, and disdain all the hardships. My life has not been a life of multiple tragedies, just an array of different kinds of *let downs* that feel like a chain of broken promises to myself, and maybe... from God. Trials and tribulations are inevitable. Our sadness at going through them doesn't mean our path should be altered. We need to be sure that we are led by God, and believing for what He wants us to believe in. Our primary aim is to have His Kingdom come, His Will be done on earth as it is in heaven. Sometimes we just need forgiveness for not using wisdom, and for having the wrong attitude toward what is happening in our lives. No matter the oppressive trial, no matter the joyous triumphs, we need our eyes fixed on Jesus to make our path straight. There is a joy in what's straight ahead. Even if we can't see it now, just keep looking!

Dear Lord, Forgive me. Forgive me for my lack of follow through, for my good intentions that do not come to fruition. Forgive me for not having an ear to hear what your Holy Spirit is leading and guiding me toward. Help me to grab hold of faith, and to exercise my faith until it functions like a strong muscle. Help my unbelief, rid me of hopes and desires that are not from you. Thank you for blessing me with a new day. May your rod and staff keep me on the straight path. Thank you for giving me a daily opportunity to rise again and serve you. In Jesus' name... Amen.

APRIL 27

How Many Times?

Then Peter came to Jesus and asked, "Lord, how many times shall I forgive my brother or sister who sins against me? Up to seven times?" Jesus answered, "I tell you, not seven times, but seventy-seven times."
–Matthew 18:21—22 (NIV)

For we are God's handiwork, created in Christ Jesus to do good works, which God prepared in advance for us to do.
–Ephesians 2:10 (NIV)

There is an author named Walt Kelly, who wrote a book entitled, *We Have Met the Enemy and He is Us.* In the soul of a procrastinator this is too often the case. We know we have no one else to blame but ourselves. No matter our reasons for seeking out avoidance activities and distractions, in the aftermath when we are even further behind on our goals, we cannot seem to forgive ourselves. If you are a consistent procrastinator your emotions are often tainted by guilt, shame, and an apparent inability to rid yourself of these negative emotions. So often a clean slate is exactly what we need to move forward. Without our ability to consciously, even vocally, acknowledge forgiveness toward ourselves, no matter how many times it takes, we carry a burden we were never intended to carry. That weight hinders us moving forward. How many times does God forgive us? Countless times. We owe ourselves countless times of forgiveness to get this life right.

Dear Lord, Help me to overcome these negative emotions that hold me back from living the kind of life that you have called me to live. Let forgiveness come quickly to others that have hurt me, and when my own actions require forgiveness, let me be quick to forgive myself as well. God, give me a vision to see the good works that you have created me to do. Let me be aware of when my own guilt is dragging me down. Create within me, through the guidance of your Holy Spirit, a plan to defeat procrastination in my life. In Jesus' name... Amen.

APRIL 28

A Little Wisdom Goes a Long Way

How wonderful to be wise, to understand things, to be able to analyze them and interpret them. Wisdom lights up a man's face, softening its hardness... Don't always be trying to get out of doing your duty, even when it is unpleasant... The wise man will find a time and a way to do what he says.
–Ecclesiastes 8:1—5 (TLB)

A prudent man foresees the difficulties ahead and prepares for them; the simpleton goes blindly on and suffers the consequences.
–Proverbs 22:3 (TLB)

It is almost a Biblical guarantee that the more that we pursue wisdom, the better our decision making becomes. Are we overextending ourselves and not taking into account the difficulties that are ahead? Just recently I promised to do something for someone who had called me at 9:00 P.M. for something that needed to be accomplished by 11:00 P.M. I love this person, they were in a rough spot, I usually stay up late, no problem I thought. The fact that the request was a *last minute* demand, or that my attention deficit disorder was not taken into account in making my commitment, means that it was not a wise move. I forgot, feel asleep, in the morning when my promise flashed across my brain... there it was, the all-too-common procrastinators' regret, guilt, and a broken promise, followed by the inevitable self-condemnation. With a bit of wisdom, that all could have been avoided.

Dear Lord, Help me to embrace wisdom in every decision I make, not just the big ones, but all the little ones as well. Keep me from offering to do something at the last minute, unless I think it through and prepare for the difficulties which that commitment may bring. Any time that I make a promise or give my word, give me the strength and foresight to carry it through. Help me to always do what I say. Help me to avoid situations that bring regret and self-condemnation into my life. Lead me into a pursuit of wisdom by spending time in your Word. In Jesus' name... Amen.

APRIL 29

Mirror Mirror

Do not merely listen to the word, and so deceive yourselves. Do what it says. Anyone who listens to the word but does not do what it says is like someone who looks at his face in a mirror and, after looking at himself, goes away and immediately forgets what he looks like. But whoever looks intently into the perfect law that gives freedom, and continues in it–not forgetting what they have heard, but doing it–they will be blessed in what they do.
–James 1:22–25 (NIV)

The book of James has always been one of my favorite parts of the Bible because it deals with what is considered "rubber meets the road Christianity." If all you had was James to guide your Christian life, you would probably be alright. Years ago, when I was managing a Christian rock band, I wrote many lyrics and had to rely on others to put the music behind my words. One of the greatest thrills of my life was hearing my words wrapped in the perfect music, joyfully received by those who heard it. The value doesn't come merely in the listening, but in embracing what is heard. My homage lyrics to this song started out, "Tell it like it is James, the World ain't my friend. Must be a doer of the Word to be a winner in the end." There is strength in always knowing who we really are. We should never forget who we can be as doers, versus who we will be if we don't do God's Word. The believer who hears the truth, and doesn't follow it, forgets who they are. Doers reap freedom and blessing, and never forget who they really are.

Dear Lord, Let us hear your voice clearly. Let us spend time in your Word so that we can more easily recognize your voice. I thank you that you still speak to us, through scripture, through teachers, through music, through your quiet voice that whispers with authority into our minds. Help us to not forget who we really are because of our relationship with you. Let us know the freedom and blessings of obeying your laws and doing what you have called us to do. In Jesus' name... Amen.

APRIL 30

Too Much Confusion

The Philistines drew near to attack Israel; but the Lord thundered with a mighty voice that day against the Philistines and threw them into confusion; and they were routed before Israel.
–1 Samuel 7:10 (RSV)

Now some cried one thing, some another; for the assembly was in confusion, and most of them did not know why they had come together.
–Acts 19:32 (RSV)

For God is not a God of confusion, but of peace
–1 Corinthians 14:33 (RSV)

Confusion is a terrible thing, used in some instances by the Lord to confound the enemies of God, leading those enemies to destroy themselves. So why do we procrastinators often put ourselves in a state of flustered confusion? For me, as a student loving the research part of a paper, going beyond the sane boundaries of note taking, the night before a paper was due confusion would hit hard. How to organize? What goes where to create logical order? I need more caffeine! (coffee, Red Bull, pills, etc...) How will I ever finish this on time? As a teacher, surrounded by mounds of ungraded papers, room in chaos, not being able to locate missing assignments, grades due tomorrow, confusion would paralyze my brain.

Chaotic thoughts would create a cluelessness as to what to do first. *What now? What next?* At times I would emit a rather primal scream to hopefully clear the cluttered thoughts. Cathartic yelling is best employed at a sporting event, not really a solution to the problem at hand. All any of us need is a clear, realistic plan that we would be willing to follow. All we need to do is sacrifice a bit of personal freedom to higher priorities and save ourselves from the brain battering effects of confusion. Unfortunately, the oaths that we loudly swear to ourselves, "I'll never do this again!" often fade after the immediate crushing blows of confusion have dissipated.

Dear Lord, Help us to embrace organization and planning, instead of avoiding it. Remind us of past results and the negative feelings that we have experienced in relation to our procrastinating ways. Let us be seekers of peace, not pursuers of "last minute rush" motivation. Help us to be mature, learning from our mistakes. Help us to seek you daily, praise you often, and develop a grateful heart as we seek your plan for our lives. Reveal to us what we need to do this day to fulfill your plan, and to have our minds be at peace. In Jesus' name... Amen.

MAY 1

Letting Down our Nets

When He had finished speaking, He said to Simon, "Put out into the deep water, and let down your nets for a catch." Simon answered and said, "Master, we worked hard all night and caught nothing, but I will do as You say and let down the nets." When they had done this, they enclosed a great quantity of fish, and their nets began to break.
–Luke 5:4—6 (NASB)

Simon Peter and the others that fished with him were professional fishermen. They knew how to do their job, and they worked hard. Sometimes our diligence, our knowledge, and our hard work, does not yield the results we are looking for. That can bring discouragement. We need to take heart, be willing to try again, not lose faith, and first and foremost, listen to Jesus. We may certainly come up empty sometimes even though we are doing all the right things. But, when we listen and obey a specific direction from our Lord and Master, eventually we will be rewarded for our efforts and we will reap an abundant return for our labor, just as Peter did by putting his faith in Jesus into action.

Dear Lord, Please save us from fruitless time and effort. Life is too short to waste any of our resources. Let us be like Simon Peter, though exhausted and disappointed, was willing to obey your word. Help us to realize that no time and energy put into doing what you have asked us to do, leaves us empty handed. You are a God of abundance, and desire to bless us abundantly. Keep us willing to go out into deep waters, any time, at your command, so that we may partake of your supernatural provision. In Jesus' name... Amen.

MAY 2

Too Many Words

Much dreaming and many words are meaningless. Therefore fear God.
–Ecclesiastes 5:7 (NIV)

It has been fairly easy to talk about the dreams and visions that are part of my life. As time goes on however, it seems as if the talking has not turned into the necessary effort needed to bring these dreams into reality. There must be starting, planning, action, and execution. As procrastinators, that is often what we do not do. The words describing our hopes and wishes are sweet in our mouth, as if the mere talking about them would turn them into a reality. It does not work that way. Probably the more we talk, the less time, sweat, sacrifice, and energy, we invest into transforming our dreams into reality. Fear of God is not a popular perception these days. However, maybe more fear of God would result in less empty words, and that would be a good thing.

Dear Lord, Forgive my empty words, and unproductive talk. Have I fooled myself into thinking that the more my dreams were spoken about, the more likely they were to come to pass? Wisdom now shows, this is not so. Unless the work is actually started, in progress, or near completion, let me keep it locked in my heart, only spoken to a chosen few. Lord, it seems as if we live in a world that has ceased to fear you; sin is no longer a cause of shame and repentance. Help me to know how to fear you and respect you in a way that brings out the best in me, without passing condemnation onto others. Let my words be meaningful, not meaningless. Let me be a person of action today. In Jesus' name... Amen.

MAY 3

What Happens Tomorrow

For I know the plans I have for you, says the Lord. They are plans for good and not for evil, to give you a future and a hope. In those days when you pray, I will listen. You will find me when you seek me, if you look for me in earnest.
–Jeremiah 29:11—13 (TLB)

You people who say, "Today or tomorrow we are going to such and such a town, stay there a year, and open a profitable business." How do you know what is going to happen tomorrow? For the length of your lives is as uncertain as the morning fog–now you see it; soon it is gone. What you ought to say is, "If the Lord wants us to, we shall live and do this or that."
–James 4:13—15 (TLB)

Because I grew up in the United States and have enjoyed the diverse culture and the standard of living prevalent here, I always thought that I could never live anywhere else. After I visited Ireland, home of my ancestors from my father's side, I changed my mind. Suddenly, not having a completely mapped out future seemed very freeing. If God told me that he wants me in Ireland, Morocco or Tibet, who am I to argue with my Heavenly Father? What does this have to do with procrastination? Sometimes by procrastinating we create a box for ourselves, limiting our options and possibilities. If we constantly push today's business into tomorrow, the tomorrow that God has created for us may never arrive.

Dear Lord, In all my requests let me seek your will before my own. I thank you that you always have my good in mind, which includes a hope-filled future. Help me to not casually seek you, but when I seek, let it be with my whole heart and my entire being. Let me not be quick to make plans of my own. Lead me to do today what must be done today. Do not let my whims of the moment carry today's work into a tomorrow that may never come. In Jesus' name... Amen.

MAY 4

What Really Happened

Two of them were going to a village called Emmaus, ...They were talking with each other about everything that had happened. As they talked and discussed these things... Jesus himself came up and walked along with them; but they were kept from recognizing him. He asked them, "What are you discussing together as you walk along?" They stood still, their faces downcast... "About Jesus of Nazareth," they replied. "He was a prophet, powerful in word and deed before God and all the people. The chief priests and our rulers handed him over to be sentenced to death, and they crucified him; but we had hoped that he was the one who was going to redeem Israel... Jesus continued on as if he were going farther. But they urged him strongly... When he was at the table with them, he took bread, gave thanks, broke it and began to give it to them. Then their eyes were opened and they recognized him, and he disappeared from their sight. They asked each other, "Were not our hearts burning within us while he talked with us on the road and opened the Scriptures to us?" They got up and returned at once to Jerusalem.

–Luke 24:13—21, 28—33 (NIV)

As believers we may become discouraged, focused on all the negative events at hand, and not be able to see that Jesus is right there with us. As procrastinators we can often ping pong between extreme optimism and pessimism. "I'm sure I can do this," "No problem," "This is a great idea!" All that can quickly change to- "What was I thinking?" "There is no way!" An attitude of dismay and discouragement, or even hopelessness can take over. As soon as these disciples recognized that Jesus was with them and that Jesus was alive, their entire attitude, perspective, and direction changed. They immediately went back to Jerusalem, witnessed to others, and joined in a common purpose to spread the good news.

Dear Lord, Please help us to constantly be aware of your presence. You are always with us. Help us to not focus on setbacks and discouraging facts. Let us be quick to muster our faith and embrace the eternal joy that you bought for us with your life on the cross. Keep us moving in the right direction, in line with your purpose, our hearts on fire with your Holy Spirit, your Word, and your Presence. In Jesus' name... Amen.

MAY 5

Doing as We Wish

Don't continue doing things the way we're doing them at present, each one of us doing as we wish. Until now you haven't arrived at the goal, the resting place, the inheritance that GOD, your God, is giving you. But the minute you cross the Jordan River and settle into the land GOD, your God, is enabling you to inherit, he'll give you rest from all your surrounding enemies. You'll be able to settle down and live in safety.
–Deuteronomy 12:8—10 (MSG)

According to the Merriam-Webster Dictionary, to wish means, "to have a desire for (something, such as something unattainable) // wished he could live his life over." Maybe I grew up reading too many fairy tales because the activity of wishing for unattainable things became part of the fabric of my life. Negative thoughts and feelings toward my undesirable circumstances were transformed by trying to wish them away, not really devising a plan to overcome them. I believe the long-term effect of this wishing attitude led me to be rebellious and to do what I wanted, whenever I wanted to do it. It feels like having control, but leads nowhere. Like many procrastinators, living in a world of wishing just brings you emotionally close to a phantom of your goal, *never* allowing you to possess the real thing. Right now, I want what works, not what I wish. God's plan, the inheritance that he desires for me to possess, the experience of longed for attainment, is what I now desire. It is all about where God wants me to be, and what he has for me. Simply wishing, then doing whatever we want in the moment, will not get anyone into God's Promised Land.

Dear Lord, Give me ears to hear the directions you have for me. Help me to create the plans and steps to reach my part of the Promised Land. Help me to do what I need to do to grow my faith, to expel all doubts, to submit to discipline, to have a warrior's courage in defeating all obstacles and enemies before me. Give me discernment to recognize when I am drifting into a world of wishes, chasing imaginary outcomes that lack substance. Help me this day to quiet all other voices and desires that would take me off the path that you have set for me. In Jesus' name... Amen.

MAY 6

At Least a Few Rounds

For they had gone up to Bethel and wept in the presence of the Lord until evening. They had asked the Lord, "should we fight against our relatives from Benjamin again?" And the Lord had said. "Go out and fight against them"... but the men of Benjamin killed another 18,000 Israelites...
–Judges 20:23—25 (NLT)

In the Book of Judges, Chapter 20, there is a story of a horrible deed that leads to the tribes of Israel wanting to wipe out the tribe of Benjamin. Realizing the gravity of the situation they didn't want to do anything without seeking God in the matter. God gave them permission, instructing them to send the tribe of Judah. Then 22,000 men died the first day of this losing battle! Then 18,000 of their men died on the next day, losing again! It wasn't until the third day of battle that they had the victory. These men wept before God, sought his direction, fasted all night, offered sacrifices, went into battle believing for victory, and still had a loss of 40,000 soldiers! This story from Judges teaches us that our victory is not guaranteed without losses. Sometimes our losses may be devastating, multiple, and heart wrenching events which leave us saying, "I really thought I heard from you Lord, but look what happened!" We perceive our middle of the story as if it were the end. It is not the end, even though it may feel like it is.

Dear Lord, Sometimes, such hard things happen in life, we really don't know if we are hearing from you at all. Help us to understand that life is often a fight, and it is common for the victory to come after losing a few rounds. Help us to have the strength to keep fighting with faith in what we have heard from you, no matter how dire the outcome seems to be. Build within us the knowledge that following you and your words does not provide a life free from oppressive obstacles. You are leading us, not on a pain-free path, but on a path which creates followers who become overcomers and victors, not victims. In Jesus' name... Amen.

MAY 7

Plans Have Power

Set up the tabernacle according to the plan shown you on the mountain.
–Exodus 26:30 (NIV)

May he give you the desire of your heart and make all your plans succeed.
–Psalm 20:4 (NIV)

Commit to the Lord whatever you do, and he will establish your plans.
–Proverbs 16:3 (NIV)

But the plans of the Lord stand firm forever, the purposes of his heart through all generations.
–Psalm 33:11 (NIV)

Reading through Exodus where the text goes into minute details about the materials needed, the articles to be used, and the overall dimensions of the tabernacle, frankly, it's a bit boring to me. Any portion of the Bible like that, as in David's plan and Solomon's execution of the plan to build the temple... boring! However, what it illustrates about God's ways for creating his design for us here on earth... that, I find fascinating. Creating an exact plan for anything just feels contrary to my nature because I am a *go with the flow* type of person. I like spontaneous things and last-minute activities. But, that is not the way God works. I need to admit that God has a better way than I do. Maybe I have failed so many times before: to lose weight, finish a large project, get schoolwork done on time, simply because I did not have a good plan to follow. Cruising through life with a hope and a desire that something constructive will manifest out of thin air, definitely does not work. Having a God inspired plan that will create a structure that leads to success, that will work.

Dear Lord, I need to know the broad strokes and the fine details of how to live my life. You gave your kings, prophets, and warriors specific plans to achieve victory, I also need a plan. Help me to listen to your Holy Spirit today. Help me to not resist the confines and limits that are part of your plans for me. May I be open to the counsel of others that have wisdom and godly advice. Let me embrace the order and certainty that comes with your explicit directions. In Jesus' name... Amen.

MAY 8

My Shepherd

The LORD is my shepherd; I shall not want.
He makes me lie down in green pastures;
He leads me beside the still waters. He restores my soul;
He leads me in the paths of righteousness
For His name's sake...
Psalm 23:1—3 (NKJV)

I am the good shepherd. The good shepherd gives His life for the sheep... I am the good shepherd; and I know my sheep, and am known by My own. As the Father knows Me, even so I know the Father; and I lay down my life for the sheep. And other sheep I have which are not of this fold; them also I must bring, and they will hear My voice; and there will be one flock and one shepherd.
John 10:11, 14—16 (NKJV)

My shepherd knows me. Jesus knows my faults and weaknesses, and my strengths and abilities. Certainly, I need to be more like one of his sheep, calmed by his protective presence and attentive to his voice and directions. While my Lord is truly a good shepherd, I am not so good as a sheep. Going off in my own direction, easily distracted, at times wandering away beyond the sound of his voice. Beyond his voice is really the last place to be, because he is good. He knows the best way, the way to eternal life, to still peaceful waters and purpose. There are many more sheep that he wants to gather in with those of us who are now believers. Others can be gathered in, if our ears are tuned to His voice and like good sheep, if we follow him closely, obeying his words. Good sheep gather others and are not prone to wander away from their shepherd.

Dear Lord, Thank you for giving us your only son to die on a cross for our sins. Forgive us for our lack of trust. Truly, you only want what is best for us. No matter what we face, what our flaws are, you lead and guide us to a better place. Help us to know you more deeply, to follow you more closely, to be willing to obey you more readily, and to delight in hearing your voice. In Jesus' name... Amen.

MAY 9

Times of Trouble

**In times of trouble, may the Lord answer your cry.
May the name of the God of Jacob keep you safe from all harm.
May he send you help from his sanctuary
and strengthen you from Jerusalem.
May he remember all your gifts
and look favorably on your burnt offerings.
May he grant your heart's desires
and make all your plans succeed.
May we shout for joy when we hear of your victory
and raise a victory banner in the name of our God.
May the Lord answer all your prayers.**
–Psalm 20:1—9 (NLT)

There have been many times of trouble in my life. Some of my own making, other times through circumstances totally out of my control. Life can feel like being in the midst of a heavy fog. Not knowing where to turn, and not knowing what to do in the midst of trying difficulties can make us feel oppressed and downhearted. For me, praising God for who he is, and thanking Jesus for what he did for me on the cross, has helped me to lift my head. The words of this Psalm impart hope. Like King David, I too pray for safety, help, strength, that God remembers my sacrifices and service, that he will grant my heart's desire, that my plans succeed, and that I will taste victory. Being in the midst of trouble should never hinder us from looking to God with a grateful heart and praise on our lips. The right spiritual perspective can be a refuge for a soul deeply wounded by life's afflictions.

Dear Lord, May I never cease to praise you for who you are, and for what you have done for me on the cross. I lift up every person now struggling with troubles and difficulties. I pray that they will not lose faith, and that their hearts would be uplifted and encouraged. I pray for an outpouring of answered prayers that would be like living water to their thirsty souls. I also ask for victories to spread among your people so that they could share powerful, wonderful testimonies of your goodness and your faithfulness. Help us to always look to you as our source of peace and protection. In Jesus' name... Amen.

MAY 10

Like Blackbirds in My Head

When we worship the right way, God doesn't stir us up into confusion; he brings us into harmony.
–1 Corinthians 14:33 (MSG)

Ephraim is fickle and scattered, like a flock of blackbirds, their beauty dissipated in confusion and clamor, frenetic and noisy.
–Hosea 9:11—12 (MSG)

Sometimes, when I have an unbearable number of things to do, it makes my brain feel like a blender. So much life noise with thoughts churning around at high speed, gives me a headache, making it impossible to focus on one single thing. Nothing illustrates this phenomenon any better than my poster from the band Blenderhead. You can see it by searching- "Images: Blenderhead, Prime Candidate for Burnout." With all the noise and confusing thoughts in my head, it would be nice to have a way out. There is only one way out that works for me when I am in that state. Make a list. Some procrastinators make lists to avoid doing what they should do. Others, like me, use lists as an organizational tool to halt thoughts spinning out of control, and to create a step-by-step way out of the headache and mind-numbing paralysis into productivity.

Dear Lord, When there is too much to do, and time is pressing down on me, and tasks whirl through my brain adding to my mental and emotional pain, I need help! Help me to slow everything down, worship you, listen to you. Help me to make a list, to order my thoughts and actions into a tangible plan. Free me from being frozen over what to do. With each item written down, the blender in my head is relieved of pressure; my list creates a safety valve and a way out. Thank you for any tool that provides victory over confusion, and anything that leads to productivity. Grant me peace and order in my thinking. In Jesus' name... Amen.

MAY 11

Ready for Battle

Your strength must come from the Lord's mighty power within you. Put on all of God's armor so that you will be able to stand safe against all strategies and tricks of Satan. For we are not fighting against people made of flesh and blood, but against persons without bodies—the evil rulers of the unseen world, those mighty satanic beings and great evil princes of darkness who rule this world; and against huge numbers of wicked spirits in the spirit world. So use every piece of God's armor to resist the enemy whenever he attacks, and when it is all over, you will be standing up.
–Ephesians 6:10—13 (TLB)

Often, life is a battle. Battles are within us, or with others, with dark spiritual beings, or with circumstances totally out of our control. If we don't realize we are in a battle, opposition can overwhelm us like a flood. We don't want to just survive; we are designed to thrive. Let us be poised for victory on every front. We should not be chained to past mistakes. Quitting should never be an option with God on our side. Covering our heads with the helmet of salvation, blocking our ears from the accusations and taunts of our Enemy, we are moving forward to capture territory. As a Christian, my eyes are fixed on Jesus, the author and finisher of my faith. But my feet are planted in the soil of the Old Testament. Today my inspiration comes from God who has woven our history before time itself. It comes from the Hebraic Reggae music and lyrics of Matisyahu, who worships the "God of Abraham, Isaac, and Jacob." I can put his "Live Like a Warrior" on repeat and transform myself into an attitude of victory! Musical expressions of spiritual conquests help me to move forward, singing of my victory, even before it happens, faith in action with God on my side! Today these lyrics are my prayer. In Jesus' name…

"Today, today, live like you wanna,
Let yesterday burn and throw it in a fire, in a fire, in a fire
Fight like a warrior,
Today, today, live like you wanna,
Let yesterday burn and throw it in a fire, in a fire, in a fire,
Live like a warrior"

MAY 12

My Soul's Hope

So I will not be silent; I will sing praise to you.
Lord, you are my God; I will give you thanks forever.
–Psalm 30:12 (GNT)

My soul is glad because of God my Savior
–Luke 1:47 (GNT)

But don't be glad because the evil spirits obey you; rather be glad because your names are written in heaven.
–Luke 10:20 (GNT)

Procrastinators are notorious for being "in the moment," not necessarily in a good way. Rather than choosing an outlook that embraces deferred gratification and long-term goals, we tend to just perceive the here and now, be ruled by our feelings, and we make choices based on pleasure instead of wisdom. For me, there is a constant tension between the best course and what *feels* the best. The big picture includes my soul's hope, my salvation, the blessing of being part of the Body of Christ, fulfilling my God-given destiny, and having Heaven as my eternal home. I struggle because I do not see that big picture often enough. If my soul's hope and the joy of knowing that my name is written in the Lamb's Book of Life was ever before my eyes, that pleasure would outshine all else. But… there's a cheesecake calling my name, a DVR full of movies I want to watch, and taking a nap would feel great right now.

Dear Lord, Help me to focus on all that you are, and all that you have provided for me. Let the pleasure and joy of your kingdom bring healing to my soul. I confess that when my focus is on my wounds and disappointments, I become blind to your grace and the goodness all around me. May my soul's hope be restored by the joy of my salvation. Today, guide me to make my decisions based on your words and wisdom, not my immediate circumstances and feelings. In Jesus' name... Amen.

MAY 13

We Got to Pray

Praise be to God, who has not rejected my prayer or withheld his love from me.
–Psalm 66:20 (NIV)

But Jesus often withdrew to lonely places and prayed.
–Luke 5:16 (NIV)

But in every situation, by prayer and petition, with thanksgiving, present your requests to God.
–Philippians 4:6 (NIV)

I pray that out of his glorious riches he may strengthen you with power through his Spirit in your inner being.
–Ephesians 3:16 (NIV)

In my battle against procrastination there is one thing that I have discovered. Praying "on target" prayers have made a huge difference in bringing about victory in my life. My prayers, day after day, have battled unseen forces, and these prayers have been rewarded by positive, life changing results. My prayers are out there, born of a sincere and struggling spirit that desires freedom from the snare of procrastination. They are there to help others who have difficulty finding the correct words to connect with God's triumphant battle plan. There is certainly nothing wrong in taking time away from other obligations to make prayer a priority; Jesus did. There is also nothing wrong with praying for ourselves. We need to gain victory before we can help anyone else. There are dark powers that are at war with God's people. They aim to defeat us and rob us of our destiny, which will in turn rob others of their opportunities for salvation. Time is short; we have got to pray!

Dear Lord, I thank you and praise you for the opportunity we have as believers, to come before you knowing that you hear our prayers. Give us discernment in seeing the root of our own problems, not just the manifestations. Help us, by the power of your Holy Spirit, to pray those prayers which you desire us to pray, so that your will may be done on earth as it is in heaven. As we dedicate our time to pray, may we be encouraged by victories in your name. May we grow spiritually strong in prayer, so that our personal triumphs will blossom into winning wars against our enemies. Loosen the power of grace, mercy, forgiveness, and love in our hearts. Remove anything within us that hinders your will being done. In Jesus' name... Amen.

MAY 14

Sowing the Good Stuff

Remember this: Whoever sows sparingly will also reap sparingly, and whoever sows generously will also reap generously.
–2 Corinthians 9:6 (NIV)

Some truths are harder to accept than others. I recall so many times when the seeds of my procrastination were producing things that I didn't want to deal with. Bad results made me wish for solutions, hope for deliverance from my difficulties, and pray for some miracle to resolve the mess I had created for myself. If only I could just accept one of life's most important truths, "We reap what we sow." Searching outside myself to be rescued should not be viewed as a solution. It is all on me. I need to create within myself someone who does not procrastinate! I need to sow good seeds: starting my tasks within a reasonable time frame, choosing long term good over instant gratification, embracing my responsibilities instead of ignoring them, incorporating a daily devotional time that is founded on God's Word, seeking wisdom for every decision, sowing my time and efforts into the local church, praising and thanking God. There are many kinds of good seeds that I could sow in order to prevent a crop of anxious results. What a difference, what a tremendous harvest would be mine, if I was just sowing the good stuff!

Dear Lord, Help me to see that all my actions have consequences. I cannot eat junk and reap health. No one can sow lies and reap truth. All our actions plant seeds that will come to fruition in the future. Guide me every day to realize what I am sowing. Help me to see the possible consequences clearly. Today, let me sow responsibility, self-discipline, truth, respect, generosity. In Jesus' name... Amen.

MAY 15

God Removes Our Guilt

Now God says he will accept and acquit us—declare us "not guilty"—if we trust Jesus Christ to take away our sins. And we all can be saved in this same way, by coming to Christ, no matter who we are or what we have been like.
–Romans 3:21-22 (TLB)

If we confess our sins, he is faithful and just and will forgive us our sins and purify us from all unrighteousness.
–1 John 1:19 (NIV)

We are His. We Follow Him, the one who died on a cross for our sins. Every wrong thing we have ever done, every detour off the righteous path he laid out before us, Jesus covered it all. Whenever we feel guilty, which happens often, it hinders us from being the person we should be. This is not just about being a procrastinator, it is about coming clean with whatever we need to confess. How do we, as Christians, remove the weight of guilt? The act of our confession and our repentance releases the mercy and forgiveness of God, but often it is hard to shake off guilty feelings. We need to get our feelings in line with the love, mercy, grace and forgiveness given to us. God removes our guilt. It's done, we don't remove it. We just need to receive the spiritual truth that God removes our guilt, over and over, again and again.

Dear Lord, I am so grateful that Jesus died for me. His great love for me by suffering upon the cross is beyond my comprehension; let it never be beyond my appreciation. I thank you and praise you for who you are and the tremendous depth of your love for me. When I recognize that guilt is dragging me down, give me the discernment as to whether it is a useless disruption of my emotional state, or a sign that it is time for me to come clean about some sin in my life. I pray that the emotions of gratitude and love for all that you have done for me, would prompt me into a time of worship, and usher in your presence and relief from my guilty feelings. May I be quick to confess my sins and move forward in freedom from guilt. In Jesus' name... Amen.

MAY 16

Not Where I Want to Be

The words of the Lord are pure words, like silver refined in a furnace on the ground, purified seven times.
–Psalm 12:6 (ESV)

Trust in him at all times, O people; pour out your heart before him; God is a refuge for us.
–Psalm 62:8 (ESV)

But understand this, that in the last days there will be times of difficulty.
–II Timothy 3:1 (ESV)

There are times when people are invited to give their lives to Christ, the message may be perceived as, "Surrender to Jesus, then magically your problems will go away. Get ready for a totally wonderful life." The apostle Paul, who experienced blindness, beatings, shipwreck, stoning, hunger, rejection, and execution, would probably refute that idea. We are never free from trials and hardships, health battles, or loved ones dying. It is just life. Being in a place watching a loved one suffer from a life-threatening disease, seeing your children becoming addicts, or having no financial resources to meet needs and wants, is not a place I want to be. When I am in a place that I don't want to be, it is simply time to realize that I am being refined in the fire. We need to pour out our heart to the Lord, realize he is our refuge in times of difficulty and trust him. We may not be where we want to be, but the Lord is leading us to where we need to go, molding us into the person we need to be.

Dear Lord, I thank you for the gift of my salvation. Help all your people to find comfort and not lose heart during difficult times. You are sovereign, and you see the purpose behind all things. May we not quit, but cling to you all the more when there are hardships and dark places in our life. Help us to see beyond our current circumstances, and to have faith in your plan for our life. May we always have a flame of hope for better days, and a joyous anticipation of our eternity in heaven. In Jesus' name... Amen.

MAY 17

Opportunity Costs

But don't begin until you count the cost. For who would begin construction of a building without first getting estimates and then checking to see if he has enough money to pay the bills?
–Luke 14:28 (TLB)

"No," the king replied, "I will buy it for the full price; I cannot take what is yours and give it to the Lord. I will not offer a burnt offering that has cost me nothing."
–I Chronicles 21:24 (TLB)

There is a term in Economics that applies to every aspect of life, not just the price of exchanging goods and services; it is "opportunity cost." Whenever we attain or achieve something, it has come at the cost of something else. In order to gain one thing, something else must be sacrificed. In common terms, we cannot have our cake and eat it too. When I was in college I had to give up a few parties to pass my classes, as a mother I gave up potential income to stay home and raise my three children, and presently in order to finish my book, it costs me an average of two-three hours a day. We all need to ask ourselves, "What do I really want to accomplish in my life? What do I need to give up, to get the life that God wants me to have?" As long as we procrastinate, we lose our opportunity, and it could cost us our destiny.

Dear Lord, Give us vision to see all that we can be, and help us to muster the will to pay the price to get there. Let us seek wisdom and make realistic plans today, not merely indulge in far-fetched wishes. Create within us the determination of a great athlete. May we be willing to sacrifice and work hard to achieve our goals today. Convict us of wasted time and laziness. May we count the time and effort we put into building a life according to your will, a small price to pay. In Jesus' name... Amen

MAY 18

Into Our Hand

David said to the Philistine [Goliath], "You come to me with a sword, a spear, and a shield, but I come to you in the name of the Lord of Hosts, the God of the armies of Israel, whom you have reviled. This day the Lord will deliver you into my hand. And I will strike you down and cut off your head... so that all the earth may know that there is a God in Israel. And then all this assembly will know that it is not by sword and spear that the Lord saves. For the battle belongs to the Lord, and He will give you into our hands."
–I Samuel 17:45—47 (MEV)

I confess that there have been many times when personal victories were not for my hands to possess. There were circumstances that became my Goliath, and I could not ignite the faith and courage to destroy my internal and external enemies. Now I see that David handled his battle well because of his previous experiences that the Lord had brought him through. We must be ready to confidently realize the Lord is on our side. Whether we battle procrastination, discouragement, fear, negative self-talk, or financial lack, we possess the God-given resources in our hands to conquer our enemies. Let us move forward into areas that need to be conquered, to grow as God's warrior, so that when we are confronted by our Goliath, we will be ready to defeat our enemy by our own hands.

Dear Lord, Let me develop the confidence and faith I need to defeat your enemies; they are my enemies as well. I desire to expand your kingdom knowing that without you I can do nothing. No matter what task, situation, or enemy that I face, let me always have the confidence that you are with me, that the battle is yours and not mine. Help me to conquer territory for your kingdom this day. Help me to make your name acknowledged and revered throughout the world. In Jesus' name... Amen.

MAY 19

Self-Control

Better a patient person than a warrior, one with self-control than one who takes a city.
–Proverbs 16:32 (NIV)

Like a city whose walls are broken through is a person who lacks self-control.
–Proverbs 25:28 (NIV)

I think having a self-control problem is something that all procrastinators have in common. I can't count the number of times I have prayed for God to just zap me instantaneously with that superpower. I want the power to control myself, to lose those extra pounds, to not hit the snooze button countless times before rolling out of bed. I'm already late before my day is even started! I desire the discipline to accomplish any goal set before me. I do not envy many people, but when I witness the life of a friend who is disciplined and very self-controlled, I must confess that am definitely envious. How do they do it? Why them and not me? Oh yeah, that's right, self-control is a fruit and not a gift. This means that it requires hard work in order to grow and nurture it within myself. Too bad, I really would prefer to just get zapped!

Dear Lord, My lack of self-control has been a burden to me for far too long. While I realize that it is my responsibility to take charge of this area in my life, I admit that I can't seem to do it on my own. Plant your words deep within me, renew my mind, guide me by the power of the Holy Spirit. Help me to realize when I am out of control, and recalibrate my emotions, my impulses, and my decisions. If I am going to defeat procrastination I must embrace a lifestyle of self-control today. Without you, I can do nothing. Grant me the grace to change myself in this area. In Jesus' name… Amen.

MAY 20

In the Future

Know also that wisdom is like honey for you: If you find it, there is a future hope for you, and your hope will not be cut off.
–Proverbs 24:14 (NIV)

For I know the plans I have for you, says the Lord. They are plans for good and not for evil, to give you a future and a hope. In those days when you pray, I will listen. You will find me when you seek me, if you look for me in earnest.
–Jeremiah 29:11—13 (TLB)

No one really knows for certain what their future on earth will be. Even our future in heaven is a mystery of what "no eye has seen, nor ear heard of the wonderful things" awaiting us. Countless times I have made decisions based on how I thought those decisions would impact my future, only to be mistaken. Being too attached to the specifics of what I thought would result from my decisions often led to being disappointed. If my decisions are based on wisdom, knowing he has my future in his hands, and doing the work that needs to be done today, I will free myself from unnecessary emotional let downs. Procrastinators do what we do to avoid negative feelings about ourselves. By embracing God's will for our lives, we can rest in hope, and trust his loving kindness. The prize we then seek is gained through obedience, not in a fulfilled list of expected results here and now. The future is sweet, when we are moving forward in wisdom.

Dear Lord, Forgive me for all the times that I let disappointment cloud my gratitude for all that you have done for me. I confess that I want my own way, I want quick rewards and good consequences for all my efforts. Help me to detach myself from seeking specific results, and content myself with seeking you, acting in wisdom, trusting you to work the details out on my behalf. Help me to grow in confidence and hope in the future that you are creating for me. Help me to follow you obediently, day by day. In Jesus' name… Amen.

MAY 21

Never Say Never

Jesus looked at them intently, then said, "Without God, it is utterly impossible. But with God everything is possible."
–Mark 10:27 (TLB)

Then everyone will be praising the name of the Lord Jesus Christ because of the results they see in you; and your greatest glory will be that you belong to him. The tender mercy of God and of our Lord Jesus Christ has made all this possible for you.
–2 Thessalonians 1:12 (TLB)

How many times have I said, "I'll never_____________!" I could fill in that blank with, "get this assignment done on time," "finish my screenplay," "lose weight and get in shape," "pay off my debts," "finish my degree," "get my book published," etc. Surely you have some goals you could fill into your own blanks, things you believe may never happen. Sometimes working on heartfelt desires is like rolling a rock uphill, one which inevitably rolls back to the bottom again. Those Greeks were pretty insightful with their myths; while Sisyphus was eternally condemned to this activity, thank God we are not. We should never condemn ourselves to a Neverland where all dreams do not come true, and all our aspirations expire before we die. Whenever an attitude that promotes "that will never happen" instead of "with God all things are possible," we need to take that thought captive, and declare faith into our situation.

Dear Lord, Help us to be people of faith over frustration. Help us determine what actions are unfruitful and need to be abandoned, so that our time and energy will be well spent. You are an almighty God; you have created the heavens and the earth! May we never doubt that all things are possible for you. May we surrender more and more of our dreams, our priorities, our time, and our resources into your hands. May whatever we do bring glory to your name and sustain our spirits as we spread your kingdom throughout the earth. In Jesus' name... Amen.

MAY 22

What's Wrong with Being Perfect?

And having been perfected, He became the source of eternal salvation for all those who obey him.
–Hebrews 5:9 (NASB)

For by one offering He has perfected for all time those who are sanctified.
–Hebrews 10:14 (NASB)

The Law of the Lord is perfect, restoring the soul; The testimony of the Lord is sure, making wise the simple.
–Psalms 19:7 (NASB)

Perfectionism is a trap. We want to be perfect; we strive to be perfect. A gymnast once in a blue moon can get a perfect score. Jesus even said, "you shall be perfect as your Heavenly Father is perfect." Yet, in pursuing the unrealistic goal of perfection, we fall short and are depressed, rarely allow the time needed to tweak every perceived error, then quit because it is impossible. Progress beats perfection every time. Did Jesus pick perfect people to be his disciples? No! The only perfection possible for us is God's perfect will flowing through us. When that happens, when in obedience our will embraces the Lord's perfect will, that's when perfection happens for us. To try to be perfect with what we create, how we parent, or in our career, is a spiritual stumbling block. We will trip over it again, and again, until we realize, only God is perfect, and we don't have to be. Perfectionism feeds an unsatisfying procrastinating life. Are you a perfectionist? Time to let it go.

Dear Lord, I thank you that you are perfect, so I do not have to be. You have done for us what we cannot do for ourselves… earn salvation. Thank you Jesus, for being the perfect sacrifice, the Lamb of God who takes away the sins of the world. Let me be someone who seeks to walk in, and do, your perfect will. Help me to avoid unproductive efforts that can never produce a perfect result. Help me to earnestly work toward progress and finished outcomes. In Jesus' name… Amen.

MAY 23

The Right Road

Your word is a lamp to my feet and a light to my path.
–Psalm 119:105 (MEV)

In all your ways acknowledge Him, and He will direct your paths.
–Proverbs 3:6 (MEV)

I consider myself to be a road warrior. I have traveled across the entire United States by myself twice and driven on the opposite side of the road along the slender rock-walled lanes of Ireland and England. If there is adventure to be had by being behind the wheel of a car, I am up for it. While it is common to take wrong roads and exits from time to time, thankfully I am not one to go too far off my intended course before correcting it. There was one time while crossing through Montana that the pavement turned into a winding dirt and gravel path slowing my progress, darkness and fierce thunderstorms gathered to my left, and a herd of bellowing cattle were roaming freely and nervously to my right, and my GPS signal disappeared! It was scary, and doubt crept in as to whether or not I was on the correct way to where I was headed.

Life is like that. We find ourselves in unfamiliar territory, danger, and unpredictable forces gather around us. It does not mean that we have lost our way, or that we are not on the right road. I was on the right road, just hit a rough patch. When we live a life submitted to God there will be times of opposition, times when we question our direction, but with an attitude of surrender, the Holy Spirit will guide us to where we need to be. That could mean going back to where "we missed it," or proceeding through all hindrances until we arrive at our God-given destination.

Dear Lord, Thank you for lighting our way in this world. You are a holy and righteous counselor, the navigator for our souls. May we be diligent in reading and listening to your words, following your lead, and undaunted by rough terrain that can cause us to trip and stumble. Give us discernment as to when we are heading in the wrong direction. Let us be people that are quick to repent and correct our course. May we always stay on the road that you have made for us to travel on, even when the way gets harsh. In Jesus' name... Amen.

MAY 24

Crisis Tends to Rule

For God is not a God of disorder but of peace.
–1 Corinthians 14:33 (NIV)

Whenever I planned to do something that brought out the procrastinator in me, the negative results were totally my fault. My avoidance, my fears, my lack of effort, or my irresponsibility always created varying degrees of disorder, chaos, and anxiety. When I started to write a blog, that would later become this book, there was hardcore determination that nothing would stop my daily entries for five days a week, week after week, month after month.

Now, everything has changed. Crisis has intervened and reared its ugly demanding head. When a family member is in medical crisis, emergency needs supersede everything else. So, no need for guilt or berating myself for unmet goals. Life in times of crisis has demands that must be met first, beyond individual hopes and plans. Unforeseen troubling circumstances may alter the pace of my progress, but it can never take me off course unless I let it. A crisis, by its very nature, severely alters our present. It may rule for a time, but it cannot rule me past its due season. Eventually even a crisis must bow down because only God rules and reigns forever.

Dear Lord, I need your comfort, your words, your presence. Chaos, discouragement, and sadness are invading my heart and soul. I need you now more than ever. Help me to realize that putting important goals on pause during a time of crisis is not procrastination or failure; it's wisdom. Grant me peace in my present situation. You are good. You rule and reign over all. In Jesus' name… Amen.

MAY 25

It's Like Hockey

I'm not saying that I have this all together, that I have it made. But I am well on my way, reaching out for Christ, who has wondrously reached out for me. Friends, don't get me wrong: By no means do I count myself an expert in all this, but I've got my eye on the goal, where God is beckoning us onward–to Jesus. I'm off and running, and I'm not turning back. So let's keep focused on that goal, those of us who want everything God has for us. If any of you have something else in mind, something less than total commitment, God will clear your blurred vision–you'll see it yet! Now that we're on the right track, let's stay on it.
–Philippians 3:12—16 (MSG)

Viewing Stanley Cup playoff hockey as the weather turns hot around here seems strangely out of season. As I watch hockey being played at the highest level it strikes me, how hard it is to actually score a goal. Sometimes there are so many obstacles of sticks, men, and movements, blocking the way of a puck into the net, it seems almost impossible to score. It's analogous to life; the limited space and time allowing the goal to happen is daunting. When time is ticking away, the pressure and intensity increases, best efforts must come forth or you lose. I find that I cannot be casual about the time that is allotted to me on this earth. None of us should take it for granted. Today, I need to wisely assess what is blocking my efforts to reach my goal and push them aside. Without actively clearing a path, too much interference will prevail, and my goal will never happen. Whether life is at the start, a full sixty minutes in hockey terms, or near the end with only two minutes left, the clock is still ticking, there is still an opportunity to win.

Dear Lord, I thank you for the time and the opportunities that you present to me every day. Help me to not waste a moment. Help me to recognize all the superfluous things that get in my way and push them aside. Help me to ruthlessly clear a path to my goal, to vanquish all obstacles, and to clearly see the straight line to pursue my victory. In Jesus' name... Amen.

MAY 26

Not Worth Putting Off

But all who humble themselves before the Lord shall be given every blessing and shall have wonderful peace.
–Psalm 37:11 (TLB)

But I have no regrets. I couldn't be more sure of my ground—the One I've trusted in can take care of what he's trusted me to do right to the end.
–2 Timothy 1:11—12 (MSG)

One thing that robs us of peace is regrets. Dwelling on some missed opportunity or mistake can be like living with a cloud over your head. It can actually suck the life out of you. Unfortunately, due to my procrastination and other issues, regrets linger in my brain. When my opportunity to take a wonderful trip to Europe was in jeopardy, I had many choices to make. Part of me felt if I don't do this now, it may never happen. Much was at stake, whether I stayed home, or left for Europe. Thankfully, God provided for me in a most unlikely way. I was able to travel to Europe with my beloved granddaughter, because a long-lost friend came back into my life and we were able to meet one another's unique needs. Thus, no regrets! Because of God's provision, a dream that I could not give up became a blessed reality. London, Stonehenge, Rome, Venice, Florence, Assisi, Paris, Versailles and more, became the experience of a lifetime. If I had put that trip off somewhere in the future, like so many other things that I have delayed, it might have never happened. I am amazed at how my Heavenly Father provided for me so that rather than one more regret, I experienced a dazzling treasure that has enhanced my life. Some things are too important to put off.

Dear Lord, We do not know how much time we have on earth. Help us to not put off our dreams and help us to live with no regrets! As St. Francis said, in his often-quoted prayer, "Lord, make me an instrument of your peace." Help me to develop a peaceful life, one where haunting regrets have no place. In Jesus' name… Amen.

MAY 27

In the Morning

How precious it is, Lord, to realize that you are thinking about me constantly! I can't even count how many times a day your thoughts turn toward me. And when I waken in the morning, you are still thinking of me!
–Psalm 139:17—18 (TLB)

Let me see your kindness to me in the morning, for I am trusting you. Show me where to walk, for my prayer is sincere.
–Psalm 143:8 (TLB)

I have not been a morning person since I was a child. As soon as the light would open my eyes, it was time to play and get out of bed with abounding energy. My childhood attitude was like... let's get this party started! Since my teen years, I've been a complete night owl. Certain jobs have necessitated me rising at 5:00 A.M. Odd that I consider that an "ungodly hour," when much scripture, and Jesus' prayer habits, show early morning to be a rather godly time. Whether it is an inherited internal clock, nocturnal media habits, difficulty getting a good night's sleep, or laziness, hitting the snooze button is often my first procrastination act of the day. My snooze button finger probably has a callous on it. Knowing that the alarm is set for my ideal time to rise matters not. I will sleep, delay, ignore, and waste the first portion of the morning, when I should take advantage of God's precious attention to me, in preparing for the rest of the day. That needs to change!

Dear Lord, Help me to recalibrate my daylight hours and any habits that hinder my inclination to start my day in a way that pleases you. Help me to quit my repeated "snooze button" habit. Help me to embrace your design and not to fight it. Help me to realize that every minute counts, and delays at the start of my day often translate into rushing around in anxious moments later. May I greet you every morning like a child, happy to see my loving Daddy, bounding out of bed, looking forward to the day's plan, receiving a precious hug first thing in the morning. May my wasteful minutes and hours be transformed into devotional focused productivity. In Jesus' name ... Amen.

MAY 28

I Think I Can... I Believe I Can

Abram believed the LORD, and he credited it to him as righteousness.
–Genesis 15:6 (NIV)

Then they believed his promises and sang his praise.
–Psalm 106:12 (NIV)

When he had gone indoors, the blind men came to him, and he asked them, "Do you believe that I am able to do this?" "Yes, Lord," they replied.
–Matthew 9:28 (NIV)

Anyone that has grown up reading *The Little Engine That Could* has embraced an important life lesson. In order to accomplish anything in life, you must first think that you can do it. There is a very intricate connection between thinking something can come to pass and believing that it will. Thinking is where the momentum starts, yet it is believing that sustains the drive until the mission is accomplished. Without belief in accomplishing a particular goal it could just stay in the netherworld of thought, without ever manifesting in the real world. As the little engine shows us, there is some intense action required. I must exert energy until the goal is accomplished. It is not just, "I think I can. I think I can." But it is also, "I believe I can." For me- I thought I could overcome procrastination, then I believed I could. I am acting on that belief, now I know I can. Praise God!

Dear Lord, Reveal to us the power of right thinking combined with belief. Help us to have our mind submitted to you and your ways, so that we may have "right thoughts." Help us to cast down doubt and unbelief and overcome inaction. Help us to stay focused and diligent, working toward our goals, so that we may enjoy the exhilarating finish. Let us be focused on the prize, and also looking forward to a heavenly reward, hearing you say to us, "Well done, good and faithful servant." In Jesus' name... Amen.

MAY 29

If Then

In all this you greatly rejoice, though now for a little while you may have had to suffer grief in all kinds of trials.
–1Peter 1:6 (NIV)

[Jesus said] "However, do not rejoice that the spirits submit to you, but rejoice that your names are written in heaven."
–Luke 10:20 (NIV)

There is often a great divide between what we currently experience, the reality of present disappointments, and our lofty aspirations. There have been times when I was inclined to think, *Surely God, if you really loved me, then this heartbreaking thing would not have happened!* It is spiritually unhealthy to ping pong if/then scenarios like this around in our brain. These "ifs" launch us into a negative state where we are blaming God for our circumstances, or we are doubting his sovereignty, goodness, or love. The antidote for our disappointment is simply to rejoice in who God is, and what Jesus did for us on the cross. Trials, pain, confrontation with evil forces will come. That is not an *if,* but a *when.* We live in a fallen world. When there is a time of suffering or grief, then we must rejoice that our names are written in heaven, engraved in the Book of Life. We must learn to rejoice in the Lord, even if it is the last thing that we feel like doing.

Dear Lord, Help me to guard my thoughts and my heart. May I not blame you when negative things happen. Help me to quickly recognize when my emotions are forging a chain of doubt and depression. Give me a revelation of the power of thankfulness and praise. You are great, and greatly to be praised, and you have given your son a name which is above every other name- Jesus. May my rejoicing in who you are, your great love, and the gift of salvation, lift my spirit above the hurt and pain. Help me to spread salvation to those who do not know you yet. In Jesus' name... Amen.

MAY 30

Courage Counts

Courage! We must really act like men today if we are going to save our people and the cities of our God. May the Lord's will be done.
–2 Samuel 10:12 (TLB)

Then he continued, "Be strong and courageous and get to work. Don't be frightened by the size of the task, for the Lord my God is with you; he will not forsake you. He will see to it that everything is finished correctly."
–1Chronicles 1:28 (TLB)

We Christians are God's house–he lives in us!–if we keep up our courage firm to the end, and our joy and our trust in the Lord.
–Hebrews 3:6 (TLB)

"Success is not final. Failure is not fatal. It is the courage to continue that counts."

When I first read the above quote, I was impressed by how powerful and applicable they are to leading a purpose-filled life. Maybe that is why this saying is often wrongly attributed to Winston Churchill. Let's face it, has any world leader faced the odds his country did during WWII? The man was known for inspiring courage in his deep resounding voice. However, it is just as likely to be first written in an old newspaper ad or spoken in a coach's speech to ignite his team. We require courage when we are facing gigantic odds, scary enemies, or have no assurance of a favorable outcome in a difficult situation. We must be brave when there is a prize worth fighting for, worth dying for if necessary, and definitely worth living for! Often procrastinators cannot face the possibility of failure or rejection. Our fear becomes a paralyzing shadow keeping us from our calling. By all means let us be strong and work. No matter who first uttered these words, they are still true and powerful. God knows we all need truth and power, and courage to continue when it counts the most.

Dear Lord, Help us to let go of all our fears and be bold. Loosen within your people the courage of brave soldiers, true disciples, and martyrs who have lived and died for the cause of Christ. Give us discernment to recognize our real enemies. Let us be people whose work saves others and does your will. Open our eyes to see that you are always with us, and that no task before us is beyond our ability with you by our side. Let us have courage that is true until the end. In being this way, may we greatly expand your kingdom on earth as it is in heaven. In Jesus' name... Amen.

MAY 31

What Was Sown Today?

And Isaac sowed in that land, and reaped in the same year a hundred fold. The Lord blessed him.
–Genesis 26:12 (RSV)

May those who sow in tears reap with shouts of joy! He that goes forth weeping, bearing the seed for sowing, shall come home with shouts of joy, bringing his sheaves with him.
–Psalm 126:5—6 (RSV)

The point is this, he that sows sparingly will also reap sparingly, and he who sows bountifully will also reap bountifully.
–2 Corinthians 9:6 (RSV)

I often wish that I could escape the truth of the sowing-reaping principle. Especially when it comes to eating bountifully and reaping extra pounds around the middle. But, the principle is a consistent one that proves to be true. If one sows into their studies today they could reap a scholarship, a diploma, or advance a career tomorrow. One of the most precious seeds that we sow is our time. A new business or creative venture can only mature into reality through time and effort, daily. Those of us in the U. S. can be rather spoiled by a culture of instant gratification. Sowing while weeping implies the difficulties and sorrows people may endure in order to possess the fruit of their labors. We must do what needs to be done to sow into the life that we want, the productive life God wants for us. Today, take time to examine what you have sown into your own life, and what you are sowing into the lives of others.

Dear Lord, Keep me diligent in sowing into my future every day. Let me sow into my spirit by reading your word, sow into my soul by giving you thanks and praise, sow into my resources by being generous. Let me also sow blessings into others, and plant seeds in prayer that will produce a harvest for your kingdom. Let my head not hit the pillow tonight without sowing actions that will produce the life that you want for me. In Jesus' name... Amen.

JUNE 1

What Not to Do

God is not unjust; he will not forget your work and the love you have shown him as you have helped his people and continue to help them. We want each of you to show this same diligence to the very end, so that what you hope for may be fully realized. We do not want you to become lazy, but to imitate those who through faith and patience inherit what has been promised.
–Hebrews 6:10—12 (NIV)

Who were they who heard and rebelled? Were they not all those that Moses led out of Egypt? And with whom was he angry for forty years? Was it not with those who sinned, whose bodies perished in the wilderness? And to whom did God swear that they would never enter his rest if not to those who disobeyed? So, we see that they were not able to enter, because of their unbelief.
–Hebrews 3:16—19 (NIV)

When I read about the journey of the Hebrews out of Egypt, through the Red Sea, being turned away from the promised land until all that generation died in the wilderness except faithful Caleb and Joshua, something just hits me. How sad, yet typical, is the way our human nature sabotages us. If you want to know how NOT to follow God, and NOT reach your reward, this story reveals the answer. What not to do?... 1) Be critical of your leaders. 2) Refuse to look forward and yearn for the illusions of past. 3) Decide you would rather have someone go between you and God, instead of having an intimate relationship with him. 4) Believe the bad reports spoken by those that do not believe in God's Word. 5) Be rebellious in big and small areas of life. 6) When you see miraculous signs and wonders still doubt God's power. 7) Lose your faith. 8) Be a complainer.

Dear Lord, You are great and have done mighty deeds. If there be any rebellion within us, may we recognize, repent, and rid ourselves of this dangerous sinful attitude. Grant us eyes to see who you really are and the plans you have for us. Help us stick to the path you have determined for us, without complaining. While we keep our focus on what we must do, give us conviction of our errors when we do something that we should not do. Guide our steps, so that we will enter into your will this day, and all the days of our lives. In Jesus' name... Amen.

JUNE 2

Watch Out

You're addicted to thrills? What an empty life! The pursuit of pleasure is never satisfied.
–Proverbs 21:17 (MSG)

Watch out for the Esau syndrome: trading away God's lifelong gift in order to satisfy a short-term appetite. You well know how Esau later regretted that impulsive act and wanted God's blessing–but by then it was too late, tears or no tears.
–Hebrews 12:15—17 (MSG)

Esau was Isaac's first born, ahead of his twin brother Jacob. Being the first born he was to inherit special blessings, rights, and privileges from his father. Too bad for him, he sold his birthright to Jacob for a bowl of soup! Not being able to defer gratification cost him more than he could imagine. I share something in common with him, deferring gratification is a continual struggle for me. Thus... the extra pounds, the unfinished projects, currently unfulfilled dreams. I would rather go to a concert than study, watch a movie instead of putting extra time into a long-range goal, sleep in instead of exercise in the morning, etc. When it comes to forgoing the pleasurable thing, to do the *should do now* thing, like many procrastinators, I just give in to what feels better in the moment. To say that I hate self-denial may be an exaggeration, but not much of one. It is one thing to enjoy myself and be thrilled by some of the pleasures that life offers, it is quite another to sell my destiny for instant gratification. Time for a change!

Dear Lord, Help me to be victorious in the area of deferred gratification; it seems so much harder than it should be. Give me insight, grow within me a resistance to immediate pleasure that sacrifices long term gain. Lusts of the flesh takes many forms, competing for my time and attention. Help me to listen to your voice, instill your will within me. May the lure of world's excitements continually fade. May my greatest pleasure be in doing your will, in being a disciplined disciple, and in having the joy of you working through me for the rest of my life. In Jesus' name... Amen.

JUNE 3

The Land of Now or Later

"Or, God's kingdom is like a jewel merchant on the hunt for excellent pearls. Finding one that is flawless, he immediately sells everything and buys it."
–Matthew 13:45—46 (MSG)

A dozen or so yards from the beach, he saw the brothers James and John, Zebedee's sons. They were in the boat, mending their fishnets. Right off, he made the same offer. Immediately, they left their father Zebedee, the boat, the hired hands, and followed.
–Mark 1:19—20 (MSG)

They arrived at Jerusalem. Immediately on entering the Temple Jesus started throwing out everyone who had set up shop there, buying and selling.
–Mark 11:15—17 (MSG)

When I looked up the word, "immediately" in Bible Gateway, there were 48 references to this word. The gospel of Mark is particularly characterized by the theme of immediate action, some translations using the term, "straight away." The choice between doing something now or later is a common procrastinator's dilemma. It is also the source of unnecessary domestic conflict as well, "Honey, please fold the laundry." "Yes, dear." Four hours later, spouse returns expecting to see laundry folded, yet there it is bunched up in the basket, wrinkles firmly set in. What happens now? Frustration in one person, self-defense on the other, "I told you I'd do it." In one person's mind, later is as good as now, for the other- immediate action was the only acceptable course. In the greater scheme of things, what's the big deal about a load of laundry? Domestic tranquility for one thing. In the much bigger picture, how do these little things reflect how we handle life's weighty, more important issues. If we constantly dwell in the land of *Later*, and not the land of *Now*, we need to calibrate our bearings.

Dear Lord, Give me constant discernment as to what needs to be done now, and what can wait until later. Help me to be sensitive to the expectations and needs of others around me. Guide me on a path of action, so I do not depend on what life throws at me to determine my course. Holy Spirit set my compass to follow you, no matter what storms may hit, no matter how far off course that I find myself. Create within me the desire to be a person of immediate action, to be someone that dwells in the land of Now, not Later. In Jesus' name... Amen.

JUNE 4

Patience

Put on then, as God's chosen ones, holy and beloved, compassion, kindness, lowliness, meekness, and patience
–Colossians 3:12 (RSV)

So that you may not be sluggish, but imitators of those who through faith and patience inherit the promises.
–Hebrews 6:12 (RSV)

Preach the word, be urgent in season and out of season, convince, rebuke, and exhort, be unfailing in patience and in teaching.
–2 Timothy 4:2 (RSV)

"Be unfailing in patience," now that is a tough one! I want what I want now. Waiting is not my strength. When the car in front of me doesn't immediately accelerate when the light turns green, or my husband has moved the pepper grinder and I can't find it in the midst of my culinary exploits, I can become downright volatile. My study of procrastination has revealed to me just how important patience is in overcoming this major flaw. Whether we are talking about a great wine, a brilliant novel, or the Grand Canyon, some valuable things in life take time. Many of the things that we put off in life, it's simply because they take too long to accomplish, and we are unwilling to put in that much time. We don't want to wait. It is too uncomfortable and annoying; we want it now! We need to value patience and work toward developing it. Patience provides us with a quiet pool of emotional reserve. Patience becomes our comforting *still waters* within. We need to avoid easily triggered frustrations and exert our power to calm the anxiety that pushes us to avoid what we should be doing now.

Dear Lord, Help us to realize the importance of patience in our battle to defeat procrastination in our lives. Help us to be vigilant in recognizing when impatience is rearing its ugly head. Let us develop an awareness of our triggers in this area so that we may learn to relax and let go of useless frustrations and anger. Prompt us by your Holy Spirit to a place of still waters when our impatience begins to accelerate. You desire to convince, teach, and exhort us to be all that we can be. Let it start today, being done within your time frame, not ours. In Jesus' name… Amen.

JUNE 5

The Good Side of Never

"The Lord reigns! Yea, the world is established, it shall never be moved; he will judge the peoples with equity."
–Psalm 96:10 (RSV)

I will never forget thy precepts; for by them thou hast given me life.
–Psalm 119:93 (RSV)

Cast your burden on the Lord, and he will sustain you; he will never permit the righteous to be moved.
–Psalm 55:22 (RSV)

Sometimes the word *never* haunts me. The thought that I may never finish the work that God has assigned to me, is probably my greatest fear. While the cliché, "Never say never," is of some comfort, it doesn't carry the weight that it should in my emotions. I have seen my beloved New England Patriots come back after being down by astronomical odds, and still become winners, it gives me a bit of courage to think that the same could happen to me. But life is more than a football game, and *never* seems so permanent, so absolute. What does God's Word say about *never* that could possibly encourage me? The Lord God is sovereign, what he establishes will never be moved, and he rules with justice. If I never forget his words and laws, I have life. I can let God carry my burdens so that they do not weigh me down along the path that he has given me. He will never let me be moved off his calling for my life. The good side of never, as revealed in these scriptures, can prevail over nonproductive worry and the specter of *never.*

Dear Lord, Let me not be defeated by the feeling that I will never accomplish what you have called me to complete. I thank you that you are a good, sovereign God. I thank you for giving me life and countless opportunities to expand your kingdom. Grant me the confidence to know that my life will never end on earth until your will has fully been done in me. I thank you that by my faith in your son, you consider me to be righteous. Let gratitude for the eternal life which you have given me, empower me and help defeat the powers of darkness that war against me. In Jesus' name...Amen.

JUNE 6

Perhaps Only One

But the Lord answered her, "Martha, Martha, you are anxious and troubled about many things, but one thing is necessary. Mary has chosen the good portion, which will not be taken from her."
–Luke 10:41—42 (ESV)

My choice is you, God, first and only. And now I find I'm your choice! You set me up with a house and yard. And then you made me your heir!
–Psalm 16:5—6 (MSG)

All of us have been in circumstances when there are too many things to do, too many obligations and deadlines, or an array of fires to put out. All we can do is throw up our hands and say, "Lord, help me. What should I do first?" The answer is so simple that it is often ignored. "Seek ye first the Kingdom of God." I know how Martha feels, every procrastinator does. Feeling overwhelmed and frustrated looking for a scapegoat. Martha did the right thing, going to Jesus, but she took the wrong posture. What she needed to do, what we all need to do, is be on the floor at the feet of Jesus, hugging his legs like a child that refuses to let go, listening to every word coming out of his mouth, deeply aware of his ever-present healing love.

Dear Lord, Keep me on my knees in an attitude of submissive thankfulness. Let me envelope myself in your presence until all the demands that surround me disappear for a blessed respite. Build me up in my spirit as I feed on your word and your love for me. Remind me in the midst of life's demands that you have chosen me. You meet my needs, and I am an heir to the Kingdom of God. As I move close to you as my first choice, in faith, you will show me the next steps to take. In Jesus' name... Amen.

JUNE 7

Wonderful Things

However, as it is written: "What no eye has seen, what no ear has heard, and what no human mind has conceived"–the things [wonderful things] God has prepared for those who love him–
–I Corinthians 2:9 (NIV)

You asked, 'Who is this that obscures my plans without knowledge?' Surely I spoke of things I did not understand, things too wonderful for me to know.
–Job 42:3 (NIV)

Lord, you are my God; I will exalt you and praise your name, for in perfect faithfulness you have done wonderful things, things planned long ago.
–Isaiah 25:1 (NIV)

Recently, a friend in church said to me, "The process just doesn't look like the promise." Amen to that! When you've had plans and dreams on hold forever, or you've seen them crash and burn, it is hard to believe that God truly has a wonderful plan for your life. You may have thought you knew what they were; you may have a parade of missteps and false starts leading to nowhere. I just may be twirling a baton at the head of that parade! Plans may have come to nothing so far, but that doesn't mean they have expired. Experience is one thing; truth is quite another. God loves us, and God is good, and God is the creator of wonderful things, on earth as it is in heaven. We are the ones that don't see the big picture. To move forward in life, we must believe that God has wonderful things, marvelous and glorious things, in store for all of us that love him.

Dear Lord, Let any vision that I have, not in keeping with your plan, fade from my mind and no longer stir any desire for fulfillment. Give me your plan, let me see my life the way you see it. Mark my path clearly in the direction of those most wonderful things, things which you have prepared for me from long ago. Let me never lose trust in your love for me and let me always believe that wonderful things will be within my reach. In Jesus' name... Amen.

JUNE 8

What Fruit?

But the fruit of the spirit is love, joy, peace, patience, kindness, goodness, faithfulness, gentleness, and self-control. Against such things there is no law.
–Galatians 5:22 (ESV)

Since all of these "Fruits of the Spirit" are of God, and I love God, they should all be embraced with equal zeal by me, but no. It is kind of like real fruit, I love watermelon, but honeydew, not so much. The fruit of love, and letting it flow freely to almost anyone in my path, yes. Patience? I have exorbitant amounts of patience with children, yet with bad drivers and technical difficulties, barely any.

Then there is the mysterious, elusive fruit of self-control. When it comes to my anger, appetites, overindulgence in escapism entertainment, or controlling my time wisely... where is self-control? What does that fruit taste like? Procrastinators often lack the self-control necessary to get somewhere on time, to complete projects, or to even start something that should have been started years ago! Since I have begun this writing project, the *Procrastinators Daily Devotional*, I have been actively doing something that exercises my self-control. Rather than think about my lack of it, thank God... this self-control fruit is actually starting to grow! When it is finished, only then will I know how good it tastes. Yet, I know for sure it will be delicious.

Dear Lord, Self-control is so important in overcoming the inefficient tendencies of procrastination. Help me to be the person you want me to be. Let me start every day devoted to you. Give me the will, the tools, the support, the positive habits, so that I will leave my procrastinating ways behind. As I dedicate time and effort to develop self-control, it seems to grow within me. Jesus, I love you and thank you for the finished work of the cross, and all that your gift of salvation means to me. I ask for all these things in your name... Amen.

JUNE 9

Where's the Hope

We put our hope in the Lord; he is our protector and our help... May your constant love be with us, Lord we put our hope in you.
–Psalm 33:20, 22 (GNT)

The Lord is near to those who are discouraged; he saves those who have lost all hope.
–Psalm 34:18 (GNT)

Whenever we attempt to change ourselves for the better it seems as if obstacles, beyond what we could predict, come out to challenge and hinder us. Good intentions often end up as fodder for pessimism and defeat. If we hope in our intentions, that is a risky venture. It is far better to hope in God, in God's unfailing love, faithfulness, and grace. We may fail, he doesn't. We have a firm foundation to hope for a good outcome, to look forward to fulfilling the change we desire, when we trust and hope in the Lord.

Dear Lord, You have created us in your image, for us to be creative and victorious in this life. Help us to be battle- ready when obstacles rise up to defeat us. We have disappointed ourselves many times. Help us to realize that we have not disappointed you. You have loved us and saved us, despite any failures that we dwell upon. Protect our spirit, let us not give up in defeat. Help us to look forward to the next battle, the next challenge, with hope in you. Keep hope burning in our hearts, purifying us from despair and discouragement. Guide us to victory. In Jesus' name... Amen.

JUNE 10

Not Alone

Two can accomplish more than twice as much as one, for the results can be much better. If one falls, the other pulls him up; but if a man falls when he is alone, he's in trouble. Also, on a cold night, two under the same blanket gain warmth from each other, but how can one be warm alone?
–Ecclesiastes 4:9–12 (TLB)

Therefore, since we are surrounded by so great a cloud of witnesses, let us also lay aside every weight, and sin which clings so closely, and let us run with perseverance the race that is set before us, looking to Jesus the pioneer and perfecter of our faith... Therefore lift your drooping hands and strengthen your weak knees, and make straight paths for your feet, so that what is lame may not be put out of joint but healed.
–Hebrews 12:1–2, 12–13 (RSV)

After listening to the magnificent voices of Kelly Clarkson and Pink sing the song "Everybody Hurts," I was moved to tears. I felt touched by the common human experience of emotional pain that crosses all cultures, all over the world. If we are not able to be touched by someone else's pain, we are in a very numb and useless state indeed, and that is sad. Hearing the blend of their powerful, beautiful voices drive home the reality that two are often better than one was an emotional spiritual experience for me. Sometimes we humans do have the ability to gloriously bring out the best in each other. We were never meant to be alone, to hurt alone, and be separated from the comfort and support of others. Thank God for people in our lives that bring out the best in us, creating lives that are a beautiful song. We were not designed to be isolated, but to be connected to others in an uplifting harmony. It is why our Lord wants us all to gather regularly and to be part of a supportive, faith filled, loving local church.

Please check this amazing duet out on YouTube:
Everybody Hurts, Pink & Kelly Clarkson, AMA Awards 2017

Dear Lord, You are great, and mighty, and worthy of all praise. You have designed us to be supportive and instrumental in the well-being of others. May we have a heart of compassion like you have. May we always be responsive to the needs of others. I am grateful that you have made me part of your Body of Believers. Help me to function within that body to my utmost. Help me to join with others in harmony to proclaim who you are, and to spread the joy of your salvation offered to all humanity. In Jesus' name... Amen.

JUNE 11

It's Just Wrong

Come to me, all who labor and are heavy laden, and I will give you rest. Take my yoke upon you, and learn from me; for I am gentle and lowly in heart, and you will find rest for your souls. For my yoke is easy, and my burden is light.
–Matthew 11:28—30 (RSV)

How do I feel when I see that one of my favorite women, in a world changing Christian ministry, has just written her umpteenth book? Sorry to say... depressed a bit. While I admire her so much, that she is so successful in advancing God's Kingdom globally, and maintains such a lovely family, somehow her achievements make me feel all the more unsuccessful. And... I've even heard her preach on the dangers of comparison! Either feeling superior or inferior to anyone, is just wrong. God values our uniqueness. Jesus' disciples all had different backgrounds and personalities, even including two brothers who wanted to put themselves ahead of all the other disciples. It's just wrong.

As a procrastinator, I am well aware that I have been late too often, and sometimes I may have missed a precious opportunity entirely. However, we all must remember our God is the God of multiple chances. We must stop carrying the heavy burden of comparison, or we may never be able to move forward. That burden presses a procrastinator's feet deep in the mire of self-condemnation and doubt. We were meant to be free, so we can keep advancing to where we belong.

Dear Lord, I thank you that you have designed each one of us to be unique. Help us to remember that we are not to compare ourselves to anyone else, but to use your words as a guide. May we all increase our time in scripture, plant it deep in our hearts that we may be transformed into the person you designed us to be. Rid us of useless self-condemnation, depression, and low self-esteem. Renew our hearts with your abundant grace and love. Help us today, to find our place submitted to your yoke and gentle hand, that we may be joined with you to produce a harvest of good things in this life and the next. In Jesus' name... Amen.

JUNE 12

Are You One of Those?

This God– how perfect are his deeds! How dependable his words! He is like a shield for all who seek his protection.
–Psalm 18:30 (GNT)

I do not claim that I have already succeeded or have already become perfect. I keep striving to win the prize for which Christ Jesus has already won me to himself.
–Philippians 3:12 (GNT)

There was a time in my life when there was a transition from my Hindu philosophical mindset to accepting Jesus Christ as my Lord and Savior. Eventually it led to embracing Jesus' perfect work on the cross for the salvation of my soul. I was participating in a Yoga class, where my teacher encouraged us to strive for "perfection" in our strenuous postures. A transforming illumination filled my thoughts during class one night, "Thank you God, Jesus was perfect, I never will be perfect, and I don't have to be, because he was perfect for me."

In an article titled, "4 Ways to Stop Procrastinating," published May 26th, 2014 on Time Magazine's Health.com, perfectionism's relationship to procrastination was addressed. "If you're so afraid of being bad (or worse, just OK) at something that you'd rather not try it at all, here's a news flash: you're a perfectionist... Carrying this to extreme you may also believe that you are only lovable and worthwhile if your performance at everything is nothing less than outstanding." Perfectionism is one of the most common characteristics of procrastinators who not only miss deadlines but are more likely to miss life enhancing opportunities and live in regret. Ask yourself, are you one of those?

Dear Lord, Reveal to me where my ambition to be perfect is driving a wedge between you and me. Help me to see how perfectionism sabotages my happiness, my future, and my submission to your perfect will for my life. Help me to be free from this inclination to measure myself by unrealistic standards, help me to realize that your love for me is not based on my performance. Let me be free from the fear of failure that so often accompanies perfectionism. In Jesus' name... Amen.

JUNE 13

In My Dreams

Don't fret or worry. Instead of worrying, pray. Let petitions and praises shape your worries into prayers, letting God know your concerns. Before you know it, a sense of God's wholeness, everything coming together for good, will come and settle you down. It's wonderful what happens when Christ displaces worry at the center of your life.
–Philippians 4:6—7 (MSG)

I marvel at how many times my dreams display the anxious, worrisome effects of my lifestyle. Too often in my dreams I am: running late, on a stage unprepared, looking for something that should be right there–but isn't, feeling the weight of something still undone. The worst is when I wake up from one of these dream-woven anxious scenarios and start to rummage through the list of all my unmet goals. The next thing that happens, I sink into a heart pounding fear that I may never finish the purpose for which God made me. While I am committed to changing my procrastinating ways in my waking hours, the shadow of my ill-managed past still infects my mind. Time to develop a prayer strategy to take down fret and worry. Being more active in prayer and attacking that list of unmet goals will lead to "everything coming together for good."

Dear Lord, You hold all of existence in your hands. You know every thought, action, and worry that holds me down. Let me be quick to bring every anxious thought captive and release them to you in prayer. Help me to have faith that you will allow me the privilege of fulfilling my purpose in this life before I enter eternity. Help my mind to settle down and partake of a sense of your wholeness. Let my thoughts turn more to Christ's goodness and finished work on the cross, and less on myself. Let Christ be the center of my existence. Let there be more focus on what he has done for me, instead of what I want to do for him. In Jesus' name... Amen.

JUNE 14

Every Passing Moment

Therefore, as we have opportunity, let us do good to all people, especially to those who belong to the family of believers.
–Galatians 6:10 (NIV)

Making the most of every opportunity, because the days are evil.
–Ephesians 5:16 (NIV)

So, as the Holy Spirit says:
"Today, if you hear his voice,
do not harden your hearts..."
–Hebrews 3:7-8 (NIV)

I had been planning for months to visit friends from church. They had set up a business in a newly renovated retail space, and yesterday I finally went there. Too bad when I arrived I found out that they had recently moved out! My procrastination means that I just missed out again. Guess I can only keep a plan cooking on the stove for so long before it just burns out. It made me wonder, how many opportunities have I missed? I have moved all over the place, but with two years in my present location I still haven't met up with all my old friends that live here. Two weeks ago, I thought, "I need to get in touch with Bruce." I found out yesterday, Bruce died just days ago. How much better it would have been to visit him during my two years here, than to go to his memorial service tomorrow. Alternate encounters were created because I missed it again. I met some wonderful people that still occupy the retail space, my circle will expand. I will meet some of Bruce's recent friends, maybe some that are on my "should see" list as well. Whenever we miss out on one opportunity, let's make sure that we make the most out of what is left. Each moment we have counts.

Dear Lord, Help us to be mindful of every passing moment. Let your Holy Spirit punctuate our thoughts and plans with an urgency when a person or situation is about to disappear from our lives. May we be forever grateful for all the opportunities you give us every day. May we daily bless someone, encourage, uplift, meet, and visit people that you want us to encounter. Keep our hearts soft and tender toward your instructions, so that blessings will triumph over sin. In Jesus' name... Amen.

JUNE 15

What's Ahead

The Spirit of God whets our appetite by giving us a taste of what's ahead. He puts a little heaven in our hearts so that we'll never settle for less. That's why we live with good cheer. You won't see us drooping our heads or dragging our feet! Cramped conditions here don't get us down. They only remind us of the spacious living conditions ahead. It's what we trust in but don't yet see that keeps us going. Do you suppose a few ruts in the road or rocks in the path are going to stop us?
–2 Corinthians 5:5—7 (MSG)

When a task creates spinning thoughts of failure and doubts in our ability to complete it, we often indulge in avoidance behaviors. According to information on the *erupting mind* website, "By doing something else instead of what we should be doing, avoidance behaviors allow us to momentarily escape our uncomfortable feeling, and by doing so, help bring psychological relief." There is a solid reason for indulging in these behaviors; they offer short term mental relief. But they are no solution to our problem, which is to complete what we should be doing. Looking beyond the present discomfort, we must encourage ourselves with God's Word to whet our appetite for what's ahead, no drooping heads, no dragging feet, no stopping. Simply engage in the work we need to accomplish and know the encouragement and comfort of our Heavenly Father's approval.

Dear Lord, You have prepared a marvelous heavenly kingdom that you desire for us to enjoy. Help us to not be trapped by our present condition. Guide us away from those behaviors that we use to avoid our work. Give us discernment to recognize when we are running away from our responsibilities, so that we may turn quickly in the direction we should go. May we be a people who have heaven in our hearts as our ultimate goal, so that the setbacks and bruises in this life will not hold us back from what's ahead. In Jesus' name... Amen.

JUNE 16

Learning to Aim Correctly

So our aim is to please him always in everything we do…
–2 Corinthians 5:9 (TLB)

Apollos and I are working as a team, with the same aim, though each of us will be rewarded for his own hard work.
–1 Corinthians 3:8 (TLB)

Let love be your greatest aim; nevertheless, ask also for the special abilities the Holy Spirit gives…
–1 Corinthians 14:1 (TLB)

Like many other procrastinators that are perfectionists, often my aim is too high. One of my college professors actually took a few points off one of my rather excellent term papers because I did, "too much." Being someone who expects more than I should of myself often means that I disappoint myself. Others also become a source of disappointment, by not living up to my standards. Aiming too high, especially concerning things that don't matter much in the long run, usually means anxiety and frustration are close at hand. As Christians this is not the kind of life we should be living. It is like trying to shine your light through a dense fog. It can't clearly illuminate anything, and guides no one toward the light.

Dear Lord, Help me to aim for the most important things in life, to please you in all I do, to be an example of love. Please bring people into my life that help me to keep my aim true and steady. Encourage me with the assurance of rewards for labor dedicated to you. Help me to approach my tasks and obligations responsibly, without delays, without unrealistic expectations. Help me to avoid procrastination, perfectionism, anxiety, and frustration which robs me (and those closest to me) of the peace and contentment that you want me to have and to give to others. In Jesus' name… Amen.

JUNE 17

The Time Between

Then David said to Solomon his son, "Be strong and of good courage, and do it. Fear not, be not dismayed; for the Lord God, even my God, is with you. He will not fail you or forsake you, until all the work for the service of the house of the Lord is finished."
–1 Chronicles 28:20 (RSV)

For which of you, desiring to build a tower, does not first sit down and count the cost, whether he has enough to complete it?
–Luke 14:28 (RSV)

You see that faith was active along with his works, and faith was completed by works
–James 2:22 (RSV)

The middle of a project can be a tough place. Stuck between the enthusiastic beginning and too far from the end to see the finish line. Energetic momentum has stalled, doubt in our abilities can throw mental obstacles into our creative path. As a procrastinator that has started several projects, and has finished few, I am all too familiar with this doldrums phase. If I focus backward, my track record would declare, "It will never be finished." But now my mind is set on God's Word, knowing that he who began a good work in me will be faithful to complete it! My obligation is simply one of time, put in the time, have courage, and do not be dismayed. God will not forsake us when we count the cost, pay the price and have faith that we will cross that finish line.

Dear Lord, You are the Alpha and the Omega, the beginning and the end. You are Lord of all creation and you have endowed us with a precious gift, the power of creation. May we never take for granted the time allotted to us on this earth to complete the work that you have planted in our hearts. May there be a powerful unity between our hearts' desires and your will for our lives. Grant our growing faith and labor to be rewarded by the joy of a finished work that will bring honor and glory to your name and expand your kingdom on earth. In Jesus' name... Amen.

JUNE 18

Changing Me

Sitting in that dark, dark country of death, they watch the sun come up. The Isaiah-prophesied sermon came to life in Galilee the moment Jesus started preaching. He picked up where John left off: "Change your life. God's kingdom is here."
–Matthew 4:15—17 (MSG)

Jesus heard about it and spoke up, "Who needs a doctor: the healthy or the sick? I'm here inviting outsiders, not insiders–an invitation to a changed life, changed inside and out."
–Luke 5:31—32 (MSG)

I really don't like change. It disrupts my comfort level. Afterall, there are bad changes as well as good. When I move into a new place, the first position my furniture takes, that is where everything stays until it's time to move somewhere else. I wish for change within myself, however, but wishing doesn't really work. As believers in Christ, we should be able to embrace change. I know that my inclination to procrastinate needs to change. God wants me to change, and He will help me. My part is faith in action. It is that powerful combination of faith in the desired result, plus the work required to make it happen that produces successful change. Positive change can be ours! No better time to start than today.

Dear Lord, You have brought all things into existence and are worthy of all praise. I have every reason to have faith that you will help me change my life for the better. May faith rise within me. May I have a clear vision of myself changed. Let the work begin now. In Jesus' name... Amen.

JUNE 19

You Don't Have To

But now that you've found you don't have to listen to sin tell you what to do, and have discovered the delight of listening to God telling you, what a surprise! A whole, healed, put together life right now, with more and more life on the way! Work hard for sin your whole life and your pension is death. But God's gift is real life, eternal life, delivered by Jesus, our Master.
–Romans 6:22—23 (MSG)

There will always be a reason to procrastinate. We need to have the Word of God infused in our mind to shoot down excuses that are robbing us of our best life. Often those excuses just mask a sin of disobedience to God...

Time to put all excuses to death!

"I've always been this way." .... Well, you don't have to be, you can be a new creation.

"I don't think that I can ever change." ... Maybe you can't on your own, but with God's help, you can.

"I get distracted too easily." ... O.K. time to sharpen your focus on what matters most and be consciously aware of when you are drifting away from your main goal.

"I hate feeling like I have no choice in what to do, why do something right now, when I can do it later?" ... Stop lying to yourself because when later comes, you won't do it then either.

"I just want to have some fun with my friends!" ...Your friends are not responsible for spending time in ways that will determine your future, you are.

Dear Lord, You are a good shepherd and a gentle master. You lead and guide us to good and proper places where our desires can be quenched by life-giving water. Help us to be quick to recognize your voice and respond in obedience. Let us be quick to recognize the lies that we tell ourselves. When fear or self-indulgence calls us to a place that we shouldn't go, help us to see that for what it is, a lure away from you. May the realization that we don't need to heed the call of sin, beckon us to alter the course of our lives in your direction. In Jesus' name... Amen.

JUNE 20

Thanksgiving, Praise, and Victory

I give you thanks, O Lord, with all my heart; I will sing your praises before the gods.
I bow before your holy Temple as I worship.
I praise your name for your unfailing love and faithfulness;
for your promises are backed by all the honor of your name.
As soon as I pray; you answer me; you encourage me by giving me strength
–Psalm 138:1—3 (NLT)

Reading these words from Psalm 138 today generated great hope for victory. God has the antidote. Like any habit that robs us of life's best, procrastination provides sustenance for an attitude of defeat. When our heart is filled with thankfulness for all that God has done for us, there is no room for feelings of impending defeat, only victory. As we sing praise or speak praise to God in the midst of our emotional and spiritual enemies, we lay the groundwork for victory. When we bow down in submission to God with an attitude of, *Not my will, but thine be done,* doors open to greener pastures. Recognizing His love and faithfulness strengthens us deep within our souls. God doesn't make promises he doesn't keep; He is honorable. Thanksgiving, prayer, praise, and worship forge our connection with our Creator. That connection builds encouragement and leads to joy and strength. Praise God for He is worthy; He strengthens us.

Dear Lord, I will humbly submit to your plans for my life. May expressions of thankfulness far outweigh any words of discouragement on my lips. May I never cease to praise you in every circumstance. Remind me continually of your great love and faithfulness, not just for others, but for me! Help me to hold on to your promises, in faith and expectation. Let me seek your presence daily, not just to ask favors from you, but merely to partake of your presence. Fill me with supernatural strength and joy. My need for you is endless. Give me a vision of victory so I can press toward what I see, knowing you have made a way for me to receive it. In Jesus' name... Amen.

JUNE 21

What Tomorrow Brings

"In a word, what I'm saying is, Grow up. You're kingdom subjects. Now live like it. Live out your God-created identity. Live generously and graciously toward others, the way God lives toward you.
–Matthew 5:48 (MSG)

Give your entire attention to what God is doing right now, and don't get worked up about what may or may not happen tomorrow. God will help you deal with whatever hard things come up when the time comes.
–Matthew 6:34 (MSG)

We should not get *worked up* about tomorrow, but many of us want to change our lives and be different in the future. If we truly want to change for the better tomorrow, we must live differently today. The inclination to always put off until tomorrow what should have been done by now, creates a wishful attitude instead of an action plan we work at to transform our life. There is no fairy godmother at our beck and call to create an altered reality for us. There is a loving God who has given us his Word, salvation through his son, and wisdom, counsel, and comfort available through the Holy Spirit. We don't need our wishes granted. We need to get to work and live out God's plan. Then, step by step starting today, we will create a much better tomorrow, instead of worrying about what tomorrow will bring.

Dear Lord, Thank you for your Word and for the work of your Holy Spirit. Help us to overcome all our fears and not worry about tomorrow. Show us what to do this day, so that we may face tomorrow in peace. Draw us to your Word and your presence. Help us to submit to the wisdom and discernment of your Holy Spirit. Convict us of wasting time if we are lingering in leisure pursuits when there is work to be done now. Let a sense of satisfaction grow within us as we meet our obligations in a timely manner. Allow us a taste of your divine approval, as we anticipate the day when we hear you say, "Well done, good and faithful servant." In Jesus' name... Amen.

JUNE 22

When?

My eyes fail, looking for your promise; I say, "When will you comfort me?"
–Psalm 119:82 (NIV)

When you hear them sound a long blast on the trumpets, have the whole army give a loud shout; then the wall of the city will collapse and the army will go up, everyone straight in.
–Joshua 6:5 (NIV)

You need to persevere so that when you have done the will of God, you will receive what he promised.
–Hebrews 10:36 (NIV)

Employees do not receive a paycheck until after they have done the work assigned to them. An entire generation coming out of slavery from Egypt did not enter into the land promised to them from God. Jericho's walls fell, not just because God promised his people that victory was assured, but because those people did what God told them to do. Too often I am like the psalmist, with my eyes not seeing clearly, saying "When, Lord?... When will you do what I long to see you do?" We can be all about, "When?" like we deserve a big reward from God without having earned it. I can sit here, eating my tiramisu cheesecake, saying "God, when will you help me lose weight?" It is time to see clearly that most of God's promises are actually conditional. *IF* we do what he says, *IF* we do what we are supposed to, only then will we receive what God has promised. Obedience, and faith that God is true to his word, produces a reality where we can enter into God's promise, and we no longer have to ask the question, "When?" Then, we can trust as we wait, knowing God will do what was promised.

Dear Lord, Help me to see clearly my own part in making your promises come true. Having faith without obedience does not produce the results that I seek. I confess that I mistakenly feel like I keep waiting on you to move on my behalf, when you are the one who waits on me! You long to give me all that you have promised. Holy Spirit light the path of obedience, and prompt me away from self-defeating acts. Help me to realize the power in my own hands to change my ways and create the future that I strongly desire. In Jesus' name... Amen.

JUNE 23

Let Me See

And the Lord said to them, "Even with a prophet, I would communicate by visions and dreams;"
–Numbers 12:6 (TLB)

After I have poured out my rains again, I will pour out my Spirit upon all of you! Your sons and daughters will prophesy; your old men will dream dreams, and your young men see visions.
–Joel 2:28 (TLB)

Long ago God spoke in many different ways to our fathers through the prophets, in visions, dreams, and even face to face, telling them little by little about his plans.
–Hebrews 1:1 (TLB)

There are so many different kinds of vision. While growing up I was probably the queen of daydreaming. Who wants to learn about fractions when you can just let your mind soar to an imaginary landscape? There, I was a great actress with tons of money to spend on doing good deeds, solving huge problems, and had a mega-celebrity style home by the ocean! The worst thing about having a fantastic visual imagination is that when life is too dreary and mundane you are tempted to escape into fantasy. How much better it is to have a clear vision. To be a marathon runner that sees the finish line, or an aspiring student that sees that diploma in their hand. Vision gives direction, purpose, and a picture of what our accomplishment will look like. Daydreams are a procrastinator's pacifier, empty, temporary satisfaction, with no substance. What we need is vision.

Dear Lord, Give me a vision of where you see me going. Create within me a picture of my goals accomplished. Let me see what my finish line looks like so that I can pursue it diligently, no holding back, no substitute empty daydreams. Build within me the means, the fervent hope, desire, and the discipline, to push me to that place of completion. In Jesus' name... Amen.

JUNE 24

Blessings of Being Uncomfortable

But in everything commending ourselves as servants of God, in much endurance, in afflictions, in hardships, in distresses...
–2 Corinthians 6:4 (NASB)

For bodily discipline is only of little profit, but godliness is profitable for all things, since it holds promise for the present life and also for the life to come.
–1 Timothy 4:8 (NASB)

Therefore, since we have so great a cloud of witnesses surrounding us, let us also lay aside every encumbrance and sin which so easily entangles us, and let us run with endurance the race that is set before us...
–Hebrews 12:1 (NASB)

There is a young woman from my hometown of Belmont, Massachusetts named Becca Pizzi; she did something truly amazing. As a single mom, working two jobs, she raised $36,000 in order to participate in an event called the World Marathon Challenge. She became the first American female to complete seven marathons, in seven days, on all seven continents! Amazing, right? Most of us have difficulty just making it to the gym a couple times a week or sticking with any healthy regimen for more than a month. During an interview she stated something that I think every procrastinator needs to embrace if we really want to change. When questioned about the mental challenges in accomplishing such a difficult goal she stated, "You have to become comfortable with being uncomfortable." So true! Unless we adjust and accept discomfort as a byproduct of positive transformation, we will never be able to change for the better. Thank you, Becca, for your words of wisdom.

Dear Lord, I must confess that I cling to my comforts and "feel good" moments too tightly. My deepest desire is to accomplish my personal aspirations, and the purposes for which you created me. Help me to embrace discipline, discomfort, commitment, and persistence as I keep the finish line in view. I know that there is an amazing blessing waiting for me when I cross that line. Help me to do today what needs to be done, to bring me into that blessing. Help me to never put off until tomorrow what I need to do today. In Jesus' name... Amen.

JUNE 25

Disgrace or Grace

You have made us a reproach to our neighbors, the scorn and derision of those around us. You have made us a byword among the nations; the people shake their heads at us. I live in disgrace all day long, and my face is covered with shame...
–Psalm 44:13—15 (NIV)

Praise be to the God and Father of our Lord Jesus Christ, who has blessed us in the heavenly realms with every spiritual blessing in Christ. For he chose us in him before the creation of the world to be holy and blameless in his sight. In love he predestined us for adoption to sonship through Jesus Christ, in accordance with his pleasure and will–to the praise of his glorious grace, which he has freely given us in the One he loves. In him we have redemption through his blood, the forgiveness of sins, in accordance with the riches of God's grace that he lavished on us.
–Ephesians 1:3—8 (NIV)

Who would choose to live in disgrace and shame if they could be transformed by God's lavish love and grace? Unfortunately, too many people do. After working with abused children who are driven to self-harm, suicide, and violence, I realized that some people honestly cannot grasp the idea that they deserve that kind of unconditional love. When life has cruelly dumped on you, you have the tendency to believe that you must have deserved it, otherwise why did it happen to you in the first place? Other people are haunted by things that they have done. They caused a destructive fallout in their family, or their loved ones have paid a heavy price because their wrong behaviors. Then, they pay that price again with heavy guilt and remorse. The Good News is it is your choice! Today you can choose the magnificent, loving grace of God that covers all guilt and shame. Today you can become blameless in his sight through Jesus' perfect love! Ask and you will receive.

Dear Lord, May my heart be forever grateful for the wonderful gifts of salvation, forgiveness, mercy, and grace which you offer me. Help me to realize that through faith in Jesus you have made me your blessed child. Open my eyes to all that I deserve as a child of God. Help me to ignore the taunts of my enemies, the negative voices in my head, the pain and shame of the past. Let your grace be my constant comfort as I walk forward in a blessed life, overcoming all insecurity and fear. In Jesus' name... Amen.

JUNE 26

Alive, Awake, and in Shape

God knew what he was doing from the beginning. He decided from the outset to shape the lives of those who love him along the same lines as the life of his Son. The Son stands first in line of humanity he restored. We see the original and intended shape of our lives there in him. After God made that decision of what his children should be like, he followed it up by calling people by name. After he called them by name, he set them on a solid basis with himself. And then, after getting them established, he stayed with them to the end, gloriously completing what he has begun. So, what do you think? With God on our side like this, how can we lose?
–Romans 8:29-31 (MSG)

What do you need to do to remind yourself that you are not dead yet, that your life is not over? You still have time if you are alive, to shape yourself beyond your self-defeating habits and be transformed into a productive, fruitful child of God. For me that reminder comes from blasting some thrashing hard industrial music like Mortal's- *Alive and Awake*, or in P.O.D.'s car crashing, death defying video- *Alive,* or Pearl Jam's emotionally intense- *Alive.* They all work for me. And, I am always encouraged, my spirit always lifted up by Hillsong Y&F, and I love their *Alive* as well. These hard rocking sounds may not be for everyone, but if loud & hard music is in your DNA... Go for it! You can find all these on YouTube-

P.O.D.- *Alive* **Pearl Jam-** *Alive*
Mortal- *Alive & Awake* **Hillsong Y&F-** *Alive*

Whatever it takes to wake up, to work on developing into our fully alive and creative selves, time to do it.
Find your own sound, your music that does it for you!

Dear Lord, Let us walk in a newness of life every day. Let us rid ourselves of comatose sleep and be fully awake. Let every breath we take infuse us with your supernatural life. Let us be aware of the power of the Living God within us, making us truly Alive! Shape me into the image of your son, that others may see Jesus in me. Thank you for the gift of our present and eternal life. May we always recognize to the depth of our being, that you are on our side, therefore we cannot lose. In Jesus' name... Amen.

JUNE 27

Cast Away

Cast all your anxiety on him because he cares for you.
–1 Peter 5:7 (NIV)

Let us not become weary in doing good, for at the proper time we will reap a harvest if we do not give up.
–Galatians 6:9 (NIV)

Now to him who is able to do immeasurably more than all we ask or imagine, according to his power that is at work within us, to him be the glory in the church and in Christ Jesus throughout all generations, forever and ever! Amen.
–Ephesians 3:20—21 (NIV)

One thing that has stopped me dead in my tracks is discouragement. It has come my way far too often, in too many forms. A disappointment is one thing, a momentary setback with a short-lived sadness; that's ok. However, when it evolves into a lengthy, direction shifting move into self-pity, a desire to quit, and loss of faith, it definitely needs to stop! It is hard to crawl out of that dark place. When one cannot defeat discouragement, as is often the case with procrastinators, depression is lurking right around the corner. Once I was so crushed when a meeting with an editor that was to lead to a book contract, suddenly evaporated. I was so sure that this was my time for that door to swing wide open, then it slammed shut in my face! It hit me as if all my hopes and dreams had suddenly been flushed away. The pain of that was so overwhelming, it took years to bounce back from that massive discouragement. I now refuse to let past disappointments or rejections, or the fear of them, determine my present course.

Dear Lord, It seems as if discouragement and disappointment are always hovering by my door, waiting to destroy my plans and my future. Help me to accept inevitable setbacks with grace, and to have faith that you have something better for me down the road. Teach me how to castaway my cares, and to rid myself of anxiety, handing it all over to you. Help me to never despair of my circumstances. Help me to always look forward to a good harvest, to not grow weary in doing good, and to never give up! Let me always seek your presence, embrace your great love for me, and feed my faith by your words. Jesus' name... Amen.

JUNE 28

Get Where You Are Going

Get going. Cross this Jordan River ... I'm giving you every square inch of land you set your foot on– just as I promised Moses ... All your life, no one will be able to hold out against you. In the same way I was with Moses, I'll be with you. I won't give up on you; I won't leave you. Strength! Courage!... Give it everything you have, heart and soul ... Don't get off track, either left or right, so as to make sure you get to where you're going. And don't for a minute let this Book of The Revelation be out of mind. Ponder and meditate on it day and night, making sure you practice everything written in it. Then you'll get where you're going; then you'll succeed... Strength! Courage! Don't be timid; don't get discouraged. GOD, your God, is with you every step you take.
–Joshua 1:1–9 (MSG)

When I hear people talk about the promises of God, it makes me wonder, *What promises are they talking about?* Is it wisdom to take a specific promise that God made to an individual, under very specific circumstances, and claim it as your own? That doesn't sound wise to me. In the case of Joshua, after the death of Moses, it seems that there is a very broad application to "the people of God" here, not only for Joshua himself. We may not be recipients of a miraculous parting of the sea, led into numerous bloody battles to claim a specific geographic territory, but all of God's people battle something. We all have areas to conquer. If we take Joshua's promises here as our own, we follow God's command to be bold and courageous, then we realize his presence is with us and know he will never give up on us. As we infuse our souls and minds with his words, we are promised victory. Truly, we can get to where we are going, praise God!

Dear Lord, Help us as "your people," to grab hold of those promises that you made to Joshua as he faced his biggest challenge. May we become the leaders in our own victories. Let us give everything over to you, experiencing new levels of trust, obedience, and faith. May our lives be evidence of the truth of your promises, as it was for Joshua, also for us! In Jesus' name... Amen.

JUNE 29

My Hand

Lord, remind me of how brief my time on earth will be.
Remind me that my days are numbered–
how fleeting my life is.
You have made my life no longer than the width of my hand.
My entire lifetime is just a moment to you;
at best, each of us is just a breath.
–Psalm 139:4—5 (NLT)

The Lord directs the steps of the godly.
He delights in every detail of their lives.
Though they stumble, they will never fall,
for the Lord holds them by the hand.
–Psalm 37:23—24 (NLT)

Our hands are one thing that sets us apart from all the other animals. They can be so loving, so hateful, so skilled, or useless. One of the first ways that we count is by using our hands and fingers. When asked, "How old are you?" eagerly a child holds up the proper number of fingers. We measure our time on earth by our hands at an early age. It may be scary to feel that our lives are as small as the width of our hands. Thankfully it is also reassuring to know that our protective, loving Heavenly Father holds us by the hand. His guidance brings us to a place where we will not waste the time given to us. The more we submit to him, the less we wander away, because he directs our steps and holds our hand, bringing us to where we belong.

Dear Lord, Teach us to be aware of the preciousness of time. Give us discernment to realize when we are putting something off that needs to be done now. Help us to realize that we risk what you have called us to do by hours of delay, turning into weeks, months, years, or even decades of wasted time. Keep us from gathering dust on our dreams. Let us walk, hand in hand with you, sensing your delight in us, directing our paths to follow you, and treasuring the time we have on earth. In Jesus' name... Amen.

JUNE 30

Out of the Rut

Don't copy the behavior and the customs of this world, but be a new and different person with a fresh newness in all you do and think. Then you will learn from your own experience how his ways will really satisfy you.
–Romans 12:2 (TLB)

Behold, I will do a new thing, Now it shall spring forth; Shall you not know it? I will even make a road in the wilderness and rivers in the desert.
–Isaiah 43:19 (TLB)

Any self-defeating habit follows a particular pattern. Every time we engage in a behavior that alters our life in a negative way, we are one step closer to establishing an almost inescapable rut. The more time spent, and the more frequently we engage in that behavior, the deeper the rut. Eventually that rut becomes a pit, too steep to escape from and too ingrained to alter. There are two ways out that will most likely yield success. One- Dig an alternate path a bit at a time, little by little, different behavior and direction will bring you to a more desirable destination. Two- Look for that onrushing stream, so immediate and powerful that it overflows into your pit, raising you up, creating a brand-new riverbed for you to dive into its sweeping flow. That river will carry you along to a brand-new place, a different and satisfying location. While we may want the second option to prevail, if we simply wait for it to happen, our pit gets deeper and deeper. Option One is always our best option because Option Two is out of our control. But, thank God it may happen to us at any time while we are busy digging a little bit at a time!

Dear Lord, Help me to be willing to do the work, bit by bit, to overcome the self-defeating behaviors in my life. Many of these patterns took years to establish, let me not avoid the labor needed to change. Let me sharpen my ears and my eyes, to see the work that you have done in an effort to set me free. Make me sensitive to all that you are doing on my behalf, keep me vigilant and always looking for your means to rescue me. Help me to look out for that river in the desert, that flow of your Holy Spirit which has the power to change me from the inside out, and bring me to that place in life, where you want me to be. In Jesus' name... Amen.

JULY 1

I'm Not Going to Lose It Today

When I came to the spring today, I said, 'Lord, God of my master Abraham, if you will, please grant me success to the journey on which I have come'...
–Genesis 24:42 (NIV)

But encourage one another daily, as long as it is called "Today," so that none of you may be hardened by sin's deceitfulness.
–Hebrews 3:13 (NIV)

Losing things is almost a perverted hobby of mine. There is the amount of "lost" time looking, anxious fretting, self-condemnation for those loud "Not Again!" moments. There is a negative energy fallout that explodes beyond my personal space, quite detrimental to those around me. Can all that emotional excrement ever be redeemed? Probably not. Is changing behavior possible in the future? Absolutely. Something as precious as time needs to be treasured, not lost. I wrote the first chapter of a book in 2002. Where are the other chapters? Still in my head. Where have those years gone? They have melted into the past and are gone forever. As a typical procrastinator I kept thinking, "Well, if I don't get to that today, I can always do it tomorrow." However, ... after over five thousand tomorrows, still no chapter two! Today is the time, to find the time, for what should be done today.

Dear Lord, I am tired of the deceitfulness of procrastination and the lies of what "could be" tomorrow. Help me to hear your voice clearly today. Direct my time, energy, and attention to what needs to be done this day. Grant me success for today's journey and use me this day to encourage others. Energize my faith to empower me to change my ways. Give me hope to find and redeem what has been lost in my life. Let me be diligent in the present. In Jesus' name... Amen.

JULY 2

Thank You, Bob

With God's help, I finally had victory over my procrastination! My book, the *Procrastinators Daily Devotional* now has 366 pages, and is complete. While drifting in and out of my dedication to writing, this entry originally appeared in 2014, and it is certainly worth sharing now.

Then I thought, 'I will die in my own home, my days as numerous as the grains of sand.
***Job 29:1* (NET)**

As I lay on the coach, contemplating the value of watching even more mind-numbing television, a thought came visually to me. Time. There it was in the hourglass, each moment a grain of sand, passing from past to present, present to future, one tiny bit at a time. What will I do with it, this bit of time, now mine? I see on television an ungodly world spreading its dominion over modern culture. What was once good is now bad, what was once sinful now celebrated as freedom, and atheism now advances with celebrity endorsements. It makes me wonder, how far can this pendulum swing? Is there any way to turn this tide around? Is there anything I can do? If people that actively assault the very idea of God's existence can dedicate their time to ridiculing my God and people of faith, can't I do my literary bit to alter the ungodly balance? God, I would love a sign, after all you are good, and you do give signs. Can I really do something that can change someone's eternity, right now?

With my multitude of self-indulgent choices looming over my depressed psyche, there it was... the hourglass image, the steady gravity of time passing away, what to do? I thought... my blog, my Procrastinators Daily Devotional, my neglected, practically nonexistent blog, now ignored for months, could my writing make any difference at all? If I cannot expand the Kingdom of God, if my writing makes no positive impact in someone's life, if I can't initiate and produce soul saving TRUTH, then... why bother blogging anything? If I sleep, eat, mess around, watch soul-sucking television, produce nothing, what's the difference? I must know that what I do can make a difference, otherwise why get out of bed?

It was at that moment, tonight, after drenching myself in televised media for multiple hours, that I decided, *Time to get off the couch, time to return to my writing.* Sensing the possible importance of actually making a difference in someone's world, I sat down to dredge up my long-ignored blog. A spark of hope in making the right choice with this particular tic of time lighted within me. As I touched my keyboard, music that had been silently humming on my computer for hours burst forth with pleasant volume, Bob Dylan's "Every Grain of Sand," from his *Shot of Love* album. What? God, you bless me with confirmation and victory. Little victories by one second, one little decision at a time. What are the chances, in the so-called disordered, random, atheistic universe, that as the image of the hourglass's flowing sand moved me to finally write at my computer, that I would be heralded into my creative space with that song? I'd say chances are... a million to one, at least. Thank God for the manna breadcrumb trail that He leaves for us to discover and follow.

"Don't have the inclination to look back on any mistake
Like Cain, I now behold this chain of events that I must break
In the fury of the moment I can see the Master's hand
In every leaf that trembles, in every grain of sand."
-Bob Dylan

Dear Lord, Please help me to not look back on my mistakes, for they are a weight that I should not carry. Please break this chain of events that pulls me away from my productivity. Help me to see my Master's hands, and to be my Master's hands in this world. You are in every grain of sand, teach me to number my days, hours and minutes, and every grain of time that passes through my hands. May it all be for your glory, used to expand your Kingdom. In Jesus' name... Amen.

JULY 3

I Want to be Wonder Woman

Finally, be strong in the Lord and in his mighty power... For our struggle is not against flesh and blood, but against the rulers, against the authorities, against the powers of this dark world and against the spiritual forces of evil in heavenly realms. Therefore put on the full armor of God... Stand firm then, with the belt of truth buckled around your waist, with the breastplate of righteousness in place, and your feet fitted with the readiness that comes with the gospel of peace... Take up the shield of faith, with which you can extinguish all the flaming arrows of the evil one. Take the helmet of salvation and the sword of the Spirit, which is the word of God.
–Ephesians 6:10—17 (NIV)

I want to be Wonder Woman, not because she is *drop dead gorgeous,* but because of her strength, values, and mostly her amazing fearlessness. Her stepping out of the trenches to fend her way across "No Man's Land," was one of the most impressive, emotionally uplifting scenes from a movie that I have ever seen. Her goals: to fight for those who cannot fight for themselves, to not stand by while innocent lives are lost, to see her mission as a sacred duty to save the world. These are priorities every Christian should embrace to some degree. We all have a mission, the consequences at stake are eternal life or death, and we must be willing to charge through an entire barrage of flaming attacks with courage, never once losing sight of our mission. Yes, I definitely want to be like Wonder Woman!

Dear Lord, Help me to always be prepared to meet life's opposition to my goals with courage and persistence. Remind me to put on my armor every day: truth, righteousness, the gospel of peace, salvation, the words of God, and of paramount importance- the shield of faith. Let me realize deep within my soul and mind that no weapon formed against me will prosper when I seek to advance your kingdom with my life. In Jesus' name... Amen.

JULY 4

The Value of Dependence

Just as a body, though one, has many parts, but all its parts form one body, so it is with Christ... If the whole body were an eye, where would the sense of hearing be? If the whole body were an ear, where would the sense of smell be? But in fact God has placed the parts in the body, every one of them, just as he wanted them to be. If they were all one part, where would the body be? As it is, there are many parts, but one body. The eye cannot say to the hand, "I don't need you!" And the head cannot say to the feet, "I don't need you!"
–1 Corinthians 12:12—21 (NIV)

This may seem an odd topic on a day when those of us in the USA celebrate Independence Day. I am very glad that our founding fathers decided to break away from England, and to no longer be ruled by a king across the ocean. By embarking on this course, they set in motion an experimental form of government that evolved into a blueprint for modern democracies all over the world. The downside of the American character, in my opinion, is how exalted the idea of being independent has become. We over-value the "I Did It My Way" bravado, claim we have the right to do whatever we want, reject submission to authority, and applaud the self-made man or woman. Not a very Christian attitude. In the Body of Christ, there is interdependence, one part relying on another, serving is more highly esteemed than recognition, humility is greater than pride. Being dependent on God or others is something for which we should be truly grateful. United together, we can more easily advance to victory, in our personal battles and in our common struggles against the enemy of our souls. In *dependence* on one another, esteeming what is best for all, not just me, our world becomes a better place.

Dear Lord, I thank you for the way in which you have designed your church. Help us to settle into our position within your Body, so that our lives will produce the greatest result in building your kingdom. In whatever we do, let us not hesitate to help our brothers and sisters in Christ do their best. Help us to not be so concentrated on our own agenda that we do not recognize the needs of others. Help humility to grow within us. May we not let pride keep us from seeking the help we need. In Jesus' name... Amen.

JULY 5

Beware the Inner Child

It's like this: when I was a child I spoke and thought and reasoned as a child does. But when I became a man my thoughts grew far beyond those of my childhood, and now I have put away the childish things.
–1 Corinthians 13:11 (TLB)

Then we will no longer be like children, forever changing our minds about what we believe because someone has told us something different or has cleverly lied to us and made a lie sound like the truth.
–Ephesians 4:14 (TLB)

When it is time for young children to do something they should, often their response is, "I don't wanna do that!" Brushing teeth or sitting down for dinner is much less desirable than playing with *Legos* or watching *Frozen* for the umpteenth time. Frequently children dig in their heels, stubbornly refuse, possibly throw a defiant tantrum. For some procrastinators, this "I don't wanna" attitude is the root of the problem. According to Mike Bundrant, retired psychotherapist and life coach, from his website AHA System, "Refusing to do what you don't feel like doing is a maturity issue. All worthwhile accomplishments involve doing a lot of 'no fun' stuff... Children have a very hard time doing what they don't feel like doing. If you still do, then part of you hasn't grown up yet." In order to overcome procrastination sometimes our inner child just needs to grow up! Time to break the rule of the inner child as tyrant over our adult life, starting today.

Dear Lord, Reveal to me the root of my procrastination. Whatever it is; it needs to be removed. Make me aware of how I am handling my "must do's." If there is a childlike refusal to do what is good for me, if there is an immaturity that hinders me from growing up and taking hold of my adult responsibilities, give me the insight and willingness to overcome my childlike urges. Help me to put away childlike thinking. Keep my mind steady and unwavering toward my life's goals. Help me to not be distracted by the desire for times of play, when I need to be working. In Jesus' name... Amen.

JULY 6

Enough Power

Thy steadfast love, O Lord, extends to the heavens, thy faithfulness to the clouds.
–Psalm 36:5 (RSV)

And without faith it is impossible to please him. For whoever would draw near to God must believe that he exists and that he rewards those who seek him.
–Hebrews 11:6 (RSV)

Be watchful, stand firm in your faith, be courageous, be strong.
–1 Corinthians 16:13 (RSV)

Faith is such a mysterious powerful force. It is a conduit to God Almighty. It is the substance of the faithfulness of our Lord toward us, and our anchor to him. It is the path to a better reality for us and for future generations. We know that faith is the substance of things hoped for, and the evidence of things unseen. I am overwhelmed by the many attributes and the power that faith possesses, but unfortunately it seems hard to access at times. Thank God for His Word. It is by His Word that our faith grows, defends and conquers!

Dear Lord, I don't want to be one of those "with little faith." It is my heart's desire to please you in all things, and faith is the key to pleasing you. Lead me to times of absorbing your words into my heart, soul, and mind. May I do all that I can to build my own faith. Help me to be strong and courageous in my faith. Let me be victorious in arenas where my faith is tested, so that I will have testimonies to encourage others in their faith. Through faith, I declare victory over my procrastinating ways. In Jesus' name... Amen.

JULY 7

A Very Good Vine

[Jesus said] I am the true vine, and My Father is the vinedresser. Every branch in Me that does not bear fruit He takes away; and every branch that bears fruit He prunes, that it may bear more fruit... Abide in me, and I in you. As the branch cannot bear fruit of itself, unless it abides in the vine, neither can you, unless you abide in Me. I am the vine, you are the branches. He who abides in Me, and I in him, bears much fruit; for without Me you can do nothing.
–John 15:1—5 (NKJV)

How do we decide, *What is the most important thing for me to do today?* Do we check our calendar, email, Facebook, Instagram, or work schedule? Nothing, absolutely nothing is more important than taking time to be intimate with God. In some old school King James vernacular, we just need to "abide in the vine" if we want to increase our productivity. We cannot let the world, our distracted minds, our feelings of guilt about carving out that time, refrain us from our primary purpose. Time to be in God's presence, absorbing His Word, immersing in the Holy Spirit, and being pruned, makes us fit for fruitful service. That is our fundamental purpose; all else springs from that.

Dear Lord, Let my desire to be close to you supersede all other desires. Tune my ears to hear you calling me, drawing me away from the things of the world to a place where we can be one. As I daily check my priorities, let nothing come before you. Guide me to carve out our time from the hours and minutes allotted to me this day for precious life-giving time with you. Let these times of us abiding together increase in frequency, deepen in fellowship, and produce fruitfulness. In Jesus' name... Amen.

JULY 8

Living Beyond the Shadows

Read up on what happened before you were born; dig into the past, understand your roots. Ask your parents what it was like before you were born; ask the old-ones, they'll tell you a thing or two.
–Deuteronomy 32:6—7 (MSG)

I will always show you where to go. I'll give you a full life in the emptiest of places– firm muscles, strong bones. You'll be like a well-watered garden, a gurgling spring that never runs dry. You'll use the old rubble of past lives to build anew, rebuild the foundations from out of your past.
–Isaiah 58:9—12 (MSG)

[Excerpts from the vision of the new heaven & new earth]
All the earlier troubles, chaos, and pain are things of the past, to be forgotten. Look ahead with joy. Anticipate what I am creating... my chosen ones will have satisfaction in their work. They won't work and have nothing come of it.
–Isaiah 65:17—22 (MSG)

Our past is such a paradox. We are always being advised to learn from it on one hand and let go of it on the other. We desire the latest innovation, but God forbid we ignore the wisdom of those elders who have lived full lives and learned life's most important lessons. After watching *The First Grader,* a profound movie based on the life of an old man from Kenya who was brutalized in a British prison camp, the strength of past events to influence the present was very evident. He is in his eighties and just wants to learn to read, but there are many social and political forces coming against him. At one point his protective teacher says to her boss, "Can't we just let go of the past?" Her boss emphatically says to her, "The past is always with us!' Like it or not, it is so true. But, the past is a shadow. Thank God, past failures, disappointments, or injustices do not have to determine our future.

Dear Lord, Help me to look forward to the glorious future that you have designed for me. Keep me from looking too long at the shadow of past injuries or failures. Keep me facing your light to keep those shadows behind me. You are a creative God; I pray for your creative energy to work through me. Bring me to a place of satisfaction in my work, create a firm foundation out of my past rubble and the solid rock of wisdom that has been passed down from generation to generation. In Jesus' name... Amen.

JULY 9

Able to Choose

I pray that your love will keep on growing more and more, together with true knowledge and perfect judgement, so that you will be able to choose what is best. Then you will be free from all impurity and blame on the Day of Christ. Your lives will be filled with the truly good qualities which only Jesus Christ can produce, for the glory and praise of God.
–Philippians 1:9—11 (GNT)

How does growing in love more and more, mix together with true knowledge and perfect judgement? I'm not quite sure, but apparently it is God's formula for us to be able to choose what is best. Possibly loving God more, or loving my neighbor, and maybe those I don't even know yet more and more, creates an unselfish environment within our mind. While we humans are often all about what feels good and pleases us, as followers of Christ, our lives need to be about what pleases Him. Many of our foolish mistakes and self-defeating behaviors come from a lack of wisdom. Do you ever hear yourself say, "If I had only known _______, I would have done something different?" If we have more love, true knowledge, and perfect judgement, we will choose what is best. Living like that, we would no longer avoid doing the most important things in our lives. Maybe letting love rule prepares our soul to lean into wisdom. That sounds very good to me.

Dear Lord, In the multitude of decisions that I make today, let love and wisdom guide every one of them. Fill me with all those good qualities which only you can produce in me. Help my mind to be free of selfish thoughts, and hedonistic schemes. Help me to be free from blaming myself for all the missed opportunities in my past. Guide me to choose what is best, so there will be no blame, or shame to carry into the future. Let a desire to love generously and judge every situation rightly, create a life in me that brings you praise and glory. In Jesus' name... Amen.

JULY 10

While You Are Young

Honor and enjoy your Creator while you're still young,
Before the years take their toll and your vigor wanes,
Before your vision dims and the world blurs
And the winter years keep you close to the fire...
The words of the wise prod us to live well.
They're like nails hammered home, holding life together.
They are given by God, the one Shepherd.
–Ecclesiastes 12:1—2, 11 (MSG)

Enjoying the Creator is something that can keep faith fueled and instill a desire to praise God. When one enjoys God, there is an abundant life that fills a believer with energy. Young people have such an enviable abundance of energy. Because this vigor comes naturally they often don't realize what an advantage it is for their life. It may take growing older to actually appreciate the value of possessing youthful energy. In the movie "It's a Wonderful Life," an old man sees George Bailey wasting a romantic opportunity and bemoans the situation by proclaiming, "Ohhh, youth is wasted on the wrong people!" If you are young, what a wonderful gift you possess. If you are a procrastinator now, don't let your years slip into your old age without accomplishing what you can do right now. You will never have more energy than you have now, and if you wait too long you may never take the time to use it later.

Dear Lord, Let none of us take our life, our youth, or our energy for granted. The inevitability of growing old and being "unable" is everyone's fate if they live long enough. Help us to value all the gifts, assets, and skills that we have to build productive lives right now. May we be full of honoring and enjoying you. In Jesus' name... Amen.

JULY 11

Gold and Silver

If anyone builds on this foundation using gold, silver, costly stones, wood, hay or straw, their work will be shown for what it is, because the Day will bring it to light. It will be revealed with fire, and the fire will test the quality of each person's work. If what has been built survives, the builder will receive a reward. If it is burned up, the builder will suffer loss but yet will be saved–even though only as one escaping through the flames.
–1 Corinthians 3:12—15 (NIV)

Recently my kitchen has been invaded by tiny little ants, and the wooden bench on my deck is infested with bees. As I struggle over decisions of how to prioritize my day, there they are, God's creatures instinctively doing exactly what they were designed to do. The Creator built instinct into every animal that creeps, crawls or flies. Humans… we have free will. God has also built within us our own individual purpose, not as obvious and as immediate as an ant, but something uniquely ours. Our eternally valuable works will benefit the entire Body of Christ, and ultimately humankind. When the Judgement Day comes, if we have been about our own God-ordained calling as diligent as the ant is for his colony, our work is silver, gold, and costly precious jewels. That sounds way better than a pile of ash to me.

Dear Lord, Let my desire for treasure be of a heavenly nature, where no moth or rust or decay can destroy. Let my calling grow within my mind and heart until it becomes like an irrevocable instinct within me. Let me learn from your creatures how to focus on my part, to the benefit of the entire community, bringing about positive results on earth as well as in heaven. Draw me away from a saved life merely saved, barely escaping the flames. Draw me close to your heart so that I can enjoy the company of other believers dedicated to a life of gold, silver, and eternal rewards. In Jesus' name... Amen.

JULY 12

There is a Good Side

Then you called out to GOD in your desperate condition; he got you out in the nick of time. He quieted the wind down to a whisper, put a muzzle on all the big waves. And you were so glad when the storm died down, and he led you safely back to the harbor. So thank GOD for his marvelous love, for his miracle mercy to the children he loves. Lift your praises high when the people assemble...
–Psalm 107:23—32 (MSG)

When the deadline approaches, and the end of a project is not yet assured to be on time, emotions are a stormy sea. When everything comes together and all is finished, what a beautiful feeling of quiet and safety there is. While the rush to finish, pressed by a deadline, can cause anxiety as well as exhilaration, is it necessarily bad? According to Dr. Mary C. Lamia, explained in her article, "The Secret Life of Procrastinators and the Stigma of Delay," the answer to that question is, "No." The following quote illustrates her findings:

> "Racing the clock emotionally stimulates those who procrastinate. Since emotions serve to direct one's attention, we might consider such deadline stimulation highly adaptive as well. Moreover, procrastinating enables some people to perform at peak efficiency, and their task delay enables them to work diligently and attain optimal efficiency... Thus, for [professionally successful] procrastinators, the energizing quality and focus provided by emotions that are activated upon nearing a deadline are essential."

The good side happens when procrastinators have an emotional push toward concentration that enhances their efficiency and ability to focus, making them more equipped to meet their deadline. The key to the good side is actually being able to finish on time. In order to be a "successful" procrastinator having a deadline, and meeting it, are essential. We do not need the rush for the sake of feeling a rush, we need that push across the finish line in order to win. I must admit, too many of my projects have no deadline. Because I am in "no rush," sadly they remain unfinished. Today that needs to change.

Dear Lord, You are the author of time, and you have created all things for your glory. Guide me in the direction that you want me to go. My multitude of tasks and obligations can feel like being in the midst of a stormy sea. In prayer, seeking your will, please give me deadlines. Tell me what needs to be done, and when. May all my actions push me toward accomplishing my goals, doing your will, and expanding your kingdom on earth. Grant me sweet times of a peaceful finish. In Jesus' name... Amen.

JULY 13

My Place

Do not let your hearts be troubled. You believe in God; believe also in me. My Father's house has many rooms; if that were not so, would I have told you that I am going there to prepare a place for you? And if I go and prepare a place for you, I will come back and take you to be with me...
–John 14:1—3 (NIV)

But the one who hears my words and does not put them into practice is like a man who built a house on the ground without a foundation. The moment the torrent struck that house, it collapsed and its destruction was complete.
–Luke 6:49 (NIV)

It is rather fascinating the way a house can progress from a thought, into a written plan, to laying the foundation, to the coordinated construction of all the elements inside and out. The idea of God just dropping a blueprint for my life into my lap seems like a good idea to me. However, it appears that our God is a *one step at a time, my child* kind of God. According to Tim Urban, a self-proclaimed master procrastinator-

> No one 'builds a house.' They lay one brick again and again and the end result is a house. Procrastinators are great visionaries–they love to fantasize about the beautiful mansion they will have built one day–but what they need to be is gritty construction workers, who methodically lay one brick after another, day after day, without giving up, until a house is built.

Dear Lord, You are the foundation for my life, set in place by sending Jesus to die on a cross for my sins. Help me to live my life according to his words and seek his presence. Let me live a life not built on fantasies but built on the gritty "day to day" work that needs to be done. Let me realize that you have already given me access to your plan, as well as the skills, and all of the abilities that I need. Lead me to do my work, one brick at a time, to build a life that brings me to a place of fulfillment and shines your glory. In Jesus' name... Amen.

JULY 14

Never Too Late

But those who wait upon the Lord [who expect, look for, and hope in Him] Will gain new strength and renew their power; They will lift up their wings [and rise up close to God] like eagles [rising toward the sun]; They will run and not become weary, They will walk and not grow tired.
–Isaiah 40:31 (AMP)

Even in your old age I am He,
And even to your advanced old age I will carry you!
I have made you, and I will carry you;
Be assured I will carry you and I will save you.
–Isaiah 46:4 (AMP)

When should we change our bad habits?... Now. What is the best time of our lives to overcome our self-defeating behaviors?... While we are still young. Do we ever get too old to improve ourselves and change?... No! No matter how old we are, as long as there is breath in our lungs, change for the better is possible. If you think that it is too late, or that you are too old, you are wrong. God can renew your strength to do things you always wanted to do, even if you have buried them away for years. Have you been a procrastinator for twenty, forty, or even sixty years? Maybe you are still alive because (forgive the obvious cliché here) God isn't finished with you yet. Do not let your age become just one more excuse piled upon years of excuses! If you do not have the energy you feel that you need, that's alright. God will renew your power, and he promises to carry you.

Dear Lord. I confess that I regret allowing my procrastination to go unchecked for too many years. I thank you and praise you that you have given me life, and that I am still alive, and still able to do what you have called me to do. Please, free me from doubts that I will just not have enough time left to do what I desire to do. Grant me the courage to challenge myself to accomplish something that I have never done, or to complete a task that I have not finished yet. Help me to embrace the truth that it is never too late. In Jesus' name... Amen.

JULY 15

Growing Blessings

[Speaking of King Hezekiah]- He worked very hard to encourage respect for the Temple, the law, and godly living, and was very successful.
–2 Chronicles 31:21 (TLB)

So encourage each other to build each other up, just as you are already doing.
–1 Thessalonians 5:11 (TLB)

Then, too, I need your help, for I want not only to share my faith with you but to be encouraged by yours: Each of us will be a blessing to the other.
–Romans 1:11—12 (TLB)

When the Bible says Hezekiah "was very successful," just what success was the writer referring to? Does it mean he was successful in his efforts to encourage his people to a godly life, or because he encouraged his people to live a godly life, God blessed him with overall success in his life's endeavors? Either way, he was a blessing as he planted seeds of encouragement and godliness. Both he and his people reaped the multiple benefits. Encouragement is something we all need, and it costs nothing to give it away and spread it around. Where encouragement is evident, blessings and success are sure to grow. When we plant those seeds in others, blessings and success will be ours as well as theirs.

Dear Lord, Sometimes we feel in dire need of encouragement to keep going. Sometimes life's obstacles seem too difficult. Help us to get our eyes off of ourselves and look to inspire others. Prompt me to be an encouragement, to act and speak in ways that bring out the best in others. Give us discernment to see what actions of ours will grow blessings and success for those closest to us, and for people we don't even know yet who are hungering for an encouraging word. I thank you that in encouraging and blessing others, it miraculously uplifts us as well. May we be people whose lives benefit others. In Jesus' name... Amen.

JULY 16

Things and People Disappear

Since everything here today might well be gone tomorrow, do you see how essential it is to live a holy life?
–2 Peter 3:11 (MSG)

"Aren't these people just so much grass? True, the grass withers and the wildflowers fade, but our God's Word stands firm and forever."
–Isaiah 40:7—8 (MSG)

[Jesus in response to the thief on the cross, dying next to him]
He said, "Don't worry, I will. Today you will join me in paradise."
–Luke 23:43 (MSG)

While sitting in my car, in the rain, in the parking lot of a closed library so that I can get a Wi-Fi signal, I experience the futility of using my phone to post a blog entry. After just publishing a draft, it disappeared. Probably because I am prone to running late, many things of mine are lost, and left behind, and too often disappear. Like my good raincoat, and I really need it right now! Within a very short time too many people I know, and some beloved pets, have passed from life to death. There is a weighty sadness when this happens. Losing an item is just annoying, losing a loved one can be a tragic alteration of life itself, accompanied by extended grief. The transitory nature of life is hitting me hard today. We simply do not have much time on earth. As Christians, there is a comforting faith that reassures us; when our loved ones who serve the Lord die, we will see them again. For other people, I fear that may not be so. Life is too short, eternity is too long, to not be busy about our Father's business, inviting, sharing, giving, and doing His will.

Dear Lord, Help me to be comfortable about sharing the gospel with others. It truly is Good News. Let today not disappear before letting people in my life know that they are valued. Help me to not rush through life with an attitude that disregards people and things, allowing them to carelessly disappear. Help me to let go of frivolous activities and overindulgence in entertainments that steal my time from more important actions of eternal significance. Let me not put off until tomorrow, one single thing, that you would have me do this day. In Jesus' name... Amen.

JULY 17

Sticks and Stones

[From the story of David and his battle against Goliath]
Saul said to David, "Go, and may the Lord be with you." Then Saul dressed David in his own tunic. He put a coat of armor on him and a bronze helmet on his head. David fastened on his sword over the tunic and tried walking around, because he was not used to them...
"I cannot go in these," he said to Saul, "because I am not used to them." So he took them off. Then he took his staff in his hand, chose five smooth stones from the stream, put them in the pouch of his shepherd's bag and, with his sling in hand, approached the Philistine.
–1 Samuel 17:37—40 (NIV)

Although he was young, David was wiser and braver than any soldier on the battlefield that day. First of all, he knew that God was on his side. As a shepherd he had mastered the sling and had killed a variety of beasts who were bigger and stronger than he was. He knew that he could not wear the king's bulky, unfitting armor. He could not do the *expected* thing. He had to do what was tried and true for him. He walked into battle knowing his abilities, exuding confidence, and he brought his enemy down. Sometimes we focus far too much on our own weaknesses and say, "If only I could get better at ________," but that is not necessary. If we move confidently in our own strengths, be dedicated to the task at hand, and know that our God is for us, like David, we can also experience major victories in our life.

Dear Lord, I thank you for the Bible. Thank you for the examples you provide in your Word; they can help me to live a victorious life. Thank you for the strengths and abilities that you have given me, help me to develop my attributes and never take them for granted. As the "Serenity Prayer" states, "God, grant me the serenity to accept the things I cannot change; the courage to change the things I can; and the wisdom to know the difference." In Jesus' name... Amen.

JULY 18

Over Your Head

Don't be afraid, I've redeemed you. I've called your name. You're mine. When you're in over your head, I'll be there with you. When you're in rough waters, you will not go down. When you're between a rock and a hard place, it won't be a dead end– Because I am GOD, your personal God, the Holy One of Israel, your Savior...
–Isaiah 43:1—4 (MSG)

God knew what he was doing from the very beginning. He decided on the outset to shape the lives of those who love him along the same lines as the life of his Son. The Son stands first in the line of humanity he restored. We see the original and intended shape of our lives there in him.
–Romans 8:29 (MSG)

No matter what we have been through, or what we are going through right now, God is with us. God will not abandon us and will ultimately usher us into a glorious eternity. In Isaiah's time, God spoke to the nation of Israel through him. Once Jesus came, God showed us how to live through the example of His Son. We are New Testament heirs to promises made in the beginning of time and living examples of restored humanity. There are times when we are in circumstances over our heads, feeling as if we are drowning. Life is not a matter of *if* hard times will come, but *when*. Jesus not only suffered for all the sins of the human race, he experienced them all on the cross. There may be no person on earth that knows your pain, but Jesus does. Thank God he did not stay on that cross; he demonstrated God's resurrection power. We are not created to be crushed between the rock and the hard place; we are intended to be shaped in Jesus' image, and partake in the glory of God.

Dear Lord, Help us to be more like your Son. He was daily seeking your presence, praying, living according to your Word, submitted to your timetable. He showed compassion, mercy, grace, healing, forgiveness, and love to all– not only to those who needed it, but to those willing to receive it. Shape us into followers that also have these attributes. Help us to find a reason to praise you no matter what our circumstances. May we never lose faith in your love for us. May we be willing to spread the knowledge of salvation to others. Help us make today, a day when we become more like Jesus. In Jesus' name... Amen.

JULY 19

The Symphony in Us

The reason I left you in Crete was that you might put in order what was left unfinished and appoint elders in every town, as I directed you.
–Titus 1:5 (NIV)

Wake up! Strengthen what remains and is about to die, for I have found your deeds unfinished in the sight of my God.
–Revelations 3:2 (NIV)

Man's uniqueness among the animals, something which makes him "God-like" if you will, is the ability to create. Whether it is amazing architecture, literature, movies, or music, all of which has the ability to draw a multi-faceted crowd into unified enjoyment. Franz Schubert's Symphony No.8 was written in 1822, six years before his death. Scholars still debate as to whether or not it was finished in an unorthodox short form or discovered long after his death as the most famous "unfinished symphony." Unfinished or not, it is considered an extraordinary, beautiful piece of music. I recommend that you listen to this famous piece of music, easily found on YouTube: 3rd Polish Nationwide Music School- Playing *Schubert's Symphony No.8*, Also known as the *Unfinished Symphony*. We all have some kind of symphony within us, that needs to be developed and nurtured. Will it be finished or not? In most cases, it depends solely on us and on what steps we make today toward completion.

Dear Lord, Awaken within us the gift of creativity, as a life enhancing force, for those around us as well as ourselves. As you hung on the cross saying, "It is finished," who really understood what you meant? Help us to realize that you are the only one who can judge whether our work is finished or not. Keep us focused on the tasks facing us this day. Help us to sleep well at night knowing we finished this day well, surrendered to you with a heart burning to bring you glory. In Jesus' name... Amen.

JULY 20

A Willing Mind

[David's words to his son Solomon] Learn to know the God of your ancestors intimately. Worship and serve him with your whole heart and a willing mind. For the Lord knows every heart and knows every plan and thought. If you seek him you will find him... So take this seriously... Be strong and do the work.
–1 Chronicles 28:9—10 (NLT)

How many times has our heart been in the right place, we have good intentions, but somehow our mind gets in the way? For procrastinators the answer would be, "Often." Sometimes we really don't even have a thought or plan to get where we need to go. Our God can intimately initiate a transfusion of God's Holy Spirit, His mind, and His heart into our life. We should then be like a baby who is crying out in need. Our God is like the attentive mother who is right there, and ready to recognize exactly what we need, meeting those needs with a loving embrace and a kiss on the cheek. Such intimacy produces a relationship in which our mind becomes open and willing, as this intimacy fills us with God's love, God's thoughts and God's will.

Dear Lord, Help me to meet you daily, to enjoy your presence. Keep distractions from capturing my unfocused mind. Help me to value intimate times with you. Infuse me with your Holy Spirit, let me gravitate in the direction that you want me to go. Let your words and your thoughts carry an authority that my own do not, directing me toward my life's purpose. May I recognize that my need for you is as great as an infant for its mother. Let my renewed spirit dominant my unruly mind. May my compliance be an act of love, not just obedience. Create within me a diligent, willing mind. In Jesus' name... Amen.

JULY 21

Weary Is OK, Worn-out Is Not

Even youths grow tired and weary, and young men stumble and fall
–Isaiah 40:30 (NIV)

Let us not become weary in doing good, for at the proper time we will reap a harvest if we do not give up.
–Galatians 6:9 (NIV)

Come to me, all you who are weary and burdened, and I will give you rest.
–Matthew 11:28 (NIV)

Sometimes we just need a break. We don't really want to quit, just quit for a few days or a week, or more. That's why there are such things as vacations. I recall having teachers in high school that seemed like they quit before the bell rang, doing the bare minimum, not maintaining discipline, doing the same thing year after year without improving or changing a thing. Being a "burn out" seems to be the common expression for those who are worn-out and just go through the motions of life. It is critical for our own joy, and for the effectiveness of the Gospel being spread to others, to never be a worn-out Christian. When we get weary, as all people do, deal with it, get some rest, or make a radical life or job change if necessary. Don't let lack of energy and tiredness become a lifestyle, or an excuse for shoddy effort and results.

Dear Lord, Help me to be someone who always has a sense of joy and purpose in my work. Let me be aware of balancing work and rest, labor and play, so that I don't get weary in doing good. Draw me to your side when I am in need of rest. Give me a discernment of how to spend my time. Make me aware if I lean toward "going through the motions." Let my work always be with enthusiasm, creativity, and being at my best. Help me to never settle for being mediocre. In Jesus' name... Amen.

JULY 22

"No Worries"

Rejoice in the Lord always. Again I say, rejoice! Let everyone come to know your gentleness. The Lord is at hand. Be anxious for nothing, but in everything, by prayer and supplication with gratitude, make your requests known to God. And the peace of God, which surpasses all understanding, will protect your hearts and minds through Christ Jesus.
–Philippians 4:4—7 (MEV)

Being on the road to victory over procrastination is a pleasant journey. In the midst of procrastinating there is worry, stress, and the avoidance of the undesirable but necessary things which need to be done. When future goals are always so far away that they feel constantly unattainable, purpose is put aside to enjoy instant gratification. After the temporary pleasurable escape, there is lingering guilt. A life encumbered by procrastination is no way to really live. There is no singular way out of it for all who are trapped by it. The good news is, freedom is available. How? Submit to God totally, rejoice and draw pleasure from him, be grateful, pray openly and honestly, develop a plan for yourself in one area. With God's help, your heart and mind protected, see your plan produce results that lead to victory, and goals attained. Worries vanish when your victory is in sight or becomes a reality. Rejoice before it happens, having faith that it will. Rejoice!

Dear Lord, I have been down this road too many times. May I always be aware of what procrastination has cost me, and do what I need to do, to be free. Give me the wisdom to make decisions that lead to results and productivity, not stress and anxiety. Help me to avoid seeking playful times, when there is work that needs to be done. Help me to not keep putting off those very things that will bring long term fulfillment and satisfaction into my life. Help me to value the peace of mind that you freely offer me. Thank you for creating a vision of an attainable future for me. In Jesus' name.'

JULY 23

I Need Help

I obviously need help! I realize that I don't have what it takes. I can will it, but I can't do it. I decide to do good, but I don't really do it; I decide not to do bad, but then I do it anyway. My decisions such as they are, don't result in actions. Something has gone wrong deep within me and gets the better of me every time.
–Romans 7:17—20 (MSG)

The Lord does not delay and is not tardy or slow about what he promises, according to some people's conception of slowness, but He is long-suffering (extremely patient) toward you.
–2 Peter 3:9 (AMP)

Procrastination has a way of taking over. The very thing that we desired to do, the actual good habit that we strive to create in order to break the spell of perpetual postponements, has not happened yet. We are so close to victory; it's within our grasp then it slips away. Just when we think our mind has been made up, and our preferred course is firmly set... what happens to us? We succumb to another procrastinator's pitfall; we lie to ourselves! A day-to-day march to victory is sidetracked by other things, the rare occurrence of a delay becomes the regular occurrence again. "I'll get to that later," is a self-sabotaging lie. We need to face the truth about ourselves, and the power of God to help us today, without delay. Thank God for his patience toward us! God's Word, the Holy Spirit, our dedication to change, and prayer make a difference. We can take over, and rule ourselves into a better future, starting today, not tomorrow!

Dear Lord, Renew me with the assurance of your calling on my life. Take the burden of lies and self-deception off my back. Put a right spirit in me, one that is true to you in all things. One that does NOT delay, one that can see clearly. Please don't let me exhaust or abuse your patience. Do not allow me to be slow in walking out my obedience. Help me to be quick to sacrifice whatever I must, in order to do your will in all things. Lead me to always seek the truth. In Jesus' name... Amen.

JULY 24

He Hears Us

I am writing this to you so that you may know that you have eternal life– you that believe in the Son of God. We have courage in God's presence, because we are sure that he hears us if we ask him for anything that is according to his will. He hears us whenever we ask him; and since we know this is true, we know also that he gives us what we ask from him.
–1 John 5:13—15 (GNT)

Then Jesus told his disciples a parable to teach them that they should always pray and never become discouraged… "Now, will God not judge in favor of his own people who cry to him day and night for help? Will he be slow to help them? I tell you, he will judge in their favor and do it quickly."
–Luke 18:1,7—8 (GNT)

There are simply too many ways to become discouraged, especially when we are trying to change deeply embedded habits. God's Word can be the most effective antidote to that discouragement. Too often I have given up praying for certain things that I knew were God's will, because it seemed as if it was taking too long for them to come to pass. I didn't stop believing that these things could happen, but I did stop praying. Procrastination can be a way to avoid disappointment; it provides a temporary "way out" for the hurt of unfulfilled expectations. But, persistent prayer with faithful expectation opens channels to receive God's answers, so they may flow into our lives. When we pray that way, God hears us and responds. Better to replace discouragement with hope-filled prayer.

Dear Lord, Let me always approach you with an attitude of praise, and with faith that you hear me. Let me never give up praying for loved ones that are not saved, those bound by addictions, and people oppressed by injustice. Revive my desire to spend time with you in prayer. Let your Word renew my thinking and guide my prayers to be according to your will. Empower the words of my prayers by your Holy Spirit. Let there be favor on my life, a testimony of how you are working here and now, so others will be drawn into relationship with your son and blessed by salvation and eternal life. In Jesus' name… Amen.

JULY 25

Waiting for Us All

"Wisdom is better than foolishness, just as light is better than darkness. The wise can see where they are going, and fools cannot." But I also know that the same fate is waiting for us all.
–Ecclesiastes 2:13—14 (GNT)

What is the same fate waiting for us all? Death. It is the cold, harsh reality for all living creatures. Regardless of where one spends eternity, death is the gate we all pass through. That reality should help us develop the proper perspective on living, and what we do with the life we've been given. While reading the book, *Old Age is Always 15 Years Older Than I Am* by Randy Voorhees, I came across two interesting quotes. Joan Baez said, "You don't get to choose how you're going to die. Or when. You can only decide how you're going to live. Now." These words were aptly followed by Larry McMurtry's, "If you wait, all that happens is that you get older." We cannot afford to spend our time waiting. There is simply too much that needs to be done. We need to decide how we are going to live… Now!

Dear Lord, Give us a hunger for wisdom. So often we wrestle with questioning your will for us, but you have made it clear, the way of wisdom is always your will. Let me not squander or waste any time that I have here. Don't let me just grow older, without growing wiser. Let me embrace this day, right now, as a precious gift. Let me not just wait. Let me dedicate this time I have on earth to do and create your will on earth as it is in heaven. In Jesus' name... Amen.

JULY 26

Goodness and Mercy

The Lord is my shepherd, I shall not want;
he makes me lie down in green pastures.
He leads me beside still waters;
he restores my soul.
He leads me in paths of righteousness
for his name's sake.
Even though I walk through the valley of the shadow of death,
I fear no evil;
for thou art with me;
thy rod and thy staff,
they comfort me.
Thou preparest a table before me
in the presence of my enemies;
thou anointest my head with oil,
my cup overflows.
Surely goodness and mercy shall follow me
all the days of my life;
and I will dwell in the house of the LORD
forever. –Psalm 23 (RSV)

I would like to share my most inspirational version of the 23rd Psalm, played and sung by Keith Green, it can be found on YouTube, search for - Keith Green-23rd Psalm. His music and life have been such an inspiration to me. If you are not familiar with his life or his music, getting to know him may definitely be a worthwhile use of your time. He had an urgency in his life. Maybe somehow, he knew he would die young. He did, in a plane crash along with dear friends and two of his little children. His urgency was echoed in the name of his evangelical organization, *Last Days Ministries.* We don't really know if today will be our last day or not.

Dear Lord, Help us to always remember that you are a good shepherd. You care for us with loving kindness and provision. Refresh and restore us, as you guide us by your authoritative hand. Help us to fear nothing, even death itself. Let us know peace in the midst of a fallen, hostile world. Instill us with courage to face all of our obstacles and enemies. Let us be constantly thankful for our salvation, your goodness, and your mercy. Knowing that we will dwell eternally with you, let us do all that we can this day to stay by your side, surrendering our will to you, that your will may be done. In Jesus' name... Amen.

JULY 27

Get it Together

How lovely is your dwelling place, O Lord of Heaven's Armies
I long, yes, I faint with longing to enter the courts of the Lord.
With all my whole being, body and soul. I will shout joyfully to the Living God...
O Lord of Heaven's Armies, my King and my God!
What joy for those who can live in your house, always singing your praises.
What joy for those whose strength is the Lord,...
For the Lord God is our sun and shield. He gives grace and glory.
The Lord will withhold no good thing from those who do what is right.
–Psalm 84:1–5, 11 (NLT)

When our thoughts are screaming at us, "Get it together!" Often the most difficult thing to decide is, *Where do I start?* We want to make good things happen in our life before our lives shift into a downward spiral or panic mode. The best place to start is being in God's house on a regular basis. When we have the attitude of the psalmist, longing to be in God's presence with our entire being, enjoying being engulfed by songs of praise, then our spirit, soul, and body are joyfully brought together. The best start to our week should be gathering with like-minded believers. That is an important way to advance through life with grace and glory. As we strive to do what is right, God will not withhold good things. The ungodliness of the world and our internal flaws can tear us apart. There is strength that comes from being infused with the Body of Christ. When we get together, it helps us "get it together."

Dear Lord, Help those that believe in you to see the value of gathering together on a regular basis. Give your people a revelation of the benefits of putting their entire heart and soul into worship, and service. Let us experience your protection, your grace, your goodness, and new levels of joy that are only possible as a result of honoring you. Gather those that are separated from your Body, into joining together with other believers. Let me always recognize the benefits and wisdom of belonging to a local church. In Jesus' name... Amen.

JULY 28

Praise Him

Oh, thank the Lord, for he is good! His loving-kindness is forever. Let the congregation of Israel praise him with these same words: "His loving-kindness is forever."... You did your best to kill me, O my enemy, but the Lord helped me. He is my strength and my song in the heat of battle, and now he has given me the victory. Songs of joy at the news of our rescue are sung in the homes of the godly. The strong arm of the Lord has done glorious things! I shall not die but live to tell of all his deeds.
–Psalm 118:1—2, 13—17 (TLB)

At one of the lowest points in my life, tired of dealing with an apparently unsolvable situation in my marriage, difficulty in handling rebellious teenagers, and ready to walk out the door, I learned a very important lesson. I was desperately seeking God for answers and he cleared my confusion. He let me know, "Leaving your family will not work my will in your life." Jesus lifted my depression and gave me a revelation of the importance of praise. Since then, praising God every day has been a priority and a consistent protection from confusion, depression and feeling hopeless. There is something that happens, an infusion from God, a focus on a positive unseen reality that can change our world and defeat our spiritual enemies. There are some things of eternal value that only happen during times of praise. Praise God always, and forever.

Dear Lord, I thank you that you are able to banish hopelessness and crippling frustration from my soul. No matter what is going on in my life, let me always praise you. Open my eyes to see the benefits of worship and praise. May I always put my whole heart and soul into times of worship, praising you from the very depth of my being. You are worthy of all praise and honor, and in your presence, I will be transformed. I will forever thank you that your steadfast loving kindness endures forever! In Jesus' name... Amen.

JULY 29

Firm Grip

[Christ as son, in charge of God's house] Now, if we can only keep a firm grip on this bold confidence, we're the house! That's why the Holy Spirit says, Today please listen; don't turn a deaf ear as in "the bitter uprising," that time of wilderness testing! Even though they watched me at work for forty years, your ancestors refused to let me do it my way; over and over they tried my patience.
–Hebrews 3:6–11 (MSG)

Emily Pronin of Princeton University designed a study in 2008 which determined that people were willing to commit to drink a half-cup of some nasty, bitter tasting concoction two weeks in the future, but could only commit to taking two tablespoons on that day. Like, let's just put this onerous task way out there in the future, not do this now! The substance of her research supported the idea that those who are more connected to their future self, report having fewer procrastinating behaviors. The children of Israel, rather than battle on the day the Lord had designed for them to take the Promised Land, declined to do their distasteful, scary duty. The result was forty years of wandering around the desert before a second opportunity came around. What is often thought of as giving ourselves an extra measure of grace for our mistakes, is actually just pushing our decisions and behavior into a feel-good-today, but bad-for-us-in-the-future direction. That is the nature of procrastination. Personally, I do not have another forty years to waste.

Dear Lord, Help us to see that some things need to be done as soon as possible, while we are still in the "now." Give us wisdom to see the negative results of putting things off into the future somewhere. Give us the faith to know that you are for us, and that you are leading us in the best direction. Let us be willing to take the difficult, bitter, and unpleasant tasks, with a better attitude, being confident that having them "over and done," rather than hanging around undone, is far better for us and our future. In Jesus' name... Amen

JULY 30

It Is New

What a God we have! And how fortunate we are to have him, this father of our Master Jesus! Because Jesus was raised from the dead, we've been given a brand-new life and have everything to live for, including a future in heaven–and the future starts now!
–1 Peter 1:3—5 (MSG)

Because of the Lord's great love we are not consumed,
for his compassions never fail.
They are new every morning;
great is your faithfulness.
–Lamentations 3:22—23 (NIV)

What a genuine gift it is to be presented with the light of a brand-new day after either a peaceful sleep, or a disturbing darkness. As a teenager, I spent a few miserable years within a web of dysfunctional relationships, anger, abuse, rebellion, and unforgiveness, that actually resulted in my physical illness. As I would lie down at night to sleep, I prayed for amnesia. I desperately wanted a brand-new life, with a totally clean slate, and no remembrance of anything. If some caring evangelical Christian would have explained to me the spiritual dynamics of being born again, I probably would have surrendered my life to Jesus right then. Maybe we have heard the cliché too often, "Today is the first day of the rest of your life," but it is absolutely true. Each new day should be held in awe for the opportunities it presents, like a mother that lovingly embraces her new baby, wonderfully anticipating the possibilities to come. Thank God for the way he has allotted time; every day is a new start with abundant opportunities, and an unwritten page for us to fill. Time to create an attitude of thankfulness for each new day.

Dear Lord, I thank you for your grand design of all things. You have created every one of us on purpose, and for a purpose. I thank you for the miracle of being "born again." When I was dead in sin, you gave me life everlasting through salvation in your Son. Help us to seize all the opportunities that you present to us today. Help our minds to accept the newness of every day, and not to be defined by our yesterdays. Let us see the future that you have called us to live. May our will be aligned with your will, so that our actions will result in the future that you have designed for us. In Jesus' name... Amen

JULY 31

Good to Know

For the eyes of the Lord move to and fro throughout the earth so that He may support those whose heart is completely His.
–2 Chronicles 16:9 (AMP)

If we don't know how or what to pray, it doesn't matter. He does our praying in and for us, making prayer out of our wordless sighs, our aching groans. He knows us far better than we know ourselves, knows our pregnant condition, and keeps us present before God. That's why we can be so sure that every detail in our lives of love for God is worked into something good.
–Romans 8:26—28 (MSG)

Whenever we are struggling with the daunting issues of our own failings or life's hard knocks, it is easy to forget that there is a depth of goodness in God's Word always available. God has his eyes on us. He prays for us, interpreting our inarticulate pains and interceding on our behalf. He knows us, and still loves us! As we surrender to the Holy Spirit to lead and guide our prayers, we cannot fail to pray God's will; it will manifest for our good and His glory. Our love for God miraculously unlocks his ever-ready, supportive love for us. That is all very good to know.

Dear Lord, I thank you for your great love for us. Help us to see you as the compassionate father that you are. You are always ready to encourage us as we build ourselves up in our campaign to overcome our trials, self-imposed hindrances and bad habits. Open our eyes to recognize the good things that you have provided for us, and to see the ways that you are currently working our lives into something good. In Jesus' name... Amen.

AUGUST 1

Sacrifice What?

When the offerings were finished, the king and everyone present with him knelt down and worshiped... So they sang praises with gladness and bowed down and worshiped. Then Hezekiah said, ... "Come and bring sacrifices and thank offerings to the temple of the Lord." So the assembly brought sacrifices and thank offerings, and all whose hearts were willing brought burnt offerings.
–2 Chronicles 29:29—31 (NIV)

Through Jesus, therefore, let us continually offer to God a sacrifice of praise– the fruit of lips that openly profess his name. And do not forget to do good and to share with others, for with such sacrifices God is pleased.
–Hebrews 13:15—16 (NIV)

We do not want to sacrifice just any old thing, big mistake. That situation did not go well for either Cain or Abel. The idea of bringing sacrifices to one's god, no matter which god it is, has been a worldwide religious activity since the dawn of time. Yet, it seems as if it is not too prevalent in modern thinking, too bloody I suppose. We modern believers may be missing an important principle that some kind of sacrifice may be mandatory in order to approach God favorably. Today, what do we sacrifice as we approach God? Maybe nothing. When it comes to following God's will, are we willing to sacrifice sleep, time, social media interaction, money, entertainment, food, drink, *our way,* or anything else that is blocking our productive path with our God? Time to examine, what will we sacrifice?

Dear Lord, Let me know what types of sacrifices and offerings you want from me. Help me to "do good and to share with others," for your Word says that these sacrifices please you. Reveal to me the vital sacrificial element in praise and worshiping you. Let there be an altar burning continually within my heart. Give me discernment to see what I am holding on to that should be offered up to you, letting it go into your hands as a pleasing sacrifice. In Jesus' name... Amen.

AUGUST 2

A Most Favorable Time

In the time of my favor I heard you,
and in the day of salvation I helped you.
I tell you, now is the time of God's favor,
now is the day of salvation.
–2 Corinthians 6:2 (NIV)

Sometimes it is hard for me to look into the onrushing future. It seems to be a ferocious, unpredictable wind, out of my control. To some degree it is, but on another level, it is entirely in my hands to build a self-directed path. To quote Christine Caine, "Let's be determined not to wait until tomorrow to do what we know in our hearts we ought to do today!" It is common to believe that there is always a tomorrow. Maybe that is why it is so easy to put off until tomorrow, things which should be either accomplished or completed, today. When I think of all the people that Christine Caine's organization, A21, has rescued from a life of horrific sex trafficking and slavery, I thank God that Christine didn't pile up years of tomorrows. She answered the call of *Now*, bringing life and salvation to so many. She saw her favorable time and offered her most to God when she heard his call to ministry.

Dear Lord, I thank you that I did not put off my salvation. You sought after me and rescued me while I was still far from you. Because of you, I need never worry about the future. Jesus knew his calling, knew what he had to do, and paid the price. Nudge me in that godly direction of doing today what needs to be done today. Give me ears to hear your voice, a heart that is quick to forgive myself, as well as others, and eyes to see the future that you have chosen for me. Help me to not live my life in an endless circle of procrastination, guide me to a path of fulfilling my purpose. In Jesus' name… Amen

AUGUST 3

The Word

In the beginning was the Word, and the Word was with God, and the Word was God. He was in the beginning with God; all things were made through him, and without him was not anything made that was made. In him was life, and the life was the light of men. The light shines in the darkness, and the darkness has not overcome it.
–John 1:1—5 (RSV)

For the word of God is living and active, sharper than any two-edged sword, piercing to the division of soul and spirit, of joints and marrow, and discerning the thoughts and intentions of the heart.
–Hebrews 4:12 (RSV)

[Jesus said...] "It is written, 'Man shall not live by bread alone, but by every word that proceeds from the mouth of God.'"
–Matthew 4:4 (RSV)

God spoke all creation into existence, and Jesus is the living word of God. There is astounding creative power in God's Word. The Word of God: instructs, illuminates, enlivens, directs, corrects, encourages, heals, reveals, fortifies, nourishes our body, soul, and spirit. There can be no greater tool to open eyes to life's most important realities. Of all the actions that we can take to become better people, save marriages, heal emotional scars, defeat evil, and allow forgiveness to flow in and out of our lives, no action is more beneficial than filling our hearts and minds with God's Word. We need it as much as food. The Word not only imparts life, the Word is alive!

Dear Lord, May all people who follow you, hunger and thirst for your Word. Renew our minds, activate creativity, instill courage, and let your words flow freely from within us to others. Let us embrace the Bible as your Holy Word. As your words take on a priority in our lives, let us be living examples of their transforming power. May their authority and the testimony of our changed lives, grow and spread salvation to a lost and dying world. May we never forget your word is life, and it is alive. In Jesus' name... Amen.

AUGUST 4

A Little A Lot

And I shall live before the Lord forever. Oh, send your loving-kindness and truth to guard and watch over me, and I will praise your name continually, fulfilling my vow of praising you each day.
–Psalm 61:7—8 (TLB)

"How can you eat an entire elephant?" my pastor, Jonathan Wilson from Newport Church, said one Sunday morning. The answer is, "One bite at a time." He oft repeated the wise advice, "Better a little a lot, than a lot a little." As a procrastinator, I would almost always pile up that huge lot of tasks to do in a very little time. Erroneously thinking, just wait until that adrenaline kicks in, "I can accomplish any monumental task in a short time under that kind of juice." Wrong. Now it is the peace of "nothing hanging over my head" that I desire. It beats that back-to-the-wall, paralyzed before initiating motivation, any day!

As we approached our family cabin, looking forward to those lazy days by the creek and leisurely addressing the typical to-do lists, seeing an entire truckload of dirty, insect infested logs that needed to be stacked, made me realize that a test was before me. Will I wait until the last day we are here and become a log stacking maniac? Or, do I do a little every day until the chaotic pile has been neatly stacked away? Hearing my former pastor's words echo in my head, "Better a little a lot, than a lot, a little," the victory was mine, and the task completed, a little at a time. Ahhh... the peace of doing it that way.

Dear Lord, As I exalt you daily, you give me access to your loving kindness, wisdom and peace. Let me be one that desires peace rather than being a delaying slacker or thrill seeker. Let me grow in the thrill of your presence, enjoying the act of praising you. Keep me focused today, fulfilling what needs to be done this day. Let me always be in the act of living my life a little at a time, accomplishing a lot. In Jesus' name... Amen.

AUGUST 5

That Won't Help

Therefore, there is now no condemnation for those who are in Christ Jesus
–Romans 8:1 (NIV)

I pray that out of his glorious riches he may strengthen you with power by his Spirit in your inner being
–Ephesians 3:16 (NIV)

So then, just as you received Christ Jesus as Lord, continue to live your lives in him, rooted and built up in him, strengthened in the faith as you were taught, and overflowing with thankfulness.
–Colossians 2:6—7 (NIV)

When you make a mistake, what do you do? Condemn yourself, feel guilty, then believe that you deserve all the bad feelings that you have just heaped upon yourself? That won't help. Procrastinators often have a pattern of negative self-talk. Those that feel bad about themselves have a tendency to feel that they deserve an unfulfilling life. You don't! If Jesus can say to the woman that committed adultery, "Neither do I condemn you," we should not continue to condemn ourselves. Look at all we deserve: glorious riches, no condemnation, strength, power, faith, and thankfulness. That is a foundation upon which we can build positive change, not guilt.

Dear Lord, Help me to overcome that condemning voice inside of me. Renew my thoughts and do not let negative feelings take hold of me and determine my fate. Let me be keenly aware of when I am sabotaging myself and stop it. Guide me away from thoughts and attitudes that will not help, and bring me to a place of strength, acceptance, and thankfulness for what you have done for me. In Jesus' name... Amen.

AUGUST 6

All I Need

Is there any god like GOD? Are we not at bedrock? Is this the GOD who armed me well, then aimed me in the right direction?... He shows me how to fight; I can bend a bronze bow! You protect me with salvation armor; you touch me and I feel ten feet tall. You cleared the ground under me so my footing was firm. When I chased my enemies I caught them... You armed me well for this fight... You made my enemies turn tail, and I wiped out the haters.
–2 Samuel 22:32—44 (MSG)

The above scripture aptly expresses all that God is able to do for us. When singing songs of praise, which I love to do, there is a sentiment often expressed to the effect that, "Jesus is all that I need." I must confess, often that is not my perception of real life. When loved ones are trapped in addiction, when children are wandering away from God, when our personal hopes and dreams have been dashed, when hard circumstances press upon us, Jesus does not FEEL like enough. Times such as these, the reality of God's Word, God's true character, and the nature of my relationship to God, are when truth needs to triumph over emotions. Feelings are fickle inklings often based on fiction that will blow our ship off course. If we don't make it past the trials of painful feelings and doubt, we may never make it into the safe harbor of God's eternal rewards. If God isn't all I need, I recognize that beyond physical life-sustaining needs, God's presence sustains me. Today, I must decide… I certainly do not need my feelings to rule my life. I do need God.

Dear Lord, You are the joy of our salvation, and the author and finisher of our faith. You have armed us with spiritual weapons to overcome all obstacles. Teach us how to fight the good fight of faith. Help us to never give in to despair. As we move forward, give us a taste of victory to sustain us through life's battles. Help us to seek your truth always, and to seek your loving presence when life is painful. May our faith sustain us during trying times. Give us vision to see the way you have cleared for us. Help me to do today, what must be done today to stay in the midst of your will. In Jesus' name... Amen.

AUGUST 7

Picasso Says

Now listen, you who say, "Today or tomorrow we will go to this or that city, spend a year there, carry on business and make money." Why, you do not even know what will happen tomorrow. What is your life? You are a mist that appears for a little while and then vanishes.
–James 4:13—14 (NIV)

After reading this verse, a history of moves made by my husband and I came to mind. Some were job related, family related, or attempts for profit. Practically none of these moves produced the results we were seeking. Because the future is unpredictable, it often creates an unforeseen disappointing reality. Therefore, it makes a lot of sense to invest in today. According to famous artist Pablo Picasso, "Only put off until tomorrow what you are willing to die having left undone." He was fortunate to live for 92 productive years! Possibly there were still many more things he wanted to do, but never did. It is most profitable for us to think and act upon, "What do I need to do, today."

Dear Lord, Only you know the measure of our days on earth, lead us in a way that makes the most out of all of them. Guard us from a fear of what tomorrow may bring as well as an over-reliance on a series of tomorrows to fulfill our plans. Let our primary goal be to serve you, simply and completely, with no reservations. If we have no more tomorrows, let us be at peace with what we did today. Guard our hearts and minds. Let your will be done in our lives. In Jesus' name... Amen.

AUGUST 8

Just Ask

Many rebuked him and told him to be quiet, but he shouted all the more, "Son of David, have mercy on me!" Jesus stopped and said, "Call him." So they called to the blind man, "Cheer up! On your feet! He's calling you." Throwing his cloak aside, he jumped to his feet and came to Jesus. "What do you want me to do for you?" Jesus asked him. The blind man said, "Rabbi, I want to see." "Go," said Jesus, "Your faith has healed you." Immediately he received his sight and followed Jesus along the road.
–Mark 10:48–52 (NIV)

"So I say to you: Ask and it will be given to you; seek and you will find; knock and the door will be opened to you..."
–Luke 11:9 (NIV)

There are things about the passage in Mark, about this blind man's healing, that make me want to dig deeper. The first thing is the blind man's loud determination to connect with Jesus. He absolutely will not be deterred by others who desired to shut him up. I admire him for that. His throwing his cloak aside says one of two things to me, either he thought, *I know that Jesus will heal me, I will be able to find my cloak with my own eyes!* Or, knowing that he would be healed, he was completely done with his old life and ready to leave every thing behind related to his past. When Jesus asks him the question, "What do you want..." the answer seems rather obvious, but this blind man had to make his request specific. He may have had a multitude of desires, but he asked for something he truly needed. Like the blind man, we also need to approach Jesus with determined faith. Let us not be ashamed of our calling out to him. God is waiting for us to ask. Our asking can open the door to our faith's reward.

Dear Lord, Sometimes our needs and wants are so great and so tangled, it is a challenge to know what our greatest need is. Please show us what to ask for. Help us to realize that when we seek your presence, you will reveal to us exactly what we need to ask for in faith. Let us determine, despite all obstacles, to seek your presence with our whole heart and soul. May we never hesitate to ask for your will, and then freely ask for what you desire to freely give us. Let the road we travel on, be one where we are following you. Help us to leave our past behind, and to do today, what needs to be done today. In Jesus' name... Amen.

AUGUST 9

Tomorrow

The Nile will team with frogs. They will come up into your palace and your bedroom and onto your bed, into the houses of your officials and on your people, and into your ovens and kneading troughs... So Aaron stretched out his hand over the waters of Egypt, and the frogs came up and covered the land. But the magicians did the same things by their secret arts... Pharaoh summoned Moses and Aaron and said, "Pray to the LORD to take the frogs away from me and my people, and I will let your people go to offer sacrifices to the LORD." Moses said to Pharaoh, "I leave to you the honor of setting the time for me to pray for you and your officials and your people that you and your houses may be rid of the frogs, except for those that remain in the Nile."

"Tomorrow," Pharaoh said.
–Exodus 8:3—10 (NIV)

When I first heard Christine Caine preach on the absurdity of Pharaoh waiting to rid his empire of this plague, considering how bad it was, it struck me of how easy it is to default to delay. Really? Frogs are in your bed, your food, covering everything everywhere, and when do you want to be rid of them? Tomorrow? How many habits, bad relationships, long term goals do we put in the tomorrow category? If it is something that needs to start today, begin today. If it is something we need to rid of, get rid of it today. But... human nature and our own inclinations often put things into that Neverland of tomorrow. At least Pharaoh knew tomorrow would bring a solution to his frog problem. For me, and many others, tomorrow usually turns into another tomorrow, again and again, until who knows *if* or *when* it will ever happen.

Dear Lord, Help us to see our problems clearly, and to ruthlessly deal with them immediately. Help us to see our goals as achievable and begin the process of achieving them today. Let us be very aware of when we fall into this tomorrow attitude. Move us to start today what needs to begin this day. Give us the strength to rid ourselves of whatever is hindering our lives today. In Jesus' name... Amen.

AUGUST 10

No Fear

And now, dear brothers and sisters, one final thing. Fix your thoughts on what is true, and honorable, and right, and pure, and lovely, and admirable. Think about things that are excellent and worthy of praise.
–Philippians 4:8 (NLT)

But Jesus spoke to them at once. "Don't be afraid," he said. "Take courage. I am here."
–Matthew 14:27 (NLT)

For God has not given us a spirit of fear and timidity, but of power, love, and self-discipline.
–2 Timothy 1:7 (NLT)

Fear is the root cause of many people's procrastination. Fear of not being excellent or perfect, fear of failure, fear of rejection, fear of not measuring up to past success, fear of looking foolish, are all fears that can make us want to hide somewhere like a frightened puppy. Fear is a flaming arrow aimed at our mind from the enemy of our soul. Fear is a dark illusion that keeps us from being all that we can be. Renewing our mind by reading aloud or committing scriptures to memory, such as these written above, have the power to replace our fears with truth. Courage, power, love, and self-discipline are ours, as we fix our minds on what is right, there is no fear.

Dear Lord, I thank you for your Word. Help me to realize that there is power to access, at any given moment, by focusing on your words, your thoughts, and what is excellent. I pray for your Holy Spirit to be with me in my struggles to overcome my fears. Help me to see my fears for what they really are, tricks of dark deceptions with no substance. Let my soul be comforted by the thought that perfect love casts out all fear; your love for me is perfect and powerful. Thank you for giving me victory over those fears that steal my joy and hold me back from doing your will. Keep me free from fear today, and for all the days of my life. In Jesus' name… Amen.

AUGUST 11

You Can't Make Me

In times of rebellion against God there was no peace.
–2 Chronicles 15:5 (TLB)

For rebellion is as bad as the sin of witchcraft, and stubbornness is as bad as worshipping idols. And now because you have rejected the word of Jehovah, he has rejected you from being king.
–1 Samuel 15:23 (TLB)

Rebellion comes in many forms. The most obvious is direct disobedience of a command from someone in authority. Sometimes rebellion is more subtle, ignoring a duty or obligation, or being passive-aggressive. Whatever form it takes, it is a self-defeating characteristic and can be the root cause of procrastination in some people. The following words from Mike Bundrant, retired psychotherapist and life coach, are very insightful.

> Inner Rebellion: You can't make me... Finally, we have the rebel– that part of you that will not be told what to do. Even you can't tell yourself what to do, right? Set any expectation and you can expect the rebel to do the opposite, and no realistic carrot or stick is big enough to make a difference... So, you resist other's expectations and ignore your own... And kiss success good-bye.

As a teenager I was very rebellious. I had some serious anger issues toward my father. I knew that doing well in school was a top priority for him, so why would I want to do well in school, and please him? I wouldn't! Due to my rebellion, skipping school, an extended illness, terrible grades, and having to repeat my junior year in high school was my self-defeating outcome. That is the trouble with rebellion, it almost always ends badly for the rebel. This is especially true if we are rebelling against God. King Saul lost his throne because of it. By rebelling, whether silently or blatantly, we can lose our true purpose as well as God's favor.

Dear Lord, You are the highest authority. Your laws and commandments are to be observed. Give us insight to recognize any trace of rebellion within us. Help us to leave rebellious ways behind and to trust that complying with your will is the way to peace. Help us to defeat any inclination to be stubbornly opposed to what is right. Lead us to have victory over self-defeating behavior, and to submit to your ways with our whole heart. In Jesus' name... Amen.

AUGUST 12

Without A Trace

O our God, we thank you and praise your glorious name. But who am I, and who are your people, that we could give anything to you? Everything we have has come from you, and we give you only what you first gave us! We are here for only a moment, visitors and strangers in the land as our ancestors were before us. Our days on earth are like a passing shadow, gone so soon, without a trace.
–1 Chronicles 29:13—15 (NLT)

There are a multitude of memorial crosses placed on the curves of country roads and many commemorative memorial plaques on benches outside hospitals. There is lots of physical evidence that someone was loved and is now missed. Those left behind fervently want some trace of their loved one's existence preserved here on earth. We do not want people that are important to us to disappear after death, just as we do not want to leave this earth without a trace. We need to remember the words of Lanny Wolfe, sung by many Christians…

"Only one life, so soon it will pass,
Only what's done for Christ shall last."

Dear Lord, Help us every day to make an eternal impact by what we do, say, give, and create. Help us to raise our children to follow you and do your will. Show us how to leave a godly legacy, not merely plaques and markers. Do not let us leave earth "without a trace," but with a trail, leading others to you and to your eternal glory. In Jesus' name... Amen.

AUGUST 13

My Confidence

But blessed is the one who trusts in the Lord, whose confidence is in him.
–Jeremiah 17:7 (NIV)

In him and through faith in him we may approach God with freedom and confidence.
–Ephesus 3:1 (NIV)

For you have been my hope, Sovereign Lord, my confidence since my youth…
–Psalm 71:5 (NIV)

There is no overcoming difficult circumstances, or victory over undesirable behaviors, without confidence. Having had several personal battles that were approached with confidence, then lost, with an *I'll-Never-Be-Able-To-This* attitude, I know that my low confidence level definitely contributed to a negative outcome. Relying on my own confidence is often a dead end rather than a highway to success. Our confidence needs to be in the Lord; he has our back and our front. Our own confidence may waver and fail, but in confessing our weakness, acknowledging our need for God's help, and being confident in our Savior, can make up for our own lack. Placing our confidence in a loving faithful God, instead of our own shaky confidence, can help us to sustain a *With-Your-Help- I-Can-Do-All-Things* attitude which leads to success.

Dear Lord, Let your Word transform my understanding of confidence. Let me have complete trust in you. You desire to help me in all trials, circumstances, and struggles, to transform me into the person you want me to be. Help my confidence to be fueled and energized by being confident in you. Renew my mind, let me have the kind of confidence David had when he faced Goliath, well trained in the skills he needed, sure of himself, but even more confident in you to insure his victory. In Jesus' name... Amen.

AUGUST 14

For You

Rejoice always, pray constantly, give thanks in all circumstances; for this is the will of God in Christ Jesus for you.
–1 Thessalonians 5:16—18 (RVS)

He was praying in a certain place, and when he ceased, one of his disciples said to him, "Lord, teach us to pray, as John taught his disciples."
–Luke 11:1 (RVS)

So much of what we need to pray for is covered in the prayer Jesus taught his disciples- "The Lord's Prayer," also known as "The Our Father." When I am unsure of what to pray, that specific prayer, is always of benefit and fitting. Seeking our Heavenly Father should be top priority in order for us to know God's will, so that we can accurately pray. When we are spending intimate time with God, talking and listening, sharing our deepest thoughts, feelings, and concerns, we become more in sync with God's heart and will. We want our prayers to be effective and fervent. That is how God's will is done in us, and we are able to pray in ways that transform earth to be more like heaven.

Dear Lord, Draw me near to you frequently throughout my days and nights. Help my thoughts, emotions, and concerns to flow freely to you. Make your will clear to me. Tune my ears that I can hear your voice. As a sheep recognizes and trusts the voice of its shepherd, I will follow you and submit to you, because you made me and know what is best for me. Guide my prayers beyond what I want for myself. Reveal your will during our times together. May the prayers I speak transform situations, that your will may be done on earth as it is in heaven. In Jesus' name... Amen.

AUGUST 15

Where Anger Leads

Then the Lord descended in the form of a pillar of cloud and stood there with him, and passed in front of him and announced the meaning of his name. "I am Jehovah, the merciful and gracious God," he said, "slow to anger and rich in steadfast love and truth."
–Exodus 34:5–6 (TLB)

But now is the time to cast off and throw away all those rotten garments of anger, hatred, cursing, and dirty language.
–Colossians 3:8 (TLB)

So I want men everywhere to pray with holy hands lifted up to God, free from sin and anger and resentment.
–1 Timothy 2:8 (TLB)

We all have our triggers in life that activate negative emotions. A pool of negative emotions within ourselves is an incubator for procrastination, after all there is no logical or intelligent reason to procrastinate, but we do it anyway. I hate to admit it, but anger is often the characteristic that stirs my emotional cauldron. While I am modifying my behavior to overcome procrastination in key areas of my life, anger is still rearing its ugly head. In her internet article "Anger Can Lead to Procrastination," Chantal Beaupre, an "Emotional Mastery Coach" states, "Among the emotions that can lead us to procrastinate, you will probably be surprised to see me include hostility or anger... We can also conclude that the thought that causes our anger is always false, irrational, unrealistic." Often anger is triggered by unrealistic expectations not being met by ourselves, or others. It can also be a subtle form of revenge against those who unleash their anger on us. For example, you are deliberately stalling some report your boss wants because he berated you in front of your coworkers last week. Anger does not work the righteousness of God, anger caused Moses to be denied entrance into the Promised Land. Anger can lead to murder, and all kinds of horrific outcomes; it needs to be defused and extracted from one's heart and soul. It will not lead us anywhere that is good.

Dear Lord, When I think of all the anger that was unleashed upon your son who died on the cross for my sins, I need to take it personally. It was my anger that compounded his suffering. I need your help; I can't rid myself of this unholy fire within me on my own. Please let your love, mercy, and forgiveness be an overwhelming force that rises within me, quenching my temper. My fuse seems so short, help me to extinguish it before it explodes. Impart grace to me, so that I may be slow my anger. May I be quick to apologize to those whom I have injured because of this. I thank you in advance for my deliverance, knowing that you desire what is best for me. In Jesus' name... Amen.

AUGUST 16

Get Over Yourself

Then he told them what they could expect for themselves: "Anyone who intends to come with me has to let me lead. You're not in the driver's seat– I am. Don't run from suffering; embrace it. Follow me and I'll show you how. Self-help is no help at all. Self-sacrifice is the way, my way, to finding yourself, your true self.
–Luke 9:23–25 (MSG)

Our self-obsession with our fears, our perfectionism, or freedom to do whatever we want to do at any given moment, creates huge obstacles for overcoming procrastination. Is it really better to think you are a great undiscovered writer and never complete a writing project, or to finally finish that book and have it repeatedly rejected? Is it preferable to produce a creation that can never live up to your perfect standards, or to not write anything today because you have an insatiable desire to binge watch a favorite TV series? What we decide to do, or *not* to do today, can often be a tangled mess of personality factors and defects. Our procrastinating ways will never leave us without being *consciously* and *forcibly* evicted. We need to get over ourselves and just get on with the work that needs to be done. Twyla Tharp, distinguished choreographer, expresses this very well in the following quote:

> "Obviously, People are born with specific talents…
> But I don't like using genetics as an excuse.
> Get over yourself.
> The best creativity is the result
> of habit and hard work."

Dear Lord, I confess that sometimes it seems as if my flaws and faults are always before me, and sometimes I focus more on them than I do on you. They seem to hinder my vision of the path that you have set for me. Help me to get over this preoccupation with my Self. Let my focus be adjusted to you. Help me to work diligently. Let me give my fears, my desires, and my will over to you. Help me to accept life's sufferings, rejections, and disappointments, knowing that I am fully accepted by you. Let me lean into self-sacrifice, ignore my temporal yearnings, and continually accept your lordship over my life. In Jesus' name… Amen.

AUGUST 17

I'd Rather Be Radiant

I will extol the Lord at all times
His praise will always be on my lips.
I will glory in the Lord;
let the afflicted hear and rejoice...
I sought the Lord, and he answered me;
he delivered me from all my fears.
Those who look to him are radiant;
their faces are never covered with shame...
Taste and see that the Lord is good;
blessed is the one who takes refuge in him...

The Lord is close to the brokenhearted
and saves those who are crushed in spirit.
The righteous person may have many troubles,
but the Lord delivers him from them all...
The Lord will rescue his servants;
no one who takes refuge in him will be condemned.
–Psalm 34 (NIV)

Every once in a while, all the shame that my procrastination has cost me comes flashing back when starting to approach that emotional/situational territory again. My response now is, "God forbid that I would ever go there again!" I yearn to be free. Praise God! Why be in a place where you are letting yourself, others, and God down again? Why be covered in the muck and mire of dishonest excuses, failed obligations, aborted dreams. Why experience the fallout of being late again, and again?... Why be weighed down with shame, fear, crushed spirit, and condemnation, when you can be radiant? God has designed us to be radiant, to reflect his image. By every means necessary, let's be radiant!

Dear Lord, Help me to fully realize the benefits of being yours. Let me be quick to grab hold of your grace that rescues, delivers, and sets free. Let me taste the glory of praising you on my lips. Thank you for the refuge of your presence. Unlock your power to transform my life. Lead me to call upon you to be rescued, whenever I feel the need. Thank you for saving me... again and again. In Jesus' name... Amen.

AUGUST 18

Immediately

But Jesus immediately said to them: "Take courage! It is I. Don't be afraid."
–Matthew 14:27 (NIV)

Immediately her bleeding stopped and she felt in her body that she was freed from her suffering.
–Mark 5:29 (NIV)

As he walked along, he saw Levi son of Alphaeus sitting at the tax collector's booth. "Follow me," Jesus told him, and Levi got up and followed him.
–Mark 2:14 (NIV)

"God can do in a *second* what you have been unable to do alone for *years*!"
Christine Caine

Many thanks to Christine Caine's ministry for promoting this thought. The Bible has many examples of the power of God, or the power of someone's decision to follow God being able to alter their life in an instant. The apostle Paul's conversion comes to mind. When the Emancipation Proclamation was issued, the hopes, dreams, and longings of multitudes of slaves were fulfilled immediately. Did their initial freedom produce all they hoped? Probably not, many obstacles remained to acquire all that Lincoln's Proclamation promised. Sometimes we just need to have the faith to believe God has delivered us in an instant, and then have the courage to acquire it. Living a life free from the burden of procrastination sounds like the Promised Land to me, and certainly worth doing whatever it takes to possess it.

Dear Lord, Help me to have faith to realize that you can truly do in a second, what I have been unable to do in years. Let me work toward possessing all that you have provided for me. Help me to be a fit conduit for your power to do what needs to be done. In Jesus' name... Amen.

AUGUST 19

Don't Listen to The Monkey

No temptation has overtaken you except what is common to mankind. And God who is faithful; he will not let you be tempted beyond what you can bear. But when you are tempted, he will also provide a way out so that you can endure it.
–1 Corinthians 10:13 (NIV)

If you have not seen and heard the following video, you should do that today. At TED.com, Ted Urban: Inside the Mind of a Master Procrastinator, TED talk. Feb. 2016.

Tim Urban's thoughts, videos, lectures, and illustrations of the procrastinator's brain are full of truth and humor. His website is waitbutwhy.com. I believe his comical approach to recognizing difficult truths about our procrastinating selves is of inestimable value. He has introduced many procrastinators to the *Instant Gratification Monkey* part of our brain. Here are his words: "Now what is going on here? The Instant Gratification Monkey does not seem like a guy you want behind the wheel. He lives entirely in the present moment. He has no memory of the past, no knowledge of the future, and he cares only about two things: easy and fun."

While I was in college this monkey was constantly at the wheel, driving my life. The result was lots of fun, but also hangovers, late assignments, all night cram sessions, and regrets. We need to realize that there will always be the monkey in us just wanting to have fun, but letting him take charge of our life, BIG mistake. Another name for the monkey could be "Temptation." An illustration of the monkey at the wheel of a person's life is on the door to my den. It helps me to confront the monkey in me. When the stick figure man says, "This is a perfect time to get some work done." and the monkey says "Nope." I say out loud, "Yes, this is the perfect time to get some work done!"

Dear Lord, Help me to be aware of temptations in my life. Sometimes I give in so quickly I don't even realize that certain things have the ability to take me away from you and to sabotage my goals in life. Help me to say, "No," to alluring distractions. Give me wisdom and discernment to guide my way. Help me to see the consequences for all of my actions, and do not let me gravitate toward what is easy and fun, when I should be doing something else. In Jesus' name... Amen.

AUGUST 20

Getting Unstuck

For God is not a God of confusion but of peace. As in all the churches of the saints...
–1 Corinthians 14:33 (RSV)

For where there is envying and strife, there is confusion and every evil work.
–James 3:16 (MEV)

You will keep him in perfect peace, whose mind is stayed on You, because he trusts in You.
–Isaiah 26:3 (MEV)

Algebra class frequently put me into a state of confusion, staring at a problem without a clue of what to do next. Nothing makes me stuck and unable to move forward more than confusion. That feeling of mental turmoil is awful. When life is peaceful and calm it seems rather simple as to what to do, and what needs to be done next. When goals are fuzzy and too many unmade decisions and undone obligations are swirling around in our heads, how can we move forward? There needs to be time set aside to gain insight into priorities. We need to know God's will and how to put one foot in front of the other to get where we need to go. Freeing ourselves from the sticky web of confusion and muddled thinking is necessary. The source of an individual's procrastination really does vary from person to person, sometimes it is just being stuck, and not knowing how to get free. In my times of greatest confusion, when critical decisions were looming overhead, God came through and gave me clarity as I sought his peace, his will, and his way for me to go. At times the way out was as simple as just making a list. Thankfully, those times have solidified my trust in Him.

Dear Lord, I thank you that you provide a way of freedom from a web of mental upheaval and uncertainty. As we put all our efforts and decisions at your feet in an attitude of surrender, lead us on a productive path that gives us peace. Help us to generate daily time in your Word and seek your presence, so that we may develop a sensitivity as to where your Holy Spirit is leading us. May you always provide clarity to release us from times of confusion. May your peace be our guide. I thank you and praise you because you deliver us from evil, and you shine your light on our path. In Jesus' name. Amen

AUGUST 21

More of Him

John answered, "No one can receive anything except what is given him from heaven. You yourselves bear me witness, that I said, I am not the Christ, but I have been sent before him. He who has the bride is the bridegroom; the friend of the bridegroom, who stands and hears him, rejoices greatly at the bridegroom's voice; therefore this joy of mine is now full. He must increase, and I must decrease."

–John 3:27—30 (RSV)

"He must increase, and I must decrease." This is a heartfelt sentiment that all Christians should declare. We don't want to be like a jealous bridesmaid or groomsman, who wishes that they were the one getting married. The most ardent desire of the followers of Jesus should be to have Jesus increase within us. As the Lord increases within us, we will then be able to shine the light of God's truth, love, and forgiveness into a dark world blinded by hurt and sin. John the Baptist was willing to lay down his celebrity status, give away his disciples and sacrifice his life, even though near the end of his life he didn't live to see the fulfillment of his mission completed. What do we need to sacrifice? How do we become more effective witnesses? What are we doing for the benefit of others? How do I decrease the *Me* and increase Jesus within me?

Dear Lord, Teach me ways to increase Jesus within, and to decrease myself. Help me to let go of things in my life that I have assigned value to, that hold little value in your eyes. Grant me the grace to be happy for others as they achieve their hopes and dreams, while mine are still not realized. Tune my ears to hear your voice with clarity, so that I will be more responsive to your words. Show me ways to increase your presence within, so that I may be more effective in being your vessel. Help me become more like your son, pouring out your love, mercy, truth, and grace to those around me. In Jesus' name… Amen.

AUGUST 22

Don't Want to Miss It

From the rising of the sun to the place where it sets, the name of the Lord is to be praised.
–Psalm 113:3 (NIV)

The day is yours, and yours also the night; you established the sun and the moon.
–Psalm 74:16 (NIV)

For the Lord God is a sun and shield; the Lord bestows favor and honor; no good thing will he withhold from those whose walk is blameless.
–Psalm 84:11 (NIV)

On August 21, 2017 Americans had the privilege of viewing a solar eclipse, a total one in some areas; likely a once in a lifetime event for most people. Information about the path of the total eclipse was available far in advance. What I *could have* done was get my special glasses ahead of time, drive an easy day trip to the beautiful city of Charleston, South Carolina and witness this event in its "total splendor." What did I do? Unfortunately, not that. That would have been awesome!

On eclipse day, running late to get my glasses, employees at 7-11 told me that they had none left, while they viewed the start of the eclipse on their own NASA approved ones! I made it to a local library that ran out of glasses an hour before I arrived, then had to borrow from other people (more prepared than me) a few seconds at a time, to witness an 86% Eclipse. I missed out! If I had not procrastinated it could have been a great day, instead of one more example of how procrastination sabotaged me once again. Sigh...

Dear Lord, We need you so much, in the big and small areas of our lives. Help us to obtain all the amazing "once in a lifetime" events that you have provided for us. As we observe the complexities and wonders of your creation, may we praise you for the world that you have made. Help us to vanquish the foe that we let undermine us, again and again. Help us to become more aware of what needs to be done in advance, so that we don't live with a multitude of regrets. In Jesus' name... Amen.

AUGUST 23

The Lord Answers

May the Lord answer you when you are in trouble!
May the God of Jacob protect you!...

May he accept all your offerings
and be pleased by your sacrifices.

May he give you what you desire
and make all your plans succeed.

Then we will shout for joy over your victory
and celebrate your triumph by praising God.

May the Lord answer all your requests.
–Psalm 20:1—5 (GNT)

After reading, and meditating on these words,
it seems as if the best thing to do is simply pray.

Dear Lord, I am constantly aware of how much I need you. Help me to recall all the times that you have come to my rescue, so that I could have faith in facing any situation. Let these words of David be my prayer. Let me never be ashamed to bring all my requests to you, big or small. Let your Holy Spirit guide me as to your will; let your desires for me grow in my heart, and may my selfish desires fade away. Give me success and the joy of victory, so I can boldly proclaim your praise, and be quick to share a triumphant testimony. In Jesus' name... Amen.

AUGUST 24

Help and Hope

Let me see how mighty and glorious you are.
Your constant love is better than life itself,
and so I will praise you.

I will give you thanks as long as I live;
I will raise my hands to you in prayer.
My soul will feast and be satisfied,

and I will sing glad songs of praise to you...
because you have always been my help.
–Psalm 63:2—7 (GNT)

There are so many emotional factors that can contribute to a person's procrastination: fear of failure or success, perfectionism stress, immaturity, hedonistic bent, rebelliousness, a sense of ultimate futility-as if nothing one ever does will make a significant difference. Add poor time management or attention deficit disorder in there and all of these personal traits produce fertile emotional soil for procrastination. We need healing, courage, and victory over our decision making that consistently defaults to avoidance or pleasure. We also need good time management tools, submission to God's authority, an openness to recognize the root of our defective ways and willingness to do the work of freeing ourselves. God is our source of restorative love, constant care, help and hope. Spending time flowing with praise that energizes our souls with thankfulness and joy, is the path toward emotional healing which produces the power to transform our lives.

Dear Lord, I confess that sometimes I feel overwhelmed with the emotional forces that hinder me. I find my hopes dashed, my expectations for positive change seemingly futile, and victory out of reach. Help me to realize that it is your desire to heal me from the inside out, that your love is absolutely relentless. Open my eyes to the power of praise and thanksgiving, so that I may experience the strength that comes from the joy of being in you. Bless me with hope and courage, that I would experience victory today, and build victory upon victory in my tomorrows. In Jesus' name... Amen.

AUGUST 25

Just Roll with the Embarrassment

And let the peace of Christ rule in your hearts, to which indeed you were called in one body. And be thankful.
–Colossians 3:15 (ESV)

I do not cease to give thanks for you, remembering you in my prayers,
–Ephesians 1:16 (ESV)

If I partake with thankfulness, why am I denounced because of that for which I give thanks?
–1 Corinthians 10:30 (ESV)

During June many couples are married, babies are born, many graduates emerge from high school or college. There is also the giving of gifts. The appropriate response to receiving these gifts, is the timely production of "Thank You" cards. I realize this concept may be a bit *old school,* but according to common good manners, still expected. I know someone that has a thank you card in the mail before the gift can even be put away, others who received gifts in May or June, see September winding down and still no thank you cards out. Showing our thankfulness in writing, within an appropriate time frame, is a good litmus test for our level of procrastination. As the appropriate time fades into months after the event, embarrassment morphs into a "what's the point now?" attitude. If this is you, just roll with the embarrassment, realize that once again negative results have been unleashed by your negative ways; just do the right thing to show your appreciation today, and do not let a simple act of gratitude like this slip into too many tomorrows again.

Dear Lord, Grow within me a grateful heart. Help me to realize the importance of showing thankfulness to you for all that you have done, and thankfulness to others for the goodness that they have shown to me. Help me to be someone who is ready to show my gratitude and prompt me before my delays turn into an embarrassment. With your help, I can have victory in small areas that can lead to big positive changes. Let me be quick to give thanks. In Jesus' name... Amen.

AUGUST 26

Armed to Overcome

For whoever is born of God overcomes the world, and the victory that overcomes the world is our faith. Who is it that overcomes the world, but the one who believes that Jesus is the Son of God.
–1 John 5:4—5 (MEV)

You are of God, little children, and have overcome them, because He who is in you is greater than he who is in the world.
–1 John 4:4 (MEV)

We can all just stay where we are in life. We may drift, stagnate, or become inconsequential for any greater purpose, if we want. Certainly, that is not what God intends for us, but even after coming to faith in Jesus as our Lord and Savior, we have free will. I don't think God intends his children to become the human equivalent of pond scum or end up in front of a video screen 24-7. Possibly, the *Old Testament* is full of so many wars and bloody outcomes to make us wake up to the fact that life is often a battle. According to Webster's dictionary, to *overcome* means to win a victory over, or to gain control of through great effort. When the children of Israel repented and sought God, then followed his plans they were victorious. No matter what form the enemy takes in our lives, God wants us to overcome and live in victory. We must all be willing warriors, ready to make His Kingdom come, His will be done on earth as it is in heaven.

Dear Lord, You are sovereign, and you reign eternally over all creation. I thank you that though we are dust, you allow your greatness to dwell within us. You have chosen to dwell within me! Help us realize that the power of our faith, coupled with your Spirit inside of us, assures us of victory. Help us to be willing to engage in the struggle against enemies that would confound us and hinder our godly purpose. Whether those enemies are our own sinful ways, or spiritual forces with deadly agendas, help us to see these enemies for what they truly are, and to never quit before a victory is ours. In Jesus' name... Amen.

AUGUST 27

Good Intentions Plus

He thought of everything, provided for everything we could possibly need, letting us in on the plans he took such delight in making. He set it all out before us in Christ, a long-range plan in which everything would be brought together and summed up in him, everything in deepest heaven, everything on planet earth.
–Ephesians 1:8—10 (MSG)

My dear children, you come from God and belong to God. You have already won a big victory over those false teachers, for the Spirit in you is far stronger than anything in the world.
–1 John 4:4 (MSG)

"Good intentions without a good strategy leads to poor results."

The preceding statement is a quote from the movie, *The War Room*. Our good intentions often become our most frequent excuses. "Well, at least I had good intentions," just doesn't get the job done. We belong to God, and the Holy Spirit is within us. If we are on the path to being productive without panic-inducing motivation, and with keeping our word, and with accomplishing what God created us to do, we need a strategy that will lead us to victory. A good plan is far better than good intentions.

Dear Lord, Help us to know deeply in our hearts that you have provided everything we need. We are part of your plan; please guide us in making a strategic blueprint that will enable us to overcome our weaknesses and strengthen our strengths. Keep us from the deception of good intentions. Let us not be haphazard, but purposeful in our efforts to rid ourselves of procrastination. Impress upon us the necessity, and the power, of fervent prayer. May we increase our times of intercessions for others, as we overcome our personal obstacles. May prayer become the foundation of our battle plan to defeat habits, emotions, and inclinations that rob us of what is best for our lives. In Jesus' name... Amen.

AUGUST 28

You Are Needed

If the whole body were an ear, where would the sense of smell be? But in fact God has placed the parts in the body, every one of them, just as he wanted them to be. If they were all one part, where would the body be? As it is, there are many parts, but one body. The eye cannot say to the hand, "I don't need you!" And the head cannot say to the feet, "I don't need you!"
–1 Corinthians 12:17–22 (NIV)

And who knows but that you have come to your royal position for such a time as this?
–Esther 4:14 (NIV)

As I look around my church on a Sunday morning, it amazes me how it all comes together. So many people are needed and there is so much to do. Whether we are in the inner circle of leadership, or on the fringe setting up the coffee; all roles contribute. Some people are overly concerned with the lack of "feeling called" into a certain role, so they sit by and do nothing. Others over commit and can barely arrive on time to do their part. Sometimes procrastinators do not want to be found out, so they let fear of failure hold them back. Serving is part of being a Christian and you are needed! Practice the ways and means that will help you defeat procrastination. Commit to a small part of a purposed-filled body of believers, stick to your role and be on time. You are needed, and you need small victories that will lead to larger triumphs.

Dear Lord, Help us to step forward into active roles in our church. Let us see the importance of every task, and do not let our pride determine the roles that we seek, or we avoid. Lead us to serve in ways that our gifts will be most fully utilized. Let us seek to help others, fulfill the needs of our church and local community, and take joy in being a valuable part of something greater than ourselves. In Jesus' name... Amen.

AUGUST 29

He Promised

The Lord gave this command to Joshua, son of Nun: "Be strong and courageous, for you will bring the Israelites into the land I promised them on oath, and I myself will be with you."
–Deuteronomy 31:23 (NIV)

You need to persevere so that when you have done the will of God, you will receive what he has promised.... "But my righteous one will live by faith. And I take no pleasure in the one who shrinks back." But we do not belong to those who shrink back and are destroyed, but to those who have faith and are saved.
–Hebrews 10: 36—39 (NIV)

There have been so many times when I thought I heard from God, then doubt crept in. Did I really hear from God, or just imagine hearing what I wanted to hear? One thing is sure, it is better to be on the side of faith and enter into the good things of the Promised Land, than to die out in the desert wandering around, doubting God and his goodness. Of the great multitude of Hebrews who walked out of slavery from Egypt, there were only two adult men who made it into the Promised Land! We need to be like those two. Joshua and Caleb believed in God's Word even when it took forty years before it came to pass. At times they must have thought, *It just may happen today!* We do not know the day of fulfillment. That's when faith and trust fortify us to hope that each new day, truly could be the day, that we see God's promise come to pass.

Dear Lord, Let us seek your presence. Let us not give up on the promises we are holding on to. Bring us into a foretaste of what you have prepared for us, so we do not lose heart or lose faith. Give us the steadfastness of Abraham, Joshua, and Caleb, to help us put our doubts aside. Bring us to a place where we are no longer slaves to our faltering ways, but obedient servants that will enter into all that you have promised to those who follow you. In Jesus' name... Amen.

AUGUST 30

Stay Close

If you seek GOD, your God, you'll be able to find him if you are serious, looking for him with your whole heart and soul... GOD, your God, is above all a compassionate God. In the end he will not abandon you.
–Deuteronomy 4:29—31 (MSG)

Come near to God and he will come near to you.
–James 4:8 (NIV)

When life doesn't seem to be going the way we want it to, it may seem as if God is far away, but that is not true. As we seek God, God comes close to us! He will be there, not only when we want God in our corner, but because he seeks us. We are that *one* lost sheep that the shepherd goes after, leaving the ninety-nine unattended. We are that prodigal son, that the father is looking for down the road, and running toward when he first catches a glimpse of his lost child. If Christ died for us, while we were yet sinners, it should not be hard to accept that our loving Father God is constantly seeking our presence, moving toward us, waiting for us to come home to him. With God on our side, so near and so immediately available to us, his help is surely there to aid us in realizing any goal we are called to achieve. Being close to God brings confidence into our challenging times.

Dear Lord, I thank you and praise you for being a loving, compassionate God. You come after us when we have strayed. Your love calls us into a relationship that is worth seeking. May our bond to you become stronger, deeper, and more full of love every day. May our seeking you produce an increasing acceptance of your will. May I always realize that you are an ever-present help, available and close to me in every moment. As I seek you, grant me the vision and tactics to confidently overcome all obstacles to your will for my life. In Jesus' name... Amen.

AUGUST 31

Roll Up Our Sleeves

A good woman is hard to find, and worth far more than diamonds. Her husband trusts her without reserve, and never has reason to regret it. Never spiteful, she treats him generously all her life long. She shops around for the best yarns and cottons... She's up before dawn, preparing breakfast for her family and organizing her day. She looks over a field and buys it, then, with money she's put aside, plants a garden. First thing in the morning, she dresses for work, rolls up her sleeves, eager to get started.... She's quick to assist anyone in need, reaches out to help the poor.
–Proverbs 31:10—20 (MSG)

It matters not if you are male or female, the "good woman" in Proverbs 31 is an example worth emulating. She is a role model living by standards hard to attain, but her ways are an example of a blessed life. She has a good spouse, is a hard worker even though she has servants, and she has plenty of money along with the wisdom of how to handle it. I'd like to be like her! Being wise in handling time and money is not only virtuous; it is a big part of having a life that is blessed. After all she is generous, well prepared, good at managing people, eager to start her day, knows a good investment, helps others, and has a heart for the poor. It is hard to imagine that any Christian would not want to be like her.

Dear Lord, Help me to be more like the Proverbs 31 woman. Remind me of the cost of being lax in paying off my financial obligations. Help me to be smart in my spending. Give me the wisdom to realize that proper management of time and money go hand in hand. Help me change my ways. Help me to keep my priorities and choices in line with your Word. May I have times of rest, but not be lazy, and have times of hard work without being too hard on myself. Help me to rise up early enough to make my days efficient and to give myself a healthy amount of sleep. As I acknowledge you and your ways with gratitude, may I walk daily in the blessings that you desire me to have. In Jesus' name... Amen.

SEPTEMBER 1

To Do for You

"Do for others what you want them to do for you. This is the teaching of the law of Moses in a nutshell."
–Matthew 7:9 (TLB)

Let everyone see that you are unselfish and considerate in all you do.
–Philippians 4:5 (TLB)

I don't mean to say I am perfect. I haven't learned all I should even yet, but I keep working toward that day when I will finally be all that Christ saved me for and wants me to be.
–Philippians 3:12 (TLB)

The book, *Procrastination- Deal With It: All in Good Time,* written by Diane Peters, is a simple presentation of the facts and problems associated with procrastination and perfectionism. Aimed at young people, it is full of myths, facts, statistics, and relational illustrations of the impact of procrastination; it is also beneficial reading for adults. One popular myth is, "When I procrastinate, I'm only hurting myself." Not true. The stress you create often has a negative impact on those closest to you. It is hard on others to feel that they cannot depend on you or trust you. If you are a member of a carpool that is always late when it is your turn to drive, or your kids feel devalued because they are always the last ones "waiting forever" to be picked up, you are hurting others. The sibling of someone who rarely pulls their fair share of work around the house knows that their reality often disproves this selfish myth. Procrastinators simply do not "do unto others" as they would have done to themselves.

Dear Lord, Help me to realize that procrastination not only affects me, but it affects others as well. I want to treat others the way I want to be treated, but I confess in this aspect of my life I do not always do that. Forgive me for the anxiety and tension that I bring into the lives of those closest to me as I perform tasks under pressure, or when waiting until the last minute, I make myself or others late. Help me to see clearly what my bad habit costs others and lead me to put their needs first. Help me to always do unto others, as I would have them do unto me. In Jesus' name... Amen.

SEPTEMBER 2

Rising in Fellowship

The eternal life which was with the Father and was made manifest to us–that which we have seen and heard we proclaim to you, so that you may have fellowship with us; and our fellowship is with the Father and with his Son Jesus Christ. And we are writing this that our joy may be complete.
–John 1:2—4 (RSV)

For a righteous man falls seven times, and rises again; but the wicked are overthrown by calamity.
–Proverbs 24:16 (RSV)

We all fall. As the Bible says, all sin and fall short of the glory of God. Falling down off the narrow path is simply being human. Even Jesus fell as he carried his heavy cross. He was able to get on his feet again because someone helped him. We all need help. When we are down, in a place that we should not be, the most important thing to do is to rise up. Having fellowship with God through our relationship with Jesus, and having the fellowship and support of other believers, is one of the best ways to rise up again. Our fellowship of faith in Christ is a very powerful network we possess in this life. It is wisdom for us to use it when we need it.

Dear Lord, I thank you for creating a vast family of believers all over the world, and you have made me an integral part. Let me be quick to extend the hand of fellowship, quick to encourage and help others rise above their oppressive circumstances. I thank you for the joy experienced in the company of brothers and sisters in the Lord. I will be ever grateful for the times someone was there for me, to clarify the truth, to give sincere encouragement, to lift me up after I fell. Today, let me rise up if I fall and let me be the one to help someone else rise up again. In Jesus' name... Amen.

SEPTEMBER 3

A Hug from God

"Look! Your God!"
Look at him! God, the Master, comes in power,
ready to go into action.
He is going to pay back his enemies
and reward those who have loved him.
Like a shepherd, he will care for his flock,
gathering the lambs in his arms,
Hugging them as he carries them…

Why would you ever complain… saying,
"God has lost track of me.
He doesn't care what happens to me"?
Don't you know anything? Haven't you been listening?
God doesn't come and go. God lasts.
He's Creator of all you can see or imagine.
He doesn't get tired out, doesn't pause to catch his breath.
And he knows everything, inside and out.
–Isaiah 40:9—11, 27—29 (MSG)

Many experts on procrastination say that those who have low self-esteem are often procrastinators. The subconscious mind would rather delay, not attempt at all, or refuse to risk a possible great reward, rather than feel like a failure. Fear of failure is one of the more common characteristics of procrastinators, and often they don't even realize that is why they are that way. God knows. He sees every strength and every flaw; it matters not to him. He loves us. We don't have to perform to a certain standard to earn his love. He loves us because we are his. He sees all our sins and failures and still loves us with an unending love. We need to be willing to risk failure, otherwise we will never taste success.

Dear Lord, Help me to keep this picture of you in my mind. Like a good shepherd, you lead us, guide us, provide for us, carry us, hug us close to your heart in tender protective love. Let the security I have in my relationship to you, erase my fears. Help me to stop falling short in my efforts, and help me to be willing to risk failure, knowing that no matter what happens, you are always there to pick me up. My fears will come and go, I thank you that you are with me forever. In Jesus' name… Amen.

SEPTEMBER 4

Night is Coming

He also who is slack in his work is brother to him that destroys.
–Proverbs 18:9 (NASB)

Give her the product of her hands, and let her works be praised in the gates.
–Proverbs 31:31 (NASB)

We must work the works of Him who sent Me as long as it is day; night is coming when no one can work.
–John 9:4 (NASB)

Life is so much easier when you work when you are supposed to work, then play, then rest and sleep when your day is done. The art of cramming has been a specialty of mine. My way was to cram as much fun into a day as I possibly could, leave too much work undone, then be tired, and produce a substandard effort in the wee hours of the morning. Naturally, this left me dragging myself around the next day. As a young college student, I could cram for exams better than anyone I knew, and pulling an all-night study session was far too common. As one ages, that lifestyle takes its toll, whether too much coffee, energy drinks or prescription drugs are involved to fuel it or not. Often procrastination is simply the result of not wanting to do the work when it should be done. We need to remember, workers thrive in God's kingdom, and slackers get left behind.

Dear Lord, Help us to realize that you have set forth a model for us to follow in your Word. Work first! Prod us to attend to our assigned tasks, to be diligent, to produce efforts and finish products worthy of honor. Let our work ethic reflect how much we value your approval. Help us to change bad habits of "play before work," into "work before play." You tell us that the harvest is ripe, but the laborers are few. Transform us into the kind of laborer that you want us to be. In Jesus' name… Amen.

SEPTEMBER 5

Power to Heal

I, the Messiah, have authority on earth to forgive sins. But talk is cheap–anybody could say that. So I'll prove it to you by healing this man.
–Luke 5:23 (TLB)

Everyone was trying to touch him, for when they did, healing power went out from him and they were cured.
–Luke 6:19 (TLB)

We should all know that Jesus came to heal the sick and free us from our sins. At times our sins are linked to our illnesses. During my college years, I was a typical example of the following profile of the procrastinating university student. According to information in Diane Peters' book, *Procrastination- Deal with It: All in Good Time,* here are some facts:

> *About 70% of university students are habitual procrastinators.
>
> *A study out of Carleton University in Ottawa found that students who tend to procrastinate have more digestive problems and sleep disorders.
>
> *Procrastinators are also more likely to get very sick when they come down with a cold or the flu. And, according to the same study they also smoke, drink, and use drugs more than people that don't procrastinate.

The power to heal ourselves from the consequences of our bad habit, starts with us. Do we really want to change, do we really want to be free? If we do, we need to press into Jesus, ignite his power to heal by our determination to receive deliverance. We start the process by realizing we have the power to heal ourselves by our choices and need to take the first step toward receiving a healing touch from Jesus.

Dear Lord, I confess that sometimes I do not see my procrastination as sin, so I have not really done the work I need to do to be rid of it. Help me to see the true cost of procrastination within myself. Let me acknowledge the physical impact of the stress, anxiety, worry, and the guilt of covering up my mistakes. Instill in me a desire to be healed from the physical, emotional, and relational injuries caused by my procrastination. In Jesus' name... Amen.

SEPTEMBER 6

On Guard

The Lord is at hand; do not be anxious about anything, but in everything by prayer and supplication with thanksgiving let your requests be made known to God. And the peace of God, which surpasses all understanding, will guard your hearts and minds in Christ Jesus
–Philippians 4:5—7 (ESV)

May he grant you your heart's desire and fulfill your plans!
–Psalm 20:4 (ESV)

You who seek God, let your hearts revive.
–Psalm 69:32 (ESV)

Setting up one's personal boundaries and plans is a good way to stay focused and emotionally protected. Personally, I have not been very good at either. One can be too open, too last minute, too whatever, to be good at guarding the heart. Procrastinators occupy a territory that comes with anxiety, stress, and regrets over unfulfilled plans. Today is the time to change, and time to protect our hearts. God's Word promises us peace if we guard our hearts and seek him with thanksgiving and prayer. Time to set new boundaries, make new plans, and strengthen the guard. Peace holds far more attraction to me today than postponement.

Dear Lord, I confess that I want revival in my heart. Now I desire peace over having things my own way from minute to minute. Help me to secure personal boundaries and realistic plans in order to guard and protect my already wounded heart. Deliver me from anxiety, from creating unnecessary time pressures. Give me discernment to make your plans, my plans. As your peace increases within my own heart, make me an instrument to share your peace with others. In Jesus' name… Amen.

SEPTEMBER 7

Watching My Step

God made my life complete when I placed all the pieces before him.
When I got my act together, he gave me a fresh start.
Now I'm alert to GOD's ways; I don't take God for granted.
Every day I review the way he works; I try not to miss a trick.
I feel put back together, and I'm watching my step.
GOD rewrote the text of my life when I opened the book of my heart to his eyes.
–Psalm 18:20—24 (MSG)

If our life feels in pieces, God can put it all together when we open the book of our heart to his eyes. The Message version provides us with a perspective-altering beautiful metaphor here. This psalm provides a prescription for wholeness. Place ALL your pieces before God, not just your good ones. As we work to bring ourselves together, He provides a fresh start. Never take God for granted, but be mindful and alert to all his ways. As we watch our step, doing what we are created to do, that sense of *having it together,* replaces falling apart. Jesus has written our name in the Lamb's Book of Life. He rewrites our story with a glorious ending. Opening up to God naturally closes off the lure of ungodly distractions and thoughts. Our steps become ordered on a narrow path which keeps us together, moving in the right direction.

Dear Lord, I thank you that you desire what is best for me. Help me to keep in step with you, and your plans for my life. As I expose myself totally to you, as I am honest in my confessions, let me see myself as you see me. Let your plan continuously unfold before me. Help me to accomplish a completed life, step by step, today, tomorrow, and all the days of my life. In Jesus' name... Amen.

SEPTEMBER 8

My Teacher Knows the Way

Make me to know thy ways, O Lord; teach me thy paths.
Lead me in thy truth, and teach me, for thou art the God of my salvation...
Remember not the sins of my youth, or my transgressions; according to thy steadfast love remember me...
Good and upright is the Lord; therefore he instructs sinners in the way.
He leads the humble in what is right, and teaches the humble his way.
All the paths of the Lord are steadfast love and faithfulness...
–Psalm 25:4—10 (RSV)

A very difficult obstacle in following the Lord, and being on the right path, is when your sins are ever before you. Past mistakes, fear, lack of faith to overcome your habitual self-defeating ways, can darken the light that God shines to guide us. While our shortcomings scream for our attention, how can we hear the Lord? God teaches us how to do what needs to be done. In times of praise and worship, he is magnified, and our failures become like a burnt offering. His Word cleanses our mind and helps us to keep negative thoughts from assaulting us. Our honesty and humility keep us receptive to God's transforming power. On the Lord's path is steadfast love, faithfulness, and forgiveness. Eventually we get to the place where we see ourselves as God sees us.

Dear Lord, Help me to dismiss all obstacles in my way. Transform my thinking, cleanse my mind, and replace memories of my past sins and mistakes by the healing power of your love and forgiveness. Free me from self-defeating habits. Lead me into an arena of victory, so that monuments of your deliverance and power to overcome will illuminate the path that you have brightly set before me. You are my teacher. Help me to humbly sit at your feet and learn from you. In Jesus' name... Amen.

SEPTEMBER 9

Ending the Feud

A wise man controls his temper. He knows that anger causes mistakes.
–Proverbs 14:29 (TLB)

As parts of the same body, our anger against each other has disappeared, for both of us have been reconciled to God. And so the feud ended at the cross.
–Ephesians 2:16 (TLB)

Dear brothers, don't ever forget that it is best to listen much, speak little, and not become angry; for anger doesn't make us good, as God demands we must be. So get rid of all wrong in your life, both inside and out, and humbly be glad for the wonderful message we have received, for it is able to save our souls as it takes hold of our hearts.
–James 1:19–21(TLB)

We should, "not become angry; for anger doesn't make us any good." Easier said than done. For procrastinators like me, who have a perfectionist bent, we hate making mistakes! We get extremely angry at ourselves, which supplies an inner reservoir of anger that can erupt all too easily. This internal source needs an outlet. Does it erupt in road rage? People we live with? Mental and verbal deluges of self-condemnation? Often inanimate objects like a malfunctioning computer become the victim of my sound and fury. Anger, and my lack of ability to forgive myself for my own mistakes, creates a barrier to my freedom from procrastination. Research by Timothy Pycyhl and others show that one of the most effective things we can do is to forgive ourselves. Reducing guilt and feelings of failure and anger, make us emotionally fit, and decreases the triggers for our procrastinating ways.

Dear Lord, I lay my anger before you. Help me to purge this destructive emotion from myself. Too often it is misplaced against me, against others, and you. Help me to see a way to rescue myself, rather than be angry at you for not rescuing me. You rescued me by nailing my guilt, my sins, my failures, and my anger to the cross. You took all that is not pleasing and productive and covered me in forgiveness. Let the wonderful message of your salvation brilliantly block out my anger and replace self-condemnation with peace. Let me not be like a tantruming child; help me to be a grateful servant with a glad heart. In Jesus' name... Amen.

SEPTEMBER 10

Procrastination-Patience Process

Being strengthened with all power according to his glorious might so that you may have great endurance and patience...
–Colossians 1:11 (NIV)

Therefore, as God's chosen people, holy and dearly loved, clothe yourselves with compassion, kindness, humility, gentleness and patience.
–Colossians 3:12 (NIV)

We do not want you to become lazy, but to imitate those who through faith and patience inherit what has been promised.
–Hebrews 6:12 (NIV)

There seems to be a tension between patience and procrastination when it comes to the creative process. It is not patient of me to keep an idea for a script in my head for a decade before writing it down, that is procrastination. Once the script is actually finished, and I continue to pursue avenues to produce my movie, that will require patience. Sometimes we procrastinate on projects due to a *What does it matter anyway?* type of attitude. Patience reminds us that being overly attached to immediate results causes additional anxiety and frustration. If the farmer procrastinates and doesn't plant in time, woe is he at harvest time. If his seeds are planted on time, patience puts negative emotions in neutral while waiting for the harvest. The x-factor in the procrastination-patience relationship equation is anxiety. More procrastination equals more stress and anxiety, less productivity. More patience equals more peace, less anxiety. In our battle to defeat our procrastination we need to find a way to fit patience into our emotional arsenal. Many times, patient people are the ones that have the endurance to prevail, while procrastinators often quit before they can finish.

Dear Lord, It is such a privilege to be chosen by you. You have called me to be productive, and to create a life complete with works that will expand your kingdom. May I never be lazy, may I never be dissuaded from working because of a defeatist attitude. Remind me that you have created me to be: holy, compassionate, humble, gentle, and patient. I confess that often I am not. Help me to consciously develop patience and gentleness, toward myself as well as others. Let your presence be a source of still waters deep within my soul, and let peace and patience prevail in trying situations. In Jesus' name... Amen.

SEPTEMBER 11

Mr. Fredrickson's Folly

[There Will Be No Delay] The word of the Lord came to me: "Son of man, what is this proverb you have in the land of Israel: 'The days go by and every vision comes to nothing'? Say to them, 'This is what the Sovereign Lord says: I am going to put an end to this proverb, and they will no longer quote it in Israel.' Say to them, 'The days are near when every vision will be fulfilled....
–Ezekiel 12:21-28 (NIV)

Hope deferred makes the heart sick, but a longing fulfilled is a tree of life.
–Proverbs 13:12 (NIV)

In the heart-warming movie *UP*, Ellie and Carl Fredrickson continue to put money aside in a coin jar to visit Paradise Falls, somewhere in South America. Sadly, due to procrastination and the ups and downs of life, this jar ends up gathering dust on the shelf. The pain of his life-long goal being unfulfilled and facing exile to a nursing home, an elderly Mr. Fredrickson is finally motivated to risk everything to float away to South America. Only now, he is without his beloved wife. Why do we let these longings just sit there, unrealized and unfulfilled? It hurts us, and the hurt grows deeper the longer these desires are unfulfilled. They may be put aside until all possibility of realization has evaporated, or... we can make them happen! Whether your desire is: to take a helicopter flight, see Paris, go to college, write a book, or hike the Appalachian Trail, just do it! Do it as soon as you can make it happen. Create a plan and follow through, let there be no delay. Let there be fulfillment instead of folly.

Dear Lord, Help us to not be in a waiting mode that extends on and on. Direct us to a way of fulfilling our desires. Help us to take the steps we need to set our priorities. Guide us, so that we may accumulate life's blessings, instead of a string of regrets. It is one thing to procrastinate and put something aside for a season, but it is quite another thing to live an entire life without doing what needs to be done to nourish our souls. Please bring us to a place where we can experience the gratification of a goal accomplished, or an adventure achieved. In Jesus' name... Amen.

SEPTEMBER 12

Not A Sin?

It is like a man going on a journey, when he leaves home and puts his servants in charge, each with his work, and commands the doorkeeper to stay awake.
–Mark 13:34 (ESV)

Blessed are those servants whom the master finds awake when he comes. Truly, I say to you, he will dress himself for service and have them recline at table, and he will come to serve them.
–Luke 12:37 (ESV)

Live as free people who are free, not using your freedom as a cover-up for evil, but living as servants of God.
–1 Peter 2:16 (ESV)

During a recent discussion about procrastination someone said to me, "I really don't think it is a sin." Of course, there is not a commandment, "Thou shalt not procrastinate!" But if sin merely means "missing the mark," as so many preachers have told me, then it is sin. It is one of those issues rarely addressed as vitally important within the church. When adultery, rampant greed, abuse, divorce, addictions, and violent acts are so obviously detrimental to our society, why is it even worthy of discussion? Our life's goal should be to hear Jesus utter those precious words to us, "Well done good and faithful servant." What kind of servants are we if we: ignore his directions, leave our work unstarted or unfinished, do not keep our word, are sleeping when we should be working, harming others with our unmet deadlines, jolting through life energized by anxiety and emotional pressure, leaving our assigned work for others to do, or if we lie to ourselves and others to cover our mistakes? Good servants do not avoid what needs to be done.

Dear Lord, Grant me ears to hear what you would say to me. How can I serve you this day? What work should I start? What assignment do I need to finish? What unmet obligations do I need to rectify? Let your word dwell in me, making me and molding me into your image. Let me be the kind of servant quick to obey, doing the very most with what you have put in my hands to do. Let me be prone to confess my mistakes, instead of covering them up. You have given me an example of how to live my life. Let me shine as a reflection of who you are, that I may guide others to you. In Jesus' name... Amen.

SEPTEMBER 13

Time to Trample

"They will fight against you but will not overcome you, for I am with you and will rescue you," declares the Lord.
–Jeremiah 1:19 (NIV)

I have given you authority to trample on snakes and scorpions and to overcome all the power of the enemy; nothing will harm you.
–Luke 10:19 (NIV)

You, dear children, are from God and have overcome them, because the one who is in you is greater than the one who is in the world, for everyone born of God overcomes the world. This is the victory that has overcome the world, even our faith.
–1 John 4:4—5 (NIV)

It would be rewarding to be able to see all the enemies of my calling lined up, and say with authority, "Off with their heads!" However, these enemies are not flesh and blood, but powers and principalities, as well as deeply embedded flaws in my own character. It's hard to enthusiastically lead a charge against these kinds of enemies, when after multiple hits of the snooze button, I resist arising from my own bed. It seems rather obvious that trying to attain victory in my own strength is pointless. Authority carries a power that is both amazingly effective, and unfortunately dangerous in the wrong hands. Spiritual authority in Jesus' name is our greatest weapon in overcoming any internal or external forces that stand in the way of our calling. To be victorious we need to faithfully use this mighty weapon more often.

Dear Lord, Sometimes it feels as if we are under attack by unbeatable forces. Help us to fully realize the power and authority that resides in the name, Jesus. Your name is above every other name. In your name, we come against fear, immaturity, rebellion, low self-esteem, discouragement, lack of focus, self-centered will, laziness, anxiety, and lies that we tell ourselves. Give us ears to hear you clearly, eyes to see your plans for our lives, and the faith to conquer our enemies. May we frequently, and effectively, use the authority that you have given us. In Jesus' mighty name... Amen.

SEPTEMBER 14

Hide and Seek

When they heard the sound of GOD strolling in the garden in the evening breeze, the Man and his Wife hid in the trees of the garden, hid from GOD.
–Genesis 3:8 (MSG)

This is too glorious, too wonderful to believe! I can never be lost to your Spirit! I can never get away from my God! If I go up to heaven, you are there; if I go down to the place of the dead, you are there. If I ride the morning winds to the farthest oceans, even there your hand will guide me, your strength will support me. If I try to hide in the darkness, the night becomes light around me. For even darkness cannot hide from God; to you the night shines as bright as day. Darkness and light are both alike to you.
–Psalm 139:6—12 (TLB)

Like Adam and Eve, or Jonah, people hide from God when they feel guilt. Often people are running away from where they should be, doing what they shouldn't do. However, there really is no point in hiding. He seeks. He sees us as we really are, then lovingly invites us into his presence. He provides protective refuge for us, in him. In his presence truth is revealed. When the truth is hard to accept we can choose to ignore it, bravely accept some painful honesty, or we can keep running and hiding. Hiding from the truth to avoid an onslaught of bad feelings can seem like a pleasurable alternative, but eventually it is a dead end. We all need an accurate mirror, not a well-placed fig leaf.

Dear Lord, Help me to realize that you are my shelter and hiding place. Open my eyes to see when I am running from you, instead of running to you. Truth can be painful and confrontational at times, but you are the Way, the Truth, and the Life. Give me courage; let me never avoid the truth about myself, no matter how much it hurts. Open up my heart and mind to the changes that I need to make to live a productive, godly life. Reveal to me the comfort that is there for me, when I find my refuge in you. I thank you that you came to seek and save those that are lost. Help me to do that as well. In Jesus' name... Amen.

SEPTEMBER 15

The Biggest Pill

In everything you do, put God first, and he will direct you and crown your efforts with success.
–Proverbs 3:6 (TLB)

So if you find life difficult because you're doing what God said, take it in stride. Trust him. He knows what he's doing, and he'll keep doing it.
–1 Peter 4:18—19 (MSG)

As long as I'm alive in this body, there is good work for me to do.
–Philippians 1:22 (MSG)

Faced with a multitude of choices revolving around, "What do I need to do today?" some things are often set in stone, like our morning hygiene routine. Every morning (when I remember, and I'm not rushing out the door anxious about being late) taking my pills is a routine thing. Vitamins, herbal supplements, and prescriptions form a little pile of varied shapes and sizes. The biggest one, the golden gelatinous fish oil pill is definitely the hardest one to swallow. As a result, it is the last one consumed. This propensity to do the hardest-to-swallow thing last is common. In our heads we know we should tackle the biggest, most difficult things first, but do we approach our lives that way? Rarely!

Some days and paths have lots of flexibility. Being a full-time mother was one of the most rewarding times of my life, and rarely did my procrastinating tendencies ever manifest. Lifestyle in those days was a balancing act between loving, playing, and the *tyranny of the urgent.* Changing a stinky diaper is done immediately. In contrast to that, during my student and career phases of life, ordering priorities or creating short and long-term plans, and using other skills essential for success were often sabotaged by procrastination. No matter what the day, or stage of life that we are in now, let us no longer avoid that big thing that needs to be done first today.

Dear Lord, Help me to not put the biggest, most important, or most difficult thing I need to do today, at the end of my list. Direct my priorities to do first things first. Develop a spiritual maturity in me, so that my inclinations will not be to put off until later that which needs to be done, now. In Jesus' name... Amen.

SEPTEMBER 16

Our Rest

Yes, my soul, find rest in God; my hope comes from him.
–Psalm 62:5 (NIV)

Finally, brothers and sisters, rejoice! Strive for full restoration, encourage one another, be of one mind, live in peace. And the God of love and peace will be with you.
–2 Corinthians 13:11 (NIV)

Come to me, all who are weary and burdened, and I will give you rest.
–Matthew 11:28 (NIV)

When life becomes a *To Do* list that is growing longer and longer, and gathering dust from extended inaction, do we really have a justifiable reason to take a rest? With God's prescribed formula of work for six days and rest for one, can we in good conscience take a break if we haven't really completed our work, or our obligations? I believe that in many cases the answer is, "Yes, we can." There is one situation that I would say, "No., we should not." One needs to examine the purpose and timing for a break. *If*… the main reason you are setting aside Me Time is to avoid doing something that you should be involved in doing right now, that's a "No!" When our body is fatigued, our brain overly cluttered, and our soul is weary, then that would be a "Yes!" Rest is needed. Unfortunately, guilt is a frequent companion for procrastinators, even when it doesn't deserve to be. Sometimes we need to recognize that guilt can encroach on valuable times of needed rest, and it is up to us to refuse to let nagging guilt steal our peace so we can have life-giving rest.

Dear Lord, I confess that sometimes I ignore my obligations. I doubt there is a benefit from always feeling guilty during times of rest and relaxation. Yet, I know that I have felt guilty even when I had a perfect right to rest. Give me discernment to recognize when my times of rest are merely an escape, or they are needed for me to be at my best. Help your people to develop balance in their lives. Let there be a sense of your presence, accessible in our lives every day, so that we may find rest for our souls at any time it is needed. Help us to set aside times to lift our burdens and be free from our weariness. In Jesus' name… Amen.

SEPTEMBER 17

Early Just Isn't My Style

Very early in the morning, while it was still dark, Jesus got up, left the house and went to a solitary place where he prayed.
–Mark 1:35 (NIV)

Waking up early in the morning is not for me. My first decisions of the day are usually to hit the snooze button several times. My day dawns clouded by procrastination. My mood when I wake up is dictated by the thought..."Is there any way that I can go back to sleep, for just a little longer, without totally messing up my entire day?" I really need to embrace the power of habit, routine, and a plan. When I hold tightly to the concept of being free to do what I want, when I want, without realizing it... I am in bondage. I could lounge my life away in entertainment and diversions, just have a good time without producing anything noteworthy. That kind of lifestyle is an option. But, if one's goal is to live a significant life, self-indulgence and having no self-restraint are not options. Usually, I don't want to wake up at all, and my selfish whims would not lead me to pray first thing. And to tell the truth, I never do the same thing as the first thing. While I understand the concept of first things first: wake up, take a shower, eat breakfast, spend devotional time. The slightest diversion can throw the simplest morning routine totally off course and "Oops! There goes my devotional time."

Dear Lord, There is no way that I can establish a good morning routine without you. Help me to turn my internal clock around and go to bed earlier. Help me to wake up feeling grateful to be able to wake up, thankful to be alive. Help me to establish effective routines and overcome the snooze addiction. On my own, and in my own power, it cannot be done. I am tired of trying and failing in this arena. With your power Lord, it can be done. Give me an attitude of being ready first thing in the morning and extinguish the desire to delay my day. In Jesus' name... Amen.

SEPTEMBER 18

All Means All

Take careful heed... to love the Lord your God, to walk in all His ways, to keep his commandments, to hold fast to Him, and to serve Him with all your heart and with all your soul.
–Joshua 22:5 (NKJV)

'And you shall love the Lord your God with all your heart, with all your soul, with all your mind, and with all your strength.' This is the first commandment.
–Mark 12:30 (NKJV)

Living a successful Christian life is not really based on doing, or not doing certain things, but on surrendering ALL. My early twenties were about seeking God and trying to live a healthy life, after damaging my body with collegiate hedonistic indulgences. I practiced Yoga regularly and read a Hindu text, the *Bhagavad Gita*, religiously. Upon first reading a passage concerning what kind of Yogi it is that God desires, the list went on and on, dismissing each logical path. My curiosity was fired up; I had to know. I wanted to be that person! In the end, the conclusion was... One who surrenders all. No longer would empty rituals, repetitious prayers, showing up for church, or even meditating with a Yoga master, going to make it. Hinduism wasn't going to get me where I wanted to go, but I thank God for the revelation that Jesus would. Not just believing that Jesus was the Son of God, who died on a cross for my sins, but in surrendering my life to him and declaring him to be my Lord and Master.

If we are on the path to serving God and overcoming procrastination, we need to lay down our life at the feet of Jesus, surrender our entire being, hopes and aspirations, sins and failures. Give it all. Entering through the narrow gate implies an act of leaving all else behind in order to enter in. Our surrender is supported by having faith in the glorious reward awaiting us on the other side. "I surrender all" is not just a good lyric from an old hymn, it is the posture we need to take to gain victory.

Dear Lord, Sometimes it is so difficult to let go, and difficult to surrender all. Enlighten my understanding of the spiritual benefits of surrendering to you. Let no distorted concept of submission keep me from laying my entire life before you. Help me to see that when you are my master, I am completely free from the bondage of sin and death, free to be the person you created me to be. Help me to readily recognize your voice, spend more time in your Word, know you more, and increase my ability to discern your will. In Jesus' name... Amen.

SEPTEMBER 19

Lesser Goals

Jesus said, "No procrastination. No backwards looks. You can't put God's kingdom off till tomorrow. Seize the day!"
–Luke 9:62 (MSG)

Your decisions should be based on whatever seems best under the circumstances, for the Lord will guide you.
–1 Samuel 10:7 (TLB)

If you want to know what God wants you to do, ask him, and he will gladly tell you, for he is always ready to give a bountiful supply of wisdom to all who ask him; he will not resent it. But when you ask him, be sure that you expect him to tell you.
–James 1:5—6 (TLB)

It is logical to think that if we are avoiding an important thing that needs to be done, we may be doing something "bad" instead. Not necessarily so. According to an ancient Indian proverb, "We are kept from our goal, not by obstacles, but by a clear path to lesser goals." Often this is the case. We can be so busy fulfilling lesser goals, that the more important ones, the kingdom goals, remain undone. How do we avoid doing what is merely good, but not what is best? We need to earnestly seek God for answers, and not put off seeking wisdom which opens our vision to reveal the right goals. We should take time to look past the obvious, clearly seen lesser goals, and believe wholeheartedly that God is ever willing to guide us to what is best.

Dear Lord, I need your wisdom, and I need to make sure that I am doing what you want me to do this day, and all the days of my life. Do not let me get led astray by lesser goals. Help me to seek you with assurance that you are willing to show me the best way to spend my time today. Draw me toward fulfilling the highest purpose that you have for my life. In Jesus' name... Amen.

SEPTEMBER 20

Presently in The Future

A good man leaves an inheritance to his children's children,
–Proverbs 13:22 (RSV)

Listen to advice and accept instruction, that you may gain wisdom for the future.
–Proverbs 19:20 (RSV)

[About the godly woman]
Strength and dignity are her clothing,
and she laughs at the time to come.
She opens her mouth with wisdom,
and the teaching of kindness is on her tongue.
–Proverbs 31:25—26 (RSV)

A psychologist from UCLA named Hal Hershfield is known for doing studies which focus on how our present self relates to our future self. One of his studies compared two groups of subjects, asking them both to decide how they would spend $1,000. One group viewed themselves in digitally aged photos as they made their decision. This group put twice as much into investing for retirement! Seeing this vision of their future-aged self, changed their perspective on the future. Procrastinators are often very disconnected from their future selves. We are less likely to save, build for our retirement (it always seems so far in the future,) and possibly more likely to depend on our children to provide for us when we become elderly, and less likely to leave an inheritance to our children. According to Proverbs, this is not what a good person does.

Dear Lord, I confess that I am not as connected to my future self as I should be. Saving for the future mistakenly seems to be something that will magically take care of itself someday. Help us all to realize that we need to be wise and responsible to provide for ourselves, and if we have children, to be a blessing to them and not a burden. Procrastinating about saving can result in dire financial consequences. Help us to grow in our understanding of what our present self needs to do, in order to be the best we can be and provide for our future self. Let us be intelligent, careful, and obedient in how we live today, so that we can create a good tomorrow for others as well as ourselves. Grant us wisdom about our finances and our future. In Jesus' name... Amen.

SEPTEMBER 21

A Good Harvest

God who gives you hope will keep you happy and full of peace as you believe in him. I pray that God will help you overflow with hope in him through the Holy Spirit's power within you.
–Romans 15:13 (TLB)

He waters the earth to make it fertile. The rivers of God will not run dry! He prepares the earth for his people and sends them rich harvests of grain.
–Psalm 65:9 (TLB)

For God, who gives seed to the farmer to plant, and later on good crops to harvest and eat, will give you more and more seed to plant and will make it grow so that you can give away more and more fruit from your harvest.
–2 Corinthians 9:10 (TLB)

The writer of Ecclesiastes tells us that there is a season for everything. There is a time to plant, and a time to reap. No one wants to labor on and on and see nothing come of it. Hope is essential. We are blessed because God gives us what we need through the power of the Holy Spirit: love, joy, peace, patience, kindness, goodness, gentleness, faithfulness, and self-control. For those who labor in the fields, God provides earth, water, seed, and he prepares us to receive a joyful harvest. In turn that harvest will produce more seed to renew the cycle of productivity again, and again. Praise God. We need to recognize the pattern he has set in motion for us to follow. As we work, plant, and give at the appropriate time, tending to the field of our endeavors, God assures us that we will reap a reward. He is on our side, and he provides us with what we need to succeed.

Dear Lord, I thank you for the grace, mercy and provision that you give to your people. Help me to realize that you are for me, and not against me. Help me to have faith that my timely labor will result in a good harvest. Help me to be patient before results manifest. Give me the wisdom to know your timetable, to recognize the season that I am currently in, and to see where and how to put forth an effort that will advance your kingdom. Help me to be diligent about doing work that benefits others as well as myself. In Jesus' name... Amen.

SEPTEMBER 22

Imagine That

And the Lord said to them, "Even with a prophet, I would communicate by visions and dreams;"
–Numbers 12:6 (TLB)

This vision-message is a witness pointing to what's coming. It aches for the coming– it can hardly wait! And it doesn't lie. If it seems slow in coming, wait. It's on its way. It will come right on time.
–Habakkuk 2:2—3 (MSG)

Sometimes I wish that God would grant me a vision of my alternate futures in side-by -side diagrams. They should be projected brightly on a wall in front of my eyes.

#1 Diagram = The chain of choices and results that will happen if I take the avoidance path..."I'll do this later." #2 Diagram = Do best choice now, to see where that leads down the road.

On the Erupting Mind (Intelligent Advice for Intelligent People) website they address the issue of "Avoidance Behaviors and Procrastination." They suggest using the power of our imagination to overcome these self-defeating behaviors. Their three-step technique involves VISUALIZATION- see yourself doing the preferred behavior using vivid imagination and engaging as many senses as possible. Then INTENSIFY to "create an exaggerated version of reality" this should stir your energy and infuse you with excitement. Finally, ACT now! Just do your task immediately. We should use our imagination to empower us to do the right thing, not to conjure up a double-minded scenario or an unreal pipe dream future.

Dear Lord, Help me to use my imagination in the right way. Let me not substitute vain imaginings and daydreams for real achievement. Let me not create a web of excuses and rationalizations that give me permission to avoid doing what I need to be doing now. Help me to create a mental picture of me in action, without fear, without hesitation, enthused about the work you want me to do. Infuse me with the power of your Holy Spirit, in order to visualize and actually become, one who defeats procrastination in my life. In Jesus' name... Amen

SEPTEMBER 23

I'm Late

When I was a child, my speech, feelings, and thinking were all those of a child; now that I am an adult, I have no more use for childish ways.
–I Corinthians 13:11 (GNT)

Fix your attention on God. You'll be changed from the inside out. Readily recognize what he wants from you, and quickly respond to it. Unlike the culture around you, always dragging you down to its level of immaturity, God brings the best out of you, develops well-formed maturity in you.
–Romans 12:1—2 (MSG)

When it comes to being on time, it is something that is getting easier for me these days since procrastination is in my cross hairs, targeted for elimination. Historically, I never set my foot out the door one minute earlier than I had to, to be on time for work. Some days my inaccurate planning, or lost keys meant that I did not make it to work on time. Late again, only a minute or two, but late none the less. Some procrastinators, myself included, hold so tightly to the idea of being free to do whatever we want, whenever we want, we resist schedules and planning with every fiber of our being. As if routines and schedules are for nitpicking chumps, trapped in ruts of their own making. There is a whole category of people whose lateness, and tendency to avoid doing anything they don't feel like doing, is simply caused by emotional immaturity. Some of us simply need to grow up and act like adults and have a realistic plan to get there on time.

Dear Lord, I confess that I want to be free from being late. I am tired of the stress, anxiety, and frustration that I feel trying to get to work, church, school, or any social function on time. Give me wisdom to judge my time realistically, and not to be engaged in activities that will hinder me getting out the door on time. Help me to realize that I cannot do anything I want, any time I feel like it. Help me to recognize when I am being immature, and when I am making poor choices trying to manage my time. In Jesus' name… Amen.

SEPTEMBER 24

Working It

We are his workmanship, created in Christ Jesus for good works.
–Ephesians 2:10 (NKJ)

Always abounding in the work of the Lord, knowing that your labor is not in vain.
–1 Corinthians 15:58 (NKJ)

Countless times I have served as a teacher at my church. There has been a broad spectrum of preparedness as I stepped into that role on a Sunday morning. God's grace was over some of the hastier preparations. Just by being there and being committed, God's work was done. Blessings flow as we serve. Sometimes going the extra mile, may have benefited me even more than my students. Our labor for the Lord is never, absolutely never, in vain. We should not be overly focused on seeing results, because that can lead to discouragement. We cannot see what God is doing behind the scenes. Like the song *Waymaker* tells us, "Even when I don't see it, You're working… You never stop working." Praying and faithfully working in whatever role we are in, does the job. Jesus is always working on our behalf; we just need to keep working it.

Dear Lord, Let our work be totally dedicated to you. Whether we are laboring in our homes, employed and making a living, volunteering,or doing the work of the ministry, give us the mindset of it being all for you. Help us to recognize our calling to serve you, using whatever skills and resources we currently possess. Let us not be slack or late, let us not avoid our personal and kingdom responsibilities. Open our eyes to see the eternal value of whatever work we do, when it is dedicated to you. In Jesus' name... Amen.

SEPTEMBER 25

Fixed and Focused

Another disciple said to him, "Lord, first let me go and bury my father." But Jesus told him, "Follow me, and let the dead bury their own dead."
–Matthew 8:21—22 (NIV)

So we fix our eyes not on what is seen, but what is unseen, since what is seen is temporary, but what is unseen is eternal.
–2 Corinthians 4:18 (MSG)

Fixing our eyes on Jesus, the pioneer and perfecter of our faith. For the joy set before him he endured the cross, scorning its shame, and sat down at the right hand of the throne of God.
–Hebrews 12:2 (MSG)

There are times when I thought, after reading about this son that wanted to bury his father, "Jesus, weren't you just a bit harsh on him?" Then I heard, what this disciple actually said was, "My dad is still alive, so after he dies then I'll follow you." If "the Way-the Truth-the Life" is in front of us, and we can see and hear him give us clear directions, should we get distracted by any other option? As an attention deficit procrastinator, it is very difficult for me to focus on any one thing, for any length of time. Distractions abound, kidnapping my eyes and attention. Computers and phones, with their insistent rabbit holes, constantly beckon. Television lures me away with exciting and escapist entertainment. It is time to be more fixed and more focused, to be alive in him eternally, instead of wasting time with the dead things of this world.

Dear Lord, I need your help continually every day. Thousands of decisions and distractions pull my attention in every direction. Give me discernment to see what paths bring life, and which are dead ends. Teach me to follow you more closely, to fix my eyes on you in such a way that when I lose sight of you, my heart and soul desires your presence once again. Help me to limit my hours of entertainment, so that hours of my life are not spent sabotaging my true purpose. In Jesus' name... Amen.

SEPTEMBER 26

Just Too Hard

Beloved, do not be surprised at the fiery ordeal among you, which comes upon you for your testing, as though some strange thing were happening to you;
–1 Peter 4:12 (NASB)

And not only this, but we exult in our tribulations, knowing that tribulation brings about perseverance
–Romans 5:3 (NASB)

And our hope for you is firmly grounded, knowing that as you are sharers of our sufferings, so also you are sharers of our comfort.
–2 Corinthians 1:7 (NASB)

See to it that no one comes short of the grace of God; that no root of bitterness springing up causes trouble, and by it many be defiled;
–Hebrews 12:15 (NASB)

For whatever reason, the task before you seems overwhelming. You may be a single mom raising her children and taking classes toward a degree, someone trying to live a normal life with an Alzheimer's afflicted spouse, or there is a web of poverty, addiction, or despair constraining you. We need God's Word to shine the light of truth into our circumstances. We need the fellowship of other believers to be supported by their love, acts of support, and the unifying power that comes with a common faith. We need Jesus. He, above all others who are being worshiped around this world, knows intimately about: pain, suffering, fear, death, being misjudged. In the Garden of Gethsemane even Jesus had a desire to step outside of God's plan for his life. We need to follow his example wherever it leads, so that we too may say, "Let your will, and not mine be done." It may seem too hard, yet we need to develop perseverance and accept God's grace. His will be done.

Dear Lord, Please deliver us from the pain and suffering of this present season, but if it be your will to work perseverance, and godly character in me, help me to submit. Holy Spirit infuse me with a supernatural comfort and sustain me with loving and supportive brothers and sisters of mutual faith in Jesus. Help me to guard against bitterness toward you in the hard times. Free me from any jealous thoughts toward others that seem to have it easy. Help me to rest in knowing your love for me is not less than for any other. When the rewards of this life seem out of reach, help me to focus on my eternal reward, and to always rejoice that my name is in the Lamb's Book of Life. In Jesus's name... Amen.

SEPTEMBER 27

Avoiding the Ditch

The wisdom of the wise keeps life on track; the foolishness of fools lands them in a ditch.
–Proverbs 14:8 (MSG)

A sound mind makes for a robust body, but runaway emotions corrode the bones.
–Proverbs 14:30 (MSG)

The one who plants in response to God, letting God's Spirit do the growth work in him, harvests a crop of real, eternal life.
–Galatians 6:8 (MSG)

As reported in Time magazine, according to cognitive scientist Tali Sharot, author of the book, *The Influential Mind,* "emotion tends to overpower reason when it comes to human decision making." This is not good news. Leaders who are able to manipulate people's emotions, can easily take populations down the wrong path. While many people think that their procrastination is mainly due to their lack of time management, most research shows that it is due to unresolved or unrecognized emotional issues that result in self-sabotage. We cannot fix something about ourselves if we foolishly believe it is one thing causing the problem, when it is actually something else.

Dear Lord, I confess that too often I am ruled by my emotions. I call you Lord, but too many times I am more submitted to my feelings and emotions than to you. Help me to be influenced by Wisdom and your Word, more than anything else. You have the path of eternal life laid out, give me the wisdom to follow it. Please quiet these emotional voices that would derail your purpose for my life. In making important decisions, in planning commitments, during my interactions with others, in changing myself into the person that you desire me to be, let me totally submit to your Holy Spirit. Help me to make reasonable and wise choices, not ones based on fleeting feelings. In Jesus' name... Amen.

SEPTEMBER 28

Hidden Things

In him lie hidden all the mighty, untapped treasures of wisdom and knowledge.
–Colossians 2:3 (TLB)

Our words are wise because they are from God, telling of God's wise plan to bring us into glories of heaven. This plan was hidden in former times, though it was made for our benefit before the world began.
–1 Corinthians 2:7 (TLB)

He knows everyone, everywhere. Everything about us is bare and wide open to the all-seeing eyes of our living God; nothing can be hidden from him to whom we must explain all that we have done.
–Hebrews 4:13 (TLB)

There is quite a contrast here in the hidden things of God, and our hidden things. God's hidden things are treasures, knowledge, glorious plans that are concealed to protect their value, to be revealed at the proper time for our benefit. Procrastinators often hide from their responsibilities, hide their feelings of stress and being out of control. Also, there is the act of covering one's tracks in the attempt to hide from the consequence of our procrastinating ways. Did I ever lie to my professors about why I was late, or why I couldn't hand in a paper on time? You bet I did. Hiding the truth, or hiding from the truth, happens all too often when you are a habitual procrastinator. Freedom from having to make up excuses is a treasure worth seeking.

Dear Lord, Help us not to hide from you, or the consequences of our actions; it is futile. Rather than laboring to bury our shortcomings, let us be people who confess openly to you, laying ourselves bare, hiding nothing. Lead us to be prospectors, yearning to find the hidden treasures you desire us to find. Thank you that you have made the glorious riches of your presence, truth, and knowledge available to us. Help us to be ones that seek and dig, for the valuable things of your kingdom. In Jesus' name... Amen.

SEPTEMBER 29

Who You Belong To

Everyone who confesses openly his faith in Jesus Christ–the Son of God, who came as an actual flesh-and-blood person–comes from God and belongs to God.
–1 John 4:2—3 (MSG)

But the fruit of the Spirit is love, joy, peace, forbearance, kindness, goodness, faithfulness, gentleness and self-control. Against such things there is no law. Those who belong to Christ Jesus have crucified the flesh with its passions and desires. Since we live by the Spirit, let us keep in step with the Spirit.
–Galatians 5:22—25 (NIV)

According to Los Angeles psychotherapist, Dr. Bill Cloke, "Poor concentration, negative internal messages, unrealistic expectations, and the inability to organize and work constructively are present with procrastination. It is part of an inner system that has many parts to it. Procrastination is principally caused by low self-esteem and self-criticism." I can see the emotional results of having a father that was very critical of others, and a mother who frequently criticized herself in my upbringing. It made an impact on how I perceived the world and myself. For many reasons, I became a *glass is half empty* person. This critical attitude tries to grow exponentially internally, often self-criticism tries to overwhelm my thoughts.

When I became a Christian there was a flood of forgiveness toward myself and others, that put me on a healing path. While we all have an inner child that seeks to control their environment, it is time for the adult to discipline that child. I do belong to Christ. God so loved me, that he gave his only son to save me. If God does not condemn me, how dare I condemn myself? Fortunately, affirmation that we belong to Jesus produces grace to silence that critical inner voice and gives strength to our spirit to overcome our self-defeating ways. Because we belong to him, we no longer have a reason to be pushed down by low self-esteem or self-criticism.

Dear Lord, I praise you and thank you for making me your child. Help me to fully embrace my position as a member of your royal family. Lead me on the path of love, joy, peace, forbearance, kindness, goodness, faithfulness, gentleness, and self-control. Quiet those inner voices of criticism and help me recognize when they are dictating my actions. Help me to be free from all influences that would pull me away from where you want me to be today. May my life be a testimony of victory, acceptance, and peace. Help me to accomplish what you desire for me to do this day. In Jesus' name... Amen.

SEPTEMBER 30

How Long Will It Take?

How long must I wrestle with my thoughts and day after day have sorrow in my heart? How long will my enemies triumph over me?
–Psalm 13:2 (NIV)

Joshua addressed the People of Israel: "How long are you going to sit around on your hands, putting off taking possession of the land that God, the God of your ancestors, has given you?
–Joshua 18:3 (MSG)

But if you see that the job is too big for you, that it's something only God can do, and you trust him to do it–you could never do it for yourself no matter how hard and long you worked–well, that trusting-him-to-do-it is what gets you set right with God, by God. Sheer gift.
–Romans 4:4-5 (MSG)

As a young person, waiting a month for something seemed like an eternity. Now that I am older, things that I thought would have happened by now, as years have passed, that seems like an eternity. There is sorrow and frustration deeply lodged in my heart, and I pray. "How long will it take for this feeling to go away? How long before this hope is fulfilled?" I am sure that the people of Israel, going around in circles in the desert complained, "How long before we enter that land God promised us?" There are some necessary components that must come together to move forward from a place of sorrowful wrestling thoughts, to finally possessing territory that fulfills God's promises to us. First, we must stop sitting on our hands and actually get to work! Then as we realize that the job is too big, we must trust God to be at the forefront of our advance. We will be too busy working and trusting to be dwelling on our own discouraging thoughts. Our vision will be looking forward, not inward. When we enter the place of promise, thank God, our wait will be over. However long it takes, it will be worth it.

Dear Lord, I confess that my own thoughts have weighed me down, hindering me from moving toward my "hoped for" goals. Help me to look ahead, and not backwards. Help me to see whether I wait on you for three days, or thirty years, your planned destiny for me never changes. Please silence the negative whispers that attack me; let me hear your encouraging voice and the comfort of your Holy Spirit above everything. Give me that clear picture of the route I need to take to enter into your promises. May I always be willing to do the work, whatever is necessary, to fulfill your plan for my life. Show me my steps for today. In Jesus' name... Amen.

OCTOBER 1

A Blessed Mystery

Praise be to the God and Father of our Lord Jesus Christ, who has blessed us in heavenly realms with every spiritual blessing in Christ... For he chose us in him before the creation of the world to be holy and blameless in his sight... With all wisdom and understanding, he made known to us the mystery of his will according to his good pleasure, which he purposed in Christ, to be put into effect when the times reach their fulfillment–to bring unity to all things in heaven and on earth under Christ... In him we were also chosen, having been predestined according to the plan of him who works out everything in conformity with the purpose of his will.
–Ephesians 1:3—12 (NIV)

I have never thought of conformity as a good thing because *marching to the beat of a different drummer* always appeared more admirable to me. This passage in Ephesians presents a lesson on the benefits of conforming to something that is ultimately as good as it is mysterious, God's will. We are chosen by him, for him. We have a destiny and a calling for a very high purpose so profound that it unifies heaven and earth. Being holy and blameless may seem too far-fetched for us to achieve, but it is ours because we are spiritually *in him,* and we are part of his pleasure and his plan. In God's time, all will be worked out. It is a blessed mystery that beckons us into conformity with the purpose of his will.

Dear Lord, You are majestic, and your ways are far above our ways. Thank you for the gift of salvation, and for choosing me to be a part of your glorious, mysterious plan. Mold me and conform me into being an active and timely instrument of your will. Let my prayers always come back to this; your will and not mine be done. Give me wisdom to understand the benefits and responsibilities of living in you. Let me always be inclined to submit to your will and embrace whatever path you have prepared for me. In Jesus' name... Amen.

OCTOBER 2

I'm Not Alright

And now may the God of peace, who brought again from the dead, our Lord Jesus, equip you with all you need for doing his will. May he who became the great Shepherd of the sheep by an everlasting agreement between God and you, signed with his blood, produce in you through the power of Christ all that is pleasing to him. To him be the glory forever and ever. Amen
–Hebrews 13:20-21 (TLB)

[Listening to the following Switchfoot lyrics feels like looking in a mirror]

"No, I'm not alright
I know that I'm not right
A steering wheel don't mean you can drive
A warm body don't mean I'm alive
No, I'm not alright
I know that I'm not right
Feels like I travel but I never arrive
I wanna thrive not just survive"

Too often there is a sense of traveling the path that seems right, without the reward of arriving at an enjoyable destination. It could be that as a procrastinator there are too many starts, and not enough satisfying finishes. Jesus is a good shepherd always leading us on the right path, to still waters and soft grass to graze and rest upon. Life should certainly be about thriving not merely surviving. We need to grab hold of this promise from Hebrews, may the Lord, "produce in you through the power of Christ all that is pleasing to him."

Dear Lord, Help us to draw upon your power; it is for us, bought with your blood shed on the cross. Give us a revelation of all that being a follower of Christ means for us as we dwell on earth. Help us to be obedient sheep, ones that trust you totally and listen closely to your voice. For those times when everything within us cries, "I'm not alright," let us not hold on to our feelings and flaws. Let us be people that hunger and thirst for your Word and find our greatest pleasure in pleasing you. May we have a constant faith to override our doubts, knowing we will be alright, arriving exactly where we need to be at the right time. In Jesus' name... Amen.

OCTOBER 3

Do It Yourself Dominoes

So get rid of all that is wrong in your life, both inside and outside, and humbly be glad for the wonderful message we have received, for it is able to save our souls as it takes hold of our hearts. And remember, it is a message to obey, not just to listen to. So don't fool yourselves. For if a person just listens and doesn't obey, he is like a man looking at his face in mirror; as soon as he walks away, he can't see himself anymore or remember what he looks like. But if anyone keeps looking steadily into God's law for free men, he will not only remember it, but he will do what it says, and God will greatly bless him in everything he does.
–James 1:21—25 (TLB)

Procrastinators that don't see themselves for who they really are, have no clue how one delay after another can lead to a burdensome chaotic life. For example, there's good old John. He is so late for every meeting that his colleagues lie to him about what time he needs to show up. He has not checked the oil in his car for endless months because he can always do it tomorrow. He stashes his bills, rather than open them. One day, after finally opening his toll bill, he realizes that his late charges and fines have exponentially accumulated. Now his $2.50 toll, equals $250.00! His car breaks down on the way to work, making him late for an important meeting, again! He is fired from his job. He gets dumped by his girlfriend; she cares about him because he is a nice guy, but she is so over his irresponsible behavior. You get the idea. Reflect for a moment... maybe you know someone like him, or maybe you are him.

Dear Lord, We need to see ourselves for who we really are; a peaceful, productive, and blessed life is at stake. Help me to always seek the truth about myself. Lead me to look steadily at your laws, that I may be responsible and diligent to obey and quick to do the prudent thing. Let me see any looming chain of events that could derail my life, so that I can correct my course today. Help me to see how every aspect of my life is linked together through cause and effect. Show me the way to live a blessed life, not one that is blocked by self-imposed burdens. In Jesus' name... Amen.

OCTOBER 4

Take a Drink

He restores my soul; He guides me in paths of righteousness For His name's sake.
–Psalm 23:3 (NIV)

As a deer pants for streams of water, so my soul pants for you, my God.
– Psalm 42:1 (NIV)

My soul thirsts for God, for the living God
–Psalm 42:2 (NIV)

Why are you depressed, O my soul? Why are you upset? Wait for God! For I will again give thanks to my God for his saving intervention.
–Psalm 43:4—5 *New English Translation* (NET)

Many times in my life, the consequences of procrastination would catch up with me. The boomerang effects of my avoiding and delaying would smack me upside the head with: punishment from my father as a child, bad grades in high school, lingering guilt of multiple lies in college, migraine headaches in graduate school, overwhelming stress as a teacher with growing stacks of papers waiting to be graded, sickness of heart due to a multitude of unmet life goals. Surely, I am not alone in this respect. Guilt, stress, lies, regrets, strained relationships, and physical ailments all take a significant toll on our souls. Eventually we will dry out unless we drench ourselves in the living water. It is too difficult to alter our course and restore our souls unless we heartily and gratefully drink from the well that will never run dry. Without water our bodies die, without opening our souls to God, seeking his presence with praise and thankful adoration our soul's vitality evaporates.

Dear Lord, Thank you that knowing all our faults, you love us enough to offer us eternal life, and give us living water to revive our souls. Help us to realize that there is nowhere else to go for what we need. No matter how hurt that we get in this life, you always provide an answer. Keep us from trying to escape negative feelings by filling them with a temporal fix. Help us to fully realize our immortal status, and our need to be nourishing our souls in your presence. Draw us to a place where we will thirst for you, knowing that nothing else will satisfy. Grant us freedom from the burden of a downcast soul. In Jesus' name... Amen.

OCTOBER 5

Do's and Don'ts

To know wisdom and instruction,
to understand words of insight,
to receive instruction in wise dealing,
in righteousness, justice, and equity;
to give prudence to the simple,
knowledge and discretion to the youth–
Let the wise hear and increase in learning,
and the one who understands obtain guidance...
The fear of the LORD is the beginning of knowledge;
fools despise wisdom and instruction.
–Proverbs 1:1—7 (ESV)

Here is a partial list of "Do's and Don'ts" inspired by the book, *Procrastination: Deal With It -All in Good Time,* by Diane Peters. The fact that this book is aimed at adolescents does not diminish its value for adults. Some of us have not grown up yet, and that is part of the problem.

> **Do:** Take pride in your work. Understand the depth of any project you commit to doing. Realize your work doesn't have to be perfect- just completed. Create a plan that includes finishing on time. Think about the consequences and who will be hurt, if you do not fulfill your responsibilities. Reward yourself for steps completed, especially at the finish. Believe that you are able to change!
>
> **Don't:** Think that your procrastination only hurts yourself. Let deadlines be your single motivation. Refuse to ask questions or seek help when you need it. Invest too much sense of self-worth into your project. Take your procrastination habits and being late, too lightly. Feel that that you are a bad person because you are prone to delay, and have difficulty fulfilling obligations on time.

Dear Lord, Thank you for wisdom and advice that helps us to correct our self-defeating ways. Let us embrace the fact that having faith in you and honoring you is where our wisdom starts. Guide us to the most important piece of wisdom that will help us change, knowing that small changes can lead to big results. Help us to be doers of your Word, to do what we need to do today, and to avoid doing the don'ts. In Jesus' name... Amen.

OCTOBER 6

Why Them?

I have not come to call the righteous, but sinners to repentance.
–Luke 5:32 (RSV)

But he was wounded for our transgressions, he was bruised for our iniquities; upon him was the chastisement that made us whole, and with his stripes we are healed.
–Isaiah 53:5 (RSV)

For God did not send his son into the world to condemn the world, but that the world through Him might be saved.
–John 3:17 (MEV)

When Jesus arrived at any particular place, who were the people he chose to approach? If he was about building up his ministry, he should have sought out the most influential leaders, but he didn't. He approached struggling fishermen, ostracized women of bad reputation, lepers, and even a small tax collector who was considered to be a thief and collaborator with his people's enemies. Why them? He saw their need, had compassion for their wounded hearts, and desired to restore their lives. He knew that these people would receive him for who he really was. They were the people that are willing to transform their own lives through faith in a faithful savior, ones that recognize that they need him, ones who are willing to repent and follow him; they are the ones that Jesus desires to meet face to face. He is always willing to seek us and meet with us.

Dear Lord, I praise you for who you are, and for the saving grace you grant me through your son. Help me to fully realize your loving kindness, and the terrible price paid for my salvation. Let me never take for granted the fact that you sought me before I ever desired to know you. Let me embrace repentance as an act of obedience that keeps me under your protective blessing. Help me to live a life where I am quick to confess my sins, and quick to receive your forgiveness. Help me to be gracious and gentle with my own flaws and failures, just as you are with me. May I always maintain a grateful heart toward you for seeking and saving me. In Jesus' name... Amen.

OCTOBER 7

Today

When Jesus reached the spot, he looked up and said to him, "Zacchaeus, come down immediately. I must stay at your house today."... [Later] Jesus said to him, "Today salvation has come to this house..."
– Luke 19:5-9 (NIV)

As it has been said: "Today, if you hear his voice, do not harden your hearts as you did in the rebellion."
–Hebrews 3:15 (NIV)

[To the thief dying next to him on the cross]
Jesus answered him, "Truly I tell you, today you will be with me in paradise."
–Luke 23:43 (NIV)

In one day, we are born, on another day something can happen out of nowhere irrevocably altering our lives. An accident, a diagnosis, a birth of a baby, the death of a loved one, these are all life altering days. The day we accept Jesus as our Lord and Savior, our eternal destiny is changed; our entire perspective on life itself is rearranged. There have been many milestones, course changing days in our lives that have brought us into this present time. Right now, none of those days is more powerful than today. All we have is today. Jesus called others into immediate action; he is still calling us today.

Dear Lord. Let me hear your voice. Keep me from hardening my heart. Quiet within me an inclination to rebel. Increase a hunger for your will in my life. Let today become a testimony to your life altering, saving grace that is here and now. Use me this day to bless and encourage others. Widen my vision to see more and more of your plan for my life, nudge me to take a step in a God-ordained direction. Give me a revelation of the eternal life and power that that you have planted within me, allow that power to work in me and through me, today. In Jesus' name... Amen.

OCTOBER 8

What We Wish

Don't continue doing things the way we're doing them at present, each one of us doing as we wish. Until now you haven't arrived at the goal, the resting place, the inheritance that GOD, your God, is giving you. But the minute you cross the Jordan River and settle into the land GOD, your God, is enabling you to inherit, he'll give you rest from all your surrounding enemies. You'll be able to settle down and live in safety.
–Deuteronomy. 12:8—10 (MSG)

Deeply wanting what we wish for seems to open up into two separate avenues. The first leading to a place of fantasy where all circumstances magically work out to our benefit. As if God were a fairy godmother not a sovereign Lord. This wish land is a very comforting perfect place where we are sovereign. Yeah, that's not real life at all! We have to live in the real world. The other place wishing leads to, is an arena where we occupy the place of total authority over our own life. To do as we wish means that no one else is going to tell us what to do. No alarm clock, no deadline, no speed limit sign, no bill due date, no parental edict, no policeman, will tell us what we have to do. I can go on and on here. Sometimes, that means even God himself can't tell us what to do. When we default to just doing what we wish, we become our own Lord and Master. As Christians that should never be an option. Unfortunately, many procrastinators live in both wish lands. If Jesus is our Savior, he needs to be our Lord and Master as well.

Dear Lord, Help me to realize more and more that you are my Lord and Master. Let me recognize when I am taking authority over my life that rightly belongs to you. Help me to be aware when my self-will is exalting itself over your will. Help me to grow my faith, to submit to discipline, to have a warrior's courage in defeating all obstacles and enemies before me. Give me discernment to recognize when I am drifting into a world of wishes, chasing imaginary outcomes that lack substance. Keep me from escaping into a fantasy world that deters me from doing what I need to be doing in the real world. Help me to seek your will today and be obedient to what you want from me. In Jesus' name... Amen.

OCTOBER 9

Act Quickly

Abigail acted quickly. She took two hundred loaves of bread, two skins of wine, five dressed sheep, five seahs of roasted grain, a hundred cakes of raisins and two hundred cakes of pressed figs, and loaded them on donkeys... When Abigail saw David, she quickly got off her donkey and bowed down before David with her face to the ground... [David said to her] "As surely as the Lord, the God of Israel lives, who has kept me from harming you, if you had not come quickly to meet me, not one male belonging to Nabal would have been left alive by daybreak."
–1 Samuel 25:18—34 (NIV)

David and his men had guarded Nabal's herds as they fled and hid from Saul. When they rightfully requested food, Nabal sent an insulting message, along with his refusal to give them anything. It was a good thing for all involved that Abigail, Nabal's wise wife, acted so quickly. As soon as she heard of her husband's ignorant refusal, she commanded her household to make provisions, and personally took them to David. Due to her acting immediately, her household was saved from David's wrath, and David spared his soul from the stain of vengeful blood. When Abigail's husband died a swift death, she became the wife of David, the future king of Israel. I consider that a very nice reward for knowing when to act quickly! Although our circumstances may not be a matter of life and death, we need discernment of times that we cannot afford to delay, and we must act quickly.

Dear Lord, I thank you for your Word. The stories and examples within the Bible can greatly benefit our lives. Help me to develop ears to hear, and eyes to see, when immediate actions are necessary. Some things are simply too critical to be delayed and avoided. Help me to be obedient, especially when acting quickly is imperative. Prompt me strongly with your authoritative voice, so that I can recognize when response is needed in an instant. In Jesus' name... Amen.

OCTOBER 10

Just A Little Thing

Consider the ravens: They do not sow or reap, they have no storeroom or barn; yet God feeds them. And how much more valuable you are than birds! Who of you by worrying can add a single hour to your life? Since you cannot do this very little thing, why do you worry about the rest?
–Luke 12:24—26 (NIV)

What seems like a very little thing to one person may seem enormous to another. Jesus equates trusting in God to provide for us as, just a "very little thing." Fear and lack of trust either pushes us, or pulls us, into different ways of coping. Lack of trust can push us frantically forward in our own strength, eliminating the need to trust. The way of fear pushes us back, retreating into isolation, progress is at a standstill. Procrastinators can fall into either mode depending on their personality, or common coping methods. We need to be people who are able to do the very little thing. We should find an area where God is challenging us to trust, write it down; go out on a limb, no self-reliance allowed. We need to face a fear, be deliberate in challenging it, advance with no retreat. Our victories will become our testimonies.

Dear Lord, I confess that it is very difficult for me to live a life of, "No worries." Why should I rely on you for something that I can do myself? Teach me to fully trust you, to completely rely on you. Let me seek direction and revelation from your Word, a personal word that will help me to anchor my faith and trust in you. Help me to advance along the path that you have set out for me, eliminating fears, and expanding my trust a little bit at a time. When I pause to admire a bird in flight, let me be reminded of how valuable I am in your eyes. In Jesus' name... Amen.

OCTOBER 11

Stand for Your Plan

May he give you the desire of your heart and make all your plans succeed.
–Psalm 20:4 (NIV)

For I know the plans I have for you, says the Lord. They are plans for good and not for evil, to give you a future and a hope.
–Jeremiah 29:11 (TLB)

Commit to the Lord whatever you do, and he will establish your plans.
–Proverbs 16:3 (NIV)

One cannot read through the Bible without recognizing that God is a planner, down to the last detail. Whether it is a blueprint for a temple, a strategy to win a battle, or a way of salvation for our souls, God has made a plan. There is one for us as well. I'm feeling a weight lately that there is a definite plan in front of me, established by God, to help myself and countless others to achieve their God ordained calling. I'm a bit hesitant seeing the risks and work required by me for this design to be fulfilled. While those thoughts occupied my mind, all of a sudden my iPod provided the perfect music for the moment. Sly and the Family Stone with their upbeat, danceable, funky sound and encouraging lyrics from the song "Stand."

"Stand… In the end you will still be you…
One that's done all the things you set out to do… Stand…
There's a cross for you to bear…
Things to go through if you're going anywhere."

Dear Lord, I thank you for providing me with musical inspiration at just the right moment. Help me to listen to your Holy Spirit. Help me to not resist the risks and labor that are part of your plan for me. May I be open to the counsel of others that have wisdom and godly advice. Let me embrace the order and certainty that comes with your explicit directions. May the accomplishment of your plan fulfill my heart's desire and be a blessing to others. In Jesus' name... Amen.

OCTOBER 12

The Linchpin

Forgive us our sins, for we also forgive everyone who sins against us.
–Luke 11:4 (NIV)

Jesus said, "Father, forgive them, for they do not know what they are doing."
–Luke 23:34 (NIV)

A linchpin is something that serves to hold separate parts together that exist to function as a unit. It is a locking pin, inserted *crosswise,* and the symbolism of that should not be ignored. Our faith in Jesus is held in place, bringing all of our separate elements together by forgiveness. Without the forgiveness of our sins, bought and paid for by Jesus' sacrificial death on the cross, there is no salvation. In the parable of the wicked servant, who refused to forgive his fellow servant, he suffered imprisonment and torture as a result of his unforgiveness. According to Matthew 18:35, "This is how my heavenly Father will treat each of you unless you forgive your brother or sister from your heart." Unforgiveness is the one sin that can block God's will in our lives, probably more than any other. We all need a periodic heart check to make sure that our unforgiving attitudes are not holding us in a prison-like limbo. Some procrastinators can forgive others but cannot forgive themselves. If Jesus can forgive us, surely we can forgive ourselves as well.

Dear Lord, Help me to realize that no transgression is beyond the power of forgiveness. When I do not feel like forgiving, let me seek your will to bring me to a decision that will unlock your mercy and grace. Free me from condemning judgmental attitudes towards others as well as myself. Let me see unforgiveness for what it really is, poison to my soul. I want to be rid of the weight of unforgiveness, toward others and myself. Lead me into times of true confession and repentance, times when healing grace flows from you, to me, and to others. In Jesus' name... Amen.

OCTOBER 13

The Turning Point

Abraham entered into what God was doing for him, and that was the turning point. He trusted God to set him right instead of trying to be right on his own.
–Romans 4:2—3 (MSG)

For as long as we lived that old way of life, doing whatever we felt we could get away with, sin was calling most of the shots as the old law code hemmed us in. And this made us all the more rebellious. In the end, all we had to show for it was miscarriages and stillbirths. But now that we're no longer shackled to that domineering mate of sin, and out from those oppressive regulations and fine print, we're free to live a new life in the freedom of God.
–Romans 7:5—6 (MSG)

Having an authoritarian father is one of the common incubators of potential procrastinators. That was me, living out a typical passive aggressive path of rebellion. Education was supremely important to my father. So undone homework, late papers, and tests not studied for, became my way to do school. After sickness forced me to repeat my junior year of high school, I realized that *my education* was for me, and all that blatant rebellion wasn't worth it.

My sickness became a huge turning point for me. That change of course got me through high school, college, and graduate school. Still, my procrastinating ways surfaced and sabotaged many deadlines and projects. Writing this devotional is my new turning point, I am pushing into what God is doing for me now. Slaying the demon of procrastination in life is definitely an ongoing, multifaceted process. There needs to be a turning point to start the process. It can be today! I am praying that if you are reading this, you too will have your victorious turning point.

Dear Lord, Help us to be rid of our old ways of life, and all forms of rebellion. As your followers there is no room for us to be on our own way; remove the emotional shackles on our lives that drag us down. Make us people whose hearts are tender toward you, humble in spirit, submissive to your words, your ways, and your plans. Let your resurrection power infuse new life into us. Bring us to a revelation of what you are actively doing for us, providing us with a turning point that expresses your will and your way. In Jesus' name... Amen.

OCTOBER 14

It's an Act

But the hour is coming, and now is, when the true worshipers will worship the Father in spirit and truth, for such the Father seeks to worship him. God is spirit, and those who worship him must worship in spirit and truth.
–John 4: 23—24 (RSV)

All the ends of the earth shall remember and turn to the Lord; and all the families of the nations shall worship before him.
–Psalm 22:27 (RSV)

I appeal to you therefore, brethren, by the mercies of God, to present your bodies as a living sacrifice, holy and acceptable to God, which is your spiritual worship
–Romans 12:1 (RSV)

Two questions came to my mind today, *Why are we here?* and *What is worship?"* We are created to be here, to be in a relationship with our Heavenly Father and worship him. Worship is an act. Many things that we do with an attitude of bringing glory and honor to our God, or lifting up the name of Jesus, are acts of worship. Rather than seeing worship as the singing part of a religious service on Sunday, we must seek to produce other acts of worship. Bringing a meal to someone who is ill, encouraging a discouraged friend, doing a household chore we dislike as a favor to someone, all these can be acts of worship. Acts of conscious service can produce times when our spirit soars in intimacy with God. Many cultures have simple acts that seem like chores prepared with a prayerful attitude, such as ceremoniously serving tea or even smoking tobacco. As followers of Jesus, surely, we should not be less reverent in our actions.

Dear Lord, Open our eyes to the multitude of opportunities to worship you. May all people who follow you have a spirit willing to seek times of intimately worshipping you. Let us be people who commit acts of worship and obedience. May the way we worship you be with our entire body, spirit and soul, a sacrifice that would draw others from all cultures close to you. In Jesus' name... Amen.

OCTOBER 15

All Things

All things work together for good for those who love God, who are called according to his purpose.
–Romans 8:28 (NET)

Jesus looked at them and replied, "This is impossible for mere humans, but not for God; all things are possible for God."
–Mark 10:27 (NET)

I am able to do all things through the one who strengthens me.
–Philippians 4:13 (NET)

Sometimes the truth of God's love, the power of his name, the overcoming strength he gives us through a relationship with him, can best be expressed in a song. *Your Love Never Fails,* by Jesus Culture, found on YouTube. This song is a constant inspiration to me. The Holy Spirit moves through this group of worshipers to encourage and inspire. This song is a gift to those believers that need fuel for their faith to overcome any situation that is assaulting them. We all need something to help our spirit break free and to move forward, accomplishing all that God designed us to do. Give yourself the time to listen to this, or some other music that is dear to you that can satisfy your soul. We all need cleansing of negative thoughts that sabotage our destiny. Godly music has power, let it work within you for your own good... today.

Dear Lord, You have created all things for good. Sometimes it is hard to grasp, with the horrible circumstances that attack people in this world, that you are good and that all things do work together for good. Help me to cling to your Word. Build up the truth within my heart and mind. As I seek you, may my faith continue to grow until it becomes an impenetrable shield from every lie and discouraging thought that would take me off the blessed path that you have designed for me. Help me to realize with every breath I take, your love never fails. Thank you for your great love, mercy, forgiveness and grace. In Jesus' name... Amen

OCTOBER 16

Power in His Name

Therefore God exalted him to the highest place
and gave him a name that is above every name,
that at the name of Jesus every knee should bow,
in heaven and on earth and under the earth,
and every tongue acknowledge that Jesus Christ is Lord,
to the glory of God the Father
–Philippians 2:9—11 (NIV)

But these are written that you may believe that Jesus is the Messiah, the Son of God, and that by believing you may have life in his name.
–John 20:31 (NIV)

When this became known to the Jews and Greeks living in Ephesus, they were all seized with fear, and the name of the Lord Jesus was held in high honor.
–Acts 19:17 (NIV)

Many years ago, when I had recently taken over the management of a Christian club, I directly experienced the power of his name. We often shared our club's space with the homeless population. One night we were having a prayer meeting, and I strongly felt God wanted no one in the room that wasn't participating in prayer. I actually hated the thought of telling people to leave. (What would they think of me?) Despite a few grumbles, most of the homeless left the space willingly to wait for their ride outside. Later we were interrupted by a very tall, extremely angry looking homeless man, with a fresh scar across his face and a cast on his arm. He refused my request to wait outside, when I repeated my request, "Tonight, if you are not here to pray, you need to wait outside," once again he refused. Then when I said, "In the name of Jesus, you need to leave." Immediately, while protesting, he literally spun around and walked outside saying, "God is outside." Thankfully, so was he! After that moment, the presence of God was so strong, all of us there felt God's power as we prayed in a unique and memorable way. Since that night I have never doubted that obedience, coupled with the authority of Jesus' name, is truly the most powerful force constantly available to all believers who treasure his name.

Dear Lord, Let us never forget the power that is in your name. As disciples of Jesus, may we walk willingly in obedience to your requests, knowing that it matters not what others may think about us. It only matters that we have your approval. I thank you that you bestow us with the authority of a name that is above every other name. I pray that we always ask, according to your will. No matter the name of our obstacle, Jesus' name is greater. Give us ears to hear your word clearly, and the courage to carry out your will. In the precious, beautiful, wonderful, powerful name of Jesus... Amen.

OCTOBER 17

Help!

God is our refuge and strength,
an ever-present help in trouble.
–Psalm 46:1 (NIV)

God is not unjust; he will not forget your work and the love you have shown him as you have helped his people and continue to help them.
–Hebrews 6:10 (NIV)

In the same way, the Spirit helps us in our weakness. We do not know what to pray for, but the Spirit himself intercedes for us through wordless groans
–Romans 8:26 (NIV)

There have been times in my life when the pressures and disappointments seemed overwhelming; I could not even articulate what to pray. Episodes of fervent Spirit led prayers and crying out for God have been necessary. Life's strains can result in tears, or the short prayer, "God, Help me!" God's help has not often come to me in swift solutions to my immediate problems and pressures. But, his presence, assurance, insight, wisdom, truth, and comfort arrive to sustain me, even when solutions have not. God knows the kind of help that we need better than we do ourselves.

Dear Lord, I thank you for always being there. You are an ever-present help in troubling times. You desire good things for me, no matter my circumstances. Your wisdom is available through your Word and your Holy Spirit, guiding me away from harsh pitfalls that can be avoided. May I be someone who allows your guidance to take the reins of my life every day. In Jesus' name... Amen.

OCTOBER 18

Avoiding Confusion

For God is not a God of confusion, but of peace
–1 Corinthians 14:33 (RSV)

When we worship the right way, God doesn't stir us up into confusion; he brings us into harmony
–1 Corinthians 14:33 (MSG)

But the wisdom that is from above is first pure, then peaceable, gentle, open to reason, full of mercy and good fruits
–James 3:17 (MEV)

I hate confusion. It was a common state for me when taking Algebra classes. Most math problems just didn't seem to properly fit into my brain. That is probably why I hated math, just way too much confusion. Other times I experienced confusion as a result of my own procrastination. Having so many tasks undone made my mind painfully clogged with too many options, and no wisdom as to how to create a workable solution. I was a teacher with a mass of ungraded, unsorted stacks of papers around me and grades are due tomorrow! My chaotic thoughts stirred into a cluelessness as to what to do first. How do I put one step in front of the other to lead me out of this mental mess? To avoid that kind of procrastination induced, self-imposed confusion, we need wisdom and a plan formed ahead of time. Procrastinators are not good at that. God has not designed us to live within a state of paralyzing confusion. If we want to really avoid confusion we need to ask God for wisdom, sacrifice a bit of personal freedom for higher priorities. Then we can enjoy an end result of peaceable productivity.

Dear Lord, Help me be someone than seeks your wisdom. Help me to realize when my ways are creating a path that will lead to confusion. May my actions be reasonable and orderly as I work out a plan to do what needs to be done, in small steps rather than large unruly piles of undone tasks. Help me to come before you every day, to put each day's work before you, that your will is done in a way that leads to a peaceful, successful conclusion, instead of confusion. In Jesus' name… Amen.

OCTOBER 19

The Urge to Diverge

As for God, his way is perfect: The Lord's word is flawless; he shields all who take refuge in him.
–Psalm 18:30 (NIV)

The law of the Lord is perfect, refreshing the soul. The statutes of the Lord are trustworthy, making wise the simple.
–Psalm 19:7 (NIV)

Do not conform to the pattern of this world, but be transformed by the renewing of your mind. Then you will be able to test and approve what God's will is– his good, pleasing, and perfect will.
–Romans 12:2 (NIV)

During a Yoga class many years ago, I had a revelation. The B.K.S. Iyengar method was to strive for perfection in your postures; total concentration was called upon to put every muscle exactly into place. My revelation was... "Thank God I don't need to be perfect, because Jesus was perfect for me! I can never be perfect anyway." Personally, I hate it when I do something that is not perfect. Unsuccessfully flipping an egg causes me to groan aloud! Logically one may think that being a perfectionist procrastinator is an oxymoron, but too often it is a dysfunctional yet symbiotic fit. Bill Knaus Ed.D. has co-authored, *Overcoming Procrastination*, and also contributes articles for *Psychology Today*. He states, "Perfectionism is a risk factor for performance anxiety and procrastination. You expect a great performance. You have doubts as to whether you can achieve perfection. You have an urge to diverge and do something less threatening. You wait until you can be perfect. This is an example of a perfectionism-driven procrastination." Working on a project that may not good enough translates into countless years from start to "not finished yet." The revelation that Jesus is perfect, and we don't have to be, should be a looped message, repeating over and over again in our heads, renewing our minds.

Dear Lord, Help me to strive for results, and not perfection. Lead me away from the urge to diverge from challenging tasks to spend time with what is merely pleasing and comfortable. Give me insight to see when my standards are being held to high, for myself and for others. Let me not see my self-worth in what I do, but in who I am, your beloved child full of strengths and weaknesses. Keep me from self-condemnation and fear of not being good enough. I ask these things, in the perfect name of Jesus'... Amen.

OCTOBER 20

The Pile Up

Very early in the morning, while it was still dark, Jesus got up, left the house and went off to a solitary place, where he prayed.
–Mark 1:35 (NIV)

The Lord looks down from heaven on all mankind to see if there are any who understand, any who seek God.
–Psalm 14:2 (NIV)

But seek first his kingdom and his righteousness, and all these things will be given to you as well.
–Matthew 6:33 (NIV)

At any given moment there are simply too many options of what to do. Modern life is complicated, and our *to do* lists keep piling up. So right now, do I… pick up my den, call my 92-year-old mother-in-law, search for a job, contact a friend, get my ridiculously slow computer fixed, straighten out bureaucratic paperwork problems with the U.S. government, exercise, start a load of laundry, eat food (I always want to eat), plan out my next trip, spend another hour on social media, read my daily One Year Bible entry? Oops, I think I see a problem here. What should have been first was listed last. There is simply no victory over procrastination without establishing the right priorities for our time. First things first, time to seek first the Kingdom of God! Then time to plan out the rest of the *to do* items with the Holy Spirit's guidance.

Dear Lord, I need you all day, every day, and need to start my days with you as first priority. If I wake early or late, let me seek you first. If I cannot seem to find time, help me to expand my day by getting up earlier, or giving up things that create wasted time. Thank you for your assurance of the rewards of seeking you first. Help me to understand the measure of my days. Let your plans for my life be my priority always. Let my love for you always prevail and grow daily. Draw me to seek you and your kingdom first. In Jesus' name… Amen.

OCTOBER 21

Thank Goodness

You go before me and follow me
You place your hand of blessing on my head...
If I ride the wings of the morning,
if I dwell by the farthest oceans,
even there your hand will guide me,
and your strength will support me...
Every day of my life was recorded in your book.
Every moment was laid out
before a single day had passed...
Test me and know my anxious thoughts.
Point out anything in me that offends you,
and lead me along the path of everlasting life.
–Psalm 139:1—24 (NLT)

How can we doubt that God created us and that he has a plan for our lives? Thank goodness he knows us, loves us, and created us to expand the Kingdom of Heaven here on earth. Having been brought up Catholic, I was quite familiar with the idea of confession. However, for me it had always been a somewhat empty ritual. I gave my shopping list of superficial sins to the priest, he gave me a list of *Our Fathers* and *Hail Marys* to say, and *Voila!*- repentance and absolution were mine. When I first became a born-again Christian, I clearly remember saying a heartfelt prayer one night, "God I know my sins, things that I do wrong, but I want you to show me. Help me make a true confession. What is it about me that offends you the most?" It was the first time I heard God truly speak to me, with authority and love he said, "At times you care more about what others think of you, than what I think of you." I wept hard, knowing it was true. Thank goodness, if we ask, he will point out what we need to change about ourselves as he leads us in the right direction.

Dear Lord, Lead us into times of true confession so that we can walk a path of genuine repentance and everlasting life. Help us to live a life that shines brightly so that we may lead others to you. Help us to rid ourselves of any sin, any habit, or any attitude that hinders us and others from following you. Help us to open every part of our heart, soul, and spirit to you, so that we can fully grasp your cleansing love. In Jesus' name... Amen.

OCTOBER 22

Too Many Words

Much dreaming and many words are meaningless. Therefore fear God.
–Ecclesiastes 5:7 (NIV)

It has been fairly easy to talk about the dreams and visions that are part of my life. As time goes on, however, it seems as if the talking has not turned into the necessary labor, planning, and execution needed to bring these dreams into reality. As procrastinators, that is what we often do. The words describing our hopes and wishes are sweet in our mouth, as if the mere talking about them would turn them into a reality. It does not work that way. Probably the more we talk, the less we invest the time, sweat, and energy necessary to transform dreams into tangible existence. Fear of God is not a popular perception these days. But... maybe more fear of God would result in less empty words, and that would be a good thing.

Dear Lord, Forgive my empty words and talk. Sometimes, I have fooled myself into thinking that the more my dreams were spoken about, the more likely they were to come true. Wisdom now shows, this is not so. Unless the work is actually started, in progress, or near completion, let me keep it locked in my heart, only spoken to a chosen few. It seems as if we live in a world that has ceased to fear you, sin is no longer a cause of shame and repentance. Help me to know how to fear you and respect you in a way that brings out the best in me. Let my words be meaningful, not meaningless. Let me be a person of action. In Jesus' name... Amen.

OCTOBER 23

It Hurts

I'm standing my ground, God, shouting for help, at my prayers every morning, on my knees each daybreak. Why, God, do you turn a deaf ear? Why do you make yourself scarce? For as long as I can remember I've been hurting...
–Psalm 88:13—16 (MSG)

He won't brush aside the bruised and the hurt and he won't disregard the small and insignificant, but he'll steadily and firmly set things right. He won't tire out and quit. He won't be stopped until he's finished his work–to set things right on earth.
–Isaiah 42:2—4 (MSG)

There I was, late one Sunday night attending the lift on the rental truck, assisting the young men of Newport Church load out equipment from our venue. A large wooden cover of a speaker slipped off and crashed into the bridge of my nose. The pain was excruciating! I thought that I had broken my nose. I didn't, but the severe pain brought tears to my eyes. Once all were assured that I was *OK,* we went our separate ways. While driving home, the pain opened a floodgate of deep hurts and inner disappointments that had been submerged for years. Decades worth of hopes and faith-filled expectations were now before my eyes, either dashed to pieces or gathering dust. All of a sudden, the rush of emotional pain far exceeded the physical, and I wept uncontrollably. God literally had to slap me in the face, to wake me up. There were God given dreams that I had put to death, but he hadn't. It was resurrection time.

According to Mike Bundrant's theories on emotional reasons for procrastination, the painful experience of having multiple disappointments in life can put people into a state of ultimate futility. They put off important tasks because, why bother?... it won't work out anyway. Procrastinating as a way to protect ourselves from disappointment is an unfortunate way to handle life. Why? As Mr. Bundrant says, it "guarantees you'll be disappointed, forever. The only way to experience the joy of accomplishment is to risk the disappointment of failure."

Dear Lord, Wake us up! Let us recognize when the hurt of multiple disappointments is blocking the path that you have set before us. Resurrect things within us that we have buried, things that you desire to bring to life. Let us be brave, enduring the pain of risk. Let us no longer avoid those goals that have the power to transform our lives and the lives of those around us. Help us to not tire or quit, knowing that you will not disregard us, and that you will eventually set things right. In Jesus' name... Amen.

OCTOBER 24

Get A Grip

Dear friend, take my advice; it will add years to your life... I don't want you ending up in blind alleys, or wasting time making wrong turns. Hold tight to good advice; don't relax your grip. Guard it well–your life is at stake!
–Proverbs 4:9—113 (MSG)

I can see now, God, that your decisions are right; your testing has taught me what's true and right. Oh, love me–and right now!–hold me tight! just the way you promised. Now comfort me so I can live, really live...
–Psalm 119:74—75 (MSG)

As I started to develop pain and stiffness in my knees and hands I thought, "I'm too young for this!" But age has a way of enforcing unpleasant realities upon us. One simply cannot play a good round of golf without a firm grip. The harder I would grip something, the more it would hurt, so my grip has become slacker over the years. Dropping stuff has become almost a daily occurrence. It is certainly annoying and often a waste of time. By the grace of God, my spiritual reaction to all of this physical change has been quite the opposite of annoying. This physical world is decaying and fading away, there is no way to hold on to it anyway. Our grip needs to be an ever-increasing hold onto God. We must hold on to the Holy Spirit for guidance, and to God's Word for strength and advice. While we still have breath, we need to hold on to God's abundant love for us and live our lives well. Thank God, when my grip fails, his grip tightens.

Dear Lord, Your advice and words are life to us. May we have an increased hunger and thirst for your Word, and your presence. Thank you that you hold us tightly. Give us an increased revelation of the love you possess for us. As we hold on to you, let us see the abundant life you have for us in this present world and in the world to come. Help us to cling to eternity, and to loosen our grip on temporal things that can distract us and lead us into blind alleys and wrong turns. In Jesus' name... Amen.

OCTOBER 25

Readily Recognize

God helping you: Take your everyday, ordinary life–your sleeping, eating, going-to-work, and walking-around life–and place it before God as an offering. Embracing what God does for you is the best thing you can do for him. Don't become so well adjusted to your culture that you fit into it without even thinking. Instead, fix your attention on God. You'll be changed from the inside out. Readily recognize what he wants from you, and quickly respond to it. Unlike the culture around you, always dragging you down to its level of immaturity, God brings the best out of you, develops well-formed maturity in you.
–Romans 12:2 (MSG)

This scripture shows me how levels of immaturity influence my everyday life. There I am: going to bed too late–often way too late, eating too much of the wrong things, but not willing to sacrifice my time and appetite to get fit, currently unemployed so there is no going-to-work routine structure in my life. While I have prayed for God to zap me with self-discipline, why ask God to be doing something that I should be doing for myself? Recognizing what he wants from me, now is the time for me to just respond. Having recently recognized the detrimental effects of bad sleeping patterns has made me up my level of commitment to myself to change my bedtime, from "way too late" to reasonable. Waking up more rested has made the start of my days easier, and I am now less likely to hit that ever tempting snooze alarm! Thank God for little victories. Hopefully, I can keep that going...

Dear Lord, You have given us a great gift in free will, but I must admit that I have misused that gift by not disciplining myself in my sleeping, eating, working, and leisure activities. Help me to realize that my day-to-day life is an offering to you. As an offering, there should be a measure of sacrifice involved. Remind me that often the difficult, or tedious tasks of life are there to help me be the person you want me to be. Help me to see my immaturity for what it really is. Let faith rise within me, knowing your help is always there, to quickly embrace what is best for me instead of putting it off, again and again. In Jesus' name... Amen.

OCTOBER 26

Let Hope Rise

He does not crush the weak,
Or quench the smallest hope;
He will end all conflict with his final victory,
And his name shall be the hope,
Of all the world
–Matthew 12:20-21 (TLB)

So I pray for you Gentiles that God who gives you hope will keep you happy and full of peace as you believe in him. I pray that God will help you overflow with hope in him through the Holy Spirit's power within you.
–Romans 15:13 (TLB)

Sometimes we can get too focused on our problems and the issues that we need to overcome. Thus, we do not feel good about ourselves. I know that when I fall short of my best, I can start to lose hope and battle self-pity. We all need to constantly bring our eyes back to Jesus. Our praise and worship allow hope to rise within us. It is in times of conscious adoration that we break out of our own limited perspective. It is there that we taste Heaven. There, we can join a throng of other believers to become a part of an ecstatic cloud of witnesses. These are the times we elevate our souls and become energized with Heaven's glorious light. We need that. We need to have a triumph of hope in order to overcome the battles and temptations of life. There is an enjoyable spiritual place where we can be filled with hope, uplifted and transformed. We need to find a place, a sound, songs of praise and worship that bring us to that place of being in God's presence. Found on YouTube, here are two places that definitely do that for me: "With Everything" (Let Hope Rise) by Hillsong, live in Miami, "Rooftops," by Jesus Culture. If their style is not your taste in music, find your taste and fill up your soul with what works for you.

Dear Lord, I pray that all of us who follow you would find a place, a style, a method of being totally engaged in praising you with everything we are, with our entire being. That we would enjoy music that lifts our souls. Through your power and grace impart hope, joy, and peace for our minds and hearts as we access your presence. May we find that place today, so that hope rises within us. In Jesus' name... Amen.

OCTOBER 27

Completely, Continually, Thoroughly

Submit yourselves therefore to God. Resist the devil and he will flee from you.
–James 4:7 (RSV)

For the mind that is set on the flesh is hostile to God; it does not submit to God's law, indeed it cannot
–Romans 8:7 (RSV)

In your struggle against sin you have not yet resisted to the point of shedding your blood.
–Hebrews 12:4 (RSV)

I thank God for every time that I have struggled with some issue that seemed just too big to overcome, and God provided an insight from an unexpected source. Recently, while on a trip complicated by very discouraging circumstances, I heard Dr. Erwin Lutzer of Moody Church in Chicago on the radio. His main point was that in living the Christian life, victory is not so much an event as it is a process. Our mechanism for change is created on a daily basis when we regularly: submit *completely*, resist *continually*, and confess *thoroughly*. I realized that I cannot wake up one day to suddenly not be a procrastinator anymore. My quick temper will not disappear immediately, my excess weight will not vanish without consistent long-term effort. What I can do is engage in the process today, and this process, day by day, will eventually lead me to victory.

Dear Lord, Help me daily to submit to you, to continually resist temptation, and to thoroughly confess my sins and shortcomings to you. Awaken within me the need to be a warrior on my own behalf. Assist me in my battles against self-defeating habits and behaviors. By your Word, instill the faith within me to be an overcomer. Submitting to you means that I will have the power to resist, and I will not desire to bury my sins, but to confess them. As I embrace this process of submission, resistance, and confession, infuse me with the joy of intimacy with you. I thank you that your joy is our strength. In Jesus' name... Amen.

OCTOBER 28

Don't Walk Away

Never walk away from someone who deserves help; your hand is God's hand for that person. Don't tell your neighbor "Maybe some other time" or "Try me tomorrow" when the money's right there in your pocket.
–Proverbs 3:27—29 (MSG)

While it is probably a very good thing to be organized and abide by routines in one's life. It is also important to be sensitive to the Holy Spirit. There are certain God-ordained appointments that are not written on our calendars. While we are busy about our own business there are times when we will hear that still, small voice ... to call, write, visit, or give to someone who is in need. That person probably needs us, at that very moment, not tomorrow or next week. Of course, there are countless times that someone is begging on the side of the road with a cardboard sign in their hands, or a neighbor or church friend is asking for a favor. Our time and money are limited; what do we do? We check in with God, we deliberately rely on the Holy Spirit to guide us. Let's be God's hand when we have the opportunity, now and not later.

Dear Lord, Help me to recognize when I am in the position to help someone, that needs my help or money at that very moment. You have been so generous to me, help me to be generous with others. Give me wisdom and discernment as to how to be a blessing to others. If my time is available, if the money is there in my pocket or my account, prompt me by your Holy Spirit to do as you will. In Jesus' name... Amen.

OCTOBER 29

Missing the Mark

Desire without knowledge is not good, and to be overhasty is to sin and miss the mark.
–Proverbs 19:2 *Amplified Bible, Classic Edition* (AMPC)

I desired to be at my doctor's appointment on time. I hate being late for appointments, but because I put things off until the last minute, I hurry. I went toward the doctor's office, couldn't find it, thought there was something wrong with my GPS. There was something wrong, operator error! After I went in an entire circle of one on-ramp to another, the thought finally hit me... Hmmm, maybe she is at her other office today. Sure enough, my Google Maps was quite correct, and I was an anxious, scatterbrained, tardy mess. Seventeen minutes tardy to be exact. That's what we do when we procrastinate. We do not plan enough ahead of time, we wing it when we think we are sure, but really are not sure, of what we are doing. Yesterday, the day before my appointment, I knew what time I had to be there, but did not double check the location of the address. In short, I had a Proverbs 19:2 morning.

One version says it this way, "He who hurries, sins." I did become an angry, frustrated, self-condemning vortex of negative emotions. Yes, I would have to call that tardy mess, "sin." As a Christian, there are certain sinful behaviors that I would never ever think of doing. Yet, in my hasty mode, I must face the fact that I miss the mark, the peace of God is not in me, or around me. Procrastination is where it all starts, sin is where it ends, and I do not want it in my life. I am tired of missing that mark, what about you?

Dear Lord, Please give me the wisdom that I need to plan ahead, to avoid doing things "at the last minute." Help me to not put myself in situations that lead to a flaring temper, or anxious frustration. Your will is peace, grace, kindness, self-control. Let my will be your will today. In Jesus' name... Amen.

OCTOBER 30

God's Bandage

A cheerful heart is good medicine, but a broken spirit saps a person's strength.
–Proverbs 17:22 (NLT)

The human spirit can endure a sick body, but who can endure a crushed spirit.
–Proverbs 18:14 (NLT)

How good to sing praises to our God!
How delightful and fitting!...
He heals the brokenhearted and bandages their wounds...
How great is the Lord! His power is absolute!
His understanding is beyond comprehension!
The Lord supports the humble...
Sing out your thanks to the Lord;
sing praises to our God
–Psalm 147:1—7 (NLT)

It has been my experience that when a procrastinator's unfinished goals extend year after year, the result is a broken spirit. There I was at the *Life Focus* conference in Norfolk, Virginia, emotionally crushed and mentally confused. Where was this abundant life that Jesus promised me? Problems that seemed unsolvable in my: marriage, finances, wayward children, broken dreams, stagnant ministry, etc. had me bound up in sadness, and on the verge of leaving my family. As the Newsboys sang, "Fix Your Eyes Upon Jesus," something within me started to open up. Singing praise to God, pouring out my heart, God poured into me healing calm that soothed my mind. Dr. Tony Evans preached on "The Foundation," and the Holy Spirit spoke to me, "Leaving your family will not work the will of God in your life." Chains of confusion and sadness instantly broke off me. As I sang praises to my loving savior that night, I embraced a weapon of praise and worship that has been bandaging my wounds and has been protecting me ever since. Praise strengthened my foundation and gave me ears to hear. Thank God!

Dear Lord, I will continually thank you for being the God that heals my broken heart and bandages my wounds. In my brokenness and humility, you heard the cry of my heart and answered me. I treasure the relationship that I have with you, fostered by times of singing praise and worship, generating tangible love and intimacy. Help me to quiet the voices of discontent and frustration within my mind. Lead me beside still waters where your voice is all I can hear. Help me to always keep my eyes on you, shedding plans that lead to nowhere, and submitting daily to your will for my life. In Jesus' name... Amen.

OCTOBER 31

The Word is Life

In the beginning the Word already existed; the Word was with God, and the Word was God. From the very beginning the Word was with God. Through him God made all things; not one thing in all creation was made without him. The Word was the source of life and this life brought life to people...
–John 1:1—4 (GNT)

But Jesus answered, "The scripture says, 'Human beings cannot live on bread alone, but need every word that God speaks.'"
–Matthew 4:4 (GNT)

Heaven and earth will pass away, but my words will never pass away.
–Matthew 24:25 (GNT)

When my three children, ages 5, 3, and 10 months old, were peacefully playing in the living room, all listening to an audio version of the Bible, I went to take a bathroom break. While obeying nature's call, I suddenly felt another call telling me to leave immediately! As I entered the living room, I didn't see my baby with his brother and sister, "Where's Jacob?" I said. Their casual response was, "He was bothering us, so we put him out on the porch." The deck of our porch was approximately 6 feet off the ground, straight down was a concrete sidewalk around the entire perimeter, and there was no barrier to a crawling baby. I flew outside, clamped tightly onto one of his little legs, just as he had reached the edge! Not that he would have plunged to certain death, but within a mili-second, he very well could have! Since God's Word was playing in my ears, I feel certain that I was able to hear God's voice as he said, "Go now!" in order to save my baby's life. At that very moment, the knowledge that God's Word is life, became permanently imbedded within me.

Dear Lord, Give us a hunger for your Word. Let us have a revelation of the life-giving power of it. Let us desire it beyond food itself, knowing that it gives us eternal perspective, discernment, power over enemies, and godly wisdom. Help us to plant your Word deep within our hearts and souls. Let us tend to your Word, in faith watching it grow, protecting us from sin and death, using it to impact lives of others for your kingdom. Give us a revelation of the creative power of your Word. May your words be in our mouths ready to share. In Jesus' name... Amen.

NOVEMBER 1

Kingdom Fitness

But Jesus told him, "Anyone who let's himself be distracted from the work I plan for him is not fit for the Kingdom of God."
–Luke 9:62 (TLB)

Whoa... That's a bit harsh! When there is a need for encouragement to stay focused on the work God wants me to do, this isn't the message I want to hear. Multiple distractions are too often yanking my chain. It may be playoff time with my team in the arena for a championship, too much dust and clutter to be straightened out, new movies to see, weeds that should be yanked out, etc. I envy the horse with its blinders on, it knows where to focus, and too often I do not. For me it is often a situation of good, better, or best. I do what is good, but don't invest my time in the best. Guilty feelings over my best not being achieved at any given moment, pushes me to pursue an avenue of escape. Movies and TV shows are usually my main distractions. It is hard to finish writing my own script if I'm too busy watching other people's productions. Guilt that disappeared while enjoying that good movie, now resurfaces when the credits begin to role. While I know that God is abundant in his mercy, grace, and forgiveness, continual reliance on his patience disregards the cost of indulging in my distractions. It is best to be busy being fit for kingdom work, but that cannot be achieved if one is too busy being merely good and unfit.

Dear Lord, I confess that my fitness level is not what it should be. The continual allure of distractions is getting the best of me. Guilt is useless if it doesn't lead to conviction and changing my ways. Help me to order my days, and nights, to put first things first. May spending time in your Word and in your presence, give me the discernment necessary to silence the call to spend time off of your plan. Quiet the emotional turmoil that draws me to avoidance and escapist behaviors. May no internal urge, or external interference, keep me from following your plan. Help me to consciously increase my spiritual fitness to conquer and expand territory for your kingdom. In Jesus' name... Amen.

NOVEMBER 2

Great Lengths

But Jonah got up and went the other direction to Tarshish, running away from GOD. He went down to the port of Joppa and found a ship headed for Tarshish. He paid the fare and went on board, joining those going to Tarshish–as far away from GOD as he could get...
–Jonah 1:2—3 (MSG)

The best thing you can do right now is to finish what you started last year and not let those good intentions grow stale. Your heart's been in the right place all along. You've got what it takes to finish it up, so go to it. Once the commitment is clear, you do what you can, not what you can't. The heart regulates the hands.
–2 Corinthians 12:11—12 (MSG)

The *Virginian-Pilot* contained a story about Maggie Seymour, a Marine and graduate student at Old Dominion University, who completed a cross country run in 100 days. The article stated, "She wasn't ready to start her doctoral dissertation on soft power and terrorism– setting a new bar for procrastination tactics. 'That's probably harder than running cross-country,' she said." Really? Completing a doctorate degree is harder than running all the way across the United States in 100 days, enduring feeling, "really miserable and hurt really bad?" Maggie's accomplishment is very admirable, but she obviously went to great lengths to avoid starting on a life goal that caused more fear than an almost impossible run. We need to ask ourselves, what great lengths am I going to, to avoid completing an intimidating, impending, God-ordained goal? The good news is, God will match our great lengths to go in the wrong direction with his own greater lengths to bring us back, if we are his.

Dear Lord, Deliver us from being like Jonah. There is a great work to be done, bringing the good news of repentance and salvation to a lost and dying world. Take the fear from our hearts; infuse us with your compassion for those who do not know you yet. Let us not deliberately run away from the calling that you have put on our lives. Let us be a people who run quickly toward doing your will, instead of running away. Give us the revelation, the strength, the courage to face and the endurance to complete your work through us, despite the pain, the opposition, and our own fears. In Jesus' name... Amen.

NOVEMBER 3

The Rush

Those who live according to the flesh have their minds set on what the flesh desires; but those who live in accordance with the Spirit have their minds set on what the Spirit desires.
–Romans 8:5 (NIV)

My flesh and my heart may fail, but God is the strength of my heart and my portion forever.
–Psalm 73:26 (NIV)

According to the Merriam-Webster Dictionary, the word *rush* can mean, "to move forward, progress, or act with haste or eagerness or without preparation," or to "perform in a short time at high speed." It sounds like a description of the typical procrastinator with a deadline bearing down fast. Interesting that the word "rush" is used to explain the euphoric feeling induced by a sudden burst of drugs into one's bloodstream. Many procrastinators are driven by the rush. I personally enjoy moving fast, whether it's in a car, or an amusement ride. At times I have enjoyed the feeling of having my back to the wall, the *I better start this right now or I'll be in trouble!* feeling. It was motivating, it was a rush. The rush is very much a flesh thing, not a spirit thing at all. Seeking a rush, whether it is watching scary movies, breaking the speed limit, or the emotional jolt of performing at high speed in a short time, means that our mind is not on what the Spirit desires. More nourishment of the soul, and less feeding the need for speed, will profit us greatly in the long run.

Dear Lord, Help us to be people that withdraw from the desire of the rush. We should not be ill-prepared people who do things in haste, motivated by obligations that have cornered us into needing exhilaration to perform. Reveal to us our motives. Draw us away from fulfilling desires of the flesh which war against the spirit. Guide us to a path of solid work, steady efforts, and peace in our times of preparation and production. Mold us into followers that set our minds on what your Holy Spirit desires. Renew my thoughts and be the strength of my heart. In Jesus' name... Amen.

NOVEMBER 4

Putting It Off

Wise people think before they act; fools don't
–Proverbs 13:16 (NLT)

For the wise can see where they are going, but fools walk in the dark
–Ecclesiastes 2:14 (NLT)

Getting wisdom is the wisest thing you can do! And whatever else you do, develop good judgment.
–Proverbs 4:7 (NLT)

There are things that people put off doing all the time, procrastinators are not the only ones. Some things are insignificant, others can be very life-altering. If you ignore the gauge that shows your car is over-heating, you can totally ruin your engine and have a multi-thousand-dollar repair. As a result of not seeing that gauge, you may have to scrap your old faithful Toyota, like I did. Maybe you and your spouse really want kids someday, but are you waiting for the *perfect time* to start a family? How about keeping in mind that your bodies have been ready since you were 15 years old, and if you wait too long, you may not be alive to enjoy being a parent or grandparent.

There are people that say, "What's the point of giving my life to Jesus now? I have my whole life ahead of me." Well, maybe you don't, and you will have lost the great benefit of doing life with Jesus as your Lord and Savior. We need to be wise, not foolish. Many bad things can happen when we put things off like: going to the dentist or doctor, paying our bills, marriage counseling, helping elderly family members, finding employment, enrolling in classes, sharing the gospel, etc. We need to find out what we are ignoring, so that hopefully as soon as possible we can do that thing we have been putting off.

Dear Lord, Keep us from being short sighted. Help us to see the long-term effects of what we are putting off. Holy Spirit you are our Comforter, our Counselor, help us to be sensitive to your prompting. May a desire for wisdom grow within us. Your Word says that if we ask, you will give us wisdom. We need your guidance to make good decisions for our lives. May our choices be the right choices, not influenced by foolish self-will. In Jesus' name... Amen

NOVEMBER 5

Surviving Shipwrecks

Then Jesus told them, "I tell you the truth, if you have faith and don't doubt, you can do things like this and much more... You can pray for anything, and if you have faith, you will receive it."
–Matthew 21:21—22 (NLT)

Cling to your faith in Christ, and keep your conscience clear. For some people have deliberately violated their consciences; as a result, their faith has been shipwrecked.
–1 Timothy 1:19 (NLT)

I have been a procrastinator for my entire life. At times I have fallen into a negative outlook, thinking that change is impossible for me. If we desire change in any area of our lives, we first must believe that change is possible, in order for it to happen. Often our faith in Christ which transformed us into dedicated lovers and followers of God, comes up short when we attempt personal change. We know that God wants us to become the best version of ourselves. How can we possibly get there without faith? We need to be initiating actions that keep our consciences clear, continually praising God for who he is, renewing our minds with the Word, and exercising our faith-filled belief that a better version of ourselves is possible, starting now.

Dear Lord, Please fill my faith gap. I desire to lay every change before you, believing that a better me is possible. Time is too short for me to be overly focused on my shortcomings when there is a hurting world out there, lost without you. Holy Spirit, teach us how to put our faith into action. Let the voice of our conscience, in unity with you, speak loud and clear and keep us from harm. As we transform our own lives, clinging to faith in Christ, use us to rescue others. As Paul survived his shipwreck, going on to live a miraculous life spreading Good News, let there be nothing that comes against us that will hinder us from our mission. May your will be done on earth as it is in heaven. In Jesus' name... Amen.

NOVEMBER 6

His Name

But these are written that you may believe that Jesus is the Christ, the Son of God, and that believing you may have life in his name.
–John 20:31 (RSV)

No one speaking by the Spirit of God ever says "Jesus be cursed!" and no one can say "Jesus is Lord" except by the Holy Spirit.
–1 Corinthians 12:3 (RSV)

Therefore God has highly exalted him and bestowed on him the name which is above every name, that at the name of Jesus every knee should bow, in heaven and on earth and under earth.
–Philippians 2:9—10 (RSV)

Songs of praise to the Lord are filled with the beauty, power, and majesty of the wonderful name of Jesus. Some people may casually throw around his name in vain, as obscenity or in mockery, but on the sincere lips of a believer it is powerful. There is something about His name. While involved in street evangelism, it was easy to tell how Jesus' name was the litmus test for true believers. No matter if people said, "Yeah, I'm a Christian." When I would ask them, "Can you say, Jesus Christ is my Lord and Savior?" Real Christians would repeat that phrase immediately. Others would resist or refuse with a variety of excuses as to why they didn't need to say it. Belief and the declaration from our mouths as to who Jesus truly is, is the rock on which the church is built. Faith in Jesus, and the power in his name are special assets that belong to us. Let us not hesitate to use his powerful name on our behalf and for His Kingdom cause.

Dear Lord, Let us never forget the power of your name. Let us all exercise the authority that you have given us, as we obey your lead and follow you. Let us be faithful to do works that glorify you. We praise your holy name because it is a name above every other name. May we access your grace, your eternal life and your name, in times of trials and testing. Before we act in ways contrary to your Holy Spirit, let your name be on our lips. Let our lives be examples of your glory at work in us. We ask these things in the beautiful, wonderful, exalted name of Jesus, our Lord and Savior... Amen.

NOVEMBER 7

Forward to The Finish

I pray that God, the source of hope, will fill you completely with joy and peace because you trust him. Then you will overflow with confident hope through the power of the Holy Spirit.
–Romans 15:13 (NLT)

May you experience the love of Christ, though it is too great to understand fully. Then you will be made complete with all the fullness of life and power that comes from God.
–Ephesians 3:19 (NLT)

And I am certain that God, who began the good work in you, will continue his work until it is finally finished on the day when Christ Jesus returns.
–Philippians 1:6 (NLT)

I recall holding each one of my babies in my arms thinking... I wish this moment of peaceful, joyous, pure love would last forever. Often, I have desired to stop time in its tracks, to linger and savor a moment. However, life does move on, children grow and test our patience. It is worth reminding ourselves that our Heavenly Father loves us as completely as any mother who cradles an innocent newborn baby close to her heart. God loves us, even in our sin-tainted, unfinished state. We don't need to stop time to feel at peace with where we are in our lives, we need to look forward. There is a future and a hope for us, not entirely up to us to finish.

Thankfully, God is the author and finisher of our faith, and he will be faithful to complete his work in us.

Dear Lord, Help us to keep our gaze forward, as we are fully engaged in the present. Fill us with your love, peace, hope, and desire to remain faithful to you until the end. Let us hunger for that "crossing the finish line" exuberant feeling. May we always stay on track, knowing that your faithfulness fuels our progress through this life. Help us to resist looking backward, keep our eyes from distractions, fill us with confident hope through the power of the Holy Spirit. Let no thoughts of self-condemnation, or lack of self-confidence sabotage the race that you have set before us. In Jesus' name... Amen.

NOVEMBER 8

Small Steps

You're blessed when you follow his directions, doing your best to find him. That's right–you don't go off on your own; you walk straight along the road he set. You, GOD, prescribed the right way to live; now you expect us to live it. Oh, that my steps might be steady, keeping the course you set; Then I'd never have any regrets in comparing my life with your counsel. I thank you for speaking straight from your heart; I learn the pattern of your righteous ways. I'm going to do what you tell me to do; don't ever walk off and leave me.
–Psalm 119:1—8 (MSG)

Sometimes our biggest changes start with small steps in the right direction. The fact that I have desired to have a career as a writer for many years, believing that it was God's calling on my life, didn't matter nearly as much as taking small steps toward writing as a daily habit. It is November, and unlike other years there has been steady progress, no stopping or quitting this journey. These steps have created a sense of putting a smile on my Heavenly Father's face, lessening fears of failure, and lifting a weight of self-doubt off my heart. The benefits of not procrastinating has greatly outweighed the pleasures of doing anything else that would have pulled me off this path. While there may be other things that need to be done which are still on hold, putting first things first and embracing God's grace for the rest, has created a pattern of blessing that is bound to increase. Thank you, God! If this can happen for me, it can certainly happen for anyone.

Dear Lord, May I always seek your will for my life. Show me the direction that you have laid out for me. Reveal the cost of my procrastination and the emotional roots of it, so that step by step I may walk through this life abandoning my fears, rebellion, insecurity, immaturity, and desires of the flesh. Help me to renew my mind in order to develop different patterns of thinking, strategies to order my time, vision to keep me focused, and patience to take small steps toward big changes. Remind me of your transforming power, as well as the gifts and abilities that you have given me. Show me one thing, one small step that I can take today, to usher in victory into my life and the lives of those around me. In Jesus' name... Amen.

NOVEMBER 9

The Battle

For our struggle is not against flesh and blood, but against the rulers, against the authorities, against the powers of this dark world and against the spiritual forces of evil in heavenly realms.
–Ephesians 6:12 (NIV)

The weapons we fight with are not the weapons of the world. On the contrary, they have divine power to demolish strongholds.
–2 Corinthians 10:4 (NIV)

We know from reading the Bible that there is an unseen spiritual world. There are angels, demons, and an enemy known as Satan. We do not want to give too much attention, or dwell on the dark side, but if we do not acknowledge its existence we can more easily experience setbacks and defeats. The more sheltered our world, the less likely we are to witness powers of darkness, but surely reading news headlines should be enough to prove the presence of evil. I believe one of Satan's strongest weapons is his whispers; thoughts that worm their way into our thinking until they have bloomed into either envy, anger, bitterness against others, or crippling forms of self- condemnation. God can make us aware of how our spiritual enemies are at work in our lives. He can also arm us to overcome them through his Word, prayer, times of praise and worship, dreams, visions, revelations in an instant, and also the powerful name of Jesus. When we are in the midst of a spiritual battle we need to remember that Satan is not all knowing, but he does know our weaknesses. As a wise mentor once told me during a very dark time, "The Devil doesn't fight fair." Best to be aware.

Dear Lord, Give us discernment to be able to know when our battle is against spiritual forces of wickedness. Guide us to examine ourselves, let us recall and then renounce any gate we have opened to evil forces. Lead us to reject things that open doors to the enemy like occult practices, witchcraft, mediums and psychics, worshipping false gods, unforgiveness, jealousy, murder, and sexual sins. Protect and rescue those that have been victims of violence and all types of abuse, please heal their wounded souls and troubled minds. Help us to keep our minds cleansed by the washing of the Word. Give us the confidence to know that victory can be ours. In Jesus' name... Amen!

NOVEMBER 10

The Way We Are

There is an opportune time to do things, a right time for everything on earth ...
–Ecclesiastes 3:1 (MSG)

Christ arrives right on time to make this happen. He didn't, and doesn't, wait for us to get ready. He presented himself for this sacrificial death when we were far too weak and rebellious to do anything to get ourselves ready.
–Romans 5:6—7 (MSG)

But make sure that you don't get so absorbed and exhausted in taking care of your day-by-day obligations that you lose track of time and doze off, oblivious to God.
–Romans 13:11 (MSG)

There are some people, some families, some cultures that go very easy on themselves for being late. Like, *that's just the way we are, no point in expecting anything different.* I remember Sunday mornings in my house as an extremely unpleasant experience. The whole family would be waiting for me, then my father, and usually last was my brother. My brother took intense verbal heat for something that my father and I were equally guilty of- being late. My very angry father would drive ridiculously fast through quiet suburban streets, emotionally steaming, barely able to find a parking spot. At times we would end up in the only seats still available, located within the little vestry where the priests put on their clerical robes. A very embarrassing position for my father! We had a neighbor that was also usually late, but he was friends with the policeman on duty that would leave a spot for him in front of the church, in exchange for leaving a bottle of whiskey in the car! Being late can involve: verbal abuse of children, flared tempers over bad parking and seat locations, reckless driving, usually not bribery with alcohol, thank God! If you are part of a culture of acceptance about being or saying, "That's just the way we are," you should question as to why you are, because no good ever comes from it.

Dear Lord, Let us be a people that value time, deadlines, and limits. Convict us of our acceptance of habitual lateness, and slack regard for wasting other people's time. I confess that I have been late too often, drove too fast to get where I should be, made others wait on me, and been too quick to get angry over my hurried situation. Help me to be someone who keeps my word, who plans ahead, who creates a plan to eliminate lateness in my life. In Jesus' name... Amen.

NOVEMBER 11

Today's Self

For the grace of God has appeared that offers salvation to all people. It teaches us to say "No" to ungodliness and worldly passions, and to live self-controlled, upright and godly lives in this present age, while we wait for the blessed hope– the appearing of the glory of our great God and Savior, Jesus Christ, who gave himself for us to redeem us from all wickedness and to purify himself a people that are his very own, eager to do what is good.
–Titus 2: 11—14 (NIV)

An article published in the Washington Post by Ana Swanson entitled, "The Real Reasons You Procrastinate – and How to Stop" explains how our lack of connection to our future self feeds the procrastination habits we have in the present. She says, "The idea is that, even though we know that the person we will be in a month is theoretically the same person that we are today, we have little concern, understanding or empathy for that future self. People are far more focused on how they feel today." When I focus on how I feel today, I eat too much, stay up too late, hit the snooze button too often, and do what I feel like doing. Instead, what I should be doing is bringing myself and those around me, into a far greater tomorrow. What we are feeling today should not take priority over matters of eternal consequence, or the person we want to become in the future. I hope that the path I am now on, is one that is creating a future me that is grateful, rather than regretful, for what my present self is doing.

Dear Lord, Remind me when I am being ruled by my emotions. Quiet the commanding voice of my feelings. Let me hear your voice above the noisy demands of escapism and self-gratification. Holy Spirit take the reins of my will and draw me into a place of self-control. Lead me into times that will bring me closer to you, times of peace and contentment instead of battles within myself. In Jesus' name... Amen.

NOVEMBER 12

Feelings Fail Us

Woe to those who live only for today, indifferent to the fate of others! Woe to the playboys, the playgirls, who think life is a party held just for them! Woe to those addicted to feeling good–life without pain.
–Amos 6:3-6 (MSG)

GOD said, "What's this? How is it that you can change your feelings from pleasure to anger overnight..."
–Jonah 4:10 (MSG)

We simply wanted to provide an example of diligence, hoping it would prove contagious.
–2 Thessalonians 3:9 (MSG)

Timothy Pychyl, a member of the Procrastination Research Group of Carlton University in Ottawa, Canada, says there is a very important step in overcoming procrastination. To me, it seems absolutely vital. Instead of focusing on our feelings, we need to focus on what our next action needs to be. He states, "Recognize that you don't have to be in a mood to do a certain task–just ignore how you feel and get started." "Most of us seem to tacitly believe that our emotional state has to match the task at hand." But, that really isn't true. According to him, "I have to recognize that I'm rarely going to feel like it, and it doesn't matter if I don't feel like it." Ask yourself, "How many times has the fact that I didn't feel like doing something determined my actions, or lack thereof?" For me, it's been too many times. Our feelings will definitely fail us, diligence will not.

Dear Lord, You are a great and mighty God. Somehow our little problems can seem insurmountable, even when solutions are so simple and available. Help us to not be ruled by our feelings, but by wisdom. Help us to dedicate ourselves to maintain a work ethic that would be an example to others, one that would be contagious. May we be more diligent in seeking your presence and peace. Calm our internal storms, ease our anxieties as you guide us on a path of productivity. I thank you and praise you for being our everlasting source of love, forgiveness, mercy, and grace. Help us to share those attributes with every person in our life. In Jesus' name... Amen.

NOVEMBER 13

Good Soil, Good Results

But the good soil represents honest, good-hearted people. They listen to God's words and cling to them and steadily spread them to others who will soon believe.
–Luke 8:15 (TLB)

And we will never stop thanking God for this: that when we preached to you, you didn't think the words we spoke as being just our own, but you accepted what we said as the very Word of God–which, of course, it was–and it changed your lives when you believed it.
–1 Thessalonians 2:13 (TLB)

Live a quiet life, minding your own business and doing your own work, just as we told you before.
–1 Thessalonians 4:11 (TLB)

When we hear or read God's Word, we should have already prepared the soil of our hearts for it. As we take in God's Word, it becomes a seed that must be nurtured, so that God's words are multiplied. Holding on to our acceptable, familiar, and comfortable sins means that we are allowing destructive weeds to grow up. We need to choose whether or not we will continue to ignore, pluck out, or feed those weeds. They just may ruin what our Lord is trying to grow within us. Whatever God has planted within us, surely it is not just for ourselves, but to make the world a better place, to save others, and make us an effective force to spread his words and his ways throughout our world.

Dear Lord, I confess that I hesitate to rid myself of all the things in my life that displease you. Holy Spirit, work within me to have an aversion toward those actions, habits, and entertainments that pollute my spiritual life. Help me to care less and less about what pleases me, and more and more about what pleases you. Let your words grow in my heart that I will not sin against you. Help me to live a life that validates me as being a follower of Jesus. Prompt me to share your words, and your good news more every day. Open doors and opportunities for me to do that. In Jesus' name... Amen

NOVEMBER 14

Fear Not

God is our refuge and strength,
a very present help in trouble.
Therefore we will not fear though the earth should change,
though the mountains shake in the heart of the sea;
though the waters roar and foam,
though the mountains tremble with its tumult.
–Psalm 46:1—3 (RSV)

Behold, the Lord your God has set the land before you; go up, take possession, as the Lord, the God of your fathers, has told you; do not fear or be dismayed.
–Deuteronomy 1:21 (RSV)

According to my research, fear is a powerful underlying factor for procrastination. Often it is the fear of failure, better to believe your dream could come true than to actually do the work toward accomplishing that goal, then fail. There is also a fear of success, this isn't one that I identify with, but it blocks many people. The basis for this is, "How can one keep up the high standard once one has achieved and been recognized for it?" Perfectionists, and those known to be emotionally obsessed with being in control, can fit in this category. Let's face it; there is so much of life that is out of our control. After living in California for many years, experiencing the earthquakes under my feet, inhaling ash from far away raging fires, or seeing the mudslides wipe away multimillion dollar homes, the concept that nothing is certain was often reinforced. Life is too short and too unpredictable to let any kind of fear stand in our way, especially fear of failure or success! We have no idea what tomorrow will bring. We need to just take possession of our God-assigned territory today.

Dear Lord, You are all knowing and all powerful. Help us to rest in your goodness and protection. Strengthen us to stand up to all of our fears. Failures can provide life lessons, let us be willing to risk failure having the faith that all will work together for our good. Help us to recognize when fear plants lies into our thoughts and hinders our way to accomplish your plan for our lives. May we do today, what needs to be done today. In Jesus' name... Amen.

NOVEMBER 15

Along the Way

It means we'd better get on with it. Strip down, start running–and never quit! No extra spiritual fat, no parasitic sins. Keep your eyes on Jesus, who both began and finished this race we're in. Study how he did it. He never lost sight of where he was headed–that exhilarating finish in and with God–he could put up with anything along the way... When you find yourself flagging in your faith, go over that story again, item by item, that long list of hostility he plowed through. That will shoot adrenaline into your souls!
–Hebrews 12:2—3 (MSG)

It is truly amazing all that Jesus went through to complete his mission on earth. One reason that he was much better at handling all that pain, rejection, humiliation than we are, he knew beyond a shadow of doubt where he was headed, a place of highest honor in Heaven. He also knew that he paid the highest price for the salvation of all people that surrender to his lordship. His love and compassion for humankind was immense! How often do we lose sight of where we are headed? How often are we able to choose what is of eternal value over what we feel like doing today? Today, I need to embrace the story of what Jesus went through for me, so that my eternal destiny will not be a dim light, but a glorious beacon shining brightly to guide me every step on the way.

Dear Lord, Let me never lose sight of the sacrifices Jesus made for me, that my daily sacrifices will seem very slight and do-able in comparison. Help me to keep my eyes on Jesus, so that my path in life will not digress here and there, but keep me on the course that you have laid out for me. Help me to perceive the realities of heavenly rewards. Help me to never quit, to lay aside every sin and weight that holds me back. Grow within me a godly compassion and love for those around me. Open my eyes to others that need my help along this journey. In Jesus' name... Amen.

NOVEMBER 16

We Are His

Shout for joy to the LORD, all the earth.
Worship the LORD with gladness;
come before him with joyful songs.

Know that the LORD is God.
It is he who made us, and we are his;
we are his people, the sheep of his pasture.

Enter his gates with thanksgiving
and his courts with praise;
give thanks to him and praise his name.
For the LORD is good and his love endures forever;
his faithfulness continues through all generations.
–Psalm 100:1-5 (NIV)

Procrastinators often struggle with self-esteem issues. This makes it hard to reach for lofty goals, especially when there is a heavy fear of falling flat on your face. Being locked into that fearful point of view keeps us from changing for the better. We are his; he takes care of us and provides for us. We need to rise above our limited view and see our lives from God's perspective. The best way to do that is to enter his presence with gratitude and praise. We should not be held back by our fears, we are his. Once we are surrendered to him through joyful praise, gladness, thankfulness, goodness, faithfulness, and a love that endures forever, our self-esteem is transformed into self-assurance because... we are his.

Dear Lord, Open our eyes to the life-giving attributes of praise and worship, and the power of your Word. Deliver us from fear of failure, self-doubt, discouragement, and self-defeating behaviors. Let us surround ourselves with words and songs of encouragement that lift your name on high, lifting our spirits as well. Help us to have confidence in whatever we set out to do because we are yours. In Jesus' name... Amen.

NOVEMBER 17

The Right Plan

He thought of everything, provided for everything we could possibly need, letting us in on the plans he took such delight in making. He set it all out before us in Christ, a long-range plan in which everything would be brought together and summed up in him, everything in deepest heaven, everything on planet earth.
–Ephesians 1:7—10 (MSG)

We humans keep brainstorming options and plans, but God's purpose prevails.
–Proverbs 19:21 (MSG)

Sometimes we see our life in snapshots, quick Instagram images, as if those brief moments in time could capture the essence of who we are, and where we're going. Life is a movie, not a still frame. I lament that I cannot see God's plan and long-range purpose, but I do not need to. I merely have to do, like the words of the old hymn say, "Trust and obey, for there's no other way to be happy in Jesus, but to trust and obey." Since God holds the ultimate plan in his hands, it is wise for us to surrender all our plans into his hands as well. God designs order and purpose. We should be imitators of him, and order our lives by seeking his will, and adopting a plan for our lives. As procrastinators we are often "spur of the moment" people, impulsively wanting the freedom to do what we want, when we want. If we don't have a plan on how to get where we want to in life, we should. If we are serving, trusting, and obeying, surely God will guide and confirm the right plan for us.

Dear Lord, I thank you and praise you for all of creation, its beauty, its patterns and mysteries. Help me to order and plan my life that I may serve you, be a blessing to others, and fulfill the plan that you have for me. May I find comfort in trusting you. When confronted with decisions and options, trying to design the steps I need to take to reach my goals, let me know your wil, and hear your voice. Give me the courage and willingness to sacrifice, when I am called upon to do so. May your will be done, and my plans be in union with yours. In Jesus' name... Amen.

NOVEMBER 18

Time for Encouragement

Anxious hearts are very heavy, but a word of encouragement does wonders!
–Proverbs 12:25 (TLB)

What a wonderful God we have–he is the father of our Lord Jesus Christ, the source of every mercy, and the one who so wonderfully comforts and strengthens us in our hardships and trials. And why does he do this? So that when others are troubled, needing our sympathy and encouragement, we can pass on to them this same help and comfort God has given us.
–2 Corinthians 1:3—4 (TLB)

When I pray, you answer me and encourage me by giving me the strength I need.
–Psalm 138:3 (TLB)

The number of times that discouragement has triumphed over my attempts to reach certain goals has been countless. Encouragement, on the other hand, has been a blessing to keep going when my goal seemed impossibly out of reach. How much more would employers, parents, and married couples get in return when encouragement is the default mode in dealing with one another's issues? To be an encourager is to be a true blessing. We all need encouragement, but we also need to share that wonderful comfort and reinforcement with others. It is not wise to always be dependent on inspirational and supportive feedback; it is important that we adopt the ability to encourage ourselves. As God became my source of support and inspiration to reach my goals, miraculously the ability to encourage myself became part of my emotional arsenal. Encouragement from God's Word, others, and coming from within our own spirits, truly does wonders!

Dear Lord, I thank you for all the times that you have sent people to encourage me. Thank you for being an inexhaustible well of comfort and inspiration. May I always be a person who goes out of my way to bring encouragement to others. Help me to develop more and more the ability to encourage myself out of my discouraging moods and dark times. May I be quick to lift my head, and quick to access the power within that you have given me. In Jesus' name... Amen.

NOVEMBER 19

Just Ask

So I say to you: Ask and it will be given to you; seek and you will find; knock and the door will be opened to you. For everyone who asks receives; the one who seeks finds; and to the one who knocks, the door will be opened.
–Luke 11:9—10 NIV)

This is a verse that I have often contemplated, usually after praying several times (or several years) for something that did not happen as I wanted it to happen. Recently, I see that whatever the context of this passage, or the prayers that are inspired by it, nothing that we could want or ask for, is more important than the Kingdom of God. My faith in applying this verse to my life has been built through the years because when I seek God; I find him. When I persistently knock, at first it may seem as if no one is home, then God answers. Finally, he opens the door, and invites me into his presence. This verse is God's invitation to all people to ask, seek, and knock. God's will is revealed to us as we walk into His presence. When we pray God's will, that is the prayer that opens the door to God's answers. His will, will be done. Rather than just being an "asker," we become receivers and vessels of His will, instruments in answering our own prayers.

Dear Lord, Help me to seek you above all else. As I enter your presence, and we are together, reveal the things that you want me to pray, so that your will is done on earth, as it is in heaven. Take me from a place of unsatisfied longings into a peaceful fulfilling place with you. Let me have more and more times of submission to you, so that you can shape and mold me into the kind of vessel that is fit for your use. In Jesus' name... Amen.

NOVEMBER 20

Lazybones

Brothers and sisters, we urge you to warn those who are lazy.
–1 Thessalonians 5:14 (NLT)

She carefully watches everything in her household and suffers nothing from laziness.
–Proverbs 31:27 (NLT)

Never be lazy, but work hard and serve the Lord enthusiastically.
–Romans 12:11 (NLT)

The vast majority of procrastinators are not lazy people. On the other hand, virtually all lazy people are procrastinators. If it requires effort, it is avoided and undone. I recently had flashbacks to an early television show entitled *Dobie Gillis*. Before the actor Bob Denver was Gilligan, stuck on that island, he was Maynard G. Krebbs. He had such an aversion to work that whenever he heard the word, he would shudder all over and repeat the word, "Work!" as if it was a horrible disease to be avoided. You can find this memorable beatnik, lazy philosophical character on YouTube. He is classic early television, and definitely worth knowing.

People actually suffer from their laziness, and they don't even realize that their lack of work ethic is the problem. They are usually focused on outside circumstances as the reason for their deprivation, instead of looking in the mirror. It is always because this or that happened, not because, "I am lazy, and I need to change." The Bible is very clear on the subject, laziness and wickedness are lumped together as reasons for God's harsh judgement! To be a lazy Christian is an oxymoron. Jesus called us to be servants and productive workers, not lazybones.

Dear Lord, I pray now for those who are lazy, that they have a revelation and realize the true cause of their problem. May all who call themselves Christians be willing workers and repent of any idle ways. Help us to encourage one another to do good works. Let us speak the truth in love for friends and family that are suffering lack and deprivation in their lives because of laziness. Prompt us to pray for those we know and love that are trapped in poverty because of idleness. Lead them to turn their lives around, so that they will be able to adequately provide for themselves, and their family, and in turn help others. In Jesus' name... Amen.

NOVEMBER 21

Recognize

But what happens when we live God's way? He brings gifts into our lives, much the same way that fruit appears in an orchard...
–Galatians 5:22 (MSG)

May all the gifts and benefits that come from God our Father, and the Master, Jesus Christ, be yours.
–1 Corinthians 1:3 (MSG)

God's gifts and God's call are under full warranty–never canceled, never rescinded.
–Romans 11:29 (MSG)

Our God gives us gifts, ones that are special and uniquely ours. The first thing that we need to do is recognize our own gifts. Often procrastinators don't give themselves enough credit for talents and abilities they possess, thinking "Maybe one day I'll be able to __________, but I can't do that now." Now is the time to accept our gifts and use them generously to bless others. Once I recognized that God had given me a gift of love for people who are very difficult to love, it opened a door for a fulfilling job, teaching "Danger to Self - Danger to Others" teens, in a locked psychiatric facility. Few people are able to work in that type of environment, but I thrive in it, and was able to greatly enhance the lives of my students by being there for them. All believers are gifted in some way and are called to do something *only they can do.* God's gifts enable us, we just need to recognize them, then use them.

Dear Lord, Help all your followers realize their unique gifts. Help us to see, use, and develop those gifts that you have given us. Let us not compare ourselves to others but let us rejoice with a thankful heart for the talents, abilities, and calling that you have given to us. Open our eyes to the difference we can make in this world by living life your way. Thank you for making me a vessel fit for use. May your grace abound to us and to those whom you want us to reach. Guide us in ways to be generous with our gifts. In Jesus' name... Amen.

NOVEMBER 22

Age is No Excuse

Don't let anyone think less of you because you are young. Be an example to all believers in what you say, in the way you live, in your love, your faith, and your purity
–1 Timothy 4:12 (NLT)

Even in old age they will still produce fruit; they will remain vital and green.
–Psalm 92:14 (NLT)

Now, as you can see, the LORD has kept me alive and well as he promised for all these forty-five years since Moses made this promise... Today I am eighty-five years old. I am still as strong now as I was when Moses sent me on that journey, and I can still travel and fight as well as I could then.
–Judges 14:10—11 (NLT)

Our age, whether young or old, creates many self-imposed limits. "I'm too young to do that," or "I'm too old for that," are common excuses. It is a good thing that, as a twelve-year-old Boy Scout, Steven Spielberg didn't think he was too young to start making movies. Benjamin Franklin, at age 81, became a major architect of our Constitution rather than decide he was too old to help create a new system of government. Age is no excuse to keep putting off a longed-for result, especially when it is of eternal or unique value. Our world is now a richer place because Spielberg and Franklin didn't let their age get in their way. We shouldn't let our age hinder us either!

Dear Lord, Help us to realize that you work beyond the limitations of our human understanding. Women beyond the age of childbearing gave birth, a boy defeated a giant, and we too are able to fulfill the calling that you have on our lives, starting now. Thank you for the opportunities that you present. Help us to be free from misconceptions about our age. Let us take full advantage of the time we have now. Open our eyes. Breakdown the self-imposed boundaries that have been constricting us. In Jesus' name... Amen

NOVEMBER 23

The Freedom Trap

For, dear brothers, you have been given freedom: not freedom to do wrong, but freedom to love and serve each other.
–Galatians 5:13 (TLB)

Don't withhold the repayment of your debts. Don't say "some other time," if you can pay now.
–Proverbs 3:27—28 (TLB)

Pay all your debts except the debt of love for others–never finish paying that!
–Roman 13:8 (TLB)

Too much freedom often translates into following our immediate urges, in place of long-range goals and life priorities. Freedom to use a credit card can lead to mounting debt without the means to pay it off. Skipping out on work to go to a concert that was paid for on a high interest credit card, may feel like great fun today, but the bill and the guilt, and the possibility of losing one's job do enter the picture. We are free to charge, free to spend, free to put off paying our debts, but... eventually it catches up. My research on the Lexington Law website stated that the average American consumer now owes over $6,000 in debt. Also, many people about to enter into retirement have debts equal to recent college graduates saddled with education loans that exceed $30,000. Credit card debt in the U.S. has increased by 18% since 2013.

Temptation to freely overspend is always in my wallet. It is crazy to me that right now I have one credit card that offers me a $28,000.00 limit! My current credit card debt is not in the realm of several maxed-out cards, but it is too high, and it should not be ignored. I see that my procrastination in this area is quite costly. Just because I am able to make my payments, doesn't mean I am doing well for myself. The freedom to create debt is a trap, the urge to not pay off debts quickly or completely, is also a trap. Now is the time to create a plan to become free from the all-American debt trap. Each day this action is delayed simply costs more, and more.

Dear Lord, Your Word contains wisdom concerning the burden of being in debt. Help me to devise a plan, and have the discipline to stick to it, so that my credit card debt could be eliminated. Let me be on a path to saving, instead of borrowing. Let me not use my freedom to trap myself into constricting financial situations. Strengthen my patience and resolve. Help my willingness to say, "I can't afford that now," instead of pulling out my credit card. Open doors of opportunity for greater income to help solve financial issues in my household. I ask this for myself and a multitude of others now trapped by debt. In Jesus' name...Amen.

NOVEMBER 24

My Choice

Those who live according to the flesh have their minds set on what the flesh desires; but those who live in accordance with the Spirit have their minds set on what the Spirit desires. The mind governed by the flesh is death, but the mind governed by the Spirit is life and peace.
–Romans 8:5—6 (NIV)

Be transformed by the renewing of your mind. Then you will be able to test and approve what God's will is–his good, pleasing and perfect will.
–Romans 12:2 (NIV)

The avoidance of what should be done now, the stressful delay of the inevitable work to do, the choice of play now, pay later, all starts in the mind. Whatever our time management issues, or proclivity to distractions, our actions are mere reflections of decisions arrived at within our minds. Too often my mind just wants to escape the real tasks at hand. The unpleasant possibilities of failure, or past disappointments cloud my judgement. I return to these verses in Romans often. They remind me that the choice is always up to me. While my choices may seem to be a spectrum of opportunities, God forbid that I allow myself to be deceived again. Some choices merely feed the flesh, others breathe life into my spirit. The discerning factor to be kept in mind when making any decision needs to be, "What part of me will be fed by this?" Will it be my flesh or my spirit? It is my choice.

Dear Lord, You hold all of existence within your hands. Help me to see the big picture, and my specific part to play in your plan. Give me discernment to see the deceptions within my own mind. As I spend time with you in prayer, in your Word, and in heartfelt worship, renew my mind. Let me seek a path of life and peace in my decisions. Help me to not avoid the hard choices that take me where your Spirit leads. Let me do today, what you desire for me to do today. In Jesus' name... Amen.

NOVEMBER 25

Looking Forward

Why am I so discouraged? Why is my heart so sad?
I will put my hope in God! I will praise him again–
my Savior and my God!
Now I am deeply discouraged, but I will remember you...
Each day the LORD pours his unfailing love upon me,
and through each night I sing his songs,
praying to God who gives me life.
–Psalm 42:5—8 (NLT)

While on a New Year's Eve weekend in San Diego, I picked up my previous year's journal. As I read through a list of a dozen things that I had hoped to accomplish by the year's end, not one single goal had been completed. I cried, it was discouraging and depressing. Here I was approaching another New Year's Eve, ready to write my resolutions for the New Year. What was the point? So, I could feel this bad again next year? It is a common discouraging experience for procrastinators. That depression led to no new goals for that upcoming year, but the next New Year's Eve didn't feel any better. The result? Two years had passed without reaching any of those original goals! Turning to God, I admitted that without his help there is no way that I can overcome this bondage of procrastination on my own. Now, I am actually working toward my goals step by step. Looking forward, there is no depression for me this coming New Year! Praise the Lord! This is a new and very pleasant change. May you also look forward to the next year, free from discouragement and the knowledge that you are closer to meeting some of your goals.

Dear Lord, I thank you and praise you for being a loving God. You desire the best possible life for me, a productive life that will be used to save and uplift others. Keep us from being caught in a trap of discouragement, or despair. Keep our eyes off of past failures and give us a vision for the future. Do not let us burden ourselves with long lists, and unrealistic goals. Help us to seek you, and at your direction, focus only on those few things that are most important to you. Have us finish this year, and every year of our lives with a sense of fulfillment, and accomplishment. In Jesus' name... Amen.

NOVEMBER 26

To See Exactly

I ask–ask the God of our Master, Jesus Christ, the God of glory–to make you intelligent and discerning in knowing him personally, your eyes focused and clear, so that you can see exactly what it is he is calling you to do, grasp the immensity of this glorious way of life he has for his followers, oh the utter extravagance of his work in us who trust him–endless energy, boundless strength!
–Ephesians 1:16—19 (MSG)

Those who trust God's action in them find that God's Spirit is in them–living and breathing God! Obsession with self in these matters is a dead end; attention to God leads us out into the open, into a spacious, free life. Focusing on the self is the opposite of focusing on God. Anyone completely absorbed in self ignores God, ends up thinking more about self than God.
–Romans 8:6-8 (MSG)

The self-focused person is like the Beatles' *Nowhere Man,* "Doesn't have a point of view. Knows not where he's going to. Isn't he a bit like you and me?" Having attention deficit disorder means that staying on task is extremely difficult for me. I readily confess a need for God's help to stay focused on what I should be doing at any given moment. As Christians, we all need to recognize that our first priority is to focus on Jesus Christ, our Lord and Savior. We must pray that God will reveal *what he is calling us to do.* A desire for an open and free life, one guided by intelligence and discernment given by God, frees us from a self-focused "nowhere" life.

Dear Lord, I want access to your endless energy and your boundless strength. Help me submit more and more to your action within me. Let my attentive eyes be on you, let my vision be clear and focused on what you would have me do. Help us to develop lives that focus on the needs of others. Keep us from being self-absorbed and looking down dead ends. Today, draw me to a place of increased trust and greater dependence on you. Help me to develop a spirit that defaults to seeking you first. In Jesus' name... Amen.

NOVEMBER 27

Up and About

But make sure that you don't get so absorbed and exhausted in taking care of all your day-to-day obligations that you lose track of time and doze off, oblivious to God. The night is over, dawn is about to break. Be up and awake to what God is doing! God is putting the finishing touches on the salvation work he began when we first believed. We can't afford to waste a minute, must not squander these precious daylight hours in frivolity and indulgence, in sleeping around and dissipation, in bickering and grabbing everything in sight. Get out of bed and get dressed! Don't loiter and linger, waiting until the very last minute. Dress yourselves in Christ and be up and about!
–Romans 13:11—14 (MSG)

This scripture in *The Message* version is one of the most specifically anti-procrastination ones in the entire Bible. There are many characteristics that contribute to our inclination to procrastinate: fear of failure or fear of being letdown or rejected, attention deficit, poor time management, aversion to deferred gratification, using last minute pressure for motivation, comfortable with being consistently late, a long list of major life disappointments, tendency to rebel against authority, emotional immaturity when it comes to not getting our own way. Unfortunately, I feel as if most of these apply to me! Maybe that it why I now feel called to help others whose lives have been sabotaged by procrastination. Hopefully, with an increased devotion to God, we can all stop getting in our own way and move on to a higher calling in life.

Dear Lord, Help us to see clearly the root causes for why we do the things we do. Free us from our self-sabotaging habits. Give us a clear vision of our gifts and calling, fill us with the power of the Holy Spirit to accomplish your will. Let us be increasingly uncomfortable with our procrastinating ways. Help us to desire productivity over self-indulgence. May all followers of Christ be up and about kingdom business. In Jesus' name... Amen.

NOVEMBER 28

Charging into the Fray

Do you give the horse its strength
or clothe its neck with a flowing mane?
Do you make it leap like a locust,
striking terror with its proud snorting?
It paws fiercely, rejoicing in its strength,
and charges into the fray.
It laughs at fear, afraid of nothing;
it does not shy away from the sword.
The quiver rattles against its side,
along with the flashing spear and lance.
In frenzied excitement it eats up the ground;
it cannot stand still when the trumpet sounds.
At the blast of the trumpet it snorts, "Aha!'
It catches the scent of battle from afar,
the shout of commanders and the battle cry.
–Job 39:19—25 (NIV)

While watching battle scenes in movies, it has always amazed me how horses charge into the thick of battle with brave enthusiasm. According to God's Word, apparently they really do it, not just in the movies. Death may swiftly overtake them, it matters not. These horses evidently have no fear. I want to be like that. Not that I want to rush into fierce combat, with blood and death on every side, but I do desire to be that brave. Fear of failure is one of the most common characteristics of procrastination. Better to just think we could be a great scientist, entrepreneur, writer, etc., than to actually try and fail. The mythical land of an *I Could Have* life is more comfortable, less threatening than plunging ahead to make a better life happen. Unfortunately, a *No risk-No reward* life is what we get for our fears. I would rather have no fear and be quick to charge into the fray of life's battles, earning a possible real reward, than fearfully sit on the sidelines, fantasizing about a prize that cannot be earned by the fainthearted.

Dear Lord, Help us to rejoice in the strengths you have given us. Empower us by your Holy Spirit to be people that have no fear, people that will not shy away from intimidating situations. Let us follow your commands willingly and swiftly. Fill us with a fearless enthusiasm to follow you, no matter where it leads. Let us experience the rewards of victory and have stories of triumph to tell, and testimonies used to set others free. In Jesus' name... Amen.

NOVEMBER 29

Near Completion

They were trying to frighten us, thinking, "Their hands will get too weak for the work, and it will not be completed." But I prayed, "Now strengthen my hands."
–Nehemiah 6:9 (NIV)

I have fought the good fight, I have finished the race, I have kept the faith. Now there is in store for me the crown of righteousness, which the Lord, the righteous Judge, will award to me on that day—and not only to me, but also to all who have longed for his appearing.
–II Timothy 4:7—8 (NIV)

At one time I thought that the hardest place to be in any project is the middle, lately I am thinking it is when the work is near completion. My strength seems to give out as everything seems to be taking much longer than expected. Why does the finish line seem to keep moving just out of reach? Why do necessary undone details seem to manifest one after another, just when I proclaim, "Ah, light at the end of the tunnel!" But wait, no that isn't the end, this and that and something else still needs to be done.

Anytime we are in a place of discouragement maybe we need to remind ourselves of all that Jesus went through before he could finally declare, "It is finished." Discouragement magnifies and multiplies obstacles; faith keeps its eyes on the prize. When we are near completion, let us be like Nehemiah and pray for strength. Let us be like Paul who realized that there is a fight to be fought, there is a race to run, there is a glorious finish ahead, complete with a crown.

Dear Lord, Help us to see the finish line of our work clearly. Let us pray for strength and victory over discouragement. May we be people who keep faith and long for your appearing. Remind us that completion is ours for the taking, and that quitting before the race is over is not an option. Let your light displace dark thoughts and overcome all obstacles in our way. In Jesus' name… Amen.

NOVEMBER 30

Mindfulness

What is mankind that you are mindful of them, human beings that you care for them?
–Psalm 8:4 (NIV)

For I have always been mindful of your unfailing love and have lived in reliance on your faithfulness.
–Psalm 26:3 (NIV)

"Mindfulness" is a very popular topic these days. It is generally defined as the ability to be fully present, having total awareness of what one is doing, and to not be overly reactive or overwhelmed by what is happening. Mindfulness is also described as being completely in the present moment, not dwelling on past or future, and being observant of one's own thoughts with a non-judgmental attitude. There are some definite benefits of mindfulness. Most of us could certainly use a dose of not being reactive or overwhelmed, and the concept of "Be Here Now" (a 1960's version of mindfulness) has always appealed to me. I strongly believe that it is wise to be judging one's own thoughts. If I am not careful, my thoughts will lead me to places that I don't really want to go. Imagining and planning the future is necessary to create our best possible life. Maybe it is of greater value to know that God is actually mindful of us. The one who created the universe is mindful of me! Being centered on God's unfailing love and faithfulness seems like an upgraded version of mindfulness to me.

Dear Lord, I confess that I need your help. Let me embrace every present moment to the fullest. Help me to be observant of my own thoughts, and how to train my mind to focus on the right things. Help me to learn patience, and how to detach from stressful situations. Help me to keep situations from controlling my emotions. I thank you that you are mindful of me; it is an amazing blessing. Help me to be ever mindful of you and your great love for me. Create a mindset within me that will bring me into the center of your will. In Jesus' name... Amen.

DECEMBER 1

Thank God for Being Covered

Blessed is the one whose transgression is forgiven, whose sin is covered
–Psalm 32:1 (ESV)

Therefore I tell you, her sins, which are many, are forgiven–for she loved much. But he who is forgiven little, loves little.
–Luke 7:47 (ESV)

Repentance for the forgiveness of sins should be proclaimed in his name to all nations
–Luke 24:47 (ESV)

While pursuing a master's degree in Cinema Studies in New York City, not yet a believer–but seeking a way to God, another film student chose me to act out the part of the woman from Luke 7. She anointed Jesus' feet with her tears and wiped them away with her hair. At the time, there was no motive for me to repent... because I was blind to my sins. How do we recognize our need for a Savior, if we do not realize we have done wrong? In hindsight, it seems that God was letting me know, you will be this woman, you will love much because you will be forgiven much. God orchestrates signposts toward salvation for all who seek a way. Deliberately turning away from the error of our ways, then having faith in Jesus for his sacrifice to cover ALL of our sins, opens the door for God's forgiveness. Through repentance we find forgiveness for our failures and gain the strength to turn away from useless actions. Hopefully we will be ever ready to repent, so that we will be continuously blessed by how the Lord has covered our sins.

Dear Lord, I confess that when I recognize my sins, I do not always turn from them immediately. Help me to be quick to repent and quick to do what you want me to do. Let me recognize how truly blessed I am, so that contentment would reign over my emotions. Let your love for others shine through me and give me the grace to share the good news of your forgiveness to all nations. May my love for you always be as that woman who wept at your feet, passionate and unafraid of what others thought. Help me to move forward this day, leaving my sins behind through repentance. Your will be done. In Jesus' name... Amen.

DECEMBER 2

My Heart Hears

Hear me as I pray, O LORD. Be merciful and answer me!
My heart has heard you say, "Come and talk with me."
And my heart responds, "LORD I am coming."...

Teach me how to live, O LORD.
Lead me along the right path,
for my enemies are waiting for me.
Do not let me fall into their hands.
For they accuse me of things I've never done...

Yet I am confident I will see the LORD's goodness
while I am here in the land of the living.
Wait patiently for the LORD.
Yes, be brave and courageous.
–Psalm 27:7—14 (NLT)

God does hear our prayers, and his means to respond to us is not usually a loud audible voice, yet his words go straight to the heart. For me, God's voice comes as a thought that enters outside the loop of my own stream of consciousness. It has a weight and authority my own thoughts do not have, and the soft tone of a loving father. If we serve in combat, or are in the midst of hostile people, our enemies are external ones. For many people, our enemies are internal ones. We battle with self-defeating accusing thoughts that vie for our hearts' attention. We hear, "You'll never be able to do that. Why even try?" "You'll always be that way!" etc. These enemies are very persistent, and too often successful in inflicting wounds that can damage our hearts. Protecting our hearts with the words of our Heavenly Father brings hope and victory.

Dear Lord, I thank you that you are a loving father to your people. You hear our prayers and respond to us. Help us to fine tune our ability to hear your voice and perceive your will for our lives. Bring us to a place of victory over our enemies. Help us to be patient, and to realize that waiting on you is often necessary to prepare us for what is ahead. Let our hearts hear your voice and exclude other voices that would lead us off the path of life. In Jesus' name... Amen.

DECEMBER 3

Made of Mud

There's nothing like the written Word of God for showing you the way to salvation through faith in Christ Jesus. Every part of Scripture is God-breathed and useful in one way or another–showing us truth, exposing our rebellion, correcting our mistakes, training us to live God's way. Through the Word we are put together and shaped up for the tasks God has for us.
–2 Timothy 3:14—17 (MSG)

God makes everything come out right; he puts victims back on their feet... God is sheer mercy and grace; not easily angered, he's rich in love... He doesn't treat us as our sins deserve, nor pay us back in full for our wrongs... He knows us inside and out, keeps in mind that we're made of mud.
–Psalm 103:6—18 (MSG)

The odd combination of perfectionism and procrastination exists mainly due to fear of failure. Adopting impossibly high standards leads to fear of producing an unworthy result. When we have this frame of mind it is hard to enjoy our work, leading us to avoid it, or simply making us miserable while we work. We need to give ourselves permission to fail. As we dig into God's Word to illuminate truth about our fears, our rebellion, and our need for correction, let us recognize that we are made of mud, but our Heavenly Father is gracious and full of mercy for us anyway. Making mistakes is what humans do! Learning from our mistakes puts our feet on the path of wisdom.

Dear Lord, I thank you that you do not expect me to be perfect. Thank you for your abundant grace, mercy, and forgiveness. Help me to learn to realize failure is a part of life, often providing lessons that lead to success down the road. I thank you for your Word because through it, you provide wisdom, correction, guidance, and training. Help me to not be so hard on myself. Free me from the burden of perfectionism and unrealistic expectations. I thank you that you know me better than I know myself. Give me the courage to face my fears, and to not avoid anything that you want me to do today and in the future. In Jesus' name... Amen.

DECEMBER 4

Learning to be Relentless

That is why we never give up. Though our bodies are dying, our inner strength in the Lord is growing every day. These troubles and sufferings of ours are, after all, quite small and won't last very long. Yet this short time of distress will result in God's richest blessing upon us forever and ever! So we don't look at what we can see right now, the troubles all around us, but we look forward to the joys in heaven which we have not yet seen. The troubles will soon be over, but the joys to come will last forever.
–2 Corinthians 4:16–18 (TLB)

Many people, particularly procrastinators, find it difficult to give up instant gratification in pursuit of their long-term goals. The squirrels in my backyard are a great example of the quality of being relentless. I might as well refer to my bird feeder as a squirrel feeder. It doesn't matter how often these determined creatures are chased away, threatened, contend with the dog, or have ducked a thrown object, they absolutely do not give up! They know for sure what they hunger for, and refuse to be deterred. I want to be like that! My ultimate goal is heaven, and to live a life that results in taking as many people as possible there with me. Today, I will choose to be relentless!

Dear Lord, I confess that far too often I have let the drive for instant gratification direct my thoughts and actions. Help me to stay focused on the ultimate prize of everlasting life with you. Give me perspective to see the depth of sacrifice and suffering others have made to proclaim the gospel. Let me never take your gift of eternal life too lightly. Instill within me the drive of relentless pursuit toward those goals that you have planted in my heart. Help me to not be deterred from any task that you have assigned to me. In Jesus' name... Amen.

DECEMBER 5

Built by Him

For every house is built by someone, but God is the builder of everything... But Christ is faithful as the Son over God's house. And we are his house, if indeed we hold firmly to our confidence and the hope in which we glory.
–Hebrews 3:4—6 (NIV)

For the word of God is alive and active. Sharper than any double-edged sword, it penetrates even to dividing soul and spirit, joints and marrow; it judges the thoughts and attitudes of the heart...
Let us hold firmly to the faith we possess. For we do not have a high priest who is unable to empathize with our weaknesses, but we have one who has been tempted in every way, just as we are–yet did not sin. Let us then approach God's throne of grace with confidence, so that we may receive mercy and grace to help us in our time of need.
–Hebrews 4:12,14—16 (NIV)

There is a strange brew of confidence and dread within many procrastinators, myself included. Confidence says, "Surely I can do this. I believe that I have the skills to make it happen." The dread says, "Why do I keep putting this off? "How come I never seem to finish what I start?" "How can I finish on time?" "Will my life be over before any of my goals are fulfilled?" Naturally we assume that we are the builder of our destiny, but maybe that adds unnecessary pressure, sabotaging our motivation. God is the builder, and if our undone purpose is one that will fulfill His Purpose, he will build us into who we need to be. We must prepare ourselves by ingesting God's Word and seeking his presence in worship and prayer. As we get our thoughts and attitudes right, bolstered by faith in Jesus, we become fit for the master builder's plan. When we spend time becoming the person we were meant to be, mercy and grace will see us through to the finish, not because of us, but because God is the builder. Confidence in him will be rewarded; surely, he will help us in our time of need.

Dear Lord, You are the Creator of all things. Create a clean heart and willing spirit within me. Help me to realize that you do not oppose me when I wander away, you seek me in love, and bring me back to you. Let me be an active part in your plan for saving humanity. Lead me to your Word and your presence daily that I may be strengthened to overcome my weaknesses. Help me to build, along with you, a life that expands your kingdom and fulfills the purpose for which you designed me. In Jesus' name... Amen.

DECEMBER 6

Working for the Lord

Work hard and cheerfully at all you do, just as though you were working for the Lord and not merely for your masters, remembering that it is the Lord Christ who is going to pay you, giving you your full portion of all he owns. He is the one you are really working for... he has no special favorites who can get away with shirking.
–Colossians 3:23—25 (TLB)

I don't mean to say that I am perfect. I haven't learned all I should even yet, but I keep working toward the day when I will finally be all that Christ saved me for and wants me to be.
–Philippians 3:12 (TLB)

HELP WANTED

No matter what area of work we do: domestic chores, student, volunteering, office employment, healthcare professional, childcare, lawyer or manual laborer, it is important for us to do our job well. It is also very important to discover our strengths and gifts. God intends for us to reap joy from what we do. We are not called to gripe and complain. We are called to labor, encourage others, and proclaim the gospel by what we do, as well as what we say. Finding the right role for ourselves when it comes to employment or volunteering is essential because if we are prone to being late, or avoiding certain tasks or responsibilities, the wrong job will bring out the worst in us, not the best. We need to remind ourselves, all we do is for the Lord. Any job well done carries its own reward.

Dear Lord, Let us be people who work enthusiastically. Keep us aware of going down a path of grumbling and negativity, so that we will turn away from that direction. Help us to find our gifts and talents, so that we could increase our joy in our day-to-day labors. Let us never forget that we represent and serve you, in all we do and say. Help us maintain an uplifting attitude with co-workers and meet our assigned deadlines and responsibilities. During times when the job seems difficult, help us to remember the joy of the Lord is our strength. In Jesus' name... Amen.

DECEMBER 7

It's a Pain

For we are taking pains to do what is right, not only in the eyes of the Lord but also in the eyes of man.
–2 Corinthians 8:21 (NIV)

No discipline seems pleasant at the time, but painful. Later on, however, it produces a harvest of righteousness and peace for those who have been trained by it.
–Hebrews 12:11 (NIV)

He will wipe away every tear from their eyes. There will be no more death' or mourning or crying or pain, for the old order of things have passed away.
–Revelation 21:4 (NIV)

While my daughter was growing up, at times she earned a spanking. Before the spanking was administered she would scream hysterically, as if she were in extreme pain; we hadn't laid a hand on her yet! She was so fearfully undone at the prospect of punishment, she behaved as if she was already being tortured. As with many procrastinators, fear is painful, surely more agonizing than any task we are avoiding. According to information on the Erupting Mind website, "As procrastination is primarily caused by one's desire to avoid pain... one of the best ways to deal with and overcome procrastination is by changing how you perceive the pleasure and pain of the task... starting your task will result in the dissipation of many of your fears." Some of us need to realize that the future pain of leaving something undone, is far greater than the discomfort we would feel about doing that same task now.

Dear Lord, Help us to accept the fact that there will be pain in this life. Help us to overcome our fears which cause our unnecessary dread and avoidance behaviors. Give us the courage to change our ways and be more motivated by the rewards of timely accomplishments, instead of avoiding the specter of pain. May the prospect of any kind of momentary discomfort seem like nothing in view of the eternal rewards that you desire to see us enjoy. I thank you that we can look forward to an endless time with you where there is no fear, no pain, no suffering. In Jesus' name... Amen.

DECEMBER 8

Faith Plus

"His divine power has given us everything we need for a godly life through our knowledge of him who called us by his own glory and goodness. Through these he has given us his very great and precious promises, so that through them you may participate in the divine nature, having escaped the corruption in the world caused by evil desires.

For this reason, make every effort to add to your faith goodness; and to goodness, knowledge; and to knowledge, self-control; and to self-control, perseverance; and to perseverance, godliness; and to godliness, mutual affection; and to mutual affection, love.

For if you possess these qualities in increasing measure, they will keep you from being ineffective and unproductive in your knowledge of our Lord Jesus Christ... Therefore, my brothers and sisters, make every effort to confirm your calling and election. For if you do these things, you will never stumble, and you will receive a rich welcome into the eternal kingdom of our Lord and Savior Jesus Christ."
–2 Peter 1:3—11 (NIV)

For me, there is nothing more to do after absorbing these words than to pray.

Dear Lord, I thank you for your great and precious promises. May we continue to add the qualities of goodness, knowledge, self-control, perseverance, godliness, mutual affection, and love to our faith. May these attributes enhance our character, making us more effective in advancing your kingdom on earth. Help us to set aside time to renew our minds with your Word, enable us to be productive in this life, always growing in knowledge of you. Prompt us to do this day what you desire us to do. In Jesus' name... Amen.

DECEMBER 9

Your Season

That person is like a tree planted by streams of water, which yields its fruit in season and whose leaf does not wither–whatever they do prospers.
–Psalm 1:3 (NIV)

Sluggards do not plow in season; so at harvest time they look but find nothing.
–Proverbs 20:4 (NIV)

Even the stork in the sky knows her appointed seasons, and the dove, the swift and the thrush observe the time of their migration.
–Jeremiah 8:7 (NIV)

The Lord will open the heavens, the storehouse of his bounty, to send rain on your land in season and to bless all the work of your hands.
–Deuteronomy 28:12 (NIV)

As a native New Englander living in southern California, the lack of seasonal changes was disappointing, as well as disorienting for me. All humans have seasons that they go through from birth to death. Recognizing which season we are in, then knowing where to invest our labors, can be a valuable asset. While I had babies and young children, there was no other place I wanted to be other than at home raising my children. Whatever the cost or chaos of that season, it was rewarding beyond anything else the world had to offer me. Once children were grown, the season of furthering my education and launching a teaching career was a personal and financial blessing. During all those years, many goals and dreams were in the incubator. Now a new, yet "later," season is upon me. Like the miraculous wine at the wedding in Canaan, there is a fervent hope that the latter wine will be superior to the former. The productivity near the end should outshine whatever has come before. No matter our age or stage in life, we should be as wise as the bird who recognizes the season it is in. Let us now put our hand to the plow in our assigned field for our present season. No lamenting the past, just looking to the future harvest.

Dear Lord, You ordered times and seasons for all creation. You are a God of order, as well as change. Help all your people to recognize the season they now occupy, and the work they need to be doing. Let us not be stagnant or resisting the inevitable changes that come in life. Whether we are in the valley of frustration, or on a hilltop surrounded by abundant beauty, prepare us for what will come next. Give us discernment, and a willingness to work hard. By the time our life is over, may we see the fruit of our labors and a life that did not whither, a life that was productive and prosperous to the end. In Jesus' name... Amen.

DECEMBER 10

A Little Bit

Let the favor of the Lord our God be upon us, and establish the work of our hands upon us; yes, establish the work of our hands!
–Psalm 90:17 (ESV)

Sometimes it seems so hard to simply *get to work*. Whatever the reason for our delay, when we just do a little bit to get started, usually an emotional load is lifted. Timothy Pychyl, is a professional who researches the causes and effects of procrastination. He has much much wisdom to impart with the following words. Procrastinators need to... " break down their tasks into very small steps that can actually be accomplished. So, if it's something like writing a letter of reference, the first step is just opening the letterhead and writing the date. Even if it's an extremely small action, a little progress will typically make you feel better about the task and increase your self-esteem, which in turn reduces the desire to procrastinate to make yourself feel better."

While the basis for our uncomfortable anxious delays may be a mystery, the truth is doing a little bit of work gets the ball rolling, and our task gets closer to completion. Knowing that God's favor is upon us as we work should ease our anxiety and enhance the satisfaction and value of our work as well.

Dear Lord, You have designed us to be workers. The first disciples, in the midst of doing their jobs "immediately followed" Jesus when he called them to do so. Help us to be people who immediately do what we need to do. Let us not let little tasks feel like oppressive obligations. Help us to be starters, people who are willing to do a little bit right now. May that little bit expand into rewarding productivity. As the psalmist says, "Let the favor of the Lord our God be upon us, and establish the work of our hands!" May we do at least a little bit of what you are calling us to do today, that it may progressively build into its completion in due time. In Jesus' name... Amen.

DECEMBER 11

Going Through

For everyone born of God overcomes the world. This is the victory that has overcome the world, even our faith. Who is it that overcomes the world? Only the one who believes that Jesus is the son of God.
–Romans 15:13 (NIV)

May the God of all hope fill you with all joy and peace as you trust in him, so that you may overflow with hope by the power of the Holy Spirit.
–Joshua 4:23 (NIV)

For the LORD your God dried up the Jordan before you until you had crossed over. The LORD your God did to the Jordan what he had done to the Red Sea when he dried it up before us until we had crossed over.
–1 John 5:4—5 (NIV).

I recently heard a man share a story about how God had brought him through a very difficult time. He proclaimed that, "God is the God of the Going Through!" Many times, our way seems blocked and hindered. Our earthly mind, and other people may be saying, "No" to the path of our desired destination, but our God is a God of the "Yes." God is not a man; he matches his actions to his words. God has given us spiritual weapons of prayer, faith, joy, hope, the power of the Holy Spirit, peace in times of trust, and the light of truth to displace the darkness. We need to remember these things when opposition stands in our way. We may be stopped in our own strength, but our God is the God of going through it. With his presence and power, we can get where he wants us to go.

Dear Lord, Help us to remember your mighty deeds, and all that you have brought us through until now. Let your words replace our limited thinking. May we be people who call on your Holy Spirit for strength and guidance. Open our eyes to the power of prayers spoken in faith. Let us seek your presence so that we will be strengthened with joy. Guide us to our place in your Promise Land. Let nothing destroy our resolve as we go through dark and dangerous places. Remind us that you will make a way as we are going through it; you will bring us safely to our destination. In Jesus' name… Amen.

DECEMBER 12

Why Worry?

Therefore I tell you, do not worry about your life, what you will eat or drink; or about your body, what you will where. Is not life more than food, and the body more than clothes? Look at the birds of the air; they do not sow or reap or store away in barns, and yet your heavenly Father feeds them. Are you not much more valuable than they? Can anyone of you by worrying add a single hour to your life?... Your heavenly Father knows that you need them. But seek first his kingdom and his righteousness, and all these things will be given to you as well.
–Matthew 6: 25—33 (NIV)

How many times have you been caught in a web of anxiety and worry? Too many times for me, simply because I did not do what I was supposed to do until time was hanging over me like a guillotine. There have been times of financial worry caused by carrying a double mortgage after a move for a job. As a student there were late papers, and as a teacher there were stacks of papers still needing to be corrected when grades were due. Clothes I needed to wear for some event were buried in a mountain of laundry, no wonder I couldn't find them! All too often I'd be rushing out the door, late to some appointment, not even knowing the accurate location of where I was supposed to go, worrying about getting there on time. Good knows I worry about my children. Times of worry and anxiety can happen due to either important or trivial matters. If I had been more in tune to handle each day's task on the day it needed to be done, countless hours of worry and frustration could have been avoided. God does not want us to be in a state of worry, yet we continually rob ourselves of the peace he wants to generously give us.

Dear Lord, I need victory over worry and procrastination in my life. Help me to not leave things until the last "anxiety causing" minute. Help me to order my life into a reasonable steady pace. Give me discernment in how to prioritize my days, and as to what enjoyable activities may have to be sacrificed this day in order to obtain a higher goal. Holy Spirit empower me to change myself so that I too can enjoy a life of peace and be free from unnecessary times of worry and anxiety. Help me build a life on seeking His Kingdom first. In Jesus' name... Amen.

DECEMBER 13

I Hate Rejection

But some rejected his message and publicly spoke against Christ, so he left, refusing to preach to them again.
–Acts 19:9 (TLB)

Jesus looked at them and said, "Then what does the Scripture mean where it says, 'The Stone was rejected by the builders was made the cornerstone'?"
–Luke 20:17 (TLB)

Simeon blessed them but then said to Mary, "A sword shall pierce your soul, for this child shall be rejected by many in Israel, and this to their undoing. But he will be the greatest joy of many others. And the deepest thoughts of many hearts shall be revealed"
–Luke 2:34—35 (TLB)

The idea of creating a book that may be unpublished and unread, or applying for that dream job, or striving for a ministry position, can be accompanied by so much fear of rejection, it may not seem worth the effort. Personally, I have enough confidence in what I do, it is not failure that intimidates me, it is rejection. My five-year-old son once offered a mailman a decorated plate of Christmas cookies we had baked. The mailman rejected the offer saying, "I'm not your regular carrier." My son was heartbroken and cried, not understanding why his offering was refused. Inside me, I am a bit like a child. That is how I feel when confronted by rejection. It hurts me deeply when my efforts, my faith, or a person that is important to me seems to slam the door in my face. I need to face the fact that fear of rejection is a serious obstacle to my overcoming procrastination. Yet Jesus showed us that we need to expect that, and be willing to be rejected, mocked, hurt, or to carry our own cross in accomplishing God's purpose. If people rejected Jesus as he healed others, and performed miracles, how can we think we will escape rejection in our lives? Fear of rejection should never stand in our way, but often it does.

Dear Lord, Help us to learn from Jesus. We pray to be Christ-like. No matter how much rejection hurts, help us to never be afraid of it. Jesus went through so much persecution and rejection for us, help us to focus on the end result and the greater good, as he did. When we are doing something to advance your kingdom, let nothing stand in our way. Build up our spiritual strength and determination to overcome anything that would deter us from our calling. May your will be done in us, and on earth as it is in heaven. In Jesus' name... Amen.

DECEMBER 14

What a Relief

What happiness for those whose guilt is forgiven! What joys when sins are covered over! What relief for those who have confessed their sins and God has cleared their record.
–Psalm 32:1—2 (TLB)

I, the Messiah, have authority on earth to forgive sins.
–Luke 5:23 (TLB)

According to a study done by Timothy Pychyl, "Research suggests that one of the most effective things that procrastinators can do is to forgive themselves for procrastinating." He states that, "students who reported forgiving themselves for procrastinating on studying for a first exam ended up procrastinating less for a second exam. This works because procrastination is linked to negative feelings, the researchers say. Forgiving yourself can reduce the guilt you feel about procrastinating, which is one of the main triggers for procrastinating in the first place."

While many people see religion as simply a bunch of rules and restrictions, people who embrace the Bible and their faith in Jesus see guidelines for a good life and protection. Our God is emphatic about forgiveness. Forgiveness is powerful and it heals. It is a force not only to be used in relation to others; sometimes we need it to heal ourselves. Through forgiving ourselves we are blessed to experience a great relief from an emotional burden and are able to move forward, minus the weight of guilt!

Dear Lord, Thank you for insisting that as followers of yours, we must be people who are forgiving. I confess that sometimes it is very difficult for me to forgive myself, it seems more fitting to condemn and berate myself for my shortcomings. Free us from our tendency to be unwillingly to forgive ourselves. Let us be people who seek your grace, mercy, and acceptance. Help us to rightly measure ourselves and realize that we need the relief that forgiveness delivers. Thank you for the uplifting power of forgiveness. In Jesus' name… Amen.

DECEMBER 15

Only Ten More Days

And while they were there, the time came for her baby to be born; and she gave birth to her first child, a son. She wrapped him in a blanket, and laid him in a manger, because there was no room for them in the village inn.
–Luke 2:6 (TLB)

"I bring you the most joyful news ever announced, and it is for everyone! The Savior–yes, the Messiah, the Lord– has been born tonight in Bethlehem! How will you recognize him? You will find a baby wrapped in a blanket, lying in a manger!"
–Luke 2: 10-12 (TLB)

For people who are organized there is an enjoyable amount of work to do until Christmas Day arrives. Today, for procrastinators there may be panic setting in. Too many items left to buy, and wrap, and to ship on time. The list of things that you meant to do by now is growing, and what is not done? … That list is looming a bit too large! How about the cards, emails, cookies, travel or guest arrangements, and cleaning? I have had too many Christmas Eve nights, not finishing until early A.M. Christmas Day, minutes before my children joyfully awoke and were ready to see what was in their stockings and under the tree. Now, I want everything done ahead of time, I want to enjoy my Christmas Eve and day, free from the exhaustion and stress of last minute everything. Then, just maybe then I can have my peace on earth *and* goodwill toward men, from now until December 25th. Ahhh, to have a holiday free from the stress of "last minute," That's what I call a Merry Christmas.

Dear Lord, As time is closing in for the precious time of year to celebrate your birth, help us to put your presence and your will at the center of all of our activities this year. Guide us to use our time wisely, and may this time not be one of anxiety, overspending, and too many commitments. Guard our hearts from selfishness, frustration, and envy. As we grow closer to you, grow a state of contentment within us. May we celebrate the birth of our Lord and Savior in ways that spread joy, love, generosity, and peace to those around us. In Jesus' name... Amen.

DECEMBER 16

Image is Important

So God created mankind in his own image, in the image of God he created them, male and female he created them.
–Genesis 1:27 (NIV)

For those God foreknew he also predestined to be conformed to the image of his Son, that he might be the firstborn among many brothers and sisters.
–Romans 8:9 (NIV)

For now we see only a reflection [image] as in a mirror; then we shall see face to face. Now I know in part; then I shall know fully, even as I am fully known.
–1 Corinthians 13:12 (NIV)

When we see all that is wrong with humanity: violence, sexual misconduct, abuse, lies, greed, and more, it is hard to accept the truth. The truth is, mankind is created in the image of God. Our creator has imprinted us with all that he is. We are designed to express his love, mercy, truth, grace, forgiveness and creativity. Hard to believe isn't it? Not all truth is easy to swallow... not only when it comes to the human race, but to ourselves as individuals. We think- *Me? Created in God's image and likeness? I don't think so.* Too often, procrastinators lack of self-esteem sabotages them. If we cannot accept the greatness that dwells within, it is hard to believe that we too can accomplish something great. It starts with simply believing that God has the power to transform us into his image and bring out our God-like DNA. It happens when we are willing to become more like Jesus and submit to God's will on a daily basis.

Dear Lord, Help us to embrace who you created us to be, created in your image, and carrying your qualities within us. Help us to take on your likeness. Let us be people who spend time devoted to you, learning your ways and ingesting your words. Help us to be more like Jesus, courageous, obedient, living in touch with your will every moment. May we become radiant, projecting your light into the world, so that they can see you, in us. Today, help me to do at least one thing that will reveal who you truly are, reflecting your image to those around me. In Jesus' name... Amen.

DECEMBER 17

The Cost of Complaining

For God is at work within you, helping you want to obey him, and then helping you to do what he wants. In everything you do, stay away from complaining and arguing so that no one can speak a word of blame against you. You are to live clean, innocent lives as children of God in a dark world full of people that are crooked and stubborn. Shine out among them like beacon lights, holding out to them the Word of Life.
–Philippians 2:13—16 (TLB)

Scriptures like this cause me to reflect on my tendency to complain. Having grown up within a household where my father was often critical of others, and my mother prone to self-criticism, I developed a rather critical attitude, inclined to see the negative side of things first. It seems as if my nature needs to be constantly renewed, in order to not default to a "glass half empty" outlook. There is too much useless complaining, either inside my head or spoken out loud. Work that needs to be done, pressure to do things at a high standard, a conflict of wills within my family, unpleasant circumstances beyond my control, can too often trigger arguing, or complaining. When it comes to procrastinating, my brain can mentally construct every obstacle to keep from starting or finishing some work that needs to be done. When I see what happened to the children of Israel, wandering around in the desert, complaining and resisting God's will about entering the Promised Land, it makes me realize that complaining can be the quickest route away from what God has for his people. They literally procrastinated about entering God's best, prepared especially for them! Easily accepting the negative side of situations can be a ticket to wandering around in the desert for forty years. Who wants that when your Promised Land is within reach?

Dear Lord, Forgive me. I confess that I am too quick to see the negative side of situations, too quick to complain, too short sighted to see the big picture of what you have in store for me. You have created a Promised Land of fulfilled destiny in this life, and unspeakable glory in heaven for all of your people. Holy Spirit protect us from thinking and acting contrary to your will. Let us see our lives as you see them, let us be free from complaining and arguing. Grant us the ability to see our situations from your point of view. Give us the grace to look beyond things that trigger our tendency to complain. Help us to speak words of gratitude quickly and often. In Jesus' name… Amen.

DECEMBER 18

Our Personal Trainer

[Jesus said] I do my work, putting people together, setting them on their feet, ready for the End. This is what the prophets meant when they wrote, 'And then they will all be personally taught by God.' Anyone who has spent any time at all listening to the Father, really listening and therefore learning, comes to me to be taught personally– to see it with his own eyes, hear it with his own ears, from me, since I have it firsthand from the Father.
–John 6:43—46 (MSG)

Do you not know that in a race all the runners run, but only one gets the prize? Run in such a way as to get the prize. Everyone who competes in the games goes into strict training. They do it to get a crown that will not last, but we do it to get a crown that will last forever.
–1 Corinthians 9:24—25 (NIV)

I used to run, not much, three to four miles about three to four times a week. Now that my knees have sustained injuries and aging, running is not for me. I wonder how many phenomenal places that I would hurry to see if I knew that my eyesight was failing? While there is still time and we are still able, we need to participate in our race to the best of our ability. Even the greatest athletes have to retire when they can no longer perform with excellence. Anything of value that we do, we need to learn from the best trainers and teachers possible. God is our personal trainer, getting us in shape to earn that crown that will last forever. Let's see the course the Lord has laid out for us with our own eyes, and hear him with our own ears, refusing to quit until our race is done.

Dear Lord, I thank you that you are ever ready to teach and train us in the way we should go. Help me take advantage of the time I have, so that down the road there will be no regrets. Tune my ears to your voice; I need to hear you clearly and respond immediately. Let us not waste time with things that could hinder our race or cripple ourselves by stumbling in the dark. Grant us vision to see our way toward the prize that you have promised us. Let our faith grow as we submit to your training, so that we would experience the joy of victory now, and at the end of our lives. In Jesus' name... Amen.

DECEMBER 19

For the Night Owls

Fix your attention on God. You'll be changed from the inside out. Readily recognize what he wants from you, and quickly respond to it. Unlike the culture around you, always dragging you down to its level of immaturity, God brings the best out of you, develops well-formed maturity in you.
–Romans 12:2 (MSG)

You've picked up this bad habit of not listening. By this time you ought to be teachers yourselves, yet here I find you need someone to sit down with you and go over the basics of God again, starting from square one... Milk is for beginners, inexperienced in God's ways; solid food is for the mature, who have some practice in telling right from wrong.
–Hebrews 12:12–14 (MSG)

Procrastinators often possess a childlike immaturity which defiantly states, "I don't want to!" Becoming a mature adult means that you do things that you don't feel like doing. For many people that could be paying their bills or continuing their education. For me, it means avoiding a regular routine to get ready for bed; I resist ceasing all activities because it's time to go to bed at a *decent hour.* My inner child is screaming every night, "No one's gonna tell me when to turn off the TV and go to bed!" My lack of routine inevitably leads to– too many hours escaping in shows and movies, and a lack of sleep followed by a lack of productivity the next day. If a regular nighttime routine was created, maybe my inner child would quiet down, and accept the inevitable. Too often we prioritize what we do, by what we feel like doing. For myself, I need to stop doing what I feel like doing, and just go to bed!

Dear Lord, I confess that I enjoy the late-night hours, being left to myself to do whatever I feel like doing. I also confess much of my life is wasted that way, and I rob myself of energy that is needed the following day. Help me to grow in maturity and regulate my sleeping habits, so that I am more productive, not less productive. Help me to be motivated by wisdom and order, not my feelings. Change me from someone that avoids routine and going to sleep at a regular time. Let maturity prevail within me, change me from the inside out. In Jesus' name... Amen.

DECEMBER 20

Faith Sees

Now faith is the substance of things hoped for, the evidence of things not seen.
–Hebrews 11:1 (NKJV)

For in it the righteousness of God is revealed from faith to faith; as it is written, "The just shall live by faith."
–Romans 1:17 (NKJV)

For whatever is born of God overcomes the world. And this is the victory that has overcome the world– our faith.
–1 John 5:4 (NKJV)

Faith is a powerful force beyond my comprehension. It is a lifeline to God. Faith plays its part in our day-to-day world in silent ways; no one would board a plane without it! The Bible also says without faith, it is impossible to please God. My belief in Jesus- that he died on that cross for me, freeing me from the eternal consequences of sin and death, is the most important result of faith. Many things in my life, that I have faith for, have not yet come to pass. Thankfully, faith sees a possible future when my eyes cannot. I will put my faith in the rock-solid faithfulness of God over my unstable faith any day. Time to keep praying to see what God has for me, good things that can only be seen and attained through the eyes of faith.

Dear Lord, Let us be people who spend time in your Word, in private praise and worship, growing our faith. Place us in a local church, a community of believers that thrives on love, as well as exercising and building faith. Give us eyes to see what you desire for our lives. Let us raise our consciousness of the power of faith in our lives. Speak to us of that one thing you want us to pursue, in faith, that we will overcome all obstacles standing in our way to attain it. Let us be not only hearers of your words, but doers as well. By faith, in Jesus' name... Amen.

DECEMBER 21

Doing Your Work

Then Moses inspected all their work. When he found it had been done just as the Lord had commanded him, he blessed them.
–Exodus 39:43 (NLT)

Whatever you do, do well. For when you go to the grave, there will be no work or planning or knowledge or wisdom…
–Ecclesiastes 9:10 (NLT)

Pay careful attention to your own work, for then you will get the satisfaction of a job well done, and you won't need to compare yourself to anyone else.
–Galatians 6:4 (NLT)

Many times, especially in college when facing an assignment that I knew would take a tremendous number of hours to accomplish, just starting it seemed to be the hardest part. We need to change our internal operating system to earlier, rather than later. The following is very good advice from the website: www.eruptingmind.com. –

> The worst thing about procrastination is that the pain you have associated with a particular task is almost always worse than the actual task itself. This is why people keep procrastinating, because essentially, they fear their task so much that they don't want to confront it. However, by starting your task at the earliest opportunity, most of these fears will quickly dissipate as you will be too focused on doing your work that you won't have time to think about fear or worry

Dear Lord, Help us to defeat the fear of impending projects. Let us not avoid the responsibilities of the work that is before us. Help us have a diligent heart toward our work, whatever that work may be. Let us be people that pay attention to our own work and not compare ourselves to anyone else. Let us experience the intrinsic rewards of hard work, and as we work, know the joy of your approval. If there be any task before us right now that we are avoiding, let us take responsibility now, and begin that work so that we can move forward. In Jesus' name... Amen.

DECEMBER 22

A Risky Plan

The law of the Lord is perfect,
refreshing the soul.
The statues of the Lord are trustworthy,
making wise the simple.
The precepts of the Lord are right,
giving joy to the heart.
The commands of the Lord are radiant,
giving light to the eyes.
–Psalm 19:7—8 (NIV)

"For I know the plans I have for you," declares the Lord, "Plans to prosper you and not to harm you, plans to give you hope and a future. Then you will call on me and come and pray to me, and I will listen to you. You will seek me and find me when you seek me with all your heart. I will be found by you," declares the Lord...
–Jeremiah 29:11-13 (NIV)

According to Mike Bundrant, retired psychotherapist and practicing life coach, "chronic procrastination often has its roots in emotional life... When you procrastinate, you have more than a productivity problem. You also have an emotional obstacle in the way of your success." When that obstacle is one made up of multiple disappointments in life, we cope by protecting ourselves from the emotional pain of yet another disappointment. Risk feels like an open invitation to sorrowful consequences. Why work to set another plan in motion, only to be devastated again when it doesn't work out? Our old disappointments are so loud, we can't hear the Lord wooing us to get on track. Do we dare risk, yet one more let down in our lives? We do, **if** we can move past those painful emotions, trust in God's Word and his plan for our lives. Risking yet one more painful experience, is a necessary step toward walking into, and working out God's plan.

Dear Lord, I confess that painful disappointments have crippled my efforts to be all that I can be. I don't want to be hurt like that ever again. I need to be delivered from the fear that all my efforts, hopes and dreams, will come to nothing! The idea that my life will be lived without completing all that you have for me to do, is a foreboding oppressive cloud. Free me from this sense of futility that darkens my eyes and confounds the truth of your plans for me. Help me to focus on the possibility of future rewards, not on past hurts. As I seek you Lord, refresh my soul, give me wisdom to overcome, let joy spring up with my heart, giving light to my eyes. In Jesus' name... Amen.

DECEMBER 23

Avoiding a Troubled Mind

But Martha was distracted with much serving; and she went to him and said, "Lord, do you not care that my sister has left me to serve alone? Tell her then to help me. But the Lord answered her, "Martha Martha, you are anxious and troubled about many things; one thing is needful. Mary has chosen the good portion, which shall not be taken away from her."
–Luke 10:40-42 (RSV)

There are a lot of extra things to do during the holidays. We may have ongoing obligations that take a back seat for a while with special events, and *once a year* get togethers. My sister has a list written down scheduling all that needs to be done by its assigned date. She manages everything well because her "To Do's" are properly thought out and put into a good order. My sister and I are quite different, but I am successfully working toward being more like her in this area. Christians are too often "distracted with much serving." Overextending ourselves is the last thing we should be doing. We need to be choosing the "good portion." That means choosing the one thing that brings us closer to our Lord, not to a place of anxiety and a troubled mind. Let's be at the feet of Jesus, eager to hear his every word.

Dear Lord, Draw us close to you as we put aside precious time to listen to your words, and have a heart that beats with yours for things that are most important. Let serving you never be more important than simply spending time with you. Teach us when to say, "No," to those tasks that would take us away from our main purpose. Draw us to be where we need to be. Help us to organize our obligations, so that they may be met responsibly and on time. As we follow you, putting first things first, let us experience the precious peace of an untroubled mind. In Jesus' name... Amen.

DECEMBER 24

Rejoice!

The glory of the Lord shone around them, and they were terrified. But the angel said to them, "Do not be afraid. I bring you good news that will cause great joy for all the people. Today in the town of David a savior has been born to you; he is the Messiah, the Lord."
–Luke 2:8—11 (NIV)

For Christmas Eve and Christmas Day, I plan to celebrate and rejoice over the birth of Jesus Christ, my Lord and Savior. Time to be with family and friends, give, rejoice, forgive, feast, enjoy, and embrace the small blessings of life that are all around us. At this time of year, it seems appropriate that nothing is more important than that. I praise God that we have a time of year on our calendar, despite growing efforts to erase the meaning of Christ's birth, to publicly proclaim, exalt, and celebrate who Jesus is, and sing aloud of the power of his saving grace.

Dear Lord, May we reach out to those who do not know you, those that are lonely. May we bring joy into someone else's life during this Christmas. Thank you for bringing your son to earth and fulfilling the mission of salvation for everyone that believes. May we be like the shepherds, in awe of your birth, and a bit like the angels, singing God's glory and spreading tidings of great joy. In Jesus' Name... Amen.

DECEMBER 25

Tis the Season

Then Daniel praised the God of heaven and said:
"Praise be to the name of God for ever and ever;
wisdom and power are his.
He changes times and seasons;
he deposes kings and raises up others.
He gives wisdom to the wise
and knowledge to the discerning.
He reveals deep and hidden things;
he knows what lies in darkness,
and light dwells with him..."
–Daniel 2:19—22 (NIV)

Today is Christmas Day, it is a day to be celebrated and enjoyed. How we *do* this day is based on a few things: our faith, geography, and our season of life. A child who believes in Santa, a teenager bored by family gatherings, a young couple whose children are enthralled in the magic, and lonely senior citizens, certainly all experience this day differently. Change is inevitable, and Christmas can be a good time to reflect on Christmases past, find joy in the present, and prepare for changes in our future. We should remember that there is a future version of ourselves out there being defined in this present moment, hopefully getting us prepared for the next season. Isn't that how Ebenezer Scrooge had his life transformed? He certainly didn't like the truth about his past, present, or future. Realizing his future was not yet set, he joyfully, zealously took advantage of his new opportunity to live differently, and he became the best version of himself before it was too late. Change is possible, "God bless Us, Everyone!"

Dear Lord, Help us to keep expectant hearts filled with faith. Help us to embrace our present season of life, and find the good in it, no matter the pains and trials it may bring. Let us keep attitudes of kindness, giving, and joy associated with this season for the whole year through. May we all strive to be generous and be a blessing to others. Give us a perspective on life that places you in the center of everything. In Jesus' name... Amen.

DECEMBER 26

Our Father's Will

Father, if you are willing, take this cup from me; yet not my will, but yours be done...
–Luke 22:42 (NIV)

"...The LORD your God, who is going before you, will fight for you, as he did for you in Egypt, before your very eyes, and in the wilderness. There you saw how the LORD your God carried you, as a father carries his son, all the way you went until you reached this place." In spite of this, you did not trust the LORD your God, who went ahead of you on your journey, in fire by night and in a cloud by day, to search out places for you to camp and to show you the way you should go.
–Deuteronomy 1:30—33 (NIV)

Submitting to God's will is not always easy; it can be extremely difficult at times. Even Jesus, faced with a tortuous death on the cross, asked his Heavenly Father to provide another way. Thank God he submitted to his father's will and bought abundant eternal life for all who believe in him. Sometimes I think, *If I had seen all the miraculous works of God with my own eyes it would be much easier to obey God's will.* Then I realize, that really isn't how it works.

The Israelites lost their Promised Land through disobedience after seeing awesome miracles. Some people who saw Jesus raise Lazarus from the grave decided to plot against him! We simply have to obey, trusting the results will work God's will, not only in our life, but in the lives of others. Every step of obedience, trust, and surrender to our Heavenly Father's will reaps a great reward, opens doors of blessings, and allows us to move forward into the good things specifically prepared for us by God.

Dear Lord, You have provided precious promises and salvation for all who have faith in you and by the sacrifice of your son on the cross. May all your people trust you more and more every day. Guide us to greener pastures as we obey your commands and do your will. Let us not seek signs but seek your presence and your will for our lives. May we rely more on your Holy Spirit to infuse our conscience and lead us in the right direction. Today, help us to know what things to put aside, what actions to take, and what words to speak. In Jesus' name... Amen.

DECEMBER 27

Enough Time

I don't want you ending up in blind alleys, or wasting time making wrong turns. Hold tight to good advice; don't relax your grip. Guard it well–your life is at stake!
–Proverbs 4:10—15 (MSG)

So that you cannot live at times one way and at times another way according to how you feel on any given day. Why don't you choose to be led by the Spirit and so escape erratic compulsions of a law-dominated existence?
–Galatians 5:17—18 (MSG)

Time management is a big issue with many procrastinators. We often need help in structuring the right method to organize our time. We also need to discern the most important actions to take on any given day. I would like to share some advice, by Jonathan Lowenhar, given to improve time management and focus. As President at ETW Advisors (Enjoy The Work), (www.etwadvisors.com) an organization that gives advice to entrepreneurs and founders of new businesses, he knows this subject well. He states that if this method is followed for three weeks there will be dramatic results in improving your ability to get things done. He calls it the **"3-2-1"** method. Jonathan states, "I personally don't recommend bounding yourself to a time-based schedule. Stuff comes up all the time. You get distracted. With 3-2-1, you can be flexible. And at the end of the day, knocking out your priorities is what matters. So why let a difficult-to-follow pre-planned schedule stress you out. I've found that someone who has historically struggled with time management employs this for 3 consecutive weeks, the habit sticks."

I haven't tried this yet, but it seems like a very good idea.

> **"Every morning create a list of 6 goals that follow this pattern:**
> What are **3 things I must accomplish** today?
> What are **2 things I would like to accomplish** today?
> What is **1 thing that would be nice to get to** today?"

Dear Lord, You are the author of all wisdom. Lead and guide me into more successful ways of managing my time. May I always rely on your Holy Spirit to reveal what is most important for me to do this day. Help me to create habits that will increase my productivity. Whatever method works for me, help me to always dedicate my talent, time and energy to you. In Jesus' name... Amen.

DECEMBER 28

Staying on Track

So let's keep focused on that goal, those of us who want everything God has for us. If any of you have something else in mind, something less than total commitment, God will clear your blurred vision– you'll see it yet! Now that you are on the right track, let's stay on it.
–Philippians 3:15—16 (MSG)

Don't get off track, either left or right, so as to make sure you get to where you are going. And don't for a minute let this Book of Revelation be out of mind... Haven't I commanded you? Strength! Courage! Don't be timid; don't get discouraged. GOD, Your God, is with you every step you take.
–Joshua 1:1—9 (MSG)

It is hard to fathom the actual importance of staying on course when it comes to altering habits and initiating changes in one's life. I cannot count how many times, over decades, that I have tried to change my eating habits. There have been many times of disciplined seasons, edging close to a healthy weight and exercise, when one day of indulgence turned into a few days, a week turned into months, and "Oops! Here I am 35 pounds overweight again!" It is a roller coaster I am very tired of, but I never seem to get off this ride. This year can be the time I finally focus on that end goal and refuse to get off course. Maybe, if I can finally desire that end goal more than that fragrant cinnamon bun in front of me, and add some faith and reliance on God's help, I can stay on course and make it happen. Hmmm, maybe next year?

Dear Lord, There is nothing more important than you. Help me to stay focused on you, and your words. I come against doubt and unbelief that hinder me as I try to change my habits for the better. Let me keep inviting the Holy Spirit into my life to guide, counsel, and give me comfort when I am weak. As I focus on you, show me the individual path you want me to take. Once my path is known, steer me away from distractions and temptations. When I stumble off track, bring me back quickly, repeatedly, until I no longer look to left or the right, but have my course firmly set, in perfect aim with your will for my life. In Jesus' name... Amen.

DECEMBER 29

What Tomorrow Brings

In a word, what I'm saying is, Grow up. You're kingdom subjects. Now live like it. Live out your God-created identity. Live generously and graciously toward others, the way God lives toward you.
–Matthew 5:48 (MSG)

Give your entire attention to what God is doing right now, and don't get worked up about what may or may not happen tomorrow. God will help you deal with whatever hard things come up when the time comes.
–Matthew 6:34 (MSG)

We should not get "worked up" about tomorrow, but many of us want to change our lives and be different in the future. If we truly want to change for the better tomorrow, we must live differently *today.* The inclination to always put off until tomorrow what should have been done by now, creates a wishful attitude instead of an action plan we work at to transform our life. There is no fairy godmother at our beck and call to create an altered reality for us. There is a loving God who has given us his Word, salvation through his son, and wisdom, counsel, and comfort available through the Holy Spirit. We don't need our wishes granted. We need to get to work and live out God's plan. Then, step by step starting today, we will create a much better tomorrow, instead of worrying about what tomorrow will bring.

Dear Lord, Thank you for your Word and for the work of your Holy Spirit. Help us to overcome all our fears and not worry about tomorrow. Show us what to do this day, so that we may face tomorrow in peace. Draw us to your Word and your presence. Help us to submit to the wisdom and discernment of your Holy Spirit. Convict us of wasting time if we are lingering in leisure pursuits when there is work to be done now. Let a sense of satisfaction grow within us as we meet our obligations in a timely manner. Allow us a taste of your divine approval, as we anticipate the day when we hear you say, "Well done, good and faithful servant." In Jesus' name... Amen.

DECEMBER 30

A New Kind of New Year

Give instruction to a wise man, and he will be wiser; teach a righteous man and he will increase in learning.
–Proverbs 9:9 (RSV)

As each has received a gift, employ it for one another, as good stewards of God's varied grace
–1 Peter 4:10 (RSV)

The Master commended the dishonest steward for his shrewdness; for the sons of this world are more shrewd in dealing with their own generation than the sons of light.
–Luke 16:8 (RSV)

Many people appear to have lives far from honoring God, yet seem to be very successful. That has made me question why that is, and has even provoked a bit of jealousy at times. I wrongly thought that since I served Jesus with my whole heart, that magically God would create an upbeat, success story of my life, sort of a *happily ever after* tale. Not so. There are certain actions that we can take, based on wise principles that will produce positive outcomes, whether or not we follow God. Approaching the time for New Year's resolutions, it is good to be wise and realistic. No longer will I make a list of 12 things to change about myself. Then, feel badly at the end of the year because those goals were not accomplished. This year, I will seek God, lean on his guidance, and set 3-4 goals that when accomplished, will produce a better life, making me better equipped to bless others. This year, as I set out to slay the Procrastination Monster, God has been faithful, and my feet are on the path to victory. If it is possible for me to be free from the snares of procrastination, it is possible for anyone!

Dear Lord, Guide me through the process of approaching this New Year. Holy Spirit counsel me and impart wisdom to me so that I will set my mind on God's will for my life. Help me to cast aside comparison and envy, unrealistic expectations, frustration and hopelessness. Open my eyes to the wonderful possibilities awaiting me in the new year. Bring to mind goals, that when accomplished, will allow me to live at my best for this season of life. Give me hope, vision, and faith to trust you in every step of the way. Grant me a renewed sense of purpose with a clear vision of the ways that you want to use me to expand and build your kingdom. Grant all those who desire to be free from their procrastinating ways to have the victory. In Jesus' name... Amen.

DECEMBER 31

Too Much Wine

May God give you heaven's dew and earth's richness– an abundance of grain and new wine.
–Genesis 27:28 (NIV)

Do not get drunk on wine, which leads to debauchery. Instead, be filled with the Spirit.
–Ephesians 5:18 (NIV)

In the same way, deacons are to be worthy of respect, sincere, not indulging in much wine...
–1 Timothy 3:8 (NIV)

When he drank some of its wine, he became drunk, and lay uncovered inside his tent.
–Genesis 9:21 (NIV)

The Bible does not condemn wine, otherwise Jesus would not have made a superior lot of it at the wedding of Cana. Here it is New Year's Eve, the holiday most known for excessive drinking. It is time to address addiction, and the dangers of procrastinating when it comes to dealing with it. Are you addicted to some mind and mood altering substance? Time to face that truth that most addicts continually deny! The longer one procrastinates in dealing with their alcoholism (or any other life controlling addiction) the harsher the consequences. The price of avoiding your need for deliverance can cost: marriages, careers, freedom, fatal accidents, failing health, terrible emotional pain in your loved ones, friendships, the destruction of one's destiny, and often death. Look back and see what your addiction has cost you so far. If you do not overcome it now, there is a bleak future that awaits, with far greater costs around the bend. Avoiders may continue to deny, but reality has a way of making itself harsh and ugly, and painfully present in the future. Those of us who do not suffer from life threatening addiction, we need to step up our prayer power to see our loved ones set free.

Dear Lord, I thank you that there is freedom from addiction, and that victory is possible. I am so grateful for organizations like Alcoholics Anonymous for those seeking recovery, and for Al Anon, dedicated to helping families of alcoholics. Please open the eyes of believers that are bound by alcohol, that they may see their condition for what it really is. I pray for help, healing, and deliverance for all those bound by alcoholism, or any other drug addiction. May many who follow you, find their way to having no master over their lives but you. May the chains of addiction be broken! In Jesus' name... Amen.

REFERENCES

January

2- Sarah Young, *Jesus Calling,* Nashville: Thomas Nelson, 2004.

8- Ruth Ziolkowski, (Crazy Horse Memorial sculptor's widow)

18- Hara Estroff Marano, "Procrastination: Ten Things to Know." psychologytoday.com, August, 2003

19- MxPx lyrics, "Late Again," *Secret Weapon,* 2007

20- Johnny Kelly, "Procrastination"- Vimeo, 2007.

21- Timothy Pychyl, professor at Carleton University, Ottawa, Canada

22- Dianne Wilson, *Body and Soul,* 2010

29- Ana Swanson,"The Real Reasons You Procrastinate," Case Western Reserve University Study, 1997. Posted April 27, 2016. washingtonpost.com website

February

2- *Ground Hog Day*, produced, written, directed by Harold Ramis, 1993

4- Hara Estroff Marano, "Procrastination: Ten Things You Should Know." psychologytoday.com. August 2003

9- *AARP Bulletin,* December 2017

17- Mike Bundrant, "The Emotions Behind Procrastination: Five Scenarios You Should Understand if you Want to Get Things Done." inlpcenter.org

20- SpongeBob SquarePants, "Procrastination/I'm with Stupid," Season 2, Episode 17, 2001.

25- Joyce Meyers, *Battlefield of the Mind*, New York: Faith Words Hachette Book Group, 2011

28- J.R.R. Tolkien, *The Lord of the Rings,* United Kingdom, Allen & Unwin publishers, 1954-5

March

5- Words of wisdom from Milton Adolf

6- Tim Urban, "Wait But Why" blog. TED.com, Tim Urban: Inside the Mind of a Master Procrastinator, TED Talk, Feb. 2016

7- Tim Urban, "Wait But Why" blog. TED.com, Tim Urban: Inside the Mind of a Master Procrastinator, TED Talk, Feb. 2016

21- Dr. Timothy Pychyl

30- *Springs of Roman Wisdom,* New York: Herder Book Center, 1968.

April

6- Winston Churchill

7- Lynn Johnston, "For Better or Worse" comic strip.

18- Hal Hersfield, psychologist from UCLA Anderson School of Management, quote from: Ana Swanson, "The Real Reasons You Procrastinate—and How to Stop" April 27, 2016. washingtonpost.com.

21- Timothy Pychyl, quote from- Ana Swanson, "The Real Reasons You Procrastinate—and How to Stop" April 27, 2016. washingtonpost.com.

May

10- Poster artwork, for the band *Blenderhead.*

11- Matisyahu lyrics – *Spark Seeker,* July 2012.

15- Dr. Timothy Pychyl, quote from- Ana Swanson, "The Real Reasons You Procrastinate—and How to Stop" April 27, 2016. washingtonpost.com.

June

10- YouTube- Pink & Kelly Clarkson, "Everybody Hurts," AMA Awards, 2017.

12- Time Magazine's Health.com – "4 Ways to Stop Procrastinating," May 26, 2014.

15- eruptingmind.com: Intelligent Advice for Intelligent People. "Avoidance Behaviors and Procrastination."

24- Becca Pizzi, who ran World Marathon Challenge- 7 Marathons on 7 Continents in 7 Days. Interview- CBS This Morning. February18, 2016. https://www.cbsnews.com/news/becca-pizzi-world-marathon-challenge-first-american-woman-to-complete/

26- YouTube music videos: P.O.D.- *Alive,* Mortal- *Alive & Awake,* Pearl Jam- *Alive,* Hillsong Y&F- *Alive*

July

2- Bob Dylan, "Every Grain of Sand," *Shot of Love,* August 1981

3- *Wonder Woman,* directed by Patty Jenkins, screen play- Allan Heinberg, 2017.

5- Mike Bundrant, AHA System website

8- *The First Grader,* directed by Justin Chadwick, screen play- Ann Peacock, 2010.

12- Dr. Mary C. Lamia, "The Secret Life of Procrastinators and the Stigma of Delay," www.pyschology today.com, August 14, 2017.

19- Franz Schubert, *Unfinished Symphony (Schubert's Symphony No.8)*

25- Randy Voorhees, *Old Age is Always 15 Years Older Than I Am,* (Kansas City: Andrews McMeel Publishing, 2001).

26- Keith Green, "The Lord is My Shepherd," *Songs for the Shepherd*, April 1982.

29- Emily Pronin, Princeton University Study, 2008. cited in: "The Real Reasons You Procrastinate—and How to Stop" April 27, 2016. washingtonpost.com.

August

2- Christine Caine

4- Jonathan Wilson

7- Pablo Picasso

9- Christine Caine

11- Mike Bundrant, "The Emotions Behind Procrastination: Five scenarios You Should Understand if you Want to Get Things DONE." inlpcenter.org website

12- Lanny Wolfe, "Only One Life," 1973.

15- Chantal Beaupre, "Anger Can Lead to Procrastination' -Part 1/VividLife.me

16- Twyla Tharp

18- Christine Caine

19- Tim Urban, waitbutwhy.com

27- *The War Room*, directed by Alex Kendrick, written by Alex and Stephen Kendrick, August 2015.

September

1-Diane Peters, *Procrastination- Deal With It: All in Good Time,* Lorimer Children & Teens, Minneapolis, 2016.

5- Ibid

9- Timothy Pycyhl

11- *UP,* Pixar Animation Studios, Walt Disney Company, director- Pete Docter, May 2009.

20- "Mirror Mirror: Seeing Future Self May Shape How You Invest," Ticker Tape editors, January 9, 2015. tickertape.tdameritrade.com

22- https://www.eruptingmind.com/avoidance-behaviors-and-procrastination.

27- Tali Sharot, *TIME,* October 2, 2017.

29- Dr. Bill Cloke, "Procrastination… The Tip of the Iceberg," www.billcloke.com/all-services/procrastination/

October

2- Switchfoot, quote from the song, "Thrive," *Vice Verses,* September 2011.

5- Diane Peters, *Procrastination- Deal With It: All in Good Time,* Lorimer Children & Teens, Minneapolis, 2016.

11- "Stand" by Sly and the Family Stone, released 1969- Pacific High Recording Studio

15- Jesus Culture, "Your Love Never Fails,"

19- Bill Knaus, Ed.D. "Overcoming Procrastination,"

23- Mike Bundrant, "The Emotions Behind Procrastination: Five Scenarios You Should Understand if you Want to Get Things Done." inlpcenter.org

26- YouTube-: Hillsong, live in Miami, "With Everything" (Let Hope Rise), By Hillsong Worship, 2012 & Jesus Culture, "Rooftops." Written by Ben Williams, Lindsey Sweat, Jonathan Berlin of Bethel Church, sung by Kim Walker, 2010

27- Dr. Erwin Lutzer

30- The Newsboys, Dr. Tony Evans

November

2- Maggie Seymore, *The Virginian -Pilot*, October 28, 2017, written by Ryan Murphy.

11- Ana Swanson, "The Real Reasons You Procrastinate—and How to Stop" April 27, 2016. washingtonpost.com.

12- Ibid.

20- *Dobie Gillis,* 20th Century Fox Studios, 1959-1963

23- Lexington Law, "2019 Credit Card Debt Statistics," original post December 19, 2018. lexingtonlaw.com

26- "Nowhere Man," The Beatles, written by Lennon & McCartney, October 1965

December

10- Dr. Timothy Pychyl, quote from- Ana Swanson, "The Real Reasons You Procrastinate—and How to Stop" April 27, 2016. washingtonpost.com.

14- (Ibid)

21. www.eruptingmind.com

22- Mike Bundrant, "The Emotions Behind Procrastination: Five Scenarios You Should Understand if you Want to Get Things Done." inlpcenter.org

27-Jonathan Lowenhar, given to improve time management and focus. As President at ETW Advisors (Enjoy The Work), (www.etwadvisors.com)

Bible Quotes From-

The Amplified Bible (AMP)- Zondervan & The Lockman Foundation, Grand Rapids Michigan, 1965.

Amplified Bible, Classic Edition (AMPC) The Lockman Foundation, 1965, updated version 1987

English Standard Version (ESV)- Good News Publishers, Wheaton, Illinois, 2001, rev. 2016.

Good News Translation (GNT) & *Today's English Version* (TEV)
the American Bible Society, Philadelphia, Pennsylvania, 1966, 1976.

King James Version (KJV)- originally published by the Church of England in 1611.

The Living Bible (TLB)- paraphrase written by Kenneth Taylor based on the American Standard Version of 1901, Tyndale House Publishers, Carol Stream, Illinois, 1971.

The Message (MSG) The Bible in Contemporary Language created & translated by Eugene H. Peterson, Nav Press in association with Alive Communications, Inc. Colorado Springs, Colorado, 2002.

Modern English Version (MEV) updated version of King James edited by James F. Linsey, Passio (Charisma House), Lake Mary, Florida, 2014.

New American Standard Bible (NASB)- Lockman Foundation, La Habre, California, 1960, rev.1995.

New English Translation (NET) Biblical Studies Press, L.L.C. Copyright 1996, version revision 2019, Richardson, Texas.

New International Version (NIV) Biblica (International Bible Society), Colorado Springs, Colorado, 1978, in association with Zondervan publishing, rev. 2011.

New King James (NKJV)- Thomas Nelson, Nashville, Tennessee, 1982.

New Living Translation (NLT)- Tyndale House, Carol Stream, Illinois, 1996, rev. 2015.

Revised Standard Version (RSV)- Thomas Nelson, American Bible Society, Oxford University Press, Wayne A. Meeks, 1946, 1952 rev.

ttps://www.biblegateway.com
Throughout the writing of this book the *Bible Gateway* website was a constant companion to me. This site was extremely valuable in examining the nuances in meaning from one translation to another. In terms of finding Biblical references to certain subject matters, this site was exceedingly helpful.

TITLES

January

1- A New Year
2- The Power of Dedication
3- This Time Next Year
4- Look Back to Look Forward
5- On the Road to Somewhere
6- Better Than Belief
7- Running to Win

8- The Main Thing
9- Oh, It's Too Late
10- First Things First
11- It's All About Timing
12- It's a Beautiful Morning
13- This is the Day
14- Time for Order

15- The Destiny of Dreamers
16- Small Beginnings
17- I'd Rather be His Delight
18- Whose Plans Prevail?
19- I am Weak
20- Controlling Distractions
21- A No-Kill Zone

22- I Never Liked Doing Nothing
23- Naps Are Great
24- Are We Wrestling or Snuggling
Our Demons?
25- I Can, Because God Can
26- Not by What I See
27- What's Trust Got to Do with It?
28- I Just Want to Feel Good
29- Students Beware
30- Our Inner Child
31- Something to Show

February

1- Paying for Nothing
2- Groundhog Day
3- It May Seem Impossible
4- Watch Out for Foxes and Squirrels
5- Who Wants to Get Crushed Today?
6- Ruling Over the Flood
7- From the Inside Out

8- Plan Ahead
9- Millennials at Risk
10- Cliches Can Be True
11- What to Pray
12- Just a Little Late
13- Peace be with You
14- I Wish I Could Find It

15- Overdue Dreams
16- What's That Mirror For?
17- Mood Swings
18- Just One Thing
19- Many Times
20- Even SpongeBob Does It
21- A Break from the Past

22- The Exhilarating Finish
23- Little Steps
24- Get on With It
25- The Mind is a Battlefield
26- Didn't Want to Hear That
27- Friend or Foe
28 - "Not All Who Wander are Lost"
29- Making Up Time.

March

1- Call for Help
2- What a Mess
3- The Cost of Complaining
4- Building Up
5- Slow Down Ms. G
6- The Folly of Fools
7- No Deadlines

8- In the Margins
9- Those Annoying Pine Needles
10- An Easy Out
11- A Confident Hope
12- Real Time
13- Completed
14- Now or Later?

15- Love My Neighbor as Myself
16- Killing Time
17- Let's Celebrate
18- No Matter What
19- Wonderful Things
20- Will be Done
21- Removing Guilt

22- What Log?
23- Sometimes Late Means Never
24- Baby Boomer or Gen X, Matters Not
25- Getting Off the Wrong Road
26- Everyone Makes Mistakes
27- Comfort versus Comfortable
28- What Could Have Been

29- Sometimes
30- Unwise Reluctance
31- If You Are Lazy

April

1- Time for Resurrection
2- Hide and Seek
3- Choosing Calm
4- No Dark Paths
5- Real Rest
6- No Easy Path
7- Deep Roots

8- Maybe It Needs to be Brand New
9- Not Procrastination
10- What You Give
11- Who is Imitating Who?
12- Praise Him
13- Help Please
14- Embracing the Cup

15- Victory Guaranteed
16- Dropping Our Defense
17- Beware the Wounded Heart
18- For My Future Self…
19- Got to Find a Way Out
20- Progress Equals Joy
21- Grace Wins

22- Certainty of Eternity
23- The Size of the Task
24- Know Your Enemy
25- In the Margins
26- Making My Path Straight
27- How Many Times?
28- A Little Wisdom Goes a Long Way

29- Mirror Mirror
30- Too Much Confusion

May

1- Letting Down Our Nets
2- Too Many Words
3- What Happens Tomorrow
4- What Really Happened
5- Doing as We Wish
6- At Least a Few Rounds
7- Plans Have Power

8- My Shepherd
9- Times of Trouble
10- Like Blackbirds in My Head
11- Ready for Battle
12-My Soul's Hope
13-We Got to Pray
14-Sowing the Good Stuff

15- God Removes Our Guilt
16- Not Where I Want to Be
17- Opportunity Costs
18- Into Our Hand
19- Self-Control
20- In the Future
21- Never Say Never

22- What's Wrong with Being Perfect?
23- The Right Road
24- Crisis Tends to Rule
25- It's Like Hockey
26- Not Worth Putting Off
27- In the Morning
28- I Think I Can...I Believe I Can

29- If Then
30- Courage Counts
31- What Was Sown Today?

June

1- What Not to Do
2- Watch Out
3- The Land of Now or Later
4- Patience
5- The Good Side of Never
6- Perhaps Only One
7- Wonderful Things

8- What Fruit?
9- Where's the Hope?
10- Not Alone
11- It's Just Wrong
12- Are You One of Those?
13- In My Dreams
14- Every Passing Moment

15- What's Ahead
16- Learning to Aim Correctly
17- The Time Between
18- Changing Me
19- You Don't Have To
20- Thanksgiving, Praise, and Victory
21- What Tomorrow Brings

22- When?
23- Let Me See
24- Blessings of Being Uncomfortable
25- Disgrace or Grace
26- Alive, Awake, and in Shape
27- Cast Away
28- Get Where You Are Going

29- My Hand
30- Out of the Rut

July

1- I'm Not Going to Lose It Today
2- Thank You, Bob
3- I Want to be Wonder Woman
4- The Value of Dependence
5- Beware the Inner Child
6- Enough Power
7- A Very Good Vine

8- Living Beyond Shadows
9- Able to Choose
10- While You Are Young
11- Gold and Silver
12- There is a Good Side
13- My Place
14- Never Too Late

15- Growing Blessings
16- Things and People Disappear
17- Sticks and Stones
18- Over Your Head
19- The Symphony in Us
20- A Willing Mind
21- Weary is OK, Worn-out Is Not

22- "No Worries"
23- I Need Help
24- He Hears Us
25- Waiting for Us All
26- Goodness and Mercy
27- Get it Together
28- Praise Him

29- Firm Grip
30- It is New
31- Good to Know

August

1- Sacrifice What?
2- A Most Favorable Time
3- The Word
4- A Little A Lot
5- That Won't Help
6- All I Need
7- Picasso Says

8- Just Ask
9- Tomorrow
10- No Fear
11- You Can't Make Me
12- Without a Trace
13- My Confidence
14- For You

15- Where Anger Leads
16- Get Over Yourself
17- I'd Rather Be Radiant
18- Immediately
19- Don't Listen to The Monkey
20- Getting Unstuck
21- More of Him

22- Don't Want to Miss It
23- The Lord Answers
24- Help and Hope
25- Just Roll with the Embarrassment
26- Armed to Overcome
27- Good Intentions Plus
28- You Are Needed

29- He Promised
30- Stay Close
31- Roll Up Our Sleeves

September

1- To Do for You
2- Rising in Fellowship
3- A Hug from God
4- Night is Coming
5- Power to Heal
6- On Guard
7- Watching My Step

8- My Teacher Knows the Way
9- Ending the Feud
10- Procrastination-Patience Process
11- Mr. Fredrickson's Folly
12- Not a Sin?
13- Time to Trample
14- Hide and Seek

15- The Biggest Pill
16- Our Rest
17- Early Just Isn't My Style
18- All Means All
19- Lesser Goals
20- Presently in The Future
21- A Good Harvest

22- Imagine That
23- I'm Late
24- Working It
25- Fixed and Focused
26- Just Too Hard
27- Avoiding the Ditch
28- Hidden Things

29- Who You Belong To
30- How Long Will It Take?

October

1- A Blessed Mystery
2- I'm Not Alright
3- Do It Yourself Dominoes
4- Take a Drink
5- Do's and Don'ts
6- Why Them?
7- Today

8- What We Wish
9- Act Quickly
10- Just a Little Thing
11- Stand for Your Plan
12- The Linchpin
13- The Turning Point
14- It's an Act

15- All Things
16- Power in His Name
17- Help!
18- Avoiding Confusion
19- The Urge to Diverge
20- The Pile Up
21- Thank Goodness

22- Too Many Words
23- It Hurts
24- Get a Grip
25- Readily Recognize
26- Let Hope Rise
27- Completely, Continually, Thoroughly
28- Don't Walk Away
29- Missing the Mark
30- God's Bandage
31- The Word is Life

November

1- Kingdom Fitness
2- Great Lengths
3- The Rush
4- Putting It Off
5- Surviving Shipwrecks
6- His Name
7- Forward to The Finish

8- Small Steps
9- The Battle
10- The Way We Are
11- Today's Self
12- Feelings Fail Us
13- Good Soil Good Results
14- Fear Not

15- Along the Way
16- We Are His
17- The Right Plan
18- Time for Encouragement
19- Just Ask
20- Lazybones
21- Recognize

22- Age is No Excuse
23- The Freedom Trap
24- The Choice
25- Looking Forward
26- To See Exactly
27- Up and About
28- Charging into the Fray

29- Near Completion
30- Mindfulness

December

1- Thank God for Being Covered
2- My Heart Hears
3- Made of Mud
4- Learning to be Relentless
5- Built by Him
6- Working for the Lord
7- It's a Pain

8- Faith Plus
9- Your Season
10- A Little Bit
11- Going Through
12- Why Worry
13- I Hate Rejection
14- What a Relief

15- Only Ten More Days
16- Image is Important
17- The Cost of Complaining
18- Our Personal Trainer
19- For the Night Owls
20- Faith Sees
21- Doing Your Work

22- A Risky Plan
23- Avoiding a Troubled Mind
24- Rejoice!
25- Tis the Season
26- Our Father's Will
27- Enough Time
28- Staying on Track

29- What Tomorrow Brings
30- A New Kind of New Year
31- Too Much Wine

-NOTES-

Here are some blank pages just for you.

I have shared my scriptural revelations, personal experiences and reflections on things that I have learned from others whose wisdom exceeds mine. I pray that this book is a means for you to have victory over the common weight that so easily drags us down. It would be beneficial to check out some of the videos, music, and authors referenced in this devotional. Tim Urban's Ted Talk: Inside the Mind of a Master Procrastinator, which includes the illustrated story of the "Instant Gratification Monkey" is especially enlightening.

As you write in these pages provided here, may it help deepen your understanding of the complex binding chords of procrastination, increase the understanding of your own brand of avoidance emotions and behaviors, provide motivation for lasting positive changes, and draw you into a deeper relationship with our Lord and Savior. Time spent in devotion to Jesus is always time well spent. Ask, seek, knock, and ... write in your own words, your thoughts, your plans, and your prayers that will lead you on to your very own victory. May God bless you!— Barbara Gelnett

-NOTES-

-NOTES-

-NOTES-

-NOTES-

Printed in the United States
by Baker & Taylor Publisher Services